Plan of the centre of Ripon reproduced from the 1854 Ordnance Survey map.

A   RIPON   RECORD
1887 — 1986

The Grammar School (Fossick)

A RIPON RECORD

1887 — 1986

Edited by
Edna Ellis, Mary Mauchline,
Ted Pearson and John Whitehead

Phillimore

1986

Published by
PHILLIMORE & CO. LTD.
Shopwyke Hall, Chichester, Sussex

© The Ripon Civic Society, 1986

ISBN 0 85033 600 7

Printed and bound in Great Britain by
REDWOOD BURN LTD.,
Trowbridge, Wiltshire

CONTENTS

LIST OF PLATES

(between pages 48 and 49)

LIST OF TEXT ILLUSTRATIONS

A Ripon Record adopts the same pattern of chronology as the Millenary volume, in which the dating of events followed the civic rather than the calendar year. Up to 1949, the mayoral year ran from 1 November to 31 October and from then onwards from 1 May to 30 April.

An illustration appears at the beginning of each year of the silver medallion chosen by the Mayor as his personal emblem which is attached to the City baldric. The custom dates from 1520 but it was not established until the Victorian period. There are, however, 13 medallions missing from the sequence over the last 100 years; in these instances the City's crest replaces the mayoral badges, reproduced from a drawing by George Fossick.

ACKNOWLEDGEMENTS

A Ripon Record 1887-1986 has been produced under the auspices of the Ripon Civic Society. Publication was made possible by financial guarantees from the Society, from Ripon City Council and from the City of Ripon Festival Trust 1986.

Thanks are due to many persons and institutions for their help during the years in which this volume was in preparation. The contributions of the following are acknowledged with particular gratitude: Mr Patrick Webb, Clerk to Ripon City Council, on behalf of the Town Hall; Mr Geoffrey Willett and Mr John Hagart, of the Library of the College of Ripon and York St John; those searchers who examined the newspaper files deposited therein, in particular Miss Jean Denton and Mrs Beryl Thompson and Mrs Jill Freeman and Dr John Addy; the Ackrill Press; the *Ripon Gazette*; the staff of the North Yorkshire County Record Office, in particular Mr M. Y. Ashcroft, Miss Judith Close, and Mr Hugh Jacques; Mrs Eve Burr, who typed the manuscript; Dr W. J. Petchey, who drew the badges of the Mayors of Ripon. The maps used as endpapers are reproduced by permission of the Ordnance Survey; the drawings by George Fossick by permission of Ripon City Council; those by George Jackson by permission of Miss Winifred Jackson; those by Jim Gott by permission of the Gott family. For other illustrations the editors acknowledge permission to reproduce given by the College of Ripon and York St John Community History Project, the Ackrill Press, the *Ripon Gazette* office, and Mr W. Robson.

FOREWORD

by Lady Graham O.B.E., past President Ripon Civic Society

This record of daily life in Ripon during the last 100 years illuminates in vivid detail the changes that have taken place. Some incidents — for instance the collision between the elephant and the lamp-post — we should like to have witnessed; others — the soup kitchens of the severe winter of 1895 and the march from Jarrow which came through the town in October 1936 — we profoundly hope will never be seen again. All of us in, or near, Ripon, will have a much greater understanding of its development after reading this fascinating book.

Many Riponians living and many yet unborn will owe a great debt to all those who have inspired and produced a Record of Ripon.

Beatrice Graham.

INTRODUCTION

In 1986 Ripon celebrates 1,100 years of civic history. A hundred years ago the *Ripon Millenary* was produced to commemorate the thousandth anniversary in 1886. This companion volume records the history of the city since then, a century during which Ripon has changed more drastically than in all the thousand years covered by the *Millenary*.

A team of researchers and writers has studied and selected items from the extensive sources available, primarily the Ripon City Archives and documentary material deposited in the Ripon Community History Project Centre at the College of Ripon and York St John. The editors have endeavoured to maintain a balance between the many facets of urban history revealed, between the minutiae of day-to-day events and the matters of greater moment in the affairs of the city.

Ripon is at once St Wilfrid's City, dating from the foundation of his Minster church in 672; a medieval market town of ancient origin; a venue since the 18th century for horse-racing; a place well-endowed, notably from Victorian times, with educational establishments; and in the 20th century a military centre of great importance, especially during the two World Wars. The traditions and pageantry of these various aspects combine to enrich the life of the city, but civic occasions have become matters of ceremony rather than significance since 1974, when Ripon became part of the Harrogate District. The Yorkshire countryside—its agriculture, its farms and its horses, and the estates of the gentry who figure so prominently in the earlier decades—enfolds the city and has always influenced its history.

Planning the way ahead for one of the oldest cities in England set on the threshold of the Yorkshire Dales poses crucial questions. How far should history and scenic beauty be exploited? Should equal emphasis be laid on the promotion of tourism and light industry? Which is the more essential to the well-being of a country town of about 13,000 inhabitants? Which the more profitable in terms of finance and future growth? These dilemmas are closely allied to the problem of communications. Medieval prosperity was based on Ripon's situation between the upland country of the Dales and the plain of York; it was a focal point for transport by road and river. The old network of roads centring on Ripon, once the city's blessing, has become its greatest curse. The railway closed in 1972. Traffic clogs the narrow streets, threatening to bring about a condition of urban arteriosclerosis. Three decades of argument have divided local opinion on the merits of the alternative solutions, an inner relief road or an outer bypass. The former was ruled out of court by a public inquiry, but the construction of the latter is now scheduled for the early 1990s.

Another major dispute arose over the proposed introduction of comprehensive education. Strenuous opposition resulted in the survival of the Grammar School, a Tudor foundation, and the provision of a separate City Secondary School. Hopes that a university might be sited in Ripon during the expansion of the 1960s, encouraged by the precedent of similar schemes put forward in the reigns of Elizabeth I and James I, were not fulfilled. However, the Diocesan Training College established in 1862 now offers degree courses in association with the University of Leeds, has diversified into fields other than teacher-training, and in 1975 was amalgamated with St John's College, York, to become the College of Ripon and York St John.

The century under review is a record of some prosperity, of much poverty and hardship in the earlier days, of bouts of apathy alternating with periods of acute controversy and civic debate. Since the close of World War II a growing appreciation of the role that the arts, especially music, can play in a cathedral city and its schools has been evident. Increasingly there is concern to lift the dead hand of the past while ensuring the conservation of a heritage that will live in harmony with and contribute to vigorous urban growth and development. In the relatively short period covered in this volume, a new world has emerged. To read *A Ripon Record 1887-1986* brings a sharp awareness of the accelerating rate and the irreversible nature of the changes outlined in its pages.

1886-87. JOHN BAYNES, Slate Merchant.

Mayor 1885-86-87-88 and 1894-95: see the long account of Baynes and his ancestry in the *Ripon Millenary Record*. Born in 1830 at Ripley, he started business in Ripon in 1854, and was created Mayor again in 1894-5 as 'a distinguished citizen' though no longer one of the Corporation.

January. The final meeting of the Ripon Millenary Festival Committee was held. It was resolved that an album should be prepared, with a full set of the Millenary photographs, for presentation to the Marchioness of Ripon who had been Lady President of the Festival.

William Burniston, superintendent of the city police force from 1861 to 1875 and a Councillor from 1850 to 1883, died at South Terrace. He was interred in the Cathedral.

John Simmonds, Ripon Hornblower for 41 years, died aged 85. He succeeded his father Benjamin Simmonds who had held the office for 30 years.

February. The death occurred of William Chapman, Sergeant-at-Mace, who had succeeded Sergeant Dinsdale in 1875. Thomas Precious was appointed to the office.

May. After a long-sustained controversy the City Council agreed that the police force (made up of an inspector and four constables) should be amalgamated with the West Riding County Constabulary. The City force's last appearance at the Ripon Police Court occurred on 28 September and the West Riding Constabulary assumed authority within the city on 6 October. The Old Liberty Prison and House of Correction in St. Marygate, which had ceased to be used as a prison in 1880, became the new Ripon Police Station.

June. The Mayor attended Her Majesty's Jubilee Thanksgiving Service on 21 June. Ripon celebrated the occasion during the following week. On Monday 27 June the inhabitants of Bondgate enjoyed a general holiday, when 400 persons sat down to tea; Tuesday saw a procession of 2,196 children from all the 11 schools in the city walking in procession with music, flags and banners; a grand procession was mounted on Wednesday and passed through the city to the Cathedral, led by West Yorkshire Rifle Volunteers and band, followed by choristers, the clergy, Friendly Societies with their banners, the Mayor and Corporation in their robes, and the City magistrates with the Rothwell Temperance Band bringing up the rear. The Cathedral was decorated for the occasion and the choir was composed of 120 voices. A dinner at the Victoria Rooms followed the service and in the evening there was a grand display of fireworks. On Friday the Mayor and Mayoress held a grand reception and the Jubilee celebrations ended on Saturday with a review of the Volunteer Battalion of the West Yorkshire Regiment in Studley Park.

August. The Local Government Board gave permission for the Corporation to borrow £412 to purchase a steam road-roller with wagons. In September a Fowler's machine of four hp was purchased and christened *The Wakeman*.

October. The Right Honourable W. E. Gladstone and Mrs Gladstone visited Ripon and Studley Royal. They attended a meeting at the Town Hall to receive addresses of welcome.

1887-88. JOHN BAYNES, Slate Merchant.

Mayor 1885-86-87-88 and 1894-95

November. The Local Government Board granted permission for the Corporation to borrow a further £10,000 to complete the works at Lumley Moor Reservoir. The supply was turned on unfiltered on 4 August 1888. This proved unsatisfactory and filter beds were constructed. The scheme was completed by December 1888.

March. The Hon. T. H. W. Pelham, Assistant Boundary Commissioner, started an enquiry with reference to the boundaries of the Liberty of Ripon and the Ripon Poor Law Union for local government purposes and the election of Councillors. There was universal opposition to any change in Ripon. Full details of the enquiry and the arguments put are given in the *Ripon Millenary Record*.

May. The Revd. Canon John Pulleine, rector of Stanhope, was consecrated in York Minster as Suffragan Bishop of Ripon with the title of Bishop of Richmond.

The death occurred of Thomas Hill, aged 30, City Surveyor and Sanitary Inspector to Ripon Corporation. Henry Dearden was appointed to the post.

July. Portraits of the Mayor, members of the Council and the Town Clerk in the Millenary Year, suitably framed to hang in the Council Chamber, were presented to the Corporation by Councillor Watson.

Thomas Askwith, Manager of the Bradford Old Bank, City Treasurer and Treasurer to the Ripon Board of Guardians, died aged seventy-one.

October. Under the Local Government Act of 1887, the city of Ripon would in future return one member to the County Council. The rural portion of the Ripon Union with a population of 5,966 was added to that of the Pateley Bridge Union, making a joint population of 14,597 which would also return one member. Lord Ripon was elected as the first County Councillor for the City of Ripon and became the first chairman of the West Riding of Yorkshire County Council.

1888-89. H. MANN THIRLWAY, Printer.

Born in Ripon 1851; educated at Ripon Grammar School and joined his father in 1872 in the old-established business of stationer and printer in the Market Place which had been started by his grand-father Henry Thirlway in 1815. He was a member of the Ripon Corps of Volunteers for 18 years and an expert shot. He was a Lay Reader at Holy Trinity Church and was elected to the Council in 1883.

December. The latest development in the supply of pure water to the city, the gravitation scheme from Lumley Moor, was completed. As the work had been entirely carried out during the mayoralty of Alderman Baynes, the ex-Mayoress Mrs Baynes was invited to turn on the supply at a ceremony on 10 December with a silver hydrant key. The new reservoir covered 27 acres to a depth of 32 feet and was 467 feet above the level of the Market Place. Previously the city's water supply had been by pumping river water. Up to the middle of the 18th century water was carried from house to house in skin bags on horseback. In 1777 Alderman William Askwith installed a pumping engine at the water-mill in Duck Hill to raise water from the Skell which was conveyed to the houses in elm-tree pipes. This supply tended to be impure and intermittent, and in 1865 the Corporation took over and selected a scheme designed by Stevenson & Utley to supply 100,000 gallons per day from the river Ure from North

Bridge by a double-acting steam engine of 10 hp to a reservoir at Lark Hill. The new Lumley Moor scheme has a supply capacity of 750,000 gallons per day.

April. The marriage took place at Sharow Parish Church of the Revd. J. J. Pulleine, Suffragan Bishop of Ripon, to Miss Louise Worsley, daughter of the late Revd. Wharton Worsley, Canon Residentiary of Ripon Cathedral. The Lord Bishop of Ripon officiated.

May. The Market Cross was renovated by re-pointing the stonework and coating the whole surface with oil as a preservative. The copper vane, which is in the shape of a horn, was also repaired and re-gilded. Before it was replaced, a copy of the *Ripon Gazette*; copies of the minutes of the finance committee, the highways committee and the Sanitary Committee referring to the repairs; and cards of the Mayor, Alderman Smithson, Alderman Wells and John Clarke (the craftsman who carried out the repairs) were sealed in a copper box which was in turn sealed in the main body of the copper horn. When the obelisk and vane were repaired in 1985 in preparation for the Ripon 1100 celebrations the box was opened and the contents were found to be in perfect condition. They were returned to the horn.

July. Further unsuccessful attempts were made to move the Russian gun captured during the Crimean War and placed on the Market Square near the Obelisk to another site. Agreement could not be reached with the custodians of any of the proposed alternative sites —the Drill Hall in Park Street or the ground between the Court House and Cathedral; it was decided to provide new railings to place round the gun and leave it in the Market Square.

September. The Ripon Savings Bank in the Market Square closed after 70 years of business in the city. The bank had been opened as a branch of the Knaresborough and Claro Savings Bank.

October. A new block at Ripon Grammar School, consisting of a large school hall, classrooms and a master's study on the ground floor, and a large dormitory, a clock and bell-tower and a dozen other rooms above, was opened by the Marquess of Ripon.

The New Wesleyan Mission Chapel in Water Skellgate was opened by Mrs W. Thompson of North Parade.

1889-90. THOMAS HARGRAVE, Saddletree Maker

Born in Bondgate in 1849, son of Thomas and Ann Hargrave, followed the business of his father in the old established saddletree trade in Ripon. He was elected to the Council in 1860 and became an Alderman in 1886. He occupied nearly every position in public life, being a Trustee of the Municipal Charities, a Feoffee of Jepson's Hospital, Vice-Chairman of the Board of Guardians and a Governor of the Grammar School.

November. The Revd. W. Yorke Faussett M.A., of Fettes College, Edinburgh, was appointed Headmaster of Ripon Grammar School in place of the Revd A. B. Haslam.

December. Councillor Robert Ellington Collinson, proprietor of the *Unicorn Hotel*, died aged fifty-six. He had been a member of the Ripon Corporation for 25 years; twice elected alderman and four times mayor 1877-80.

January. John Kearsley, a City Councillor for eight years and one of the main supporters of the amalgamation of the Ripon City Police with the West Riding Constabulary in 1887, died aged forty-five.

February. Two hundred pounds' worth of damage was caused by a hot-air flue igniting the woodwork of the gallery of the Congregational Church in North Road.

March. The Marquess of Ripon presented to the Corporation a portrait by Sir Thomas Lawrence of his father, Frederick Robinson, Earl of Ripon, Member for Ripon 1807-29 and Alderman of Ripon City Council 1809.

June. The Bathing Pavilion erected on the bank of the Ure was opened by Alderman Thirlway. The provision of the pavilion originated with an offer by the Dean, Dr W. R. Freemantle, to the Corporation of not more than £400 to erect swimming baths on land at the Highways Depot on Skellbank. This proved too costly as did a scheme for a swimming bath in Park Street. The Dean agreed to give £400 towards the total cost of £550 for the pavilion, which consisted of a two-roomed cottage for the caretaker and a row of twenty dressing-rooms for bathers. A charge of 1d was made for use of towel and bathing drawers.

July. A Cathedral Schools Fancy Fair was opened by the Marchioness of Ripon to raise funds to clear the existing debt and carry out sanitary and other alterations at the Girls' School.

George Greenwood retired as Workhouse Master with a pension of £66 12s per annum. Mrs Greenwood, who had acted as Matron, was granted a pension of £32 10s. Albert and Mary Burton were appointed in their place.

1890-91. THOMAS SMITHSON, Butcher and Farmer

Born in 1836, the son of Enos Smithson, a butcher. He started business in Allhallowgate in 1852 and later moved to North Street. He married three times, the wedding to his third wife taking place during his year of office as Mayor. The election of 1874, when he was first elected to the Council, was disputed by his opponents but the petition was dismissed. He was re-elected in 1887 after a period of ten years out of office.

December. Two human skeletons, one of a full-grown man and one of a youth aged about sixteen were found by workmen on the site of five old cottages in St Marygate. They were found near the surface under the brick floor of a pantry. The remains of a young woman were found in the garden behind the cottage. The bones had been buried many years previously.

January. The Ripon and District Campanological Society was formed with the object of promoting hand-bell ringing and the improvement of change-ringing in local churches.

A special service was held in the Cathedral for the dedication of the memorial bells and chimes recently added to the belfry. A new frame afforded space for two new bells; one given by a brother and sisters of the late Miss Anne Cross of Coney Garth and the other by Messrs R. Kearsley and Co in memory of the late John Kearsley. The bells were cast and hung by Messrs J. Shaw and Co of Bradford, who also fixed the Cambridge chimes provided by public subscription.

The marriage took place at the Cathedral between the Mayor and Mrs Sarah Hebden of Bingwood Terrace, Bondgate. A handsome silver salver was presented to the Mayor and Mayoress by the Council.

The 1891 Census gave the following statistics for Ripon: inhabited houses, 1650, uninhabited, 147, building, 12; males, 3,425, females, 4,086. Total, 7,511.

An application from the British Telephone Company to carry a line of wires through the city on wooden posts was granted.

May. The Half-day Holiday Movement was adopted by Ripon tradesmen, Friday afternoon being selected. Picnics at Fountains, Hackfall, Aldborough Manor and Sawley Hall were arranged for the summer months.

June. Professor Frederick Orpen Bower, Regius Professor of Botany in the University of Glasgow, was elected a Fellow of the Royal Society. Professor Bower was born at Elmscroft, Ripon, and was a pupil at Ripon Grammar School for a short period.

August. Studley Royal was supplied with electricity from a water turbine sited near the lake where there was a drop of 9½ ft. The supply was up to 100 amperes at 100 volts. Four hundred lights of from eight to 50 candle-power were installed in the Hall besides providing power for knife-and-shoe cleaners, wringing and washing machines.

October. The Church of St Mary the Virgin, North Stainley, was re-opened for divine service by the Bishop of Ripon after the addition of a chancel to the original nave built by the late Mr Staveley in 1840. The entire cost of the work was borne by Miss Staveley and Miss Lee of Old Sleningford Hall, as a memorial to Mrs Staveley, who died in 1881.

1891-92. THOMAS SMITHSON, Butcher and Farmer

Mayor 1890-91-92

November. Six Fellows of the Society of Antiquaries, London, carried out excavations in the Saxon crypt under the central tower of the Cathedral. The research showed that the plan as now laid down with the exception of the western entrance is that of the original seventh-century crypt and that, although two deposits of bones were found, there was no indication of a place of burial.

January. A deputation of property owners residing in Kirkgate waited upon the Council asking for the replacement of the stone steps that formerly led from Duck Hill into Kirkgate and which had been removed about 1880. The Council agreed to the request and Mr Boddy erected the steps at a cost of £34 4s. In addition the Highways Department relaid the whole of Duck Hill roadway and provided a new causeway on the east side and in front of the mill owned by Mr Handley.

The Council planned a celebration to recognise the forthcoming marriage of H.R.H. the Duke of Clarence to Princess Mary of Teck. However, the young Prince died on 14 January, and the Council called a special meeting to pass a vote of condolence to the Prince and Princess of Wales.

February. Mr H. M. Bower presented to the Corporation a pair of spurs made by Charles Carney of Ripon which had won a prize at the recent Industrial Exhibition 'to show what can be done in Ripon in that line in 1892'.

May. A public lamp was erected as a distinctive feature of the residence of the Mayor. It was suspended by a bracket of ornamental ironwork incorporating a gilded horn and surmounted by a spur. The lamp itself was surmounted by a crown and on the sides of the glass facing the street are the words 'The Right Worshipful the Mayor'. In the two centre glasses appeared the motto of the city 'Except ye Lord keep ye cittie, ye wakeman waketh in vain'. The lamp cost £11 and is still used today.

June. Telephonic communication was opened with other towns in Yorkshire with an office at No. 35 Market Place.

June. A portrait of the Dean of Ripon, the Very Revd. W. R. Freemantle, painted by Mr C. Watson of Ripon was hung in the Council Chamber.

August. Mr H. M. Bower presented a silver cup to be competed for annually in a race of one mile, by youths residing within one mile of the Market Cross, including pupils in the public schools within the area. The first race was won by Henry Watson who received a gold medal from the Ripon Cricket Club.

The foundation stone of the new Bondgate Bridge was laid by the Mayor on 11 August.

1892-93. J. BROOKS PARKIN, Chemist

Born 1839, the son of Joseph Parkin, schoolmaster of Markington. He was educated at Markington and Ripon Grammar School and apprenticed to John Brown, Chemist, of Westgate. He set up his own business in Kirkgate in 1867. Elected to the Council in 1870, he served for 12 years and was involved with the North Road improvement scheme and the supply of gas and water to the city. He was Chairman of Jepson's Hospital and a governor of the Grammar School at the time of its re-organisation. A churchwarden at the Cathedral, he was a strong churchman and a vigorous supporter of the rights of the established church. He was also a freemason. A triumphal arch was erected at the top of Kirkgate in honour of his entry into the mayoralty. He died while on holiday in Southport in 1896.

January. Tenders totalling £1,079 were accepted for the new Mechanics Institute to be built in Finkle Street.

After making an inspection, the Sanitary Committee ordered the rebuilding, re-siting or repair of privies and ashpits at various properties in Heath's Yard, Blossomgate, Fishergate, Ireland's Court, Priest Lane and Stonebridgegate.

The Committee administering the Poor Relief Fund was told that 340 tickets had been issued, and that 1,209 persons had been relieved with 667 quarts of soup and loaves of bread three times a week. Mr Tutin asked if poor people passing through the town might be given something from the soup kitchen after the local poor had been relieved. This was not considered desirable as it could encourage tramps to come.

The Succentor of the Cathedral, who was providing breakfasts to about 120 poor children in Priest Lane Mission Room on three mornings a week, appealed for funds to meet the weekly cost of £2 10s: £20 10s was subscribed.

The Managers of the Cathedral Schools were directed by the Education Department to reconstruct and enlarge the Infants' and Girls' Schools in St Agnesgate. The Dean and Chapter subscribed £200 and the Marquess of Ripon £100 towards the expected cost of £900.

February. The Medical Officer of Health, Dr J. C. R. Husband, reported 189 births (25 per 1,000) of which 12 were illegitimate, and 173 deaths (23 per 1,000) in 1892: 26 of the deaths occurred in the Workhouse and 22 were infants under one year old.

The Corporation recommended the purchase of Duck Hill Mill from the Ecclesiastical Commissioners at a cost of £400: 70 square yards of the site would be used for road widening.

April. Messrs Samuel Croft and Co of Ripon had some of their carriages on show at a Sportsman's Exhibition in Sheffield. These included a neat shooting drag and a Studley Royal cart which had been awarded a medal for excellence at the Ripon exhibition of 1892. The industrial exhibition, held in the Victoria Hall in Water Skellgate, later the Opera House, and opened by Lady Graham, was visited by 3,000 people in four days.

The April Horse Show in North Street attracted a fairly good entry of useful agricultural and thorough-bred horses.

A thousand yearling trout were turned into the River Ure by the Yorkshire Fisheries Board.

Two thousand two hundred men of the Tyne and Tees Volunteer Brigade were encamped on the Racecourse during Whit Week.

May. George Pickersgill of Thorpe Lodge successfully sued Peter and William Taylor of Bondgate for £15 damages for lambs lost when sheep were roughly im-pounded in the pinfold at Bondgate End. The Taylors were pound-keepers for the gate-owners of Quarry Moor Common. The charge for the release of a beast found straying was 2d.

June. The total cost of the new Bondgate Bridge was £2,175; this exceeded the estimates but included narrowing the waterway and improving the road. It had also been reported to the Council that a further £1,000 would be required for the cemetery, and the City Engineer was instructed to prepare a report on the disposal of sewage.

July. The wedding of the Duke of York to Princess Mary of Teck was celebrated by a Cathedral service for children followed by tea and games organised by an ex-ecutive committee, which resolved to spend £80 on entertainments and 8d per head for tea. The city streets were decorated and illuminated in the evening. The Board of Guardians gave the Workhouse inmates a holi-day and roast beef and plum pudding for dinner. The day was Thursday and, although the Corporation decided they could not alter the holding of the market, they asked shopkeepers to close at 2 pm. The city's gift to the royal couple was a representation of the City Horn in silver and a copy of the *Ripon Millenary Record*.

The Mayor, Mayoress and Town Clerk attended a reception given by the Lord Mayor of London for the Royal Archaeological Institute. The Ripon Corpor-ation regalia was on view at the Mansion House. In the previous month a tradesmans' token had been found in a garden at Bishopton. It was dated 1666 and bore the name Lancelot Williamson, Grocer, Ripon, and the arms of the Grocers' Company (a chevron between nine cloves) as in some of the badges on the baldric.

The Dean, presenting prizes at the Cathedral Boys' School, announced that he had given his field (now the site of Ripon House) near the school as a recreation ground for the children.

August. The St Wilfrid procession, headed by a drum and fife-band, was less enthusiastically received than usual. The Feast was held a week before the proper time for the convenience of the racing authorities, and thus the citizens lost the advantage of the Bank Holiday Monday. The racecourse receipts were also seriously af-fected. A lesson was learnt and the change of date did not happen again for many years.

A company was formed to acquire *Highfield* the late Mr R. Kearsley's mansion in Palace Road, later to become part of the Training College, for a hydropathic establishment. It was proposed to raise £20,000 in £10 shares.

September. The Cottage Hospital was closed to allow a connection to be made to a new wing which had been added to the building to provide a men's ward.

1893-94. Francis Smith, Paint Manufacturer

Born in Ripon in 1854 and educated at Jepson's Hospital. He entered the firm of T. & R. Williamson, Paint and

Varnish Manufacturers, at the age of 14 and rose to be a partner and eventually managing director. He was elected to the Council in 1883 and became an alderman in 1889. In corporation affairs he was active in the establishment of the sewage works and in efforts to maintain the canal. In politics he was a Liberal. He was a freemason, a Justice of the Peace and a churchwarden at the Cathedral. He died in 1911.

November. The Cathedral bells were rung and the flag flown in commemoration of the 'Happy deliverance of King James I and the three estates of England from the most traitorous and bloody-minded massacre by gunpowder'. In no other Cathedral is the flag hoisted in memory of Guy Fawkes—'when will similar good taste prevail in Ripon?'.

Mrs Stevenson of Harrogate, Honorary Secretary to the Harrogate S.P.C.A., gave a lecture on 'Kindness to Domestic Animals' at Ripon Union Workhouse.

New instruments, purchased at a cost of £50 18s for the Ripon City Band, were displayed in the window of Mr E. Cuss's tailors' shop in North Street.

December. There was a good attendance at a meeting in support of Women's Suffrage at the Temperance Hall, Duck Hill.

January. The year began with extremely severe frost followed by fog and snow. The intense cold caused much suffering among the poor and soup kitchens were opened.

There was much public complaint about the nuisance arising from cattle sales in the Market Place, but the majority of Market Place ratepayers were content with the situation.

The North Eastern Railway Company sought the authority of Parliament to sell or abandon the canal.

February. The Bishop consecrated the portion of the new cemetery allocated for interments according to the rites of the Church of England. The division of ground between the different denominations had given rise to some controversy as the Church people thought they were not fairly treated. In the following March a Ripon lady presented to the Corporation a hearse for the use of citizens who might not be able to afford to hire one. It was lightly constructed and designed to be hand-drawn.

March. Flames appeared as a gas supply connection was being made between the *Black Bull Hotel* and the new Mechanics Institute in Finkle Street, now the Post Office. Workmen tried to quench the flames by filling the trench with earth and water; this drove the gas into the cellar of the *Black Bull* causing an explosion and a fire in the dining room above.

April. A special meeting of the City Council received a proposed scheme for drainage and sewage disposal at an estimated cost of £17,000.

In the following month an inquiry was authorised into the anomalous position of Aismunderby with Bondgate, lying partly within the City and partly within the Rural District. As a result the union of Bondgate (population 763 and with 195 inhabited houses) with Ripon was confirmed, and Aismunderby, Whitcliffe-with-Thorpe and a small outlying part of Ripon were constituted as a new township of Littlethorpe in the Rural District.

June. Day's Menagerie stayed overnight in the Market Place and the residents were subjected to sundry screechings and roarings. When leaving the city the elephant collided with a lamp post near Trinity School and broke the pillar.

The Town Clerk's annual report listed Corporation property as follows: the gasworks and mains, water mains and reservoirs; about 70 acres of land at Lumley Moor, Lark Hill, Whitefields, the cemetery, Fishergreen and Bull Close; the Market tolls of the city and the stall house and plant in Blossomgate, seven shops in Middle Street at an annual rental of £98; the weigh-house on North Street and bathhouse at Skellbank and the buildings and land of the highways depot with the steam roller, four horses and seven carts.

Messrs R. Kearsley and Co, Varnish Manufacturers, reduced the hours of labour to 7.30 am to 5.30 pm during the week, closing as usual at 1.00 pm on Saturdays; the wages remained the same.

Mrs Boyd Carpenter opened the newly-erected Girls' Club in Water Skellgate (now the Department of Employment). A club had been meeting for five years in a house in Bondgate and had 120 names on its register.

July. The Bishop of Ripon, Dr William Boyd Carpenter, was considered to be the most eloquent preacher in the Church of England and, as Chaplain to the Queen, was believed to have preached before her more frequently than any other cleric. On being asked how he managed to address so exalted a personage and retain his composure, he replied that he never addressed her at all. He knew there would be present the Queen, the Princes, the Household and the servants down to the scullery maid, 'And I preach to the scullery maid and the Queen understands me'.

August. For some years it had been the custom to augment the normal workhouse dinner on St Wilfrid's Sunday by the addition of broad beans and parsley sauce; this year the Master and Matron thought something should also be done at tea-time and one-and-a-half-dozen large fruit tarts were served and greatly appreciated.

7,060 people visited Ripon by rail on Bank Holiday. Nine excursions and six relief trains were run.

The Hornblower was dismissed, not having discharged his duties to the satisfaction of the Corporation, and the City Bellman installed in the office temporarily. Mr Masterman, of the City Band, was subsequently appointed Hornblower.

October. The City Court dealt with an abnormal number of 'drunk and disorderly' cases; there had been much brawling in the streets, particularly in Stonebridgegate with fighting between persons of both sexes, hair being pulled and pokers used as weapons. One labourer was stated to be making his 49th appearance before the Bench.

1894-95. JOHN BAYNES, Slate Merchant

Mayor 1885-86-87-88

November. The large saloon, the entrance and staircase of the Town Hall were redecorated on the instructions of the Marquess of Ripon, the owner of the property. The full-length portrait of Mrs Allanson by Henry Melbourne was restored and rehung.

The Neptune Works (formerly the Ripon Steam Plough Works) near Albion Terrace was offered for sale but was withdrawn at £650.

December. After one of the most destructive gales on record, very few houses in the city were without damage. The spire of St Wilfrid's Church gave way damaging the ceiling, *The Hall* needed much repair and the Workhouse, Post Office and the *Unicorn Hotel* suffered damage.

January. Captain Charles Lister Oxley of *The Hall* (now Minster House) was promoted to the rank of Rear-Admiral in the Royal Navy.

Lord Ripon entertained a shooting party of seven guns at Studley Royal; they killed upwards of 5,300 head of game in three days.

The Dean formally opened the new Cathedral Hall in High St Agnesgate. Except on the south, the old walls of what had for centuries been the Free Grammar School, and later, for a few years, the Choir School, were retained and replastered. All the houses along that side of the street were pulled down and when the southern end of the schoolroom was exposed it was found to be of 'post and pan' construction and in an extremely rotten condition. In front of this wall, two feet below ground, the builders found a cobbled pavement which may have been the yard before the master's house was built. A committee room was added to the south-east corner by the hall.

Wintry weather with heavy snowfalls and severe frost caused great distress. A soup kitchen was opened for three days a week distributing 500 qts. of soup and loaves of bread. For eight weeks the Succentor of the Cathedral, the Revd. F. H. Taylor, provided free breakfasts for poor children of all denominations in the Priest Lane Mission Room where 5,000 meals were served and 9,000 buns distributed. Tickets for 225 cwts. of coal were issued to the poor and clothing provided for children.

Woodchopping for the unemployed men was organised in yards in Bondgate and the tan-yard in Agnesgate, loads of wood being supplied from the Studley and Newby estates. The Bishop wrote to the Mayor from Calais, 'We are detained here, snowbound, on our way home, but I must not delay to write and tell you how greatly grieved I am to hear there is distress in the good city of Ripon. I do not know what steps you have taken, but I am sure you will have taken steps that are wise and kind. May I send you the enclosed cheque (£10) to assist your funds? I hope to be home in a few days, when I shall be able to hear more of the conditions of the city'. There were compensations—an adventurous gentleman skated the whole distance from York to Ripon on rivers and canals.

Ladies; Mrs Smithson, Mrs Lee and Mrs Jacob were elected for the first time to the Board of Guardians.

The Medical Officer of Health reported 186 births, 19 of which were illegitimate, and 140 deaths including 81 of infants under one year in 1894. He considered the death-rate high for a non-industrial town and thought it due to the overcrowded and insanitary condition of many of the old cottages crowded into courtyards. All the property in High St Agnesgate which formerly drained into the disused millrace (presumably the underground culvert) had been connected to a new sewer.

March. The Dean of Ripon, the Very Revd. W. R. Freemantle, D.D., died in his 88th year at Wimbledon, where he had spent the early part of the year. In his will he desired to be buried with his first wife in Middle Claydon churchyard and that a cottage hospital be endowed in their memory.

April. The Revd. W. H. Freemantle, Canon of Canterbury and Fellow of Balliol since 1882, second son of Lord Cottisloe and nephew of the late dean, was appointed to the Deanery. Born in 1831, he was educated at Eton and Oxford and had been curate to his uncle at Middle Claydon and incumbent of St Mary's Bryanston Square. He married a daughter of Sir Culling Eardley.

May. The May number of *Cassell's Magazine* awarded the first prize of five guineas for a short story to Mrs Jacob of the Collegiate School—the mother of the novelist and writer Naomi Jacob.

Mrs Hill of Ripon, a painter of miniature portraits, had three of her works accepted for exhibition by the Society of Painters in Water-Colours and three, one of which was hung, by the Royal Academy. Shortly before his death, a new portrait of Dr W. R. Freemantle by Miss Mary Lascelles Leesmith had been exhibited in the Town Hall. She had had a portrait of Mrs Williamson of *Sunny Bank*, Borrage Lane, exhibited at the Royal Academy in 1893 and a view of Bishopton Bridge in the following year.

June. St Wilfrid's Roman Catholic Church, which had been closed for five months for repairs after severe storm damage, was re-opened on Whit Sunday. The holiday weekend saw a large influx of visitors and 1,412 people passed through the gates of Fountains Abbey, which were opened free of charge on Whit Monday when the usual Sunday School demonstrations and services were held.

The third exhibition of the Ripon Industrial Society in the Victoria Hall saw a considerable fall in the number of exhibits compared with the two previous years, but the exhibition was enhanced by a display of old needlework lent by ladies and gentlemen of the city. The main object of the Society was to encourage industrious habits, especially among the working classes of Ripon and neighbourhood.

July. William Prest, the last of the Ripon watchmen, died at the age of 83. He held the office for many years along with John Simmonds, the Hornblower, who died in 1887. The watchman's duties ceased in 1876 when the City Police Force was increased from two to four constables. Up to that date the watchmen, like the wakemen of old, kept guard over the city by night: their sentry boxes were placed at opposite sides of the Market Place whence every hour they started on their rounds.

The storming of the Pass of Killiecrankie: a fracas occurred between Grammar School boys and town boys in College Walk (commonly known as Killie-crankie). Stones were thrown to the danger of the public and the boys were charged with common nuisance but the case was dismissed.

The annual Mayoral Picnic for about 50 guests took the unusual form of a visit to York with the return journey made by water via the Ouse and the Ripon and Boroughbridge canals.

Mr John Lloyd Wharton (Unionist) was elected MP for the Ripon Division with a 707 majority over his Liberal opponent Mr Robert Charles Phillimore.

August. There were 61 applicants for the head-mastership of Ripon Grammar School; the Governors appointed Mr C. C. Bland, M.A., Headmaster of the Devon County School, West Buckland. The vacancy arose when, to the regret of many citizens, the Revd. W. Yorke-Fausset resigned to take up purely clerical duties.

The Surveyor submitted plans for a urinal and two W.C.s with 'penny-in-the-slot locks' on Duck Hill at a cost of £30. The Council went into committee and, on discovering that the urinal would cost £16 10s, decided that this alone should be erected. At their next meeting they discussed a scheme for the creation of a public park on the land around the Court House, including a suggestion that the Court House should be turned into a refreshment room with toilets for visitors and a new court house added to the Town Hall.

September. There was a huge attendance at the Victoria Hall when Mr Albert Chevalier paid his second visit to Ripon. He was accompanied by a vocalist, his solo pianist Mr Alfred West, and Mr Charles Bertram, a prestidigitateur. Another popular attraction was the well-known troupe of the Kentucky Minstrels who played for two nights in November.

October. The Prince of Wales was the guest of Mr R. C. de Grey Vyner at Newby Hall; it was a private visit but the station was decorated and a crimson carpet laid along the platform. The Prince spent two days at Thirsk races and attended morning service at the Cathedral.

There was excitement in King Street when the body of a 68-year-old widow was found head first in a peggy tub. At the inquest the jury returned a verdict that the deceased was 'found drowned in a peggy tub containing about two bucketsful of water, but how she came there there was no evidence to show'.

1895-96. George Frederick Samuel Robinson, 1st Marquess of Ripon, K.G.

Born in 1827 during the short premiership of his father, Viscount Goderich, later 1st Earl of Ripon (for whom see: Jones, *Prosperity Robinson*, 1967). Prominent Liberal statesman, member of Gladstone's Cabinets and Viceroy of India 1880-4. Biographies by: Wolf, *The Life of the 1st Marquess of Ripon K.G.*, (2 vols) 1921, and Denholm, *Lord Ripon*, a political biography, 1982. There are many references and a long account of the lineage of the Robinsons in *The Ripon Millenary Record*. He took a great and generous interest in local affairs, he sat as the first member for Ripon on the West Riding County Council and held many offices in the city. He gave the site and buildings in Clotherholme Road and much financial help to the Grammar School and in 1897 presented the Town Hall to the Corporation. He is commemorated by a statue in the Spa Gardens.

November. The Mayor and several members of the Corporation had approached the Marquess on the question of the mayoralty and, after some discussion, Lord Ripon agreed to accept the office for the ensuing year. In so doing he was following the custom of the former Lords of Studley, John and William Aislabie and members of his own family. His great-uncle, Frederick Robinson, was Mayor in 1785-6 and his father, the 1st Earl of Ripon, was an alderman from 1809-1835. Ripon was following a popular trend; the *Yorkshire Post* noted that some ten or a dozen towns had recently induced a member of the Upper Chamber to preside over their councils. The Marquess was a convert to the Roman Catholic Church and did not attend the usual Cathedral service on Mayor's Sunday. Instead he attended St Wilfrid's Church in his official capacity escorted by the Sergeant-at-Mace and the Town Clerk; other members of the Corporation accompanied him but not in their robes. It was arranged that the horn should be blown at the Town Hall as representing the Mayor's official residence.

December. Death of Mr George Benson, for many years Canons' Verger and Parish Clerk at the Cathedral and since 1872, Cathedral Librarian. He had first entered the Cathedral as a chorister in 1838. He traced his descent to the same Nidderdale family as Dr E. W. Benson, Archbishop of Canterbury 1882-1898.

January. The Mayor and Mayoress entertained the boys of Jepson's Hospital in Water Skellgate, now the City Club, to tea at *Studley Royal* on New Years Day.

The Revd. M. de Courcy-Ireland and the members of the Scripture Union gave an entertainment at the Workhouse. The first part consisted of a service of song, illustrated by limelight views, entitled *Angels' Christmas*, followed by recitations and a duet. Oranges, nuts and biscuits were distributed during the interval.

The playgrounds of the Boys' and Girls' Trinity Schools were enlarged and improved at a cost of £200, borne by the Ripon and Wakefield Diocesan Training College who used the schools for providing teaching practice. It was then expected that the cost of building a new workshop for manual instruction in one corner of the boys' playground would be paid for by the parish and congregation.

Messrs Hepworth and Co of the old-established brewery business in Bondgate completed extensive additions to their premises. The Brewery, known for many years as *The Crown Steam Brewery*, was the property of the trustees of the Hospitals of St John and St Mary Magdalen.

A large and fashionable audience attended the Victoria Hall to witness an assault-at-arms and gymnastic display given by the members of the H. & I. (Ripon) Companies 1st Vol. Batt. P.W.O. West Yorkshire Regiment.

February. The Council accepted Councillor Williamson's suggestions for the improvement of the Market Square. These included the removal of the fountain and the Russian gun which allowed space to be cleared between the Cross and the Town Hall to accommodate the cattle and sheep markets. This area of 706 square yards was to be asphalted and a drinking tap fixed to the Market Cross. In the event, the fountain was moved to a site near the road archway leading to the Court House, its brass memorial plate repolished and the shields adorning the upper portion of the structure re-gilded. The removal of the Russian gun, the subject of criticism for a quarter of a century, was carried out by Corporation labourers under conditions very different from the pomp and ceremony and military display which marked the placing of the trophy at the close of the Crimean War nearly forty years before.

April. A plate glass window at No. 1 Kirkgate was broken by a horse backing a trap into it. The accident occurred when the horse was frightened by a large sheet of paper wrapping itself round its head. Frequent complaints had been made concerning the large quantity of loose paper blowing about in the city on market days.

There was the usual large arrival of visitors by road and rail for the Easter holiday. Fountains Abbey had very heavy traffic; a football match was played between Ripon and the Dewsbury Masters on Monday; ladies formed a large proportion of the considerable number of cyclists in the neighbourhood. At the Easter Day service, the Cathedral was enriched by the gift of an altar-cross in memory of Mrs Bickersteth, the wife of the late Bishop, who died in 1894.

A special meeting of the City Council was held to discuss the subject of the purchase of a gold chain for the Mayoress to commemorate the year of office of Lady Ripon. Subscriptions were invited in sums of one shilling and upwards. The chain was presented at a luncheon held in the Victoria Hall on 20 August as part of the 1896 Ripon Festival.

Solicitous relatives made enquiries about the well-being of a brother and sister who lived in Tomlinson's Court in Blossomgate. They were both of a weak intellect and remarkable for their unkempt, tattered and dishevelled appearance. After the death of the brother, Elizabeth continued alone doing charring until at the age of 67 she was taken into the Workhouse. The relieving officer accompanied by a policeman visited the house to take charge of her goods and chattels and found a total of £281 11s 6d in small amounts wrapped in paper all over the place; enough dresses to clothe her for years, large quantities of calico and other materials and many new hairbrushes and bottles of eau de Cologne. One room contained three tons of coal.

Following the proposal to hold a second race meeting in Ripon an address was published by the Dean, clergy and ministers of Ripon to parents and guardians to shield young children from temptation and ensure 'that they might not see or hear what might defile their purity'. The text emphasised 'the gambling, drunkenness and deeds which it was a shame to name and which were some of the sad features of such times'.

May. The City Council considered the need for a bell or some other distinctive sound to call together the fire brigade at that time was done by a messenger, a method which it was suggested wasted precious time. It was thought the use of a bell would call too many people and the idea was shelved.

Rear-Admiral Charles Lister Oxley was appointed second-in-command of the British Squadron on the China Station and his flag was hoisted on the cruiser *Grafton*.

There was a large and brilliant gathering in the Victoria Hall when a complimentary reception and talk was given in honour of the Marquess and Marchioness of Ripon as Mayor and Mayoress of the city.

June. A foundation memorial stone was laid of an extension to the Skellgate Wesleyan Mission Chapel. Originally erected in 1889, a vestry was added in 1891 but the congregation had outgrown the building by 1896. The extension would be on the east side of the chapel, the old building being part of the new structure, the length of the original chapel becoming the width of the new premises. When completed the new accommodation would be for 380 people, nearly three times the size of the old.

July. £1,760 had been collected to date towards the £3,000 needed to complete the erection of recreation room, science room, extra student accommodation and a chapel for daily services at the Ripon Training College in answer to the recommendations of Her Majesty's Inspector of Education. The extensions were completed in September 1898. The hostel for additional students was erected to the north of the old college buildings connected by corridors. On the ground floor there were a science room, demonstrator's room, classroom and two governesses' rooms. The middle and upper floors each had 18 cubicles for students and a governess's bedroom on each floor together with the requisite bathrooms.

The inmates of Ripon workhouse, by kind permission of Lord Ripon's agent, had their annual outing to Hackfall. They were conveyed in three brakes, accompanied by the Master and Matron and the cook. They enjoyed games, walks and a substantial dinner. At tea-time they were joined by Mr and Mrs F. Smith. Local tradesmen supplied nuts, biscuits and sweets, and money to provide prizes for both winners and losers in the racing.

The Ripon Bowling Club was invited by Sir Reginald Graham to meet the Bedale Bowling Club on the historic green at Norton Conyers which is associated with King Charles II who is said to have played there when visiting Yorkshire.

Lord Grantley offered at auction a number of properties in or near Ripon at a sale held at the *Unicorn Hotel*. Three houses and shops at Nos. 7, 8 and 9 Kirkgate (whole rental £68 p.a.) were sold for £2,025 to Mr F. S. Gowland, solicitor.

August. The corporation was approached by the Ripon Naturalists' Club to take over a superb collection of birds, animals and geological specimens which had been collected at a cost of £14,000 by the late Mr Rothery of Littlethorpe Hall. The trustees of the estate had given the collection to the Club but it was not in a financial position to remove or exhibit the specimens. The Council agreed to house the collection in the Park Street Museum in space vacated by a kindergarten which had occupied one of the rooms.

The corporation decided the Millenary Festival had been so successful that each tenth milestone of years should be observed with celebration and pageantry. By February £700 had been guaranteed and Mr D'Arcy de Ferrars was again appointed Master of the Revels at a fee of 100 guineas with five per cent of the nett profits. Tom Williamson agreed to write the libretto for the main pageant *Boadicea to Victoria* to be enacted at Fountains Abbey. In April florists and others were asked to grow flowers which would be in bloom in August for use in the Grand Carnival and Battle of Flowers and £150 was allocated for prizes for the best-

decorated cars, cycles and carriages. Preparations were made for an open air play *Robin Hood and the Curtal Friar*, a children's procession illustrating nursery rhymes and the roasting of an ox. The Festival took place on from 18 to 22 August and was a tremendous success with over 800 people taking part in brilliant weather. The town was profusely decorated, the Town Hall newly painted and on the final day crowds of some 15,000 strong came from all parts of Yorkshire. The inhabitants of Kirkgate produced special decorations and illuminations, the main piece being a floral arch across the street with the motto 'Floreat Kirkgate'. Mr Moss of Moss's China Shop in the Market Place produced special porcelain items bearing the coats of arms of Ripon City, Fountains Abbey and the See of Ripon. Messrs William Harrison printed a handsome record of the festival similar to the *Millenary Record*. When the final bills came in there was a deficit of £163 18s 4d, largely because with no security guards at Studley Park hundreds of people had got in without paying. However, the Guarantee Fund stood at £1,200 and when completed there was a profit of £17 6s 4d which was given to the Elementary School Fund.

September. The death occurred of Mr H. C. Bickersteth, a son of Dr Bickersteth, the late Bishop of Ripon, at the comparatively early age of 47. He had become a partner in the firm of Messrs Robert Kearsley and Co, varnish and colour manufacturers. He was Mayor in 1883-84.

Alderman Joseph Brooks Parkin of Kirkgate and Mayor of Ripon in 1892-3 died suddenly at Southport at the age of 57. Educated at Ripon Grammar School, he was articled to Mr John Brown, Chemist in Westgate and in 1867 went into business for himself in Kirkgate (see p.4).

The dead body of Charles Barker, butler to Lord Ripon, was found in the Ripon Corporation reservoir. His hat and stick were found floating on the water and it was assumed he had slipped when walking along the path. A verdict of found drowned was returned. The water was run off at Whitefields and the reservoir thoroughly cleaned.

October. The new sewage disposal works at Fishergreen were officially opened by the Mayor on 20 October.

1896-97. THOMAS WILLIAMSON, Varnish Manufacturer

Born 1853, son of Robert Williamson and grandson of Thomas Williamson, Mayor 1848-9. Educated Ripon Grammar School, Rugby and Balliol College, Oxford. Went to the United States in 1879, where he pioneered as a cattleman in Colorado and then took up journalism—in later years he was a regular contributor to the *Leeds Mercury*. Finally returned to Ripon in 1892 and was elected to the Council in 1895; he is reported to have said of his colleagues that he would rather drive cattle from Texas to Klondike than the Ripon Corporation to a decision. An active Liberal in the family tradition, he was invited to contest the Ripon

parliamentary seat in 1899 but declined because of dissension over local issues. He was a prolific writer in verse and prose and he and his wife were preeminent in dramatic and musical activity in and around Ripon. For an account of his life and examples of his literary excursions see the memoir by his wife Alice J. Williamson, *Williamsons, with particular reference to Tom Williamson and his times.* He died at Borrage House in 1920.

The population statistics for 1896 were as follows: births, 196, 4 illegitimate (25.8 per 1,000); deaths, 132 (17.4 per 1,000).

November. The Marquess of Ripon was presented with the honorary freedom of the city at a ceremony at the Town Hall. The presentation was in recognition of his Lordship's services to the state and to the city at the end of his year of office as Mayor.

Mr Tom Williamson was invested with his robe and chain of office as Mayor for 1897 when the country would celebrate Queen Victoria's Diamond Jubilee. The Mayor's first duty was to read a letter from Lord Ripon, who was ill and unable to attend, making a free gift of the Town Hall to the Corporation.

December. Extensive improvements were completed at the Bishopton flax spinning mills of Messrs W. Waite, Sons, and Atkinson. New floors had been laid, new machinery added and electric light installed. Bishopton Mills had the advantage of water power from the River Laver and at that time of year the volume of water was sufficient to drive not only the flax mill but also the adjacent corn mill, though the latter generally only had power for night working. This water power drove the dynamo for generating electric light. Power was also given for the rope-walk machinery on the east side of the mill. The mills employed 30 to 40 people.

Councillor and Mrs Lee gave the traditional Christmas entertainment to the inmates of the Ripon Union Workhouse. Ripon seems to have been exceptional in its annual support of this event. There were the usual generous gifts ranging from toys, books, dressed dolls, sweets and crackers for the children, to tea and sugar for the women and tobacco or snuff for the men in the Infirmary, one dozen woollen shawls for the

old women, cakes, oranges and apples, and a bottle of rum from Alderman Wells for the sauce.

February. A petition was presented to the Corporation against planting trees in the Market Place and a letter appeared in the *Gazette* from a citizen objecting that these could become an interference with business, being a nuisance during wet or windy weather, bringing an appearance of desolation during winter and lastly being a useless and needless expense. The Council held a special meeting to thrash out the matter and finally decided to go ahead with the scheme. On 19 February, the ex-Mayors of the city each planted one of twelve lime trees, the gift of the Mayor and Mayoress and the ex-Mayors. The planting was followed by a civic luncheon at the *Unicorn Hotel.*

Following a cruelty to children case in Ripon, the Mayor, Mr Tom Williamson, as Chief Magistrate deplored the conditions in which many children were brought up in the city. He said he had no doubt that there was property which had seen little repair during the whole of the Victorian era and that it would be a fitting commemoration of the record reign if owners brought such houses in line with the developments of the century.

A 'Victoria Endowment Fund' was started to restore the finances of the Grammar School which was reported to be in a poor way due to payment for new buildings and a reduction in the number of boarders. The account was planned to close at the end of the year by which time £1,263 4s 1d had been raised. Early in 1898 the governors decided to reduce the boarding fee to £45 per term in an attempt to encourage an increase in the number of boarders.

The Ripon Agricultural Association held a meeting to discuss the possibility of building a covered market in Ripon for the sale of butter, eggs, poultry and fruit. The Marquess of Ripon offered a suitable site abutting on the Market Place to the Corporation for the sum of £2,500. A public subscription list was to be set up to pay for the project.

March. The Mayoress of Ripon, Mrs Tom Williamson, was presented at court by the Marchioness of Ripon at the second Drawing-room of the season at Buckingham Palace. She wore the new official chain of the Mayoress of Ripon and a cream satin dress painted with butterflies and garlands, lined with azalea pink; the train was of cream, azalea-patterned brocade and also lined in pink.

May. A deputation from the employees of Messrs T. and R. Williamson waited upon the Mayor to present him with a silver salver inscribed 'Presented to Tom Williamson, Esq., J.P., by the employees of T. and R. Williamson Ltd to commemorate his year of office as Mayor. May 1897'.

A man was brought before the Liberty Court for not contributing to the maintenance of his father, who was chargeable to the Common Fund of the Ripon Union. The man had signed an agreement to pay one shilling a week but had paid only once. The defendant said he could not afford it as he had a wife and children to keep and he also helped to support his younger brother. His wages on average came to 19s 0d per week but he was unable to work in bad weather. The court decided he could afford to make the contribution and an order to pay was made.

June. The Corporation accepted the offer by the then anonymous donors (later known to be the Misses Cross of Coney Garth) to build a Clock Tower at the junction of Palace and Princess Roads and North Road in celebration of Queen Victoria's Diamond Jubilee. The Misses Cross handed over the deed of gift and the key of the Victoria Clock Tower on the anniversary of the Queen's coronation day the following year, 1898. The Mayor and members of the Corporation received the gift before a large crowd and the dedication was carried out by the Bishop of Ripon.

The City Surveyor reported on the condition of the Town Hall following a complaint from the Postmaster that slates from the roof had fallen near the entrance of the Post Office next door. The Council agreed that the front portion of the roof be re-covered with Welsh slates and the outside brickwork and the keystones repaired as required. In consequence of the expenditure on this work, the decoration, painting and supply of curtains for the hall had to be deferred. On Mr Baynes's advice, the old bell-tower housing the disused fire bell was removed.

The trustees of the Hospital of St Mary Magdalen ordered restoration work to be carried out on the Leper Chapel. The surrounding objectionable buildings were cleared away, the walls strengthened by buttresses and the ancient tiles relaid. The oak screen and the ancient plate chest were returned temporarily for the visit of the Yorkshire Archaeological Society.

Although 20 June was the day set for the national celebration of Queen Victoria's Diamond Jubilee, festivities started in Ripon on Saturday 19 June. There was a great gathering of children for a presentation of medals in the Town Hall to those attending the Ripon elementary schools. The Council had given a grant of £25 towards the decoration of the Town Hall and general festivities. The Mayor and Corporation together with a congregation of 1,600 people attended a special service at the Cathedral on the next day, Ascension Sunday. The band of the 1st Batt. P.W.O. West Yorkshire Regiment accompanied the hymns. At 3.30 pm, 300 over-sixties sat down to a free dinner, and in the afternoon 2,400 Sunday school children joined a demonstration in the Market Place and later returned to the schools for a Yorkshire tea. In the evening of 22 June the Cricket Field was open for gala and sports. At ten o'clock the bonfire was lighted at Studley Park and a line of other bonfires on the Hambledon Hills could be seen in the distance. This was followed by a fireworks display. Bondgate had its own celebrations; 320 children sat down to tea followed by 650 adults in the grounds of Bondgate Grange. Later there were children's sports and a Punch and Judy Show. The entrance to Bondgate had a decorative arch in the shape of an ancient gateway. In the midst of a very crowded day the Mayor and Mayoress paid the district a visit.

July. Mrs Lee, one of the Board of Guardians at the Workhouse, submitted a resolution to answer the problem posed by the refusal of the children to eat their daily porridge. She proposed that they should be served bread and butter with jam and tea on alternate days or milk if they would drink it. Mr Hargrave objected saying that half the children in Ripon would be glad to have jam and butter for breakfast and suggested that there was plenty of good dripping from the best of beef available. The Guardians agreed to the proposal but the Local Government Board would have to sanction any change of diet.

The Mayor invited representatives from Ripon's organisations to meet the Marquess of Ripon at a commemorative luncheon on St Wilfrid's Saturday 31 July to celebrate the formal presentation of the Town Hall to the citizens of Ripon. It was stipulated that each delegate was to be an active, not honorary, member of the Societies represented. Local Friendly Societies, Political Clubs, Cricket and Football Clubs, the Mechanics Institute, the Cottage Hospital, the Volunteers and Scientific Societies accepted. As the Council Chamber was inconvenient and too small for the ceremony, it took place in the Town Hall garden, where the Marquess formally handed over to the Mayor the deed of conveyance.

August. Dr Charles Husband received at his home in St Agnesgate a deputation who presented him with an address in appreciation of his services as a medical practitioner in the city during the previous half-century. He had been a prominent figure in the public life of Ripon for more than that time. As a doctor he always kept abreast of advances in medical science and was a constant campaigner for better conditions for the poorer classes. He was born at Green Hammerton, educated at Whixley School and London University and started practice in Ripon as a surgeon in 1844. He was elected to the City Council in 1853 and retired in 1862 acting as Mayor in 1860. He was appointed Medical Officer to the Board of Guardians in 1853, Coroner for the Ripon Liberty in 1870 and in 1876 Medical Officer of Health, and retired from these posts early in 1897. Dr Husband died in September 1898.

September. Mr James Fairburn of Caxton House died in his 79th year. He was a native of Ripon and entered his father's printing business on the east side of the Market Place.

The Mayor received a Diamond Jubilee medal from the Queen. These medals, diamond in shape, were made in gold and silver bearing a likeness of Her Majesty in 1887 and 1897.

Mr Arthur Cardew, barrister-at-law, an assistant Charity Commissioner, opened an inquiry at Ripon with reference to charities and endowments in the ancient parish of Ripon. This was part of a general inquiry into all the charities of the West Riding of Yorkshire; the only previous inquiry had been in 1818, the findings of which were published in 1820.

A memorial stone was laid at the Drill Hall of a recreation room for the Ripon Detachment of the 1st West Yorkshire Regiment. The stone, which faced the

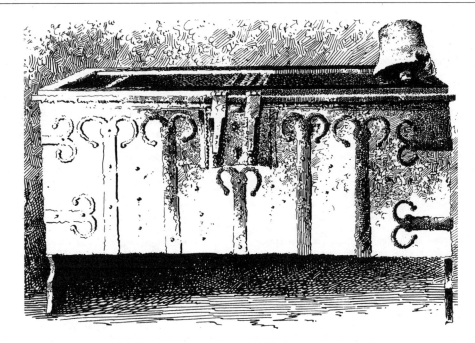

1. Old chest in St Mary Magdalen (Fossick)

2. The old leper chapel of St Mary Magdalen (Fossick)

drill yard, bore the following inscription: 'This stone was laid by Colonel G. Kearsley V.D. commanding the 1st V.B. West Yorkshire Regiment, September 29th 1897 to commemorate the 60th year of the reign of Her Majesty Queen Victoria'.

The Mayor marked his appreciation of the Town Clerk's services by presenting him with framed portraits of the Mayoress and himself in Court dress, each of which was signed.

The Mayor decided to break with tradition when inviting his guests to the annual tea and entertainment on 22 and 23 October. Instead of all the guests being citizens of age 60 and over, as hitherto, the Mayor's list was representative of the Queen's record reign with 360 guests born in each of the six decades: 60 born between 1837-47; 180 from the next three decades; and in the last two decades, those born between 1877 and 1897, boys and girls aged one to twenty who had made the best attendance at elementary school. The different decades were differentiated by different colours in the flower decorations at the tables. The youngest guest, a Jubilee baby of four months, received a silver spoon. In the evening a thousand people were present when Charles Dickens's *A Christmas Carol* was presented.

1897-8.   JOHN BANKS LEE, Draper

Mayor 1882-3, 1884-5. Born in Stokesley in 1838, educated at Grewelthorpe and Masham Grammar School. Came to Ripon in 1859 and joined his uncle in the Drapery and Millinery business of Rayner and Lee. Elected to the Council in 1872. See entries in *Ripon Millenary Record*.

November. At a meeting of the feoffees of Jepson's Hospital, attention was drawn to the dilapidated condition of the tombstone in the burial ground of the Cathedral of the late Zachariah Jepson, founder of the Bluecoat School. The Town Clerk was requested to have the tomb rebuilt and re-lettered.

Councillor Lee said he was sorry to see that the Sanitary Inspector had ordered the removal of earth closets in Queen's Head Court and the substitution of water closets. He was satisfied that earth closets were more healthy and, as water closets were usually badly constructed and were in direct communication

with the main drain, they were generally very injurious and dangerous. Alderman Kearsley said that they had thought about the matter very carefully and had decided that, as the closets were very near the houses, water closets would get rid of the smell.

At the Municipal Elections there were surprise results when Mr William Harrison, who had been a Councillor for ten years, was rejected and Mr John Briscoe Briscombe, who put up as an Independent, was elected on his first attempt.

Ex-Councillor Harrison presented a small book, edited by the Dean, giving an account of the presentation ceremony of the Town Hall to the City by the Marquess of Ripon. The new Mayor directed that the gift be laid among the archives.

The annual Martinmas fair was attended by large numbers of both farmers and farm servants who came for hiring. There was a miscellaneous collection of shows, shooting-galleries, roundabouts and other diversions on the west side of the Market Place and the roadway on two sides of the Square and in High Skellgate was occupied by cattle. There were complaints from pedestrians having to dodge frequent charges of frightened animals and having to avoid stepping on the greasy, filthy surface of the tarmacadam. The postmaster complained that cattle and sheep standing in the roadway obstructed the entrance to the Post Office.

The City Council resolved that the cobbles on the Market Place should be removed and replaced with concrete in order to provide a more sanitary flooring for the cattle fairs. The Board of Agriculture finally took action in July 1898 when it issued an order prohibiting the sale of any cattle, sheep or swine in or at any market or fair, or on any highway or thoroughfare in the municipal borough of Ripon after 1 October. The order was later withdrawn with respect to the sale of cattle when the north side of the Market Place was provided with a concrete base.

December. General William Harrison Askwith, Colonel Commandant R.A., died in London. Born in 1811 at Pickhill, he was educated at Ripon Grammar School, received his commission signed by George IV in 1829 and commanded the firing party at the funeral of William IV in 1837. He was the eldest brother of Mr T. Askwith of the Old Bank, Ripon.

When the Mayor enquired how best the city might provide a permanent memorial to celebrate the Diamond Jubilee, the Queen expressed a wish through the Prince of Wales that something should be done for the poor and suffering. It was decided, in order to fulfil these sentiments, to enlarge the scope of the Nursing Institute which had been started for the gratuitous care of the sick and poor with a bequest of £1,000 given by the late Lady Mary Vyner. A fund had been opened in April and by December donations had totalled £281 12s 7d and subscriptions had reached £56 19s 6d. At the first annual meeting in February 1898 it was reported that two extra nurses had been employed. A lease for five years on No. 2 Bondgate Green had been taken and furnished with gifts from friends to provide accommodation.

January. The announcement of the death at the age of 42 of Mrs Emily Oxley, wife of Admiral Charles Oxley of *The Hall*, was received with deep regret. She was the eldest daughter of the late Mr Robert Kearsley and she left a family of seven children. In December 1898 a white marble monument was placed in the south-east corner of the nave of the Cathedral. The design, by Admiral Oxley himself, represents emblematically the deceased lady, her husband and children in cherubic form with wings, looking towards the final reunion of mother and family.

The Marquess of Ripon was re-nominated as County Councillor for Ripon. He had held office for nine years.

February. There was a large attendance at the Town Hall when, under the auspices of the Ripon Agricultural Association, Councillor Tom Williamson gave a lecture describing his own experiences entitled *Ranching in the Rockies, or Farming in the Far West*.

March. Councillor Williamson again appeared in the press, this time as correspondent for the N.S.P.C.C. Ripon Branch. In his letter he attacked property-owners stating 'there have recently been found cases in Ripon where ten human beings have been herded together in a space scarcely adequate for a self-respecting litter of pigs'.

The City Surveyor prepared a plan for a new street from Fishergate, west of the Market Place, principally through Lord Ripon's property, much of it insanitary, to the junction of Park Street and Blossomgate. The proposed tramway through the City from the railway station to Studley Park would have used this route.

The Ripon Cathedral clergy made a welcome discovery in a collection bag. After a service in the Cathedral in connection with the bi-centenary of the S.P.C.K. the offertory amounted to £24 3s 9d. A day or two later, after a hint had been given by an anonymous caller, the collection bags were re-examined and a £50 note was found.

Mr Thomas Simpson of Rayner Street, gardener and botanist, died at the age of 86. He was an acknowledged authority on the habitats of various species with many references in Baker's *Flora of the North Riding* and received a silver medal from the Linnaean Society for his exhibition of rare British ferns.

April. Both hackney and farm horses were on view at the annual horse show held in Ripon Horse Fair.

May. An interesting event took place at the residence of the Mayor, Mr J. B. Lee. He had become a grandfather soon after taking office; a few weeks later the Mayoress presented his worship with a son. Councillor and Mrs Lee were given a silver box surmounted by a silver cradle at a gathering held at the Town Hall in August to celebrate the event. This was the third time in the last twenty years that a silver cradle had been presented to the Mayor and Mayoress in office to commemorate the birth of a child, the other recipients being Mr and Mrs Collinson in 1878 and Mr and Mrs Bickersteth in 1884.

An application was made to the City Council for the erection of a verandah in front of the Ripon Club (now Boots' the Chemist) which would be the full width of the pavement with five supporting pillars fixed in the kerb.

The news of Mr Gladstone's death was received with regret by inhabitants of Ripon of all political shades and to large numbers it was a cause of genuine sorrow. Many blinds were drawn and the flag on the Town Hall flew at half mast. On Sunday his life and death was the subject of a discourse delivered from every pulpit; most church attenders wore mourning and in nonconformist churches mourning drapery was hung from pulpits and communion tables.

June. The Marquess of Ripon offered for sale at auction the *Studley Hotel*, Market Place, and the *Royal Oak*, Kirkgate. Both properties were withdrawn at £3,075 and £2,950 respectively.

Amongst a gift of books to Ripon Museum Library was a bound volume of *Play bills of the Ripon Amateur Dramatic Society* 1851-1855. The first performance was in the Public Rooms but later the society removed to the Georgian Theatre Royal.

August. A committee of the Victorian Nursing Institute recommended the establishment of a Ripon Branch with an annual subscription of 2s 6d for persons earning up to 30s per week and 5s for those earning more than that amount.

Mr Frank Benson, the distinguished Shakespearian actor, brought his Old English Comedy Company to Ripon. The Company attracted large audiences to open-air performances in the gardens at *Sunny Bank*, kindly placed at his disposal by Mr and Mrs R. Williamson. A performance of *As You Like It* was given in the afternoon and *Twelfth Night* was played in the evening.

The Mayor and Mayoress added another item to the year's hospitality when they held a garden party in the grounds of their residence *North Bridge House*. More than 100 guests including the Marquess and Marchioness of Ripon accepted invitations. Mr H. Taylor's band discoursed sweet music on the lawn.

September. A new wooden bridge over the Skell to Borrage Lane was completed.

The visiting committee to the Workhouse agreed that fish should be given for dinner on Fridays which would then consist of 8 oz potatoes and 3 oz of bread. Previously Friday had been a meatless day, and the meal had consisted of only a plate of rice which was not sufficient to sustain an able-bodied man.

Eight members of the Cathedral Bellringers Society assisted by two ringers from Middlesborough and Stockton-on-Tees rang a date touch consisting of 1,898 changes (i.e. same as the years A.D.) and known as treble two royal in Kent Variation, in one hour and 19 minutes.

October. The Dean and Chapter agreed to the fixing of lightning conductors to the Cathedral towers.

On the first Sunday in October a handsome brass cross, flower vases and altar linen, the gifts of three friends of St John's Church, were used for the first time.

The Littlethorpe Brick and Tile Co. was registered with a capital of £10,000 in £10 shares to acquire certain lands, brickworks and buildings in the township of Littlethorpe.

H.R.H. Princess Christian was a guest of the Bishop of Ripon and Mrs Boyd Carpenter at the Palace when she visited Ripon to open the three-day bazaar to raise funds for clearing the public elementary schools of debt. Miss Clara Butt, the famous prima donna, gave a recital in aid of the fund. £1,715 was raised towards the £2,000 needed.

1898-99. ARTHUR WELLS, Wine Merchant

Born in Ripon 1857 and educated at Mr Stephenson's School at Bishopton Close. He was employed first at the Yorkshire Bank and then joined the family firm of wine merchants. Elected to the Council 1887. He was an active supporter and a member of the Operatic Society. He was keenly interested in sport: athletics, rugby, golf and racing (chairman of the Racecourse Company for 29 years) and especially cricket. His score of 152 on the Ripon ground was a long-standing record; he was President of the Ripon Club and a Vice-President of the Yorkshire C.C.C. He died in 1934.

Population statistics for 1898: births 192, illegitimate 16 (25.1 per 1,000); deaths 148 (19.3 per 1,000); mortality by age, 26 under one year, 11 aged one to five years, 7 aged five to fifteen years, 4 aged fifteen to 25 years, 39 aged 25 to 65 years, 61 aged 65 years and over.

January. The Ure rose high above the level of the Sharow Road and floods, the worst since 29 January 1883, cut off any approach to Hewick Bridge along the Boroughbridge Road. Travellers had to follow a circuitous route to Hutton Bank, through Sharow and Bridge Hewick, to join the main road nearer to Boroughbridge.

February. The Marquess of Ripon, President of the Ripon Club, attended a social gathering and invitation ball at the Club to inaugurate a new billiard room. An excellent programme of music was provided. Considerable changes had been made to the premises on the Market Place: the old billiard room became the reading room and the previous small readers' room now became a retiring room for writing or taking tea.

The Corporation recommended that the Rt Hon J. L. Wharton M.P. should be asked to bring pressure on the North Eastern Railway Company to adopt telephonic communication between Ripon Station and the city, as a direct approach by the Council had failed.

Mr W. A. Stanley, the well-known, eloquent and versatile reciter, gave one of his attractive entertainments in the Public Rooms with a programme of dramatic scenes and humorous character sketches.

A new infirmary was opened at the Union Workhouse with tea and entertainment provided by various friends.

At the A.G.M. of the Naturalists' Club, Mr C. Watson showed his photographs of the skull of Eugene Aram, a gardener at Newby Hall who had been executed at York for the murder of Daniel Clarke in 1759, and the old house in Bondgate where Aram was said to have lived. A copy of the house photograph would be placed next to the skull which was preserved in the Museum.

3. *Eugene Aram's house (Fossick)*

March. Ripon Women's Liberal Association had a well-attended meeting in the Temperance Hall to hear papers read by Mrs T. Williamson 'The abilities and disabilities of women for citizenship', and Mr Storey on 'The duties of citizenship'. Mrs Thompson, a lady visitor from America, gave a pleasing rendering of the song *Happy Birds*.

An Inspector of the Local Government Board held an inquiry in Ripon to consider an application by the Mayor and Corporation to amend the Ripon Corporation Act 1886, so that the days on which fairs should be held and the tolls, stallages and rents laid down in the Act could be changed. Another enquiry was held in December with respect to an application by the Council to borrow £1,500 to pay for resurfacing of the Market Place insisted on by the Board of Agriculture to improve conditions at the cattle fair. This would replace the cobbles laid 100 years before. The Town Clerk gave the following facts: population 8,500, outstanding loans £75,927 and Corporation property value £135,517.

The Hon. and Very Revd. the Dean of Ripon was detained at the Deanery with a knee sprain following a bicycle accident. He was out riding with Archdeacon Danks when his front wheel caught in a rut causing the two machines to collide. Both clergymen were pitched from their bicycles with the Dean falling on top. Fortunately both reverend gentlemen escaped without serious injury.

A local syndicate purchased land on the west side of the city in the direction of Bishopton for building houses. The site between Skellbank and Bishopton comprised 24 acres and was bounded on the south by the River Laver, above which, along a natural terrace, the land runs from the corner of Studley Road and Grammar School Lane.

April. The interment took place at the Cemetery with military honours of Private Jesse Davidson, aged 40 years, a member of the Ripon detachment 1st Volunteer Battalion P.W.O. West Yorkshire Regiment and one-time Ripon Hornblower.

In the Report of the Education Committee of the Ripon Diocese, it was asserted that the Training College was one of the best-equipped of the provincial colleges in England. The Inspectors praised the work of the College and gave a high opinion on the behaviour of the students. The College Chapel was dedicated and two new wings were opened on 11 May.

May. The Council resolved 'that the room at present occupied (in the Town Hall) by the Church Institute, be occupied as a Mayor's reception and committee room'. The room, still the Mayor's Parlour, had been used for the previous 27 years as a free library and a reading and news room for local working men and apprentices.

After a long period of protest, criticism, and jokes, pertinent and impertinent, Ripon was brought up-to-date by the provision of lavishly-equipped public lavatories within the pavement of the Square and underground in front of the Town Hall. The cost of the work was £500 and it was proposed that flower beds and a seat should be placed above the structure.

June. The Ripon Racecourse Company received Lord Ripon's permission to remove their grandstand from the Red Bank course which had been originally erected in 1865 at a cost of £2,800. The stand had been used by the Volunteers in camp as the officers' mess. It was expected that future encampments would be on the new racecourse on the York Road. The Scarborough volunteers in camp on the old racecourse were warned against poaching on Lord Ripon's estate either for game or fish.

Several businesses with premises in the Market Square changed hands. Mr J. E. Parker retired from his grocery business at 15 Market Place which was taken over by Messrs W. B. Moss & Sons of Otley and Hitchin. Mr J. Grisewood transferred his drapery business from the east side of the Square to the west side and Messrs Hepworth removed to premises on the north side where they remained until 1983.

A notice board appeared facing the Studley Road indicating the 'Site of the *Fountains Abbey Hotel* and Pleasure Grounds' (later to become the *Ripon Spa Hotel*). The new hotel was planned as a three-storey building with 20 to 25 bedrooms on the first and second floors, some with sitting room, bathroom and dressing room. A lift was included and stabling for 15 horses, and the whole would be controlled by a limited liability company.

July. The West Ripon Estates Company was registered with a capital of £10,000 for the purpose of acquiring land for building in the area. Subscribers included R. H. Bowman, surgeon, F. S. Gowland, solicitor, J. S. Hurst of *Copt Hewick Hall*, H. Kearsley of *Woodside*, Tom Williamson of *Borrage House*, and others. Building would commence almost immediately on a group of semi-detached villas in a field beyond the *Fountains Abbey Hotel* site to be let on an annual rental of £35 to £40. In December the company gave 2,200 square yards of land to widen Clotherholme Lane to a width of 40 feet. At the same time, Church Lane was widened to the same width.

American visitors took a special interest in the ancient *Hen and Chicken Inn*, soon to be demolished in Fishergate with its massive stone foundations, stucco-plastered walls and heavy beams. Another road widening scheme was announced for the corner of High Skellgate and Westgate when a new bank building for the Yorkshire Banking Company would be set back another six feet behind the then building line.

On the retirement of Miss Ling, the first headmistress, Skellfield School was taken over by Miss Boycott and Miss Tarver. At a gathering to introduce the two ladies, the Dean of Ripon reminded his audience that Miss Boycott was the niece of Captain Boycott whose exploits in Ireland in 1880 had caused the name to pass into the English language.

The Railway Company fitted new gates at the third lock as part of its obligation to keep the Ripon canal in repair despite its little use.

The Ripon and District Steam Laundry recently set up by the Misses Burrill and Supple on the right bank of the Skell near the railway arch on Fishergreen was proving a highly successful and efficient business employing 25 people.

August. The sixth annual sports of the Ripon City Swimming Club were held at the Corporation Bathing Pavilion on the Ure.

The Race Committee complained that mounted police arrived too late to stop large numbers of people, variously estimated between two and 500, from rushing the turnstiles and entering without payment after an affray at the racecourse.

The Gas Company erected four Kitson oil lamps at each corner of the Market Place. It was estimated that these would be cheaper to run that the existing Bray's lamps which would be used elsewhere.

The Duke of York arrived at Ripon Station on a private visit to the Marquess of Ripon.

The Town Clerk was informed that Ripon Station would be equipped for the despatch of telegrams from 23 August. This proved a great boon, not only for travellers by rail, but also to residents living in Ure Bank and North Road.

The Mayor used his casting vote in favour of the proposal to connect the Town Hall, Town Clerk's residence and the Gasworks with the telephone exchange, as nearly half the council were opposed to the use of the telegraph and the telephone.

The Sanitary Committee instructed the City Surveyor to prepare plans and estimates for the construction of eight weirs on the Skell between Borrage Bridge and the railway bridge.

September. The self-binder perfected after years of experimentation by Colonel Kearsley and manufactured at his engineering works had proved of great benefit to farmers who found it difficult to secure labour in the collection of the harvest.

The annual outing of the inmates of Ripon Workhouse was to Grantley Hall and Studley Hall. Mrs Bower of *Elmscroft* provided one tier of the bridescake made in honour of her son's recent marriage.

The Town Clerk applied to the Charity Commissioners for a new scheme which would empower the trustees of Dr Richardson's Charity to devote its income to the maintenance of the Maison de Dieu Hospital in St Agnesgate which had had a deficiency of £16 6s for the past year. The income from Dr Richardson's trust had been £18 4s.

To celebrate the birthday of one of the Misses Oxley, all the children from the Workhouse were invited by Admiral Oxley to a garden party at *The Hall*. There was tea on the lawn and games until dark and each child left with a silver threepenny piece.

Over 50 members of the League of Pity (Children's Branch of the N.S.P.C.C) accompanied by their mothers, attended an At Home at Studley Royal. Mr Tom Williamson (honorary correspondent) proposed the vote of thanks to Lady Ripon and said that the Ripon League was the largest in the York and mid-Yorkshire district.

October. A statue of St Wilfrid was placed in a niche on the facade of the imposing new premises of the Knaresborough and Claro Banking Company in the Market Square.

The Mayoress of Ripon, Mrs A. Wells, presented the Mayor with another child, their fourth son. Alderman Wells declined to take office as Mayor for a second term; Councillor Henry Kearsley, who was next invited, intimated that he could not accept because he objected to wearing the Mayoral chain and gown (the only time he wore a robe of office as a councillor was when the Corporation were presented to the Prince of Wales); finally Councillor Wilkinson agreed to be Mayor.

The Mayoral banquet, a return to the old custom after a break, was a brilliant and successful event.

Alderman Lee when Mayor had preferred to give the old people a tea.

The Mayor received a letter from the Lord Mayor of London asking for the city's support for the Patriotic Relief Fund set up to help the refugees from the Transvaal and Orange Free State and the widows and orphans of troops killed and wounded in the South African campaign.

The Highways Committee recommended important improvements to Skellbank. The City Surveyor was instructed to drain the spring in the Old Mill race, fill up the race, widen the roadway and add the remainder of the land to the Highway Depot in Mill Lane. The Committee also decided to extend tree planting along Studley Road past the cricket field to the City boundary.

It was suggested that the lamp which had traditionally been mounted over the gateway to the residence of the Mayor-in-office since 1892, should in future be a pillar lamp and that the lamp-standard at the entrance to the carriage drive of the present Mayor's house, *Green Royd* in Studley Road, should be used.

An appeal was made by the Victoria Nursing Institution for winter gifts, particularly tam o'shanters, woollen socks, mufflers, flannel shirts, vests and cardigans for the Kimberley and Mafeking garrisons.

The list of local men killed or wounded in the Boer War continued to grow. Second Lieutenant Reginald Guy Graham, 21 year-old heir of Sir Reginald Graham of Norton Conyers, was amongst those severely wounded.

1899-1900. RICHARD WILKINSON, Brewer

Born at Crayke in 1856, educated in Leicestershire, and began his career by teaching in Portsmouth. In 1874 he left teaching for a post with the Midland Bank in Leeds, later transferring to the Knaresborough and Claro Bank and coming to Ripon. In 1888 he went into partnership with T. F. Hepworth who had taken over the brewery previously owned by Messrs R. Lumley & Company, and on Hepworth's death in 1892 he became managing director. He was elected to the Council in 1896. He was a freemason, active in the Ripon Agricultural Association and the

Constitutional Club, and a keen golfer on the Studley Royal Course. In 1903 he left Ripon to live in Canada and died in Winnipeg in 1909.

Rainfall in 1899 was 27.73 inches, the wettest month being January and the driest March.

The birth rate in 1899 was 22.8 per thousand and the death rate was 14.4 per thousand. The death rate was the lowest ever recorded for the city despite the epidemic of diarrhoea which had resulted in a higher than usual infant death rate.

November. The Public Notice was published of the proposed Ripon Corporation Act which was to be put before parliament as a Private Member's Bill. The main provisions were to take water from Aldfield Spa; to set up Baths and recreation grounds; to advertise the city; to extend control on Hackney carriages and lodging houses; to have borrowing powers and to levy rates.

At the Annual General Meeting of the Ripon Church Institute it was announced that Miss Darnborough had given land to build new premises in High Skellgate.

Miss Schofield and Miss Sturdee visited Ripon and held revival meetings at a number of chapels in the city. It was the first time that such meetings had been held led by women at the Wesleyan Chapel, Coltsgate Hill.

The grandstand on Red Bank was bought from the Racecourse Company for £275 and given to Lady Ripon and her committee for conversion into a convalescent home.

Heavy storms washed away the roadway at High Cleugh and prevented the Corporation from extracting gravel from the river bed.

December. The Ripon Board of Guardians reluctantly adopted the Local Government Board's new diet table. There were complaints that the new diet list did not include meat and potato pie which had proved the most popular dinner at Ripon Workhouse. The Board decided to withdraw the customary allowance of beer. There was a compromise agreement with the North and West Riding County Councils to increase the number of Guardians from seven to ten members. Bishopton Parish had been added to those served by the Ripon Board.

The Council decided to reduce the wages of gas-lamp lighters from 10s to 7s per week.

Mr René Bull, the famous war correspondent for the magazine *Black and White*, gave an illustrated lecture on 'The War in South Africa'. He showed 200 slides of scenes and incidents, many of which were taken under difficult conditions, during the investment of Ladysmith and General Buller's campaign.

Two boys aged nine and ten were drowned while sliding on ice on the Ripon Canal on Christmas Day: special prayers were said at the Cathedral Sunday School's Service on Holy Innocents' Day.

January. Numerous letters from Ripon men serving in South Africa were published in the press throughout the year. A National Day of Commemoration and Intercession was marked in Ripon on 7 January by the Mayor and Corporation joining a public procession ending at the Cathedral where a special service was held.

A pillar gas lamp was provided to mark the Mayor's residence. The city gas supply was a recurrent topic at Council meetings where complaints were voiced about the high price and poor quality of the gas and the inadequate street lighting, the lamps not being lit when the moon was full. At the end of the year the *Gazette* commented 'The discussion showed that, whatever the illuminating quality of Ripon gas, its explosive character is undeniable'. Perhaps this comment was prompted by a gas explosion which had occurred in January causing damage at Metcalfes' Furnishers in Kirkgate and injury to Mr Metcalfe.

February. Improvements at the Dispensary and Cottage Hospital included the installation of a lift and a new system of outpatient tickets to help the poor.

The Ripon Volunteers were given an enthusiastic send-off at the station on 3 February when the crowds were so great that some mothers complained that they were denied access to the platform. On the same day a meeting set up a Ripon Soldiers' Clothing Fund.

A very heavy snowfall and severe frost caused problems, −20°F and −32°F being recorded on successive days. Schools in the city were closed, farmers were unable to get home from market, a train was caught in a snow drift between Baldersby and Melmerby, and voters were deterred from voting at a municipal by-election. The Poor Law Guardians refused to give extra help to the poor for fear of setting a precedent, but the Marquess of Ripon arranged for the distribution of coal tickets.

Improvements were carried out at the Town Hall and were said to have given it a less 'prison-like appearance'.

Professor Piazzi Smyth, the pioneer photographer, Egyptologist and Astronomer Royal for Scotland, died at his residence *Clova*. A rumour that he had bequeathed his home to the national hero Baden-Powell proved unfounded. He is buried in Sharow churchyard beneath a pyramid tomb.

March. The relief of Ladysmith was announced by the Mayor in the Market Place on 1 March. There was great rejoicing and children were given a half holiday. The Revd J. G. W. Tuckey, later a Canon of Ripon, was one of the garrison.

Unfounded rumours of a pro-Boer meeting in the city led youths to riot in the town centre. Damage was caused to the property of local people believed to be pro-Boer and large numbers of police were drafted in to prevent a recurrence on the following day.

There was an increase of 20,000 in rail visitors to Ripon in 1899. It was thought this might have been the result of advertising by the Council.

May. The Council went ahead with concreting the Market Place despite protests from the public at the disappearance of the cobbles.

On 18 May the news of the relief of Mafeking arrived and there was wild rejoicing. A service of Thanksgiving was held in the Cathedral on 20 May, the following day was declared a General Holiday at the request of the Mayor, and a celebration ball was held in the Victoria Rooms on 25 May.

June. An effigy of the Boer President Kruger was paraded through the streets and burnt at the Market Cross. The Deputy Mayor attended in case the Riot Act needed to be read but this was not required.

Rain marred the opening ceremonies on 28 June at the new Racecourse when Councillor Wells laid the corner stone of the grandstand. The first flat race was won by Mr Vyner's *Mazawattee* and the first steeplechase and hurdle meetings were held in October.

September. Severe floods which had damaged bridges and riverside footpaths in March prompted the West Ripon Estates Company, who were developing Mallorie Park, to propose closing the footpath over their land from Borrage Lane to Bishopton Bridge. The Corporation eventually decided to pay the company to make a new footpath.

On 27 September there was no contest in the Parliamentary Election as the Liberals failed to put up a candidate, and there was a walkover for the Conservative and Unionist, Mr Wharton.

October. As a precaution against a private company getting in first, the Corporation decided to apply for a provisional order enabling them to supply electricity to the city. The Order received the Royal assent in January 1901 but the city was not supplied with electricity until after World War I.

The Council approved the building of a new gas holder at a cost of £4,000. The price of gas was increased from 3s 4d per therm to 3s 9d per therm.

1900-01. JOHN SPENCE, Timber Merchant

Born at Grewelthorpe in 1838 and joined his father's firm, timber merchants who once operated the sawmill at Bishopton. He was elected to the Council in 1873 and retired in 1890 but returned to take up the mayoralty. He was a member of the Agricultural Association, a Justice of the Peace, a member of the Board of Guardians and a Ripon Rural District councillor. He lived at Ashley House, Ure Bank, and died in 1926.

November. There was no contest in the Municipal elections but Councillor Wilkinson, although elected

unopposed, declined to continue as Mayor for a second year.

The Council resolved to promote a parliamentary bill to obtain water from South Gill Beck; they also decided to pay for recreation grounds and public baths and to cover the Aldfield Spa scheme.

The City Surveyor was directed to have all the streets in Ripon named and numbered before the next census.

December. Lieutenant Freemantle, the Dean's son, gave an account of his experiences in South Africa as an army surgeon at a lecture on 20 December.

January. It was reported at the meeting of the Ripon Board of Guardians that the introduction of the new dietary table had increased the food costs by 25 per cent. The Guardians agreed in principle to the boarding out of children of the deserving poor but in practice none were boarded out from the Ripon Workhouse. Outdoor relief rates were increased from 4s to 5s per week for single persons and 8s to 9s per week for married couples.

Difficulties arose over the funding for the St Wilfrid procession. The organisers denied the accusation that the procession had become a drunken event, maintaining that the men were not allowed to call at public houses en route. The directors of the Racecourse Company when approached for help declined to spend shareholders' money on the event. The City Council were also asked to subscribe. The City band agreed to play in the Market Place in the evening after the procession.

The Liberal Club premises in Kirkgate were bought from Lord Ripon, the President of the Club. The facilities comprised a reading room, a large assembly hall and a billiard room.

The Bishop of Ripon, Dr Boyd Carpenter, the Queen's favourite minister, was called to take part in the last rites performed when Queen Victoria lay dying at Osborne. He was a close friend and had written a personal letter to Her Majesty every month over a period of years, and had a large photographic collection which included a copy of every photograph taken of her.

The Queen died on 22 January and the nation went into deep mourning. Advertisements appeared in the *Gazette* from outfitter firms announcing 'special attention given to all orders of black goods'. On the following day the Mayor read the proclamation of the accession of King Edward VII. Memorial services were held at the Cathedral and all local chapels and churches on the day of the Queen's funeral in London, 2 February.

February. Elizabeth Dixon, a 70-year-old spinster, was found dead in a cottage at Sharow. She was thought to be one of the deserving poor and had been taken into Ripon Workhouse whenever she had been ill. After her death it was found that she had a bank account of £160.

At the Annual Meeting of the Yorkshire Fishery Board it was agreed to give 500 trout to the Ripon Angling Club to replenish the stock in the River Ure. The appearance of salmon in the Ure was reported.

There was opposition to the holding of the Ripon Corporation Water Race, as the Council had refused to pay compensation.

Controversy arose over the financing of the Aldfield Spa Water Scheme. It was decided to organise a poll among ratepayers on the basis of the Poor Rate Register. Initial difficulties had to be ironed out which arose from the number of double registrations. Two polls were carried out: 872 for and 558 against on 28 February; 995 for and 680 against on 3 July.

Lord Ripon informed the Mayor of his decision to give up his seat on the West Riding County Council (W.R.C.C.) due to age and ill health. The Marquess nominated, and the Dean seconded, Viscount Mountgarret as his successor.

The Ripon Cricket Club organised a bazaar to raise funds for the new pavilion. Lord Hawke, Captain of Yorkshire, agreed to perform the opening ceremony.

March. The Council decided the annual lighting cost of £30 for the Clock Tower was too high, and proposed to reduce the lamps to a single gas light costing £12 per annum.

The Fishergate widening scheme was held up because no alternative site could be found for *The Grapes Inn*.

The Public Rooms Committee closed its library and the books were given to the Corporation.

A scheme for a light railway to run from Ripon to Kirkby Malzeard was shelved after objections were received from the Marquess of Ripon and Earl de Grey because it was proposed that the line should cross the Studley carriage drive.

April. The Bishop of Ripon inaugurated a Million Shilling Fund to provide for new churches, clergy training, maintenance of vicarages, improvement of benefices, church schools, colleges and foreign missions.

The death of Dr William Stubbs, Bishop of Oxford, eminent historian and former pupil of Ripon Grammar School, occurred on 25 April.

June. Mr John Metcalfe, who had carried on business as Tailor and Draper in Kirkgate, died aged 81.

The Linton Lock Commissioners on a visit to Ripon by boat were stopped nearly two miles from the city due to the accumulation of weed in the canal and had to complete the journey on foot. It was proposed that a new company should be formed to take over the management of the canal from the Railway Company.

The results of the 1901 census were published. The population of Ripon was 8,225, an increase of 714 in the ten years since the last census. The increase was largely attributed to the extension of boundaries to include Sharow and Bishopton. The Dean of Ripon was appalled at the declining birth-rate and in a letter to *The Times* he declared 'our three great groups of colonies in Canada, Australia and Africa can absorb all the surplus population for years to come. In the presence of these possibilities, is not the wilful diminution of our race a crime against humanity and its Author?'.

The Marquess of Ripon made a strong condemnation of the refugee camps in South Africa in a letter to the *Leeds Mercury*.

The Marquess of Ripon continued as Chairman of the Grammar School Governors and led the negotiations with the Corporation in the dispute over the sale of land required for a widening scheme for Clotherholme Lane.

July. Mr W. Hemsworth, antique dealer in Fishergate, secured and sold to the Corporation 'a plan of the River Ure from Milby Staith, near Boroughbridge, to Ripon in the county of York, drawn from a survey thereof taken by Mr Ellison in 1736 and corrected from a view and observation taken in 1766 with a scheme for rendering the same navigable by John Smeaton FRS'.

The Mayor opened a subscription list to provide funds for the national celebration of the 1,000th anniversary of the death of King Alfred, who by tradition had granted Ripon's first charter, and for the erection of a statue in Winchester. A commemorative banquet in Ripon was proposed.

August. A plea was made to the Dean and Chapter to provide umbrella stands at the west door of the Cathedral as the floor swam with water on wet days.

Baldersby Park, occupied for many years by the Dowager Viscountess of Downe, was offered at auction. The estate included the mansion, deer park, ten farms, 50 cottages, 2,078 acres of land, the villages of Baldersby and Baldersby St James, the Manor and Lordship of Baldersby with an annual rent roll of £2,901. The offer was withdrawn at £72,000 but sold by private treaty a few weeks later to Mr Brennard of Manchester.

Dr Crow, Cathedral Organist, announced his resignation.

September. The Bishop of Ripon officiated at the funeral of the Empress Frederick of Germany in Hamburg.

The Corporation considered the purchase of High Mill in Skellbank as a step towards making a through road to Studley Road via the then Skellbank cul-de-sac.

October. It was decided that the funds raised for the golden wedding celebrations of the Marquess and Marchioness of Ripon should be used to provide a nursing institution on a site at the corner of Dispensary Lane and the end of Somerset Row. Earlier suggestions had included a convalescent home, a library and a recreation ground. The City Council's own contribution was the presentation of an illuminated address and the erection of a statue.

The Corporation unanimously decided to buy the three-and-a-half acre Drill Field in Park Street for £5,000 for the erection of the Baths, the Pump Room and the development of pleasure gardens.

1901-02.   JOHN SPENCE, Timber Merchant
November. Giacomantanio Dirosa and Dominic de Notto, travelling musicians of Stonebridgegate, successfully sued James Baul of Galphay for £11 16s 6d damages caused when his wagonette overturned a piano organ they were playing in Church Lane.

Mayor 1900-01-02

Neither plaintiff spoke English and an interpreter was obtained from York.

The seemingly endless debates by the City Council on the Spa Scheme and the future of the Ripon Canal caused a correspondent writing under a pseudonym in the *Gazette* to declare 'if these be thy Gods O Israel let ratepayers beware'.

December. The Duchess of Bedford who was a guest of the Bishop and Mrs Boyd Carpenter gave a lecture on 'Rescue work among women' during her stay at the palace. She expressed the view that quiet but effective work in this field had been going on in Ripon for some years.

January. There was an outbreak of fire at the *Alma Inn*, Bondgate Green, which destroyed an outbuilding. The Fire Brigade got it quickly under control before it spread to the main building.

The Marquess of Ripon made a gift of £200 to the Fund for the Nurses Home in celebration of his Golden Wedding.

A number of cottages, the copyhold yard formerly used as a tanyard and adjoining gardens in High St Agnesgate were sold at auction and bought by Abel Trees who later built Skellfield Terrace.

The village of Bishopton became more definitely connected with Ripon by main drainage, a new footpath and the promise of gas lighting along Clotherholme Lane.

The Ripon Volunteers secured land midway between Trinity Lane and the Grammar School playing fields as a Drill Field with entrance from Clotherholme Lane near *Clova*. The old Drill Field in Park Street was being laid out under advice from Mr Simpson, the landscape gardener at the Cemetery, as the new pleasure ground to be part of the Ripon Spa complex.

Mr Charles H. Moody was appointed organist and choirmaster at the Cathedral and also the conductor of the Northern Three Choirs Festival. Born in 1874, he was on his appointment to Ripon the youngest English Cathedral organist.

February. The Coroner's jury sitting on the death of a woman from severe burns strongly recommended the provision of an official ambulance for taking injured persons to hospital instead of the stretchers available at the Drill Hall, Police Station and Church Institute.

Four weeks' continuous frost caused the River Ure to freeze over for the first time in seven years.

The Ripon Horn was carefully examined after being stripped of its silver bands and covering during an overhaul. The inside was particularly inspected to determine whether Ripon's ancient charter had been secreted there. Mr T. Pratt M.R.C.V.S. pronounced the horn to be genuine but there was no evidence to indicate its age and therefore this must still remain in doubt.

March. Three hundred and sixty applicants came forward for the post of headmaster of the Cathedral Boys School.

April. Mr R. Williamson presented to the Ripon Museum a sword used by Cromwell's forces in the Civil War which was found in a peat bed at Kirkby Malzeard. The Museum Sub-Committee purchased another sword of similar date and Mr Parker of Blossomgate added to the collection the gift of a sword of later date bearing a finely carved handle.

A thousand medals and 1,000 commemorative coronation mugs for distribution to Ripon school children were ordered by the City Council.

May. The Rt Hon. Viscount Mountgarret was presented with the freedom of Ripon as a mark of esteem and in gratitude for his generosity not only in Ripon but in the County of York generally.

The Marquess of Ripon decided to demolish cottages and outbuildings obstructing the view between the house at Studley Royal and Lindrick Lane and to rebuild them on the opposite side of the lane.

Plans were published for the Queen's Arcade with 21 lock-up shops to be built when the Middle Street buildings were removed. The arcade was to have an imposing entrance from the main street. Plans were also passed for two large shops and dwelling houses in Queen Street.

Aldfield Spa water was made available to the public at the Bath House, Skellbank.

The Water Sub-Committee resolved to implement a house-to-house inspection throughout the City to determine the reason for the doubling of the amount of water used in Ripon to 35 to 40 gallons per head per day.

June. The two-day programme of festivities planned to celebrate the coronation had to be postponed because of King Edward VII's illness. However, the medals and cups were distributed to Ripon school children, and, in response to Lord Cranborne's telegram announcing the King's illness, the day was marked only by lighting a bonfire and showing the firework display at Studley Park.

Colonel Kearsley opened bank accounts with half-a-crown each for the blue-coat boys of Jepson's Hospital in commemoration of the coronation.

The Council made the first moves in a road-widening scheme for Westgate by the purchase of some of the properties on the north side. It was also suggested that the Corporation should secure photographs of Ripon streets prior to these alterations and those proposed for Fishergate and Queen Street and present them for safe custody to the Ripon Museum.

July. The foundation stone of the Victoria Nurses Home was laid by the Mayoress of Ripon, Mrs J. Spence.

A new cricket pavilion was opened by Mrs A. Wells, wife of the President of the Club. Alderman Wells was a life-long exponent and enthusiast for the sport.

The foundation stone of a new Masonic Hall in Water Skellgate was laid before a large and distinguished Provincial gathering of Brethren and guests. The new Lodge was formally dedicated in the following March.

A consortium which included the Marquess of Ripon, Lord de Grey, Sir Christopher Furness and other influential local people announced plans for a private limited company which would purchase the *Unicorn Hotel* from Lord Ripon, pull down the present hotel and replace it with a large and commodious hotel with stabling for about one hundred horses. Messrs Bland and Brown, well known architects in Harrogate, were commissioned to submit designs and plans.

August. The Mayor of Ripon received an invitation from the Earl Marshal to attend the coronation on 9 August wearing robes and chain. This was a special honour given in recognition of the City's antiquity as no other mayors from boroughs with populations of less than 20,000 inhabitants were invited. Brilliant weather favoured the day itself. The first ceremony was the laying of the foundation stone of the bandstand in the new Spa Gardens by Mr Robert Williamson. This was followed by a procession to the Cathedral for a Thanksgiving Service and later by a civic lunch at the Town Hall. In the afternoon, members of the Council dressed as 'Ancient Wakemen' played cricket against their opponents 'The Ancient Britons of all England'. This was succeeded by a ladies versus gentlemen cricket match. At three o'clock there was a demonstration of day and Sunday school children with banners and flags which was followed by special teas served at the schools.

Mr C. H. Moody gave an organ recital to mark formally the completion of the renovation of the Cathedral organ.

September. Mr W. O. Thorpe, the Ripon Sanitary Inspector, presented a report on the sanitary arrangements in the poorer quarters of the town, particularly the crowded courts in the city centre. The Inspector was very scathing about the system of night soil removal and recommended the universal installation of water closets.

October. A handsome table and a set of comfortable chairs were purchased by the City Council for the furnishing of the Mayor's Parlour at the sale of the late Captain Oxley's effects. A new carpet and a number of pictures were also added.

The old High Mill in Skellbank was demolished by Corporation workmen as part of road improvements.

The Power and Traction Company produced plans for the laying of a tramway from Ripon Station to the City and on to Studley Park.

1902-03. WILLIAM TOPHAM MOSS, Varnish Manufacturer

Born 1849, the son of William T. Moss of Ure Bank who sat on the City Council 1855-62. He was educated at Jepson's Hospital and Ripon Grammar School. From school he entered his father's firm, and in 1925 completed 60 years as commercial traveller for Moss's Varnish Works. He sat on Sharow Parish Council, was elected to the City Council in 1898 becoming an alderman in 1904. From 1913 to 1930 he was the Ripon member on the West Riding County Council. Much involved in public work, he was also Chairman of the Ripon Board of Guardians and President of the Working Men's Club. He lived in The Crescent, died in 1930 and was survived by his daughter Mrs Ede.

Rainfall for 1902: 28.92 ins., a second year of drought and the lowest since 1893 when 27.92 ins. was recorded.

November. Improvements were completed to Holy Trinity Church by altering the entrance at the northeast corner and removing the porch within the building to give more space for additional seating. A new entrance was made through the vestry.

December. Demolition of the Middle Street block of buildings was started beginning with homes at the Old Market Place end. Due to the failure of the Corporation to effect an agreement with Rayners, the drapers who owned the property facing the Market Place, the building would have to be left intact until a new deal could be made. Arbitration awarded Mr Rayner £4,827 11s for the property in 1905.

The Mayor asked that Ripon, as a Cathedral City, should pay fitting tribute to the memory of the departed Archbishop of Canterbury William Temple, and requested that citizens would close their shops and draw down their blinds between the hours of 12 noon and 2 p.m. on the day of the funeral.

January. The Station Master's Office (North Eastern Railway Company) was connected to the National Telephone Exchange with an extension to the Goods Office.

The Bishop of Ripon, Dr Boyd Carpenter, was caused

4. Old Museum, Park Street (Fossick)

5. Old Middle Street from the Market Place (Fossick)

considerable embarrassment when the London newspapers stated he was to be the new Archbishop of Canterbury. The rumours were promptly contradicted.

Alderman Wells presented to the Ripon Museum a silver bronze tablet with five figures in relief of Buddha, which had been brought from the Chinese Summer Palace by the late Captain Lumby, sometime Librarian at the Ripon Public Rooms Library. Negotiations were concluded for the Corporation to take over the Museum premises in Park Street from the Naturalists' Club and Scientific Society for later incorporation in the planned Ripon Spa complex. The artefacts were to be stored in the cellars of the Town Hall. In fact, the Town Hall became for some time the City Museum and Library with the books housed in the Mayor's Parlour, the staircase and landings filled with cases of butterflies and other objects, and birds, beasts and reptiles in the hallway.

February. The City Engineer submitted a detailed report for the layout of a tramway system in Ripon, which was adopted by the City Council.

Complaints were made about the dangerous manner in which Moss's China Shop was demolished without scaffolding or hoarding and only a workman standing in the road to warn the public. The site was taken over partly by the Corporation for the widening of Westgate and partly by Freeman, Hardy and Willis for the new shoe shop at the corner of the Market Place. The road between Deanery Road and Agnesgate was also widened and iron railings were

installed at a cost of £40 on the Cathedral burial ground side.

March. At the Annual General Meeting of the Ripon Public Rooms Company it was again announced that no dividend would be paid because of a drop in attendance at some of the shows presented. Mr Tom Williamson said that Ripon audiences were capricious and critical, preferring light opera to choral concerts and high-class music recitals.

A young girl had to have a hand amputated after an accident with flax-spinning machinery at Bishopton Mills.

The River Ure caused serious flooding at North Bridge with the water covering the fields to Spring Bank, isolating the Boat House and Bathing Pavilion, extending across Sharow Road to the north and to Albion Terrace to the south.

Mr G. Watson gave an exhibition of his paintings and photographs at his Kirkgate Studio. There were portraits of the Marquess of Ripon, the Mayor of Ripon in his official robes, and Sir Reginald Graham, Bart.

April. A child died from burns as a result of a fire in Stonebridgegate when a mother left two children aged three and four by an open fire while she went to buy milk. The woman appeared for the fourth time in 12 months at Ripon City Court the following week on a drunk and disorderly charge.

June. The new bandstand in the Spa Gardens was opened by the Mayor. A recital was given by the band of the Ripon Detachment of the 1st Battalion of the

West Yorkshire Regiment.

Strong representations were made to the City Council for a road to be built between College Road and Crescent Parade.

Miss Constance Cross of *Coneygarth* presented a handsome altar frontal to the Cathedral.

July. As a result of an application to Mr Andrew Carnegie for funds to provide a Ripon Library, the Town Clerk was asked to supply full details of the new Mechanics Institute and the use to which the rooms were put. As the Trust was willing to grant only a small sum, the application was later withdrawn.

Application for a licence to slaughter pigs on premises in Borrage Green Lane was turned down by the Council because of the many objections presented by local residents.

A sounding board for the pulpit in the Cathedral nave was presented by Mr G. Simpson of *South Lodge*.

The Mayor and Mayoress hosted a civic summer outing for 80 guests to Bolton Abbey and Hall. The party was taken by train to Otley and musical numbers played by Mr Arnott's quartet en route. Charabancs and wagonettes met the party and took them to Farnley Hall to inspect the art treasures. Lunch was provided at Ilkley and the afternoon was spent at Bolton Hall.

The Hon. and Very Revd the Dean of Ripon was presented with the Freedom of Ripon in recognition . of his services as Honorary Chaplain and his great interest and activity in the municipal life of the City.

August. A scheme was approved to improve Holy Trinity Church by abolishing the south transept gallery and rearranging the east end of the nave. The proposal was in effect a restoration as the church was consecrated in 1827 originally without the gallery, and its removal would allow more air and light.

September. Edward Howard was appointed Ripon Hornblower at a salary of £12 per annum following the resignation of John Masterman.

A room at the Residence was put at the disposal of the Navy Mission Society, which had made Ripon an important centre for its operations among the large number of men employed in building the Leeds and Harrogate Waterworks above Kirkby Malzeard and Masham on the Dallowgill Moors.

Mr and Mrs Tom Williamson produced performances of the musical comedy *Jasmine Jolly* or the *Merry Maids of Melmerby,* the proceeds of which were given to the fund for developing the scientific and commercial curriculum at Ripon Grammar School.

October. The new Nurses' Home was officially opened by the Marchioness of Ripon. The Home was a golden wedding present to Lord and Lady Ripon who handed it over to the Nursing Institute.

1903-04. WILLIAM TOPHAM MOSS, Varnish Manufacturer

Total rainfall for 1903 was 37.51 ins.

November. The Mayor headed a deputation to Beverley to inspect the North Eastern Railway's services of motor omnibuses with a view to organis-

Mayor 1902-03-04

ing a similar service to run from Ripon Station to Fountains Abbey.

Mr T. Precious retired from the office of Sergeant-at-Mace after seventeen years' service.

The annual Martinmas Hiring Fair saw a large gathering of farmers and servants. Hiring of domestics took place at the Temperance Hall, farm labourers on the Square, with the showing of cattle confined to the south corner of the Square.

December. An otter was seen in the river Skell below Bondgate Green Bridge where it attacked five swans. However, the swans also went into the attack and the otter retreated.

The death took place of Mr William Wells J.P., Mayor of Ripon 1869-70.

The *Unicorn Hotel*, the *Crown Hotel* and two shops, William Harrison (Stationers) and Mr J. C. Etherington (Drapers) were withdrawn at auction as bids amounting to £14,500 did not reach the reserve prices. Mr Harrison's notice to quit due to the impending sale led him to offer the remaining stock of the *Millenary Record* to Ripon citizens at half price.

January. The West Riding Education Committee made proposals for the taking over of voluntary schools. Before any takeover the trustees must put the school buildings into satisfactory repair. The County Council would pay a rental of 2s 6d per week per child and have complete control including the appointment and dismissal of teachers. Religious instruction would be given for half an hour on two mornings weekly in those schools taken over by the Council. The managers of the Wesleyan Schools in Ripon were the first to express interest.

The Ripon Board of Guardians agreed to provide a new wood-chopping shed so that tramps could be properly housed for their work and separated from the regular inmates of the Workhouse.

The Ripon Training College authorities announced that they were willing to accept non-conformist students to training courses.

Eleven poor widows residing in North Street between the corner of Allhallowgate and the Crescent received 5s each from the Ann Kettlewell Charity. The rent of a field in Bishopton amounting to £4 10s left by Ann Day was distributed among ten applicants resident in the old township of Bishopton.

Mrs Mary Hammond died at *Caxton Lodge* which she bought in 1897. Previously she had continued the milling business at Sleningford Mills after the death of her husband Christopher Hammond leaving her with six young children. Not only did she continue the business but she kept abreast of new developments and installed improved machinery at the mills.

A portrait of the Marchioness of Ripon in water colour by Mr G. Watson of Ripon was presented to the Nurses' Home by Colonel and Mrs G. Kearsley.

February. The City Engineer completed improvements at the Coltsgate Hill corner of College Road. An entrance was made through the College wall and a new road staked out to Crescent Back Road, but as the latter will be a road it was only open to foot passengers. The land which was earmarked for a through road to North Street across the front of Brewster Terrace was sold for building.

Colonel Kearsley of the British Ironworks retired after 50 years with the Company which would in future be known as Kearsley and Company (Engineers) Ltd. Mr J. G. Kearsley took over as Managing Director.

The Ripon and District Co-operative Society selected the site of the old *Black Horse* at the junction of Park Street and Westgate for their new premises. The *Black Horse* was one of the oldest hostelries in Ripon, the licence being given up in the 1890s when it became a Temperance Hotel. It gave the Society much-needed stabling and warehouse accommodation. By setting back the premises, it was possible

6. *The old* Black Horse *(Fossick)*

to widen the road and provide a footpath on the south side.

March. The Council decided to lower the roadway at the top of Coltsgate Hill at the entrance to College Road by four feet.

A motion before the Council was agreed that 'a suitable shelter for the protection and shelter of the cab and coachmen be provided at an estimated cost of £60, the details and site for which shall be left to the Highways Committee'.

April. The West Ripon Estates Company set up to develop land on the west side of the city decided to use old names to retain a link with the former ownership by the then Studley Estate. The name chosen for the new road between Skellbank and Bishopton was Mallorie Park Drive and the new house then occupied by Mr Gowland in Clotherholme Lane was to be known as *Aislabie*.

As part of the Tercentenary Celebration of the James I Charter, the Mayor offered prizes for the best essays by school children on the history of Ripon since 1604.

Attempts were made in the Council to adjourn the Spa Baths scheme until 1906 on the grounds of bad trading conditions obtaining in the city. The majority supported the scheme, stating that if the sulphur water should prove a failure the baths would always be useful to Ripon.

One of the two posting establishments in the city, Mountains Ltd. of Fishergate, decided to stop its regular service to the Station although a few cabs and omnibuses would be retained and the establishment would be carried on as a restaurant. Mr Mountain's family had a long connection with the carriage and omnibus traffic in Ripon; his father, who died in 1856, was the owner and driver of the last coach that ran between Ripon and Leeds. The sole right of entry to the North Eastern Railway Station Yard at Ripon was granted to the other posting establishment, the *Unicorn Hotel*.

May. A. S. Heslop, aged 14, a boarder at Ripon Grammar School, lost his right hand as a result of an explosion of a small phial containing dangerous chemicals which he had purchased in Ripon contrary to regulations. The explosion occurred when Heslop was showing other boys the phial as they waited to go to Brimham Rocks on a Whit Bank Holiday picnic. Heslop had a dreadfully lacerated hand, but as he apparently was not suffering from shock, he was sent up to his room to await medical attendance and it was not until much later in the day that the hand was examined and the decision was taken to carry out amputation.

June. The Cathedral authorities complained about the increasing irreverence of visitors who came to see an ancient historic building and finding a service about to begin, took seats in the choir and often remained seated throughout, showing a lamentable attitude to worship.

Richard Jackson and Company of 27, 28 and 30 Westgate (General Drapers, Costumiers and Milliners) decided to close the drapery side of the business but to continue the clothing and outfitting.

Sir Oliver Lodge gave a lecture at the Training College under the title of 'The influence of recent discoveries on our views of the universe'. Much of the lecture was given over to the importance of the discovery of radium by the Curies. The invitations had to be limited to 100 because of the size of the lecture room.

The City Mace was re-gilded; Hugh Ripley's monument in the Cathedral was restored as were the tablet and the railings around the cannon in front of the Cathedral in preparation for the tercentenary celebrations.

A new by-law was made by the Corporation defining streets and open spaces in which markets and fairs could be held — Market Place, the Old Market Place, Queen Street and Fishergate.

The Rustic Bridge was repaired after an accident occurred when a child fell into the river. Alderman A. Wells's children were being taken for a walk by the nursemaid and Master Christopher, aged two, fell through a hole on the bridge into the Skell below. Fortunately the river was low and the child suffered no harm other than a wetting.

July. An accident occurred in Studley Park when a party from Blackburn were travelling in Mr Bielby's horse-drawn charabanc; the back and front wheels on the driving side collapsed and the vehicle heeled over, pitching the 25 passengers onto the driveway.

The Ripon Tercentary Festival to celebrate the granting of its Charter by James I in 1604, began on 14 July with the splendour of a Cathedral Service and a recital by the North Eastern Cathedral Choirs from York, Durham, Ripon and Wakefield. Hundreds crowded into the Residence grounds to witness the Pageant and Pastoral Play, *King James and the Wakeman*. The Festival was spread over three days which saw bright and glorious weather. Friday was a day of 13 hours of continuous entertainment. It began with the stone-laying ceremony by the Mayor and Mayoress of the future Spa Baths. Under the stone were buried copies of the *Ripon Gazette* and *Ripon Observer*, minutes and financial reports of the Ripon Spa development scheme, the programme for the Festival, and coins, a crown down to a penny, minted in 1902 and 1903. The Mayor, Corporation and distinguished guests processed to the Cathedral for a Civic Service and back to the Town Hall for luncheon. The Pastoral Play was shown again and the evening had music and dancing in the Spa Gardens and on the cricket field, ending with a pyrotechnic display. The surplus of £50 remaining after the Festival was donated to improving the children's playground.

August. The North Eastern Railway Company set up a motor bus service between the station and Studley and as stated in the *Ripon Gazette* — 'Though late in the season, the regular tourist regards the innovation with satisfaction as it affords a ready and convenient mode of reaching Studley Park at a fixed and moderate charge'.

The Prince of Wales made a four-day visit to Studley and enjoyed grouse shooting on Dallowgill Moors.

September. The Marquess of Ripon personally conducted members of the Trades Union Congress over the ruins on their first visit to Fountains Abbey.

Although the Motor Car Act allowed a speed of 20 mph, the Ripon City magistrates felt that this was too fast for Ripon's narrow and congested streets and suggested a limit of six to eight mph.

An Auction Sale was held to dispose of items, including gold and silver articles, taken in default of paying the new Education rate. Protests continued and in March 1905 a number of people came before the City Court charged with the same offence. They objected that they were Protestants and could not pay money for the teaching of doctrines they had opposed all their lives.

Improvements to the Ripon and Wakefield Diocesan Training College were completed during the summer vacation. These included three laboratories added to the north wing, an extension on the other side of the wing and a combined gymnasium and art room which would now serve as a concert room.

1904-5. JOHN BANKS LEE, Draper

Mayor 1882-83, 1884-85, 1897-98, 1904-05, 1906-07

Rainfall in 1904 was 33.5 ins. The average over the past 10 years had been 38 ins.

November. Severe snow storms caused roads to be blocked on the west of Ripon, to Pateley, Galphay and Kirkby Malzeard. Seventy workmen were employed to clear the drifts.

December. The contractors for the Spa Baths gave the traditional roofing supper at the *Studley Royal Hotel* to 60 workmen engaged on the project.

January. A sensational outrage at the Coal Office at Ripon Station occurred when the clerk in charge was held up and the cash drawer rifled. The robbery was due to drink rather than desperation as all the men were well-known Ripon loafers.

There was exceptionally severe weather with 15 to 20 degrees of frost. The canal and the Ure were frozen and hundreds of spectators on the canal bank gave Bondgate Green the appearance of an ice carnival. It was said to be possible to skate down the canal and along the Ure to Boroughbridge. The frost accentuated the unemployment position.

The Town Clerk's report on Municipal Charities stated that £250 was distributed to poor households at Christmas. Ripon was fortunate in having charitable sources and the amount of money distributed publicly and privately was abnormally large in proportion to the population. The vexed question of old age pensions remained and the Maison de Dieu was greatly in need of funds. The newly formed Benevolent Association, later the Ripon Charity Organisations Society for the Relief of Unemployment and the Poor, was to arrange for wood-chopping. Attention was to be directed to seeing that proper persons were recipients of gifts, as during the Christmas season they had reached 'most unworthy objects'.

Dinners for poor children were provided at the Temperance Hall at 1d per head and 200–250 children attended.

February. An animated discussion on unemployment took place in Council. The Mayor pointed out that the Corporation could not give work to all the unemployed, but they would allow space and a shed for wood chopping at the Highways Depot. Wages would be fixed at 4d per hour and no man would earn more than 10s in any one week.

March. Property for a new Post Office was purchased in North Street.

April. A Horse Show Day was held on Bondgate Green with a good parade of animals. It was suggested that instead of trotting the horses on the Ripon side of the Bridge, it would be well to cross to the opposite side where there would be more scope on the Green.

June. The Mayor tendered his resignation when the Corporation approved payment for the band for playing on the Lord's Day. He was urged to reconsider his decision and did so when the Town Clerk suggested that neither should money be collected nor the band paid.

July Dr William Boyd Carpenter completed 21 years as Bishop of Ripon and was presented with a portrait.

September. A property sale closed without the disposal of a single lot. The auctioneer hoped a day would come when there would be more trade in Ripon: the town was looking to the Spa to lift it from the lethargy of past ages.

The Mayor announced that instead of giving a tea and entertainment to the inhabitants over 60 he proposed to distribute 100 blankets among the poor.

October. Seven motorists out of 24 were convicted for exceeding the speed limit (20 mph) on the Harrogate Road. Some motorists were so delighted with the speed of their vehicles that they drove back again to see what they could do on the return run.

The Council Chamber was redecorated; it had previously been occupied by the Freemasons and the ceiling gilded with their mysterious but well-known designs.

Princess Henry of Battenburg and Princess Victoria Eugenie (Ena) arrived, 21 October, for their eagerly-awaited Royal visit. Great crowds were attracted to the city and the streets were decorated. The Cathedral was thronged for the service on Sunday morning and the Princesses visited Fountains Abbey on the Monday. The inauguration of the Spa took place on Tuesday and afterwards the Princesses opened a Schools Bazaar in the Victoria Hall. £1,094 was raised over three days.

1905-6. GEORGE SIMPSON, Ship and Insurance Broker

Born 1845 in Manchester where he attended school and Owen's College (later the University). He entered merchant offices in Manchester and Liverpool and established his own firm of Ship and Insurance Brokers in 1870. He was Lloyds' Agent in Manchester and Chairman of the Manchester Shipping Lines Association. Elected to Manchester City Council in 1900, he quickly resigned because, although a firm Conservative, he strongly disapproved of the introduction of party politics into local government. He was a lieutenant in the Manchester Rifle Volunteers. His wife was a Yorkshire woman, Miss Dyson of *Braithwell Hall*, and he came to live at *South Lodge*, Ripon, in 1901. He took an active part in the life of his adopted city and was a popular choice when the Corporation sought a mayor outside their ranks.

November. The Ven. Lucius Smith, Archdeacon of Ripon, was appointed Bishop Suffragan of Knaresborough.

A census of the Roman Catholic population taken by Father de Vacht totalled 383 souls with 98 children on the school register.

Mr George Simpson of *South Lodge* accepted the mayoralty. Because of the increasingly onerous duties of office, the Council decided to invite someone outside the Council to undertake it. The inhabitants of High and Low Skellgate decorated their streets and erected a floral arch as a tribute to Mr Simpson on his inauguration.

The scavenging carts were fitted with rubber tyres to enable these chariots of the night to move with less noise.

A shed was to be provided in Allhallowgate and it was hoped to furnish it and provide something homely where a working man might smoke his pipe in some degree of comfort. If funds could be raised, a wash-house and copper in the poverty-stricken area of Stonebridgegate, where the inhabitants of the worst courts had no means of keeping clean, would be provided.

December. A scheme was laid before the Council to improve the approach to the new Hydro by widening Park Street. Skellbank was to be opened up to provide a direct approach for vehicles from Harrogate to Studley via the new road known as Mallorie Drive. Despite strong protests from Temperance members the Council agreed that after a lapse of a number of years the inmates of the Workhouse should be allowed beer with their Christmas dinner.

January. A meeting was held at the Grammar School of old boys who had long felt the need for a club to keep them in touch with one another and with the school. An Old Riponian Club was formed with an annual subscription of five shillings, half of which was to be devoted to the publication of the School Magazine (*The Riponian*).

The Highways Department, using 1,500 tons of hard core, filled in the hollow in the road between the Crescent and the *White Horse Hotel*, so giving an easy gradient from the Clock Tower to the top of North Street.

Mr H. F. Lynch, the Liberal candidate, was elected for Ripon at the Parliamentary Elections with a 313 majority. Free Trade was the major issue.

Robert Williamson, the head of one of Ripon's oldest and most esteemed families, died on 26 January at the age of 80. He was educated at Ripon Grammar School and in France. He married in 1851 and went to live in Borrage Lane at *Sunny Bank*, where he built up a collection of rare prints and pictures. He inherited the family varnish business on the death of his father, Thomas Williamson, who had been Mayor of Ripon in 1849 and in 1867. Robert Williamson, like his father, was interested in politics and was nominated to stand for Ripon, but stood down in favour of a Cabinet Minister, Mr Goschen, in 1880. He was a great sportsman, a mainstay of the old Ripon Cricket Club in the top-hat days of cricket, and in later years a keen golfer, being an original member of the Studley Royal Golf Club. He left an estate valued at £51,055 gross.

February. The Ripon Co-operative Society completed their improvement at the junction of Westgate and Park Street, opening their new premises on the site of the old *Black Horse Inn*. Hitherto the Society had occupied two shops in Kirkgate, one for general groceries and one for boots. During the excavations, amongst other finds were a Roman pottery ewer and a barbed arrow head.

The City Council reached a settlement with Sir Christopher Furness over the widening and improvement of Park Street and Studley Road, which would follow the development of the *Elmscroft* Estate as part of the Spa Hydro scheme. This involved the demolition of all the buildings and the old wall between the Spa Gardens and the Cricket Field including *Pickle Hall* and the cottages. Sir Christopher gave 1150 square yards of land for the road widening and for a footpath running from the gardens to the old Bath House on Skellbank. The Corporation provided the site of the Town Clerk's house, *Avenue Cottage*, which was valued at £600 and constructed the footpath and the new boundary walls between the estates.

7. *The old Bath House and St Wilfrid's Well (Fossick)*

ℜipon Historic Festival,

1906.

Celebration of the 1,020th year of Ripon's Civic Life.

THURSDAY, FRIDAY & SATURDAY,
JULY 19th, 20th & 21st.

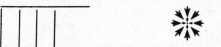

Pageant, Play & Revels

To be held in the Beautiful

ELMCROFTS PARK

and the

SPA GARDENS Adjoining, . . .

. . . . . . within 150 yards of the Market Cross.

Over!

8. Advertisement of Ripon Historical Festival, 1906

14. Collage of advertisements from 1906

March. The Spa Committee discussed the desirability of repeating the pageantry of the Millenary and Historic Festivals of 1886 and 1896. The Mayor suggested that surplus money from the event should go towards the provision of a museum in the Spa Gardens.

The custom of ringing the Pancake Bell was still followed in Ripon on Shrove Tuesday, although the County Council refused a holiday for school children.

There was a special gathering of ex-students of the Ripon Training College to dedicate three new stained glass windows by C. E. Kempe for the chapel — a gift of students leaving the College in 1903, 1904 and 1905. In June 1907, the Bishop of Ripon dedicated another window, the subject of which was Alfred the Great as associated with Christian education.

The Post Office staff vacated their old premises in the Market Place and moved into the new office in North Street.

Canon Goodier received gifts of a silver dish engraved with the Ripon crest, a Broadwood piano and a cheque for £106 on his retirement from Holy Trinity Church after 28 years' service.

The Town Clerk gave notice that the Corporation would supply Spa water in 10-oz. stoppered bottles delivered each morning, except Sunday, to citizens' own homes at a charge of 1s per week. Sulphur water could be had at the Spa Baths by citizens at 1d per glass whether hot or cold, whereas others paid ½d for cold and 2d for hot.

The shareholders of the Ripon Public Rooms decided to sell the Victoria Hall and adjacent buildings in Low Skellgate. The first hall on the site was built in the stormy days of the 1832 Reform Bill, when the use of the Town Hall, erected by the Tory owner of Studley Royal, was denied to all who did not support the Studley nominees. As time passed it became the recognised meeting place for all political parties, so the need for a larger public room was met in 1885 by the building of the Victoria Hall at a cost of £2,803 and with a capacity of seating 1,000 people. It had a stage 40 ft by 20 ft and a proscenium 20 ft by 20 ft. The buildings put up for auction included the Victoria Hall, the *King's Café*, the Edward Room and a chapel occupied by the Catholic Apostolic Denomination. The reserve price was not reached and the property was retained by the directors who thought the shareholders would be willing to continue casual letting rather than allow the city to lose its only large public hall.

An application was made for a provisional licence for the new Spa Hydro; later it was proposed, but never carried out, that the licence of the *Crown Hotel* in the Market Place (now Morrison's Supermarket) should be transferred to the Hydro. The ground floor of the *Crown* would become shops and the bedrooms transferred to the *Unicorn Hotel*.

April. The Town Clerk was ordered to obtain information from other towns as to what action could be taken to minimise the nuisance arising from varnish manufacturers, because as the Mayor pointed out in a letter to Tom Williamson, 'As a Corporation,

we are bound to keep in mind that (wisely or unwisely) the ratepayers have been committed to an expenditure of some £30,000 in the purchase, laying out and construction of a park and spa ground, pump room and baths, all with the expectation of getting a return from visitors and new residents, who should be attracted by its fine *natural* air'. Mr Williamson pointed out that the varnish industry was an integral part of Ripon's well-being, and if it vanished like the cloth trade, there would be a gap difficult to fill. The nett rateable value of Ripon's varnish works was £800; the number of heads of families employed 100; average weekly wage 30s per week, i.e., £7,800 per annum, virtually all spent in Ripon, and a railway revenue of not less than £10,000 per annum.

May. The use of vacuum cleaners was suggested to help keep down the great volume of dust liberated during spring cleaning in the Cathedral in the first week of May when the building was closed to the public.

The City Council named the eight members to represent the Council on the Board of Governors of the proposed Secondary School for girls. The County Council had three members, the Rural District Council had three members and Leeds University one member.

Mr J. E. Jones of York presented to the city a set of engravings of Fountains Abbey for display in the Council Chamber.

The residents in the Market Place objected to the nuisance caused by the weekly cattle market. It was felt that Ripon should follow Knaresborough by stopping street cattle sales, particularly as the city had a growing claim to be a health resort. These objections were reinforced by a protest from the Ripon Club after the May cattle fair — the Club's windows overlooked the Market Place. Mr Tom Williamson also entered the fray by writing to the Local Government Board, asking what residents could do to make the Council move the Statutory Cattle and Sheep Markets to a more suitable site. The Council informed the Board that it was due to Mr Williamson's action that the Corporation had felt impelled to remove the old cobblestones in the Market Place and relay them in concrete to allow for adequate cleansing at a cost of £1,487 and that the Board of Agriculture's Inspectors were completely satisfied with the arrangements.

Efforts were being made to synchronise the clocks at the Cathedral, the Town Hall, the Clock Tower, the Post Office and the Railway Station to enable passengers to catch their trains on time.

The Kirkby Light Railway Company applied for the making of a light railway (gauge three ft) between Ripon and Kirkby Malzeard, passing through Sharow, North Stainley, Clotherholme, Studley Roger, Azerley and Laverton. The railway would run for five miles and seven furlongs, starting 460 yds from the north end of Ripon Station, crossing the River Ure, Palace Road and Kirkby Road through Ellington Banks.

The large stone ball surmounting the eastern turret at the end of the north transept was dislodged with other masonry when the Cathedral was struck by lightning in a violent thunder storm. A finial, also knocked off, reached the Deanery Wall in Minster Road.

June. The Bishop of Ripon announced that the Governors offered exhibitions of £15 to £30 per annum to graduates of any University to train for the Ministry at the Ripon Clergy College.

July. The employees of Messrs Kearsley took a trip by train from Leeds to Paris as their annual excursion. They joined other parties amounting in all to 700 people from Leeds, Bradford and Hull; the 48-hour visit was organised by Thomas Cook.

The Bishop of Ripon, well known for his gesticulations to emphasise points during his sermons, sent the cushion on the pulpit desk flying when he preached in London at the Thanksgiving Day Celebration to a crowded congregation in the Chapel of the Foundling Hospital. The cushion narrowly missed the auditors seated near the aisle.

The Ripon Historic Festival, similar to those held in 1886 and 1896, was held on 19, 20 and 21 July in Elmscroft Park, where the new Spa Hydro was in the course of erection. The celebrations included a reception for visiting mayors and VIP guests at the Pump Room, a luncheon, a grand tournament of knights in armour, the Queen of Beauty competition, a Pageant of Ripon history, ballet by school children, Maypole dancing, a grand dance and procession through Ripon streets. Special trains were run from all parts of the county, together with one excursion from London. The Festival was considered a great success ending as it did with a deficit of less than £180.

It was announced at the Ripon Grammar School Speech Day that a Rifle Corps was to be formed and that the school was to be divided into 'houses' named after distinguished persons connected with the school.

August. Bank Holiday traffic at Ripon broke all records with the highest-ever receipts at the racecourse, attendance at Fountains Abbey (3,224 people and 218 bicycles) and the number of passengers at Ripon Station needing 44 trains between 4.05 and 10.20 pm to get them away.

A new clock with a second dial on the south side was installed on the Cathedral tower at a cost of £300.

September. The last obstacle for the road widening scheme to Fishergate was removed by the Corporation accepting £400 for the surrender of the licence of the *Grapes Inn* awarded by the Compensation Authority. A total of £2,726 was the estimated cost of the improvement scheme. The Inn was demolished and the debris removed in two days. The roadway was put in order and a footpath straightened, and this great improvement was completed by mid-October.

The Manager of the *Unicorn Hotel* stated that 18 visitors took rooms during St Wilfrid's week but found the noise from the fair too loud and had left the city early. The Council decided that in future only one person would be allowed to run steam roundabouts and the organs could play only for up to 30 minutes per hour and stop at 11 pm.

10. Old Fishergate from the south (Fossick)

Four boys, three aged 10 and one aged 13, were summoned at Ripon City Court for throwing stones to the danger of the public in St Agnesgate. The Corporation had brought the case because of the damage done to gas lamps and to the gardens where seats had been smashed, ten rhododendrons torn up and all the apples stolen. The parents were ordered to pay 6s costs and to administer a proper thrashing in the presence of a policeman, except in the case of the 13-year-old, who had already been thrashed, and the court regarded this as sufficient.

October. A silver communion chalice for use in the Chapel of St Mary Magdalen was presented by Miss Anne Goff who had worshipped there for 35 years.

Complaints were laid by farmers and merchants attending the Ripon Corn Market against vendors of pills, pots, parrots, canaries and other articles crowding the Market and plying their trade with such vehemence that the legitimate business of corn sales could not be properly carried out.

1906-07. JOHN BANKS LEE

Mayor 1882-83, 1884-85, 1897-98, 1904-05, 1906-07

Rainfall in 1906 was 26.12 ins.

November. New dormitories were built over the school room at Jepson's Hospital to provide accommodation for ten more boarders.

A new organ costing £600 was dedicated at St John's Hospital Chapel. The money had all been raised by local residents. The chapel was now used parochially and was thus easing the work of the Cathedral.

The Mayor presiding at the Ripon City Court pointed out the increasing number of parents who were sending their children to school without shoes. Some of the local charities took steps to alleviate the situation.

December. A Bible belonging to Mr Richard Johnson, Mayor of Ripon 1814-15, was presented to the Corporation and placed in the city archives.

January. The competition for plans for a girls' secondary school at Ripon was won by Messrs Cannon and Chorley of Leeds. The land was bought from the College and total cost of the project was estimated at £7,500; one half would be borne by the W.R.C.C. and the rest by local councils. There was considerable local opposition.

A scheme was proposed whereby Old Age Pensions could be paid from the Ripon Municipal Charities Fund. In the first instance five old people were selected.

Cadet Ingilby S. Jefferson, the son of a Ripon surgeon, aged 13 and serving on the Training Ship *Conway*, took out a patent for an improved marine water tube boiler.

William Storey of Bishopton Flax Mills, in refuting the allegation that very low wages (as little as 5s per week) were paid to the girls working at the mill, stated that the pay range was from 8s to 23s a week according to the type of work done. Christopher Jeffry, aged 16, had to have an arm amputated after it had caught in a carding machine at the mill.

The Ripon Corporation objected to a proposal to build a level crossing over Palace Road in the plans for a Ripon–Kirkby Malzeard light railway. The Board of Trade Enquiry confirmed the plan but stipulated that engines should stop before the crossing.

February. Viscount Mountgarret was again elected unopposed as Ripon's representative on the W.R.C.C.

Lord Goschen, Liberal M.P. for Ripon 1880-85, died.

The Marchioness of Ripon died on 28 February in London. The body was brought to Studley for burial in St Mary's Church amid general public mourning.

March. Charles Parkinson, an ex-Liberal agent for the Ripon division, was sued for unpaid bills for printing work carried out for the Liberal Party. The Party paid but claimed no knowledge of the work until the summons was served and reserved the right to sue Parkinson.

A fire which broke out at the Bishop's Palace on 9 March caused damage estimated at over £500. The Bishop helped the staff to put out the fire.

April. Plans were published for a Ripon City Golf Course open to any person willing to pay the subscription and to be landscaped on land acquired from the Ecclesiastical Commissioners on Ripon Parks. The inaugural meeting of the Club was held in February 1908.

Canon McColl, canon of Ripon Cathedral since 1884, a noted political pamphleteer and a close friend of Mr Gladstone, died in London on 5 April.

A family quarrel, following a stormy meeting of the Trustees and a General Meeting of the Ripon Band on 24 April, led to H. T. Beckwith being found guilty at the Ripon Court of assaulting his brother S. L. Beckwith. The brothers had taken different sides in a decision of the Trustees to disband the group and sell the instruments. The dispute was finally settled after the intervention of two City Councillors. In the meantime members of the band had continued to rehearse using borrowed instruments.

May. Following the completion of the street widening schemes involving Fishergate, Middle Street and Queen Street, there was general protest against similar plans for St Agnesgate and Skellbank on the grounds of expense and spoiling the city's character.

The York District Wesleyan Synod met at Coltsgate Hill Chapel from 6 to 9 May.

William Shepherd was charged at Ripon City Court for aiding and abetting Alfred Jones, a local bookmaker, in a case of welshing on Ripon racecourse.

The public was allowed to attend a council meeting for the first time on 27 May. This was by ticket only, each councillor having the disposal of two tickets. On this occasion eight people attended but as time passed this number dwindled.

June. The Board of Education issued new grant regulations which produced a radical change in the composition of the governing body of the Ripon Grammar School. Under the edict, no class could exceed 35 pupils and the grant per pupil was reduced unless certain conditions were complied with. To secure the highest grant the school should provide up to 20 per cent of the total entry as free places for elementary school pupils and the governing body should have a majority representation from local authorities. The Governors accepted the change of composition, but rejected the increased grant on the grounds that acceptance of the free place scheme would destroy the boarding side of the school. However, the continued burden of debts forced the acceptance of 20 per cent free places two years later.

A new anthem 'Before the ending of the day' composed by Mr C. H. Moody was sung for the first time at St Paul's Cathedral on Tuesday, 18 June.

Ripon United Football Club were runners-up in the contest for the Harrogate Whitworth Cup during 1906-7 season.

July. Thomas Brian of no fixed abode was sent to prison for seven days hard labour at Ripon Court for begging in Markington. On being charged, he said that he was not begging but only 'collecting coppers'. The *Gazette* commented 'instead the coppers collected him'.

The *Gazette* reported on the inquest into the death of the Rector of Wath, who had committed suicide by an overdose of laudanum after setting fire to the rectory. His conduct had been unstable for some time, his daughters feared violence and he was facing divorce proceedings.

General Booth of the Salvation Army visited Ripon as part of a motorcade tour of the country. He was greeted by the Mayor and Corporation and the Dean and Chapter at the Town Hall, who all accompanied him to a meeting in the Victoria Hall.

September. The City Council offered a reward of £5 for information leading to the conviction of vandals who had cut down or damaged trees and gas lamps in various streets in Ripon.

The Admiralty announced that Vice Admiral Sir F. C. B. Bridgeman, of *Copgrove Hall* near Ripon, would fly his flag as C-in-C of the Home Fleet on the battleship *Victorious* until the new *Dreadnaught* was ready.

Abnormally high temperatures during September ensured an excellent harvest in the Ripon area.

October. A police trap set on Littlethorpe Lane caught several motorists travelling at between 25 and 30 mph, who were charged with driving a motor car at speeds dangerous to the public.

A much-needed new science block was opened at Ripon Grammar School by the Marquess of Ripon on 23 October. The need for this had been pointed out by the Board of Education Inspectorate in 1902. The W.R.C.C., who first refused financial help, in the end gave only half of the £1,000 grant requested. The rest of the funds were raised by subscription headed by the Marquess for £500 and Viscount Mountgarret for £100, and a great three-day bazaar in the Victoria Hall. The bazaar had 12 stalls, a lunch and supper room and orchestral, dramatic and gymnastic performances. This latter event was so successful that after paying for the laboratories there was £300 over, which was used to build a sanatorium.

1907-08.   HERBERT MORRIS BOWER

Born at *Elmscroft* (later the *Spa Hotel*) and educated at Repton and Trinity. After leaving Cambridge he was called to the Bar but did not practice. He was for a time a captain in the 5th West Yorkshire Regiment and in charge of the Infantry Record Office. He was a magistrate on the West Riding, Liberty and City Benches, but had no previous municipal experience before becoming mayor. He was a talented musician, well-known as a viola player and took part in many concerts and festivals. An expert linguist and scholar, particularly interested in folklore, he published books, articles and translations. He left Ripon in 1920 and died in 1940.

November. A gymnastics display at the Victoria Hall was given in order to popularise the idea of setting up a public gymnasium in the city.

Mr S. P. Austin of Hollins Hall presented the Corporation with six young swans which were placed on the River Ure, between the North Bridge and the Bathing Pavilion.

Mr H. M. Bower J.P., a barrister, accepted the office of mayor. He was not a member of the Council, but was handsomely elected at a by-election caused by raising two councillors to the status of Alderman.

The lack of sun in the summer led to the vine outside the Ripon Club in the Market Place producing only sour green grapes instead of its usual ripe ones.

George Henry Brown, a farm worker, was ordered at Ripon City Court to pay £5 damages for accepting 10s as hiring money at the November Hirings and then continuing with his previous employer without refunding the money.

December. The City Surveyor and Sanitary Inspector, Mr William Mitchell, was arrested on a charge of obtaining money by making false entries in the Corporation's wage book. He later pleaded guilty and was sentenced to six months' imprisonment with hard labour by the City Court.

January. Mr W. H. Hutchinson was appointed Clerk of the Peace for the Ripon Liberty in the place of Mr F. D. Wise, of the same firm of solicitors, which had already filled this office over the past 84 years.

The Dean and Chapter published the details of a

new scheme whereby Ripon canons would be freed from parochial duties elsewhere and provided with residences within the City. They would also take up other responsibilities such as religious education and missionary work.

The Revd Samuel Reed retired as precentor of Ripon Cathedral after 30 years' service to take up the living at Bishop Monkton.

The death of Mrs Sarah Smithson, a former Mayoress of Ripon, was announced. Mrs Smithson had been well known for her work for the poor as a Poor Law Guardian, a member of the Committee for Elementary Schools and the Committee of the Nursing Institute.

February. Kirkby Malzeard Church was burnt down in the early hours of the morning of 8 February. The outbreak was attributed to the over-heating of a stove pipe.

The death rate for 1907 was 12.8 per 1,000 and was the lowest ever recorded in Ripon. The birth rate was 21.1 per 1,000.

All the arrangements were completed for the building of the new girls' secondary school. Messrs William Avery and Sons (Leeds) were the contractors and Mr A. E. Huggan of Scarborough was the clerk of works. The first sod was cut by Alderman Moss on 2 March and he laid the foundation stone containing a small metal box of mementoes on 30 May.

Heavy rain followed by violent gales caused the Rivers Ure and Skell to flood. Considerable damage was reported and no Saturday night market was held.

March. The Mayoress played on a new piano purchased by public subscription and given to the Ripon Hospital.

Buglers of the Ripon detachment of the Volunteers sounded the Last Post at the Drill Hall and other places in the City on 31 March, to mark the end of the Army Volunteers movement. On 1 April, a meeting was held at the Drill Hall to inaugurate the new Territorial Army detachment.

April. A serious accident occurred at the White Swan Laundry when the flue of the main boiler collapsed causing considerable damage. However, prompt action by staff averted an explosion and there was no one injured.

May. The Mayor and Mayoress attended a special service held at the Cathedral as part of the Empire Day celebrations, after which their Worships visited the six public elementary schools in the city where they addressed the children, made presentations and were suitably entertained.

June. Revd Isaac Albert Smith M.A., Vice Principal of St Paul's College, Cheltenham, was appointed as the new Principal of the Ripon and Wakefield Diocesan Training College. The post had become vacant by the appointment of Canon Garrod as Residentiary Canon of Ripon Cathedral.

Heavy rain led to a wall of water over eight feet high (one estimate was 12 ft) sweeping down the Laver Valley, causing damage to farms and to the new work being carried out at High Cleugh to improve the river course and banks.

A new Corporation tar boiler to provide facilities for the first tar spraying of roads in Ripon caught fire when being tried experimentally in Kirkby Lane. Work started in June and North Road between North Bridge and the Clock Tower was completed by the middle of July.

Five people were injured in a motor charabanc accident in North Street on Saturday 27 June.

July. Mr Jennings of *Aismunderby House* provided 115 window boxes for all the houses in Bondgate.

A new history of Ripon and Fountains written by Mr G. Parker of Kirkgate House was published.

Mormon missionaries were mobbed in Ripon Market Place on the evening of Sunday 5 July but escaped injury with the help of the police.

On 24 July, the Mayor opened the new sanatorium at Ripon Grammar School and said it was hoped that plans for a swimming pool would reach fruition soon.

September. New West Riding by-laws laid down speed limits of 10 mph for traffic in most of Ripon's streets and only six mph for the narrowest and most awkward ones.

The Ripon City Band was presented with an ebony and silver baton by the combined Ripon Friendly Societies in recognition of their freely-given help on Hospital Sunday.

The Littlethorpe Brickworks were acquired by Mr J. Spence J.P. for the sum of £1,200.

Canon Waugh provided an avenue of lime trees along the central footpath in the open space in St Agnesgate on the south side of the Cathedral.

The Victoria Hall, after extensive renovation, was re-opened as the Victoria Opera House.

October. Ripon magistrates and Councillors expressed great concern that neither the Fire Brigade, the Police Station nor the Railway Station were connected to the Telephone Exchange. The West Riding authorities refused 'for the present' to authorise the Police Station connection.

The Marquess of Ripon resigned his post as Lord Privy Seal on age and health grounds.

On 13 October, a roofing party was held at the *Unicorn Hotel* to mark the progress of the building of the new Girls' Secondary School, the future Ripon High School.

1908-09. HERBERT MORRIS BOWER

Rainfall in 1908 was 24.52 ins. with March and July the wettest months (3.64 ins.) and June the dryest month (0.97 ins.).

November. When a Police Sergeant stopped a horse-drawn curry with no driver, he found a man asleep in the back who claimed that another man had agreed to drive him from Masham to Ripon.

Miss Ellen Fraser addressed a Women's Suffrage Meeting in the Assembly Rooms on 24 November.

December. Improved passenger facilties were completed at Ripon Station providing more shelter over the platform, a larger waiting room, a tea-room and better sanitary arrangements.

Miss M. Davie, Headmistress of Truro County School for Girls, was appointed from 106 applicants

Mayor 1907-08-09

as the first Headmistress of the Ripon Girls' School. Mr H. R. Benson was appointed caretaker. Three pupils of Trinity School were the first girls to win exhibitions given by the Alderman Underwood Education Foundation for the new school.

New altar rails and additions to the choir stalls were completed in St John's church, Bondgate.

A local Old Age Pension Committee, formed to investigate applications in Ripon for State Old Age Pensions under the new Act, completed its work on 29 December; 210 claims were investigated; 148 authorised for 5s per week, 41 for smaller amounts, 18 refused and 3 adjourned for further consideration. An extra clerk was taken on at the Ripon Post Office so that the first pensions could be paid on New Years Day.

January. Mr C. H. Moody resigned his conductorship of the Ripon Choral Society after the performance of *Faust*, because of languid interest. The Precentor, the Revd E. H. Swann, agreed to take over.

Sir Christopher Furness M.P. of *Grantley Hall* was given the Freedom of the Borough of West Hartlepool.

The last case of children being brought publicly before the Magistrates was taken in Ripon in January before the New Children's Act came into force on 1 April.

Ripon Girls' Secondary School was opened with 12 scholars and three teachers on Friday 2 January, when Alderman Moss presented each pupil with a copy of *Sesame and Lilies* by John Ruskin.

The death of Mr Richard Wilkinson, Mayor of Ripon 1899-1900, occurred in Winnipeg, Canada at the age of 52.

February. The severe frosts each night enabled Riponians to enjoy skating on the canal, but the Councillors complained of inadequate heating in the Chamber where they had to retain their overcoats.

The Ripon Operatic Society performed *The Gon-*

doliers at the Victoria Opera House, on 17 and 19 February.

March. The Board of Guardians reported an increase in vagrancy in the Ripon area, with 254 in March this year as compared with 124 last March. It was proving difficult to find work for tramps in the Workhouse although the alterations at the Ripon Railway Station and the new Leeds Waterworks were providing extra employment for Ripon men.

The Magdalens Recreation Ground ('Paddy's Park') was extended by the gift to the city of over an acre of land by Mr F. D. Wise.

The death occurred of Mr John Baynes J.P., four times Mayor of Ripon.

The Bedale Hunt met in the Market Place for the first time for about 10 years.

April. The Corporation started a new method of avoiding the dust nuisance on roads by the application of Akoma (hydroscopic salt) which absorbs and retains moisture. During dry weather fortnightly applications would be necessary.

The Ripon City Golf Course on Palace Road was formally opened on Saturday 24 April. Nearly 200 members were present. Sir Christopher Furness M.P. was unable at the last moment to carry out the opening ceremony.

Two men were badly scalded in an accident at the Ripon brass foundry of Messrs Summerfield and Stampe.

May. Technical classes were transferred from the Mechanics Institute to the new Girls' Secondary School in College Road.

An exceptionally brilliant and lengthy display of the *aurora borealis* was seen in the northern sky on 18 May.

July. The Marquess of Ripon died on 9 July. The funeral service at St Wilfrid's Catholic Church was on 14 July, preceded by a 'lying in state' the previous night and followed by a funeral procession to the burial place in St Mary's, Studley. A Requiem Mass was sung at Westminster Cathedral.

On 21 July Viscount Mountgarret officially opened the new Ripon Girls' Secondary School and Technical Institute at an open-air ceremony.

September. The Dean and Chapter decided that the Cathedral Choir should in future wear scarlet instead of blue cassocks as the Dean declared 'Scarlet is a royal colour and has a special fitness for our Cathedral by reason of its association with King James I'. The choir first wore the new colour on 26 December.

A roller-skating rink was opened at the Victoria Opera House, where a special floor had been laid. One hundred and thirty skaters and numerous spectators attended.

The Marquess of Ripon's exhibition awards for pupils to attend Ripon Grammar School and his University Awards were given permanent provision in his will.

October. The death of Mr Thomas Smithson J.P., Mayor of Ripon 1890-92, was announced.

1909-10. FRANCIS GEORGE METCALFE, Tailor

Born 1854, son of John Metcalfe and twin brother
of J. H. Metcalfe who had the house-furnishing shop
in Kirkgate. He was educated at the Cathedral
Schools and apprenticed to his father's business
of tailor and milliner which he carried on. He was
elected to the Council in 1904, Alderman in 1910
and retired from the Corporation in 1928. He was
a Poor Law Guardian and Overseer, a Freemason,
a member of the Conservative Party and a churchwarden at the Cathedral. He died in 1933.

Rainfall in 1909 was 29.33 ins.

November. The Ripon Temperance Society held
a conversazione at its headquarters on Duck Hill
to celebrate its 75th anniversary.

December. Ripon Police Station, together with
other stations in the West Riding, was at last linked
with the exchange of the National Telephone
Company.

January. 1910 saw two parliamentary elections in
the campaign of the Liberals in the House of Com-
mons to restrict the powers of the House of Lords.
The *Gazette* supported the Liberal candidate
(H. F. Lynch) and printed the famous 'Peers or
People' manifesto in full. Miss Amelia Pankhurst
also supported the Liberal cause at two suffragette
meetings in the Market Place. Both candidates visited
Ripon on polling day, 21 January, when there was
a clash between opposing supporters with banners
and sandwich boards in the Market Place which
had to be stopped by the police. Results were
received by the *Gazette* at 11.45 am on the next
day: Hon. E. L. Wood, Unionist, 6,363, H. F. Lynch,
Liberal, 5,119, Unionist majority 1,244. Later Mr
Wood and his wife, Lady Dorothy, arrived by train
and were drawn through the streets to the Market
Place where the successful candidate made a speech
from a window of the *Unicorn Hotel* and still later
from the balcony of the Constitutional Club in Water
Skellgate.

A new comet was seen from Ripon on four nights
at the end of the month. Halley's Comet was not
seen until 29 May.

February. As usual at this time of the year, very
cold weather (up to 20° of frost) led to distress
among the poor in Ripon. The Poor Relief Fund
Committee set up a soup kitchen in the Stall House
in Blossomgate distributing 450 tickets for soup and
bread and £30 worth of coal during the first week.

The Ripon Orchestral Society was set up with
Mr W. Broome, the deputy organist at the Cathedral,
appointed as conductor and the Society gave its
first concert at the Victoria Opera House in October.

The Governors of the Secondary School for Girls
in College Road agreed to change its name to Ripon
Girls' High School at the suggestion of both the
Board of Education and the West Riding County
Council. They also decided that no more free
scholars would be admitted for the time being as
the numbers already complied with the Board of
Education requirements. Fees for paying pupils were
£5 19s 6d per annum. From this time the girls were
allowed to take examinations for exhibitions awarded
by the Alderman Underwood Trust and the Dr
Richardson Trust.

Thomas Hargrave J.P., died at age 60. He was
elected to the Council in 1880, was the Mayor 1889,
retired 1898. The family business, saddle-tree makers,
was then the foremost firm in one of the oldest
industries in the city.

March. Viscount Mountgarret was returned unopposed as Ripon's representative on the W.R.C.C.

Structural alteration plans were agreed to con-
centrate all City Council public offices in the Town
Hall. The City Collector's Office opened during
March as the first of these changes.

The last traditional Easter Egg rolling competition
in Skellbank Fields near Bishopton Bridge took place
on Easter Monday as the public footpath was due
to be closed for the completion of the newly-
constructed Mallorie Park Road. A petition against
closure was signed too late for the Quarter Sessions
on 9 April, when the final decision to close the
path to the public was made.

April. Bostock and Wombwell's Royal No. 1
Menagerie visited Ripon and set up in the Market
Place. This travelling show continued in existence
until World War I.

A team of Yorkshire and Durham ringers rang
a peal of 5,088 bob majors with Kent variations at
the Cathedral in 3 hrs 18 mins.

Mr C. W. Judson, member of the well-known
family of druggists, died. The family business,
carried out in premises on the north-east corner
of the Marcket Place, was founded in 1814 by his
great-grandfather, Thomas Judson, last Mayor to
be elected under the Charter of King James I, 1835-6.
His grandfather, Thomas Judson junior, was also
Mayor in 1862-3. The business had to close in 1911
when the Studley Estate Officer gave notice that
the site was required for building operations.

May. King Edward VII died on 6 May and the
nation went into mourning. The Bishop of Ripon
was one of the prelates officiating at the State Funeral
in London on 21 May. In Ripon, banks, businesses
and public offices closed, the race meeting was

cancelled and public houses were closed from 11.00 am to 4.00 pm; the Mayor and Corporation processed from the Town Hall to the Cathedral for a memorial service at 1.00 pm. A collection was made for the families of the victims of the recent Whitehaven Colliery diaster.

The new King, George V, was proclaimed by the Mayor in the Market Place and at the west door of the Cathedral.

June. A letter was received from Ripon, Wisconsin, U.S.A., inviting the citizens of Ripon, England, to attend an historical pageant on 14 June. The City Council sent congratulations but no representative actually travelled to the U.S.

New electrical treatments including Ionisation, Faradisation, Galvanisation, High Frequency Currents, Vibratory Massage and Radiant Heat were installed at the Ripon Bathing Establishment taking their supply from the adjacent Spa Hydro Company at a cost of £200. Mr and Mrs Sochon were to be in charge at a salary of £100 per annum.

Sir Christopher Furness of *Grantley Hall*, who had largely financed the building of the Spa Hydro, was raised to the peerage.

July. A bullock escaped from the cattle market and smashed the window of Messrs Jackson, drapers, in Fishergate.

The County Commissioner agreed that Ripon should have its own Boy Scout centre separate from Boroughbridge.

September. A thorough renovation of the spire and weather vane of the (now demolished) congregational church in North Street was carried out.

October. Zion Chapel in Blossomgate celebrated its golden jubilee.

Ripon Oddfellows celebrated the centenary of the founding of the Order and the 75th anniversary of St Wilfrid's Lodge with a torchlight procession of members wearing robes and regalia.

Mr Walter Fennell of *Aislabie* agreed to take office as Mayor and as he was not a member of the City Council he agreed to be a candidate at the forthcoming election.

1910-11. WALTER FENNELL

Born 1860 in Wakefield. Educated at Rossall and entered his father's business. He retired to Ripon in 1907, to *Aislabie*. For a short time he was a student at Ripon Clergy College but gave up his intention of taking orders on health grounds. He was a supporter of Church Schools and did much for the promotion of sport, especially athletics and gymnastics, as a council member of the National Society for Physical Education. Mrs Fennell was a prominent worker for the Girls' Friendly Society. When nominated for the Council in 1910 he particularly asked for support without any party consideration.

Rainfall in 1910 was 30.9 ins. Wettest month January (5.25 ins.). Driest month September (0.27 ins.).

December. Mr H. Norman Rae J.P., was adopted as Liberal candidate for the Ripon division at the second Parliamentary Election in this year. The

meeting on 3 December in the Assembly Rooms behind the Café Victoria was so crowded that Mr Rae could not get through the entrance and mounted an outside ladder to an anteroom to appear through a doorway near the platform. The Marquess of Ripon, with a different political allegiance from his father, supported the sitting Unionist M.P., the Hon. Edward Wood, both on the platform and by the use of his cars on polling day, 13 December. The election results were flashed by 'limelight' on the *Ripon Gazette's* screen at the Café Victoria in the Market Place: the Hon. E. L. Wood, 5,894, H. Norman Rae, 5,020. Unionist majority 824.

January. Lord Furness purchased the Brimham estate, including the hunting lodge, from Lord Grantley.

A subscription list to raise funds for the improvement of local church schools to bring them up to the standards required by the Board of Education reached £2,000.

February. The District Inspector of the Local Government Board criticised the Ripon Board of Guardians for allowing children to be kept in the Workhouse. He also found the number of casuals was too high and the fluctuation was too great to warrant improvement being made to the casual wards.

Mr John King, corn and flour dealer, was thrown into the River Laver when driving his trap across a ford between Birkby Nab and Clotherholme. Mr King was rescued by a local farmer but both pony and trap were lost.

April. At a public meeting on the anniversary of the King's death, it was decided to launch a fund to provide a new hospital wing as a memorial to Edward VII.

A break was made in the ringing of the Curfew in order not to interfere with the performance of Dvorak's *Stabat Mater* by the Cathedral and local voluntary choirs augmented by the Ripon Choral Society.

May. The Estate of the late Mrs Kenny fronting on Park Street and Church Lane, which later became the Spa Park, was put up for auction.

June. Lord Masham presented the Bishop of Ripon with a new cope to wear at the Coronation ceremony.

Bishop Gordon of Leeds, a former pupil of Ripon Grammar School, died at the age of 80. Ordained in 1859, his first mission was at the Chapel in Low Skellgate where Roman Catholics worshipped before the building of St Wilfrid's Church.

Miss Minnie Davie resigned her post as first Headmistress of Ripon Girls' High School. She was appointed in 1908 and opened the school a year later with 12 pupils, against 'not a little prejudice' arising from the opposition to any higher education for girls.

Mr C. W. Judson left £2,500 for the creation of Almshouses and the proceeds of the sale of his house, *Woodlands* at Woodside, to be invested for their upkeep.

House building was started on the land between the cricket field and Mallorie Park Drive towards the River Laver.

Mr Francis Smith J.P., Mayor 1893-94, died at the age of 57. He had risen to the position of Partner and Managing Director of T. and R. Williamson, Varnish Manufacturers, having joined the firm as a boy of fourteen. He was a Churchwarden at the Cathedral and an active Freemason.

The 1911 Census showed that Ripon had a population of 8,218, a decrease of 12 since 1901.

Viscount Mountgarret of *Nidd Hall*, County Councillor for Ripon, was made a Baron of the United Kingdom in the Coronation Honours List.

The Corporation gave instructions that Ripon Market should be held on Wednesday to make way for a two-day celebration of the coronation of King George V on 22 June, and the following day, Friday 23 June. £250 expenses were voted by the Council, which was nominally described as a salary for the Mayor.

The Town Hall and Market Cross were decorated and the Mayor and Mayoress gave souvenir coronation medals and boxes of chocolates to all Ripon school children. The Dean gave Coronation New Testaments to the older children at the Cathedral Day School.

On Coronation Day, the Mayor and Corporation, representatives of the Services and Public Bodies, processed along North Street, Coltsgate Hill, Blossomgate, Market Place and Kirkgate to attend a special service at the Cathedral. After the service the congregation processed to the Market Place to hear addresses by the Mayor and the Dean. The Territorials fired a '*feu de joie*' and the ceremony was concluded by the singing of the National Anthem and the sounding of a fanfare of trumpets. In the afternoon, there was a mass meeting of children in the Square, a special tea at the schools followed by a grand Sports Competition. The evening celebrations included games and fireworks on the cricket field with music by the bands. There was more music on Friday. The old people were entertained to tea in the Victoria Hall, but the children's Maypole and Morris Dancing had to be abandoned because of rain. However, the Military Tattoo and Torchlight Procession in the evening took place in spite of the weather.

August. Miss A. R. Piggott of Newnham College, Cambridge, was appointed Headmistress of Ripon Girls' High School.

King George V arrived on a four-day private visit to Studley Royal, where he joined the Marquess of Ripon's party for the grouse shooting. Queen Alexandra and the Empress Marie of Russia followed on 15 August, visiting Ripon Cathedral and shops in the city on 21 August.

Dr Boyd Carpenter resigned his office as Bishop of Ripon after 27 years in the diocese. He preached his last sermon at the Cathedral on 8 October.

September. Mrs Glasier spoke at a meeting in the Market Place on the need for an independent Labour Party.

1911-12.   WALTER FENNELL

Mayor 1910-11-12-13, 1921-22

Rainfall in 1911 was 25.65 ins.

November. The Revd. Henry Haigh, President of the Wesleyan Conference, visited Ripon for the golden jubilee celebrations of the Coltsgate Hill Wesleyan Chapel.

An elegant structure on wheels, intended to act as a cabmen's shelter, arrived on site — the north side of the Market Place — and was formally opened on Tuesday 23 November. The fund to pay for the shelter had been set up by the Mayor who also promised to supply papers and magazines for cabmen to read during waiting time. In the event the fund was not needed owing to a bequest by the late Miss Carter, the daughter of Mr Thomas Carter, Mayor 1867-69.

Dr Thomas Woolley Drury, Bishop of Sodor and Man, became Bishop-designate of Ripon. His formal election by the Dean and Chapter took place on 22 December.

Admiral Sir Francis Bridgeman G.C.V.O., K.C.B., who resided at *Copgrove Hall*, was appointed First Sea Lord.

December. The Revd E. Dalton D.D., President of the Primitive Methodist Conference, who had started his ministry in Ripon 40 years earlier, revisited Allhallowgate Chapel.

A large Unionist public meeting was held in the Victoria Opera House to protest against Home Rule for Ireland. Lord Hugh Cecil attended.

The City Council, after lengthy discussion, accepted the offer made by Miss Adelaide Julia Darnborough to give *Thorpe Prebend House* to the city following the expressed wishes of her late brother, the Revd John William Darnborough. This offer had been made several times previously, but the Corporation had hesitated to accept because of the funds which would be required to restore the property to its original condition. In the latter half of the 19th century the house had not been well kept and in the 1890s had been bought by Mr James Wright, a plumber, who had divided the building into five cottages. It was at this time that Revd Darnborough had become interested in the property. The Darnborough family had been well known in Ripon for centuries; Christopher Darnborough was the Wakeman in 1542 and by his will left money for the repair of North Bridge. Thomas Darnborough was Mayor in 1842-3 and perhaps because of this, his son was determined that some good use of the old building be made that would retain something of its former dignity. This wish his sister, Miss Darnborough, faithfully carried out. An arrangement was made with the Council for the matter to be allowed to stand over until the rents from the cottages had accumulated to such a sum as would pay for the necessary alterations. Miss Darnborough's final offer was made when £150 had accumulated to which she added an extra £200 towards the total estimated cost of £600.

The James Grayson collection of stuffed birds, animals and British birds' eggs was given by his son Albert to the proposed Thorpe Prebend Museum.

January. The Revd Canon Cust Nunn, Rural Dean and Vicar of Sharow, retired after 40 years' association with the Church in the Ripon area.

February. A book of poetry *Poems of the Chase* by Sir Reginald Graham of Norton Conyers was published by Hatchard, Piccadailly.

Very severe frosts again caused the Mayor to call together the Relief Committee and arrangements were made to provide a soup kitchen and tickets for groceries and fuel.

The weather also made several stretches of ice locally available for skaters. The Yorkshire Amateur Skating Championships were held on 1 February on the Carlton fishponds, Snaith. Mr F. G. Mills of Ripon was fourth in the finals although in the heats he had been the fastest competitor.

Dr Drury, the new Bishop, was enthroned in Ripon Cathedral in the presence of over 250 clergy, the Mayor and Corporation and a large body of other laity. Afterwards, the Bishop was presented with an address from the Corporation at a lunch given in his honour at the Victoria Opera House.

The city was plunged into almost total darkness for two hours due to a failure in the gas supply after air had got into the pipes. During March, a coal strike reduced passenger services on the railway to Ripon and steps were taken to save gas by holding church services earlier, closing shops earlier and not lighting some street lamps. The City Council met in the afternoon instead of the evening. It took some time to re-establish the full railway service. Ripon Agricultural Association passed a resolution against the 'Daylight Saving Bill'.

March. Local people were urged to support the Corporation, itself affiliated to the National Footpaths Preservation Society, in its attempts to prevent encroachments on public footpaths. An investigation was set up to enquire into the closing by barbed wire of the footpath along the River Skell from the Rustic Bridge to Whitcliffe.

April. Special sermons were preached and music played at services in the Cathedral and other city churches and chapels on Sunday 21 April in mourning for the loss of the *Titanic*.

This month was the driest April in Ripon for 60 years.

May. The memorial statue of the 1st Marquess of Ripon was unveiled in the Spa Gardens by Sir Hugh Ball, Lord Lieutenant of the North Riding. Lord Ripon is depicted in peer's robes and court dress and wearing the insignia of the Garter. The statue was modelled by Mr F. Derwent Wood and cast in bronze by Singer and Company of Frome, Somerset, at a total cost of £1,417 18s. The balance of £393 was divided between the Cottage Hospital and the Victoria Nursing Institution.

The Mayor presided at a meeting in the Town Hall at which a Ripon branch of the Royal National Lifeboat Institution was set up.

June. Messrs Abbott and Company gave assurances that everything possible would be done to avoid causing a nuisance from the noise of machinery in their proposed new furniture factory in Kirkby Road.

Dr Boyd Carpenter, former Bishop of Ripon, was made a Knight Commander of the Royal Victorian Order.

At a Public Meeting called by the Mayor it was decided to retain the practice of the last 20 years in Ripon for half-day closing on Fridays. It had been suggested that this should be changed to Wednesday now that closing was compulsory by law instead of voluntary as hitherto.

The Revd C. H. K. Boughton, B.A., Vice Principal of Wycliffe Hall, Oxford, was appointed to the Ripon Clergy College in succession to the Revd J. Battersby Harford, who had been appointed a Canon Residentiary of Ripon Cathedral.

The Ripon and Wakefield Diocesan Training College celebrated its Golden Jubilee on 8 June with a service in the Cathedral, which 600 former students attended, and which was followed by a luncheon at the Victoria Opera House.

Mr Alfred Barlow, Chief Assistant Surveyor for York, was appointed Ripon City Surveyor in place of Mr T. P. Frank.

July. The Headmaster of the Grammar School announced at Speech Day that the Governors had agreed to provide a swimming bath for the school. It was proposed that the boys would help in digging the hole and that once the bath was completed the Corporation would provide water cheaply.

August. Mr Harold Slack, the Nottingham airman,

11. *Thorpe Prebend House (Fossick)*

12. *Banisters in Thorpe Prebend House (Fossick)*

flew over Ripon in his Bleriot monoplane on 2 August during his 12,000-mile tour over England.

Mrs R. A. Lonsdale was killed by a slow-moving car when she stepped off the footpath at the top of Kirkgate.

September. A preparatory department, for pupils under 10, was started at the Ripon Girls' High School.

October. The reduction in vagrancy in Ripon in recent months, originally attributed to employment on the Harrogate Water Works projects, was now said to be general throughout the country because the officials could not distinguish between workers and the tramps on the evidence of insurance cards.

The Council agreed to provide a water trough and a covering of clean sand in the Market Place following complaints concerning cattle on market days. They refused to provide pens and suggested a change of site for the cattle market. This idea was vigorously rejected by the Agricultural Association.

Lord Mountgarret of *Nidd Hall*, Member for Ripon of the W.R.C.C., died at the age of 65 on 2 October.

St Wilfrid's Roman Catholic Church was consecrated by the Bishop of Leeds. A consecration ceremony can be performed in the Catholic Church only when a building is free of debt. This was now the case and coincided with the golden jubilee of its foundation and thus provided a happy opportunity for a double celebration.

1912-13. WALTER FENNELL

Mayor 1910-11-12-13, 1921-22

November. Lady Frances Balfour addressed a Women's Suffrage Meeting in the Edward Room.

Lord Furness of Grantley Hall died on Sunday, 10 November aged 60. He was a native of West Hartlepool and his interests were mainly outside Ripon, in shipping, coal and iron, particularly in County Durham. However, he provided the main stimulus for the opening of the Spa Baths by the purchase of the *Elmscroft* Estate and on the site of the mansion building and equipping a first class Spa hydro-hotel at a cost of £30,000. He was buried at Winksley.

The Bishop of Ripon dedicated new reredos panels and a new stained glass window in the chapel of the Ripon and Wakefield Diocesan Training College.

December. The Hon. E. Wood, M.P. for Ripon, had a lucky escape when the taxi in which he was travelling was crushed between two tram cars in Sheffield.

January. Reports in the newspapers showed that 1912 had been a bad year nationally for both trade and agriculture with the lowest potato yield ever recorded and a decrease of the sheep population by over one and a quarter million head. There was real poverty in the city with a number of families responding to the weekly newspaper advertisements for emigration schemes to Canada (offering farms on the prairies with payments spread over 20 years) and to Australia. The positive effect of this was reflected in the numbers of pupils at the Cathedral Schools in 1911 and 1912.

There was little response for the first time to the annual appeal for subscriptions to the Poor Relief Fund, despite the need to open the Soup Kitchen at the Stall House in Blossomgate during the bad weather. The lack of support may well have been because of the new National Insurance Act which awarded the unemployed 7s 6d per week. The high unemployment in the city was due to the lack of any large industry in the area which in turn was partly due to the obstruction of local land owners. The Spa scheme had not had a good season and there was a serious proposal that the Baths should be shut. One attempt to bolster the local economy was the setting up of a Territorial Committee to try to persuade the War Office to site training camps for the Territorial Army in the vicinity of Ripon. These tentative negotiations laid the foundation for the full-scale developments of 1915 when the Army Camp was established.

Another disappointment was the relatively poor response to the King Edward Memorial Fund which at the closure of the account stood at £131. However, it was decided to continue with the planned extension to the Hospital.

February. The Studley Bowl was sold to the South Kensington Museum (now the Victoria and Albert Museum) for £3,000. One thousand pounds was to be invested to augment the living, £1,000 to be kept as a repair fund and £1,000 to be spent as the churchwardens wished. There was one letter of protest from the son of a former incumbent of Studley Church, who suggested that the bowl might have been part of the Fountains Abbey plate and should have remained in the district.

The medical men of Harrogate, Ripon and district first refused to join the medical panel under the new National Insurance Act, but a week later decided to serve under protest.

There was an exciting incident when a young heifer being driven to the cattle sale in the Market Place bolted at the corner of Westgate into Knowles Brothers, Drapers, and bounded upstairs into the showroom on the first floor. It was finally persuaded to leave without doing any damage.

In a recruiting drive for the Army, the sum of 2s was paid to every N.C.O. and man of the 3rd Battalion West Yorkshire Regiment who recruited a new member.

March. It was suggested that the upper part of the Ripon Canal should be closed and a landing stage erected at the rear of the first lock so that the Littlethorpe Road bridge could be lowered. Members of the City Council opposed this as it was thought that canal traffic would increase because of a recent rise in the railway freight rates. Also, it was feared that this would be the thin end of the wedge towards the complete closure of the canal.

April. The Mayor and Mayoress entertained Ripon Corporation employees and their wives to tea at the Assembly Rooms when an important announcement was made concerning the care of infants in the city. Prizes were offered for the best cared-for babies born during their three-year mayoralty. The scheme was intended to help 'deserving wives' of working men whose wages were not more than 25s per week.

The departure of several Ripon families emigrating to Canada was reported in the local press.

The Ripon Shop Assistants' Society held a whist drive and dance in the Assembly Rooms in aid of funds to press their case for shorter working hours. Their present hours were 8 am to 7 pm on weekdays and to 10 pm on Saturdays.

The Ripon Industrial Society held its seventh exhibition in April in the Victoria Opera House with a larger number of entries, 1,005, than in 1911, when there were only 570. The exhibitions were held to encourage craft work in the city but in recent times numbers had declined. The first exhibition had been held in 1889 followed by larger projects in 1892, 1893 and 1895, but the numbers of exhibits had fallen each time so it was not until 1907 that the next exhibition was mounted. In 1909 there were 1,020 entries, 500 of which were from schools. In that year the Education Department refused to allow competitive work to be done in school hours. In 1913, most entries were in the art and craft sections (lace, needlework, crochet, painting, hand-wrought silver and copper craft, jewellery and wood carving). There was no entry in Sir Reginald Graham's prize design section for a detached bungalow to cost not more than £250, and only one entry in the Kearsley mechanical drawing competition for lads under twenty-one.

May. The Judson Almshouses in Locker Lane, built by the bequest of £2,560 left by Mr C. W. Judson, were completed. These consist of five houses for occupants over 70 years of age receiving old age pensions or with small private means. Preference was given by the Trustees to married couples.

The Corporation decided to purchase for £12 12s the 40 pen-and-ink sketches drawn by Mr G. Fossick of old buildings in Ripon which have now disappeared. It was proposed to have them framed for display either in the Town Hall or the Museum.

The swimming bath at the Grammar School which the boys had helped to excavate was nearing completion at a cost of £160, towards which £104 11s had previously been collected.

After complaints to the Mayor, the Water Department was charged with the task of cleaning and supplying clean water to the 'Fevers Fountain' near North Bridge. This drinking fountain (now discarded in the Spa Park) inscribed 'Erected for the use of the public by John Fevers of Ripon 1875', consisted of a 7½-foot square lower trough for cattle and horses and a 5½-foot diameter upper basin for the general public, served by means of spring taps projecting from the mouths of four boldly carved animals' heads. The upper basin is supported by a massive shaft of stone, octagonal in shape with grotesque carved figures at each of the four angles and each holding a shield bearing respectively J., S., the horn and the spurs. The base has small animals such as frogs and lizards creeping round. The fountain was erected at a cost of £130.

The Hornblower and the Bellman both applied for new hats and uniforms to be provided. This was granted for the Hornblower but the Committee decided that the Bellman had not performed his duties satisfactorily and instructed the Town Clerk to dismiss him. The Committee also ordered that estimates be obtained for new buttons inscribed 'Ripon Corporation' for Council employee uniforms to take the place of brass buttons marked 'Ripon City Police', used after the amalgamation of the Ripon Borough and West Riding Police Forces in 1887.

June. The first visit of a Lord Mayor of London to Harrogate for the opening of additions and improvements to the Royal Baths, the Pump Room and the Valley Gardens (costing £14,000) took place on Saturday 7 June. On Sunday, the Lord Mayor paid an unofficial visit to Ripon with no ceremony or uniforms, when he saw the Regalia and witnessed the setting of the Watch. The Mayor and full Council entertained him for tea, after which he visited Fountains Abbey before returning to Harrogate.

Efforts were made to re-establish lace making in Ripon. A class was formed using a classroom at the Girls' High School on Monday, Wednesday and Friday, 4.30 to 6.00 pm, at a charge of 6s for 26 lessons. The W.R.C.C. provided a grant. A private class for 10 students was also started by Mrs Harker at the Kirkgate Linen Warehouse with a charge of 12s for 12 lessons, and half-hour lessons for children at 2d per lesson.

Lord Scarbrough put forward a new recruiting scheme for the Territorial Army and a proposed new Drill Hall and headquarters for the 5th Battalion West Yorkshire Regiment in Somerset Row (now Hugh Ripley Hall).

There was very little business at the Ripon June Wool Fair, the local dale farmers relying more on direct sales from the farms.

The foundation stone was laid on 19 June of a new wing to Skellfield School.

It was agreed that the arrangement whereby the Horn was first blown at the Mayor's residence and afterwards at the Market Cross should be restored so that visitors from Harrogate could witness the setting of the Watch ceremony and still catch the 9.29 pm train. It was argued that this arrangement would not be a breach of continuity as, when the Mayor had resided at an unreasonable distance from the Market Place, the Horn had been blown at the Town Hall steps and afterwards at the Market Cross. It was also decided to revert to the custom of four blasts of the Horn, one at each corner of the Market Cross.

July. The Ripon Tradesmen's Association had an excursion to Blackpool on Friday 11 July when the shops were closed all day instead of the usual half day. Two hundred and thirty people went on the trip at a cost of 5s, leaving Ripon by train at 4.55 am and returning at 9.24 pm, to arrive back at 2.0 am on Saturday morning.

Concern was expressed by the Ripon Gas Company when a firm of electrical engineers applied to the Board of Trade for a licence to supply electricity to the city.

There was a celebration in the city with decorated streets, games in the evening and a Rose Ball in the Victoria Opera House to celebrate the 50th anniversary of the first landing in England of Queen Alexandra and to raise funds for her charity.

It was decided to use the Lark Hill Hospital as a health resort for very poor children in the city, as an experiment. The Hospital had been erected at the time of one of the several smallpox scares of the 19th century at the highest point within the city, 200 ft above sea level, on the site of the old service reservoir which supplied the city when the water was pumped from the River Ure. In the early years of the 20th century it had been used as a sanatorium for consumptives.

August. On 12 August King George was met at Ripon Railway Station by the Marquess of Ripon when he arrived for a three-day visit to Studley Royal for the grouse shooting en route for Balmoral. He was driven through Ripon and greeted with loyal cheers. There was a temporary breach of etiquette when the Royal Standard was inadvertently placed on the Town Hall — this was rapidly replaced by the Union Jack.

The 18th Ripon and District Horticultural Show was opened by the Marchioness of Ripon on Residence Field, now the field adjoining Cathedral Close.

For the first time civic business was suspended during the month of August when no Council meetings were held.

A light note appeared in the *Gazette* on 21 August in appreciation of the Marchioness of Ripon: 'She has immense personal charm and has grown middle aged without losing her wonderful looks. They have ripened but she is still the handsomest woman of her age in society'. The article went on to state that her knowledge of opera was consummate and that she had probably attended more performances at Covent Garden than any other woman of her day.

September. It was decided that the Ripon Home for Girls in Bondgate should no longer employ a governess and that the girls should attend the Cathedral Girls' School where they would mix with other children of their own age. The home was founded by Dean Goode in 1862 and now accommodated 40 girls with the object, in the words of the first matron, 'of befriending poor girls of good character, more especially those that are motherless, by training them in habits of industry, giving them instruction calculated to fit them for domestic service or as mothers of a household of their own . . .'.

Large crowds gathered at the racecourse to witness Mr Blackburn, the aviator, who was accompanied by Dr Christie, land after a flight in a monoplane from Harrogate.

The will of Mr Hurst of Copt Hewick Hall was published, showing a gross estate of £292,930. Bequests included Ripon Cottage Hospital (£300), Victoria Nursing Institute (£250) and Copt Hewick Church (£3,000).

The Board of Guardians published a report emphasising the difficulty of discriminating between genuine workmen and ordinary tramps. It was proposed that professional vagrants should be issued with a bread and cheese ticket on leaving casual wards so that they could claim half a pound of bread and 2 oz. of cheese for a midday meal. A register of all casuals was to be kept so that the government would have the necessary statistics to decide how far it was desirable to establish labour colonies and put professional vagrants under control.

1913-14.   THOMAS HARRISON, Plumber

A native of Ripon, he carried on business in North Street as a plumber and gas fitter. He contested several elections and eventually became a member of the Council in 1899 but was forced to retire through ill-health. He was a director of the Northallerton Gas Company, a Freemason and a director of the Victoria Opera House Company. Returning to the Council in 1908, he died in December 1913 shortly after his installation as Mayor. The Council elected H. Mann Thirlway in his place.

H. MANN THIRLWAY, Printer and Stationer
Mayor 1888-9, see *Ripon Millenary Record*. Born 1851 to a family long established in Ripon, his shop at the top of High Skellgate next to the *Wakeman's House* was one of the best known in Ripon; the business had

moved there in 1815. For many years a leading figure in the city and the 'Father' of the Council, he died in 1937.

November. The death was announced of Mr William Basil Wilberforce, a lineal descendant of the famous slave abolitionist, at his residence *Markington Hall*, which he had greatly improved and restored during recent years.

The art-nouveau pulpit in the Cathedral, the work of Harry Nicholson and a gift from the late Revd Stallis, Vicar of Far Headingley 1896-1906, was completed. It consists of a metal drum roughly square with semi-circular bays showing rich repoussé copper decoration and supported on marble pillars. Round the base is a series of rich panels with groups of child angels supporting figures of saints associated with the early churches of St Cuthbert of Durham, St Chad of Lichfield, St Hilda of Whitby and St Etheldreda of Ely. The present wrought-iron hangings for the sounding board were designed by Sir Albert Richardson in 1960.

It was proposed to revive the Ripon Scientific Society so that members could assist the honorary curators of the City Museum at *Thorpe Prebend House* in the arrangement, classification and care of specimens. There were 19 applications for the post of caretaker at an annual salary of £5 with house, gas and fuel free.

The low attendance at the Ripon Martinmas Fair and Hirings reflected the changing social conditions and mode of hiring farm labour and domestic servants. Annual wage quotations were: farm foreman £28 to £30, ploughman £23 to £26, ploughboys £15 to £17, young boys £6 to £8; capable women servants £20 to £22, strong girls £15 to £18 and young girls £7 to £9.

The Gas Committee ordered improved gas street lighting to be placed in many parts of the city.

December. The Mayor, Alderman Thomas Harrison, Printer, died on 10 December. The last Mayor of Ripon to die in office was James Bowman in 1834.

The Bishop of Ripon was presented with a Pastoral Staff at the Diocesan Conference held at Leeds. It cost £219 raised by public subscriptions ranging from 1d

to £5, and consisted of a richly cast wrought silver head on an ebony staff enriched with precious stones and enamel. The main decoration was the arms of the Province of York and the Diocese of Ripon.

January. The Corporation decided to leave the traditional extra street lamp which had been erected opposite the late Thomas Harrison's house in North Street to provide additional street lighting, and to place a lantern over the gateway to the new Mayor, Mr Edward Taylor's residence in *Claremont*.

The Sanitary Inspector reported that among the registered workshops in the city were: Bakehouses 11; Dressmakers and Milliners 16; Tailors 7; Boot and Shoe repairers 8; Laundries 3; Cabinet-makers 10; Plumbers 8.

February. Under the Poor Law Institutions Order 1913 the title Ripon Workhouse was abolished in favour of the new name 'Poor Law Institution'. The Board of Guardians also discussed the hours for retiring to bed for the inmates, and it was decided that the rising hour of 6.15 am in summer and 6.45 am in winter should remain but that the time for retirement (8 pm) should be extended to 8.30 pm. This was a compromise with the minority who suggested 9 pm.

April. The City Council instructed the Town Clerk to report to the Local Government Board under the Housing of the Working Classes Act that no new houses were required in Ripon as there were 24 empty cottages available at rents from 1s 6d to 5s 6d per week.

A lady Health Visitor was to be appointed for carrying out the provisons of the Public Health Acts and the Notification of Births Act.

A new Tourist Guide for Ripon had been prepared by Canon Garrod. The City Council agreed to renew a grant of £100 for advertising the city. William Harrisons were asked to quote for printing 5,000 copies, but in the event were unable to carry out the work in time for the Easter visitors. The North Eastern Railway Company agreed to produce it.

The General Purposes Committee had a problem to solve over the official opening of the Thorpe Prebend Museum. Mrs Fennell, the Mayoress during the period of the negotiations, had been asked to perform this duty but Miss Darnborough, the donor of the building, was emphatically opposed to the opening by a woman. Alderman Fennell came to their rescue and agreed to do it. The Museum was opened to the public on 25 June and attracted 1,130 visitors in the first fortnight.

May. The Ripon Territorial Company vacated the Drill Hall in Park Street which they had occupied for half a century to go to new premises specially built on Skellbank. The old building was originally erected as a theatre towards the end of the 18th century by a Recorder of Ripon, George Hansell, the eldest son of another George Hansell who was Town Clerk 1723-1757. The younger George died in 1778 and was buried in the north aisle of the Cathedral. The first performance was played by Mr Butler's Company on 20 August 1792 with the announcement 'The scenery and decorations are excellent and the manager endeavours to provide a respectable dramatic corps, with novelties of the day, for the gratification of the public, during the season'. In the 19th century, the building was acquired by the Marquess of Ripon and became a military riding school. This was in the days when the Sergeant Major and the headquarters of the Yorkshire Hussars were in Ripon before moving to York in 1860. The Ripon Rifle Volunteers were set up in 1860 with the first drills being held in the Temperance Hall on Duck Hill, then a new building. Later the Marquess provided the old Riding School rent-free as the regular Drill Hall. After the move of the Volunteers to the new Drill Hall on Skellbank the Park Street building, the adjacent house and spacious yard was converted to a motor garage and it is now used by the National Bus Company as its Ripon Depot.

The Dean and Chapter gave the sounding-board which had been erected over the old pulpit in the nave of the Cathedral in 1903 to Christ Church, Meadow Lane, Leeds. This circular board consisting of 300 wooden sections made by a New York firm at a cost of £50 had considerably improved the acoustics in the Cathedral.

A report of a recent upsurge of vagrancy in the district suggested that the tramps making up the increase in number were not genuinely of the vagrant class, but navvies with stamped insurance cards under the recent Unemployment Acts. It was inferred that these men spent their earnings on drink, then sought the casual wards for a night's lodging, followed by a demand for release in the morning as bona fide working men.

The Ripon two-day Spring Race meeting attracted more crowds than usual and extra police had to be drafted in to cope with the very heavy traffic. It was arranged that horse-drawn vehicles and motor cars should use different routes to and from the course so as to avoid collision in Ripon's narrow streets with their sharp corners.

The Bishop of Knaresborough dedicated a new stained glass window in the Ripon Diocesan Training College Chapel, paid for by the 1913 students. The window commemorated the life and work of Dr Thomas Arnold of Rugby.

July. The Chapel to St Wilfrid in the north aisle of the Cathedral was formed by the erection of a screen carved by Ripon ladies taking one of the existing screens as a model. A memorial altar to Canon MacColl, Residentiary for 23 years, was erected at the east end; it was of solid oak with a plain front intended to be covered with embroidered work at a later stage. The reredos consisted of a copy of the painting *Descent from the Cross*.

The Dean and Chapter received a beautiful addition to the Cathedral plate in the form of a silver gilt paten and chalice in memory of the wife of the Revd John James Brown of *Whitcliffe Lodge* who died in 1912.

The Lord Mayor of York opened the Ripon Branch of the Y.M.C.A. in Water Skellgate.

The Corporation decided to open the bathing pavilion on Sundays from 7 am to 6 pm to prevent young men bathing promiscuously from the banks of the River Ure near North Bridge. A local by-law was passed to allow the prosecution of bathers not using the pavilion.

At the inquest into the death of Mrs Smeeton of Bondgate, who died after being knocked down by a motor car in Kirkgate, the jury suggested the imposition of a speed limit of 6 mph on the level and 4 mph on gradients for all vehicles travelling through the narrow streets of the city.

The death of Mr Marmaduke Todd, saddler of 39 Kirkgate, at the age of 82 years, marked the passing away of Ripon's oldest tradesman both in age and in date of establishment of business. Mr Todd was a native of Ripon and was a member of the fourth generation to run the family business established in 1770. The business was originally carried out in the premises at the corner of the Market Place until it was used to enlarge the then Knaresborough and Claro Bank Company building next door, later to become the National Provincial Bank. The Todd saddlery business transferred to 43 Market Place and then to Kirkgate.

August. The Feast of St Wilfrid in 1914 was memorable because it concided with the outbreak of World War I. There were not so many visitors as usual as many trains were taken off due to the State of Emergency. The official opening itself was delayed by an hour for entirely different reasons as reported in the *Gazette* '. . . at the Cathedral a strange mingling of ceremonies, marriages and funerals (that of the Bishop's wife Mrs Drury) coming close to each other, bridal couples hurrying away with the melancholy sound of muffled peals in their ears . . .'.

The Mayor and Deputy Mayor took the salute as the local members of the Troop of Yorkshire Hussars and the Ripon Company of the National Reserve left the city for York. The local detachment of the Territorials had left during the previous week. Thus when Lord Charles Beresford later made a patriotic local appeal for recruits in the wake of Lord Kitchener's national appeal, the response would have been greater had not a large proportion of Ripon men gone to the Regular and Territorial armies.

The Ripon Rifle Club announced that without interfering in any way with existing military organisations it would give 'every able-bodied man' opportunity to come forward and fit himself to bear arms and to act in defence of his country and home, to be taught the rudiments of drill, handling a rifle and marksmanship.

The members of the Ripon Club arranged with the Exchange Telegraph Company to act as a centre for War telegrams and the Corporation agreed to display copies at the Town Hall for the information of the public.

September. It was announced that Ripon High School for Girls would begin the new term as usual in its buildings in College Road. The Ripon Red Cross Society, which had equipped the school as a hospital with 50 beds from the Training College to receive war wounded, did not yet need the accommodation; later, the Drill Hall in Skellbank was used instead, fitted with 39 beds supported by six beds in the Cottage Hospital.

The death of Mr William Harrison J.P. was announced on 17 September. He was educated in the classical tradition, being soundly instructed in Latin and Greek, which paved the way for his later interest in local antiquarian and archaeological subjects after he joined his father in the family printing business. He then came under the influence of John R. Walbran F.S.A., one of the most distinguished antiquarians of his time in the north of England, all of whose works were published by the firm. He was a very active member of the Ripon Corporation and played an important part in the promotion of the Ripon Millenary Festival of 1886, and the subsequent festivals of 1896 and 1906 and in particular in publishing the *Ripon Millenary Record and Municipal History (1886)* in 1892.

It was recommended that the Russian gun presently standing near the Cathedral should be placed in the Museum Gardens together with a suggestion that a tablet bearing the names of local heroes who fell in the Crimean War be placed in the Cathedral. It was finally decided to leave it at the north-east corner of Kirkgate opposite the west front of the Cathedral. The gun had been captured at Sebastapol in 1858 and placed in the Market Place, where it stayed for many years, although proposals for its removal were made several times: to North Bridge in 1873, to a site near the Drill Hall in Park Street in 1889, and it was not until 1896 that the gun was moved to its position near the Cathedral.

October. At a meeting of the Ripon Industrial Society, it was decided to postpone indefinitely the holding of the next exhibition and also that the balance of £25 should be spent to encourage local industry.

Fifteen men offered themselves as a result of a recruiting drive for the newly-formed 5th (Reserve) Battalion of the West Yorkshire Regiment. Eleven of these recruits were passed by the medical board and entrained for York the next day.

The Ecclesiastical Commissioners made a free gift of the site of the old King Street mill and the adjacent land to the city for a children's playground.

Improvements with new classrooms at a cost of £2,395 were made at Ripon Church Day Schools with money raised by subscription and offerings in churches.

Following a letter in the *Gazette* drawing attention to the expectation of a further 60,000 refugees arriving in Britain from Belgium, a ladies' committee was set up to arrange for the reception of a number in Ripon. Mrs Moss and Mrs A. Wells saw the Belgian Consul in Leeds to arrange the distribution of clothing and an appeal was made for the housing of refugees in the city and the Mayor set up a Relief Fund. Mr C. H. Moody, the Cathedral Organist, gave a series of organ recitals in various parts of Yorkshire and raised over £50 for the fund. Mr Tom Williamson provided a furnished house in Skellgate and Mr Rayner gave rent-free a house in Stonebridgegate. A cottage in Heath's Court, Low Skellgate, and a house in St Wilfrid's Terrace were also used. Dr Steven placed a home in Park Street at the disposal of wounded Belgian soldiers who had arrived in York. The *Spa Hotel* agreed to give accommodation for refugees. An appeal was made for persons who could speak Flemish to help with their reception. A number of events were organised to raise funds; these included a Grand Benefit Night held in the *Electric Theatre* by permission of the Campbell Cinematograph Company when patriotic films were shown with a piano accompaniment, together with the rendering of popular songs. Both events were a sell-out and raised over £50 for the Mayor's Relief Fund. The first party of six Belgians arrived in Ripon on 20 October and were housed by the Dean until a house was prepared for them. Another five refugees were taken to Copt Hewick and by the 12 November the Refugee Committee had arranged hospitality for 21 refugees consisting of four married couples, 10 children and three bachelors. Application was made for the allocation of 28 more to bring the total to 60 in the city. The refugees who included diamond cutters, a telegraphist, a secretary of a trades union and school teachers, settled down to establish a successful wooden toy industry using premises in Park Street. A shop was opened in the Market Square to retail a varied stock. One of the most popular toys was a Noah's Ark which sold for a guinea. Most of the raw materials were donated: wood, paint, polish, etc., and particularly red cigar boxes. The products created an interest outside the city and a party from Harrogate Belgian Relief Committee visited the Ripon factory with a view to starting a similar activity amongst their 300 refugees.

A 38-hp Wolseley motor ambulance presented to the army by Lord Furness was on view in the showrooms in the Market Square of Messrs Croft and Blackburn.

The Mayor of Ripon's appeal for blankets for the troops resulted in the dispatch of 100 blankets to Territorial HQ in York.

1. The Kirkgate premises in the 1920s where T. Appleton & Son, the well-known Pork Butchers, were first established in 1867.

2. Winsors Fish and Game Shop at 15 North Street dressed for Christmas. After nearly 100 years the shop closed in 1968.

3. W. B. Moss & Sons, Grocers, of Otley and Hitchin, opened in Ripon in 1899 at the corner of the Arcade in the Market Place.

4. Miss E. Burton kept a splendid stock of baby linen and children's wear in her shop in Fishergate, despite the demolition work next door.

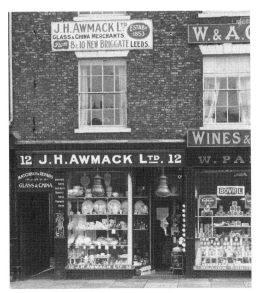

5. J. H. Awmack Ltd. Glass & China
Merchant, situated on the east side of
the Square, between Parker the Grocer
and Taylors the Cash Chemists.

6. Henry Bake, Saddler and Harness Maker, Westgate, a thriving
business in a horse-drawn era.

7. H. Key, Fish and Ice Merchant, of Low Skellgate.

8. Mr Benson, last of the saddle-tree makers, once a major industry in the city.

9. The Benson family pigging lead in King Street.

10. Horse-drawn reaping machine made by the Agricultural Engineers, Kearsley & Co. of North Street, at their Trinity Lane premises.

11. Presentation of the Town Hall, 1897.

12. Bondgate celebrated the Diamond Jubilee of Queen Victoria 1897 in royal style.

13. *(left)* The presentation of the Clock Tower by the Misses Cross took place in June 1898 on the anniversary of Queen Victoria's coronation in 1837.

14. *(below)* Whit Walk in Kirkgate at the turn of the century.

15. The Freedom Scroll.

16. Looking down High Skellgate, decorated for a royal occasion, probably George V's coronation.

17. Park Street in festive mood for the opening of the Spa Baths by two Royal Princesses in 1905.

18. The presentation of the Freedom of the City of Ripon to the Corps of Royal Engineers, on 27 July 1949.

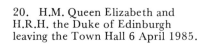

19. A modern St Wilfrid.

20. H.M. Queen Elizabeth and H.R.H. the Duke of Edinburgh leaving the Town Hall 6 April 1985.

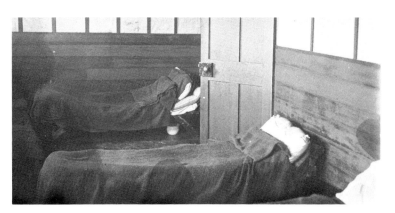

21. Inside a bedroom in the Y.M.C.A. hut at Ripon Railway Station in 1917.

22. *(above)* Church of England Soldiers' Institute in 1917.

23. *(left)* A group of soldiers of World War One queuing for the pictures at the Electric Theatre in the Victoria Hall (later the Opera House) in Water Skellgate.

24. 'Peace with Honour' in Lickley Street, July 1919.

25. Civil Defence Wardens and W.V.S. personnel 1938-45.

26. West side of the Market Place showing the *Unicorn Hotel* and the motor works of Croft and Blackburn just before World War I.

27. The junction of the Market Place with Westgate and High Skellgate when Hugh Ripley's House was owned by G. Precious; Thirlway & Co., Printers and Stationers, was demolished in 1946.

28. *(left)* The mansion of Studley Royal which was destroyed by fire in 1946.

29. *(below)* The south and west side of the Market Place in the early Edwardian period when the remaining private houses were being taken over for commercial use.

30. *(below)* York Yard, Skellgarths, pulled down in the Bedern Bank demolition of the 1950s.

31. *(bottom right)* The Claro Bank, on the same site as the Knaresborough and Claro Bank, built in 1899, showing the statue of St Wilfrid; now replaced by the National Westminster building.

32. The Victoria Hall in Water Skellgate, built 1885, later used as the Electric Theatre and then the Victoria Opera House.

33. The Bathing Pavilion erected in 1890 on the Ure above North Bridge mainly through the generosity of Dean W. R. Fremantle.

34. The Martinmas Fair which combined amusements traditionally associated with a fair alongside the more serious business of hiring labour and a cattle market.

35. A motor cycle rally in the Market Place in 1923.

36. Ripon College Staff and Students 1894 showing the Principal, Canon Badcock, and Mrs. Badcock (probably the model for the Duchess in Alice in Wonderland).

37. Miss Mercer's Room—Ripon Training College 1899.

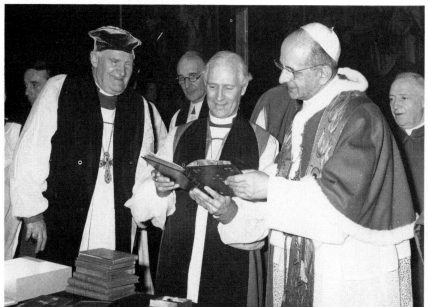

38. (*top left*) One of the Blue-coat boys from Jepson's School in the late Victorian period.

39. (*top centre*) Mr. Tom Williamson in court dress for the occasion of Queen Victoria's Diamond Jubilee, 1897.

40. (*top right*) Tom Hawley as Hornblower setting the Watch in 1953.

41. The Rt. Revd. J. R. H. Moorman, DD, presenting a book on Ripon to Pope Paul VI on 23 March 1966.

RIPON MILITARY CAMP

Army Territorial units had held their annual summer training camps on sites to the south and west of Ripon, particularly Red Bank, for some years. On the outbreak of war the City Council suggested that the War Office should set up permanent facilities for troops in training or transit to the Front. However, before this could be done, a battalion of Territorials (400 men) had to be billeted in either Pateley Bridge or Ripon, and a search for suitable large warehouses was made. The first battalion was accommodated in Harrogate, but in November the Mayor and Corporation held a hurried meeting to arrange billeting for 2,200 Yorkshire Territorials. The West Riding Education Department agreed that half the day schools should be made available and all the Sunday Schools used. Those school buildings retained alternated for teaching; the Sunday Schools were held in the churches. It was proposed that the inmates of Ripon Workhouse be transferred to Pateley Bridge and the buildings used for troops. By the end of December, billets were found in the city for two battalions of infantry, each battalion consisting of eight companies with a total of 30 officers, 983 men and 50 horses and one Army Service Corps Company with 15 officers, 150 men and 300 horses.

Negotiations for the Ripon Camp were started early in September, and by early December Lord Kitchener had approved the proposals for a camp likely to become permanent, housing two divisions amounting to over 30,000 troops, at a total expenditure of £350,000 and with a completion date of April 1915.

The camp was planned to cover 800 to 1,000 acres, stretching from the site at Red Bank previously used as a Territorial Volunteer camping ground, across the River Skell to Cockrose Fields and the land adjacent to *Plumpton Hall*, thence along the land beyond Pateley Road and across the River Laver to Clotherholme, reaching Kirkby Road just below *Breckamore*. The main hutments were built around the site of the old Ripon racecourse at Red Bank, the adjacent land near Borrage Terrace and across the fields on the south side of Whitcliffe Lane in the direction of Quarry Moor. A second miniature town (also erected by Messrs Nicholson and Company) arose on Cockrose Fields on the farther side of the River Skell and the land across the Studley Road overlooking the Laver Valley amounting to 609 acres. Two rifle ranges were included: one shooting towards How Hill and the other west of Birkby Nab firing across the River Laver against Ellington Banks.

In all, the construction of the camp involved building 10 miles of main roads, 16 miles of secondary roads and 12 miles of footpaths at a cost of £15,231. Hard-core was provided by pulling down several buildings including the old mill near King Street, given to the city by the Ecclesiastical Commissioners to make way for a children's playground. Main 20-foot wide roads capable of carrying traction engines with 16-ton loads were built. They connected Kirkby Road and Clotherholme Road from Ash Farm through Lark Hill Farm; along Green Lane, from near *Breckamore*; bridging the River Laver and skirting the new railway from Clotherholme Road to Galphay Lane; crossing to Duck House at the farther side of Cockrose Fields to join another new road from *Plumpton Hall* to Red Bank, joining Whitcliffe Lane behind Red Bank House. Secondary roads were built from Harrogate Road through Lead Lane to Whitcliffe Lane and to the east through Grove Lane to Quarry Moor Lane.

The Camp had its own light railway (4 ft. 8½ in. gauge) laid from the Littlethorpe siding across country to a point just below *Breckamore*. It passed over the road junction of Mankin Lane and Bishop Monkton Road to the Harrogate Road near the water trough. The line then proceeded to Whitcliffe Lane at its junction with Lead Lane and so to *Hellwath Cottage*. Here it crossed the Skell, Cockrose Fields and the Pateley Bridge Roads to a point just above the gravel pit belonging to Lord Ripon. Finally, it ran alongside Galphay Lane for half a mile, crossing the Laver to a point half-way between *Straw House* and *Breckamore* near Kirkby Road. The contractors for the railway were Messrs Balfour and Company of Glasgow.

Until the line was completed in early 1915, all the materials for the camp were carried by steam haulage with contractors working seven days a week and steam traction engines running to and fro through the city all day. This use of road transport produced unprecedented congestion, the confusion becoming much worse on wet days when the roads became covered with liquid mud. Councillor Kearsley at the January Council meeting voiced the strong feeling against the desecration of the Sabbath, pointing out that whilst the Mayor and Corporation were worshipping in the Cathedral the streets resounded with passing engines and wagons.

It was realised from the outset that a camp of this size would create a demand for water, another 150,000 gallons per day, far beyond the capacity of Lumley Moor Reservoir. Ripon Council gave notice in September that it would need to exercise its rights under the Harrogate Corporation Act 1901 to tap the mains from Roundhills Reservoir at a cost of £150. The War Office agreed to pay for a new filter bed at Lumley Moor together with all the connections and meters at a cost of £1,000 and these items would remain the property of the Corporation. In the actual camp two large reservoir tanks were provided to store water from the waterworks of Ripon and Harrogate for drinking, cooking and washing, and also water from the Rivers Skell and Ure for sanitary purposes, fire services, horses and vehicle washing. When the camp reached its full capacity it consumed about 700,000 gallons per day, a figure in considerable excess of the estimated limit of 500,000 gallons per day, based on 15 gallons per head per day for officers, 8 gallons for men and 10 gallons for horses. The Ripon and Harrogate Corporations entered into a five-year commitment to supply water free of charge.

The disposal of sewage for the vast camp was another service which had to be negotiated with the City Council. A total length of 48 miles of sewers and drains were laid, with pipes being erected to carry sewage across the Skell and the Laver, and the provision of an inverted syphon for the crossing of the Ripon Canal in order for the waste to reach the Ripon Corporation Sewage Farm, east of the city, where the city and camp wastes were treated together. This was achieved at a cost of £5,940, paid by the War Office. The War Office were asked by the Council to pay the cost of a new sewer in Harrogate Road (estimated at £950), leaving the present sewer for surface water; £350 towards the extension of the sewage farm and £120 per annum towards extra labour at the farms.

The camp was lit by electricity from a power station sited alongside the Pateley Road between Bishopton and Lord Ripon's gravel pit. The military authorities asked the Corporation if they wished the city to be supplied from the same station with the object of the Council taking it over. The offer was declined and nothing was done until after the War.

The construction of the camp created enormous problems in the city due to the number of extra workmen needed to carry out the work. In October 1914 not only had billets to be found for 2,200 troops, but also for 500 workmen. Corporation workmen became unsettled because contractors at the camp were paying 6½d per hour with optional work on Sundays for double pay. Although it was deprecated by the Chairman of the Finance Committee, because the proposal would add 4½d in the pound on the rates, it was recommended that the 48 city workmen should be paid an extra 1d per hour (i.e., 6d per hour) for three months. As time went on, despite the generous wages many labourers were unable to obtain lodgings in the city and by January they were being housed in huts on the camp ground.

In January letters were appearing in the local press from citizens concerned at the behaviour and drunkenness among labourers working at the camp: intoxicated men were appearing in the streets by midday. The aid of the Navvy Society was invoked: Dean Robert Freemantle had been associated with the founding of the Society which now looked after the welfare of 100,000 men employed around the country. The Temperance Hall on Duck Hill was put at the disposal of the Y.M.C.A., who put several special social workers into the field, as a rest and refreshment room for men employed at the camp when they came into the city during the evening. A room was provided at the camp as a Navvy Mission. The Military Police took control of their own personnel in the city where the Y.M.C.A. rooms and the Primitive Methodist Schoolroom were used as rest centres. The Mission Hall in Water Skellgate opened as a soldiers' club with facilities for reading, writing and games: Messrs F. Smith and Sons' auction rooms on Coltsgate Hill were commandeered as a canteen where men were supplied with limited quantities of liquor from 12 noon to 2 pm and from 6 pm to 9 pm. Public houses were put out of bounds until 6 pm.

In early May the Cycling Correspondent of the *Yorkshire Post* wrote: 'Ripon is fast losing its air of old-world serenity and possibly for ever. There are now in fact two Ripons — the old and the new, the city and the camp. Nowhere has the war wrought a greater transformation. As you enter Ripon from the Harrogate side you pass rows of military huts coming close to the road on both sides. A railway has been brought across the road and is carried along into the heart of the camp. A new road opens out to the left and as you pass it you can see row after row of huts bordering both sides. Labourers and workmen in their leisure hours fill the Ripon streets. The camp has a striking air of permanence; water supply, roads, drainage, huts and buildings (some brick) all show that here is something which is not intended to serve merely a temporary purpose'.

Advance parties of 50 to 80 men arrived in May from the 18th Durham Light Infantry and the 16th and 18th West Yorkshires. The quarters of the Durham men were to the left of the entrance to Whitcliffe Lane, the camp running parallel with the Harrogate Road. The West Yorkshire battalions were housed on the opposite side of the road on Red Bank. The main bodies of troops came by route march at the end of the month.

The Bishop of Ripon announced at the York Convocation in May that the War Office would provide eight Chaplains for each of the two large camps in the north of England at Ripon and at Richmond. At Ripon it was proposed to have two recreation and refreshment huts, also a music and cinema hall and a soldiers' institute. He appealed to the diocese for £15,000 to pay for these projects. Later the Cutlers Company in Sheffield provided another £5,000. Lady Radcliffe of Rudding Park and the Catholic Women's League for the Leeds Diocese provided funds for a similar hut to be used for the celebration of Mass on a site given by the military authorities near the hospital.

1914-15. EDWARD TAYLOR

Born in Malhamdale and educated at Skipton Grammar School, he went to New Zealand at 21 and became a farmer on a large scale. He came to Ripon, where he bought a house in Claremont, in 1909. He was president of the Temperance Society, a promoter of the Y.M.C.A., and involved in the welfare of Army reservists. He was elected to the Council in January 1914 and his resignation as Mayor in 1915 presented the Corporation with a constitutional crisis.

November. The Martinmas Fair and Hirings was held as usual in Ripon and the military recruiting authorities took advantage to urge the men to join Kitchener's Army. Ripon City had already sent more than 300 men to the Forces and it was thought that more men should go from the rural districts. A big open-air meeting was held in the Square with recruiting speeches from the Town Hall balcony, and the Wakeman's House was opened as a recruiting centre.

December. Much alarm was caused in Ripon following the sound of the bombardment of the east coast by the German Navy.

At the annual prize-giving of Jepson's Hospital, it was reported that the number of pupils had reached a new record of 72 scholars, of whom 14 were foundation boys (one maintained by Mrs F. Smith, the widow of an ex-mayor), seven were private boarders and 50 were day pupils including 20 Cathedral choristers and probationers.

January. The New Year was celebrated with a special service at the Cathedral at 11.15 pm, bells were pealed after midnight and music was played by the city band.

The first 10 wounded men were sent from Leeds to the hospital set up in the new Drill Hall in Somerset Row, where the voluntary aid detachment of the St John's Ambulance Association now operated 50 beds.

The death was announced of the Revd William Yorke Faussett, Vicar of Cheddar and Prebendary of Wells, who had been Headmaster of Ripon Grammar School 1890-95. Mr Faussett took over the headmastership at a time when the school needed to create a wider reputation and to attract more boarders. He failed to provide the stimulus and thus had to impose rigid economies. After four years he resigned to take up parochial work and later returned to education for a number of years as headmaster of Bath College.

The idea of a swimming pool in the Spa Gardens was postponed in favour of a miniature lake at the junction of the Laver and Skell, where it was hoped the Army Engineers would plan and supervise its construction.

February. It was suggested that the Corporation should purchase and convert into a museum Hugh Ripley's old house in the Market Place, which had been up for sale for months and was in a very dilapidated condition. It was purchased by Mr S. G. Moss of Messrs W. B. Moss and Sons, grocers and provision dealers, until the Council could make up its mind.

The Hornblower's salary was raised from £12 to £14 per annum. It was left to the Mayor to decide how often the Horn should be blown outside the Mayor's residence, *Grange Close*. The Town Clerk stated that in the Mayoralties of Lord Ripon and Mr John Spence, the Hornblower did not go to the Mayor's house every night. It was decided that the Horn would be blown at the house three nights a week and the Town Hall on the other evenings, in addition to the Market Cross every night.

The Belgian toymakers completed the Noah's Ark with its animals, which was being sent to the Queen at her request. The ark was displayed in the window of Mr Todd's grocers' shop in the Market Place before dispatch.

March. Innkeepers were warned that no soldier or non-commissioned officer below the rank of sergeant was allowed to frequent licensed premises before 6 pm. They were reminded that the military could close any public house in the city and anyone serving a man on duty was liable to a fine of £100 or six months imprisonment.

A description of a Roman sword which, according to the British Museum, dated from the second or third century B.C., which was discovered in the excavations at the camp, appeared in the *Gazette*. After cleaning the sword was to be displayed in the City Museum.

The Medical Officer of Health published a pamphlet giving statistics and comparisons for births and deaths over a period of 37 years since the first M.O.H. report in 1878. 1878: births, 223, deaths, 170 (24.9 per 1,000), deaths of children under one year, 36; 1914: births, 136, deaths, 114 (13.8 per 1,000), deaths of children under one year, 12.

The death of Mr Thomas Collier, Surgeon, of pneumonia was announced less than a week after the death of his son, Dr Stanley Collier, also of pneumonia. He had been a prominent figure in Ripon for half a century since he took over the old-established practice of Mr John Haseldine Tutin, coroner for the Ripon Liberty, who died in 1867. Dr Collier also took over the Tutin family home in Westgate (now a solicitor's office).

Mr R. C. Vyner of Newby Hall died on the 19 March. He had generously supported institutions in

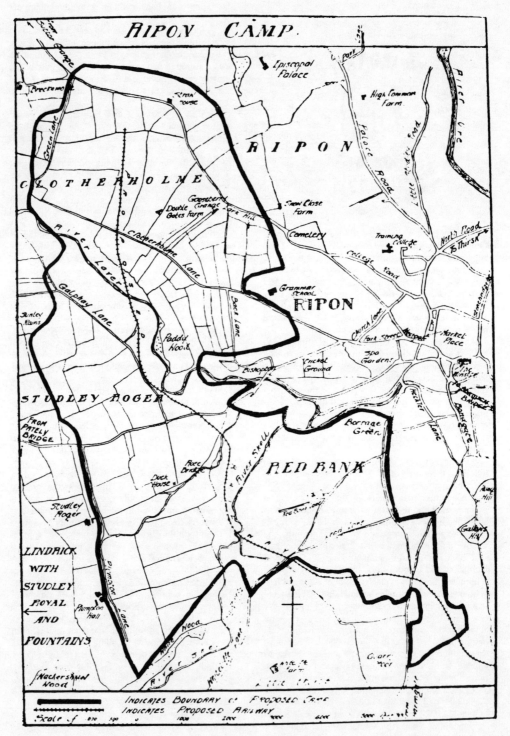

13. Map of Ripon Camp, 1918

14. Collage of advertisements from 1918

Ripon, particularly the Cottage Hospital, the Victoria Nursing Institution and the Girls' Home. Mr Vyner left property valued at nearly one million pounds. The Yorkshire estates were left in trust for Lady Alwyne Compton for life, with the remainder to her son Edward Robert Francis Compton and his heirs. The Lincolnshire and Cheshire estates and the residue went to Lady Alwyne for life, and the successors to the real estate were to assume the name of Vyner.

The Mayor, Councillor Taylor, resigned and sent a cheque to the Town Clerk for £10 to pay his fine. He complained that a Sanitary Committee had been formed of which he was not the Chairman. He maintained that this body set up to consider sewage disposal from the military camp was an *ad hoc* sub-committee and should have had the Mayor as *ex officio* chairman. He also resented the delegation of decisions concerning the camp to the various committees instead of retaining these for the full Council sitting as a committee, despite the fact that the full Council was sitting three times per week. Councillor Taylor then decided to rescind his resignation, producing a legal problem as the Town Clerk declared that the case of *Queen v. Wigan Corporation* 1885 ruled that a Mayor having resigned could not retract and therefore the Mayoralty must be declared vacant. The Town Clerk of Leeds was asked for advice, and agreed that the resignation must be accepted, and three days' notice given for a special Council meeting to appoint a mayor. In the meantime Alderman Thirlway acted as Mayor. Each of the 16 Aldermen and Councillors spoke at the special meeting, largely in criticism of Councillor Taylor's activity in the Chair of promoting schemes not in the best interests of the City. He was then re-elected.

April. A new Home Office Order was issued applying to the whole of Ripon, to the effect that public lights, shop lights, car lights and flares in the market must be invisible from above.

The Easter holiday was quieter than usual; as there were virtually no day trips, few visitors came into the city. However, the North Eastern Railway ran their motor charabanc service through to Fountains Abbey, the grounds of which were opened free by the Marquess of Ripon. The boating season opened on the River Ure and many players appeared at the Ripon City and the Studley Royal golf clubs. Work at the camp was suspended for four days, some of the workmen went home, and some got drunk, there being 13 cases before the Magistrates on Monday morning. Under the new Criminal Jurisdiction Act, fines had to include police costs and in order to diminish the number sent to prison for non-payment, time to pay was allowed. Two extra policemen were drafted to Ripon to enable more supervision to be made. War Office representatives considered closing all public houses in Ripon until work on the camp was finished. An order under the Defence of the Realm Act (D.O.R.A.) ordered all licensed premises within the city and adjacent areas, to be closed except between the hours of 12 noon and 2 pm (Sundays 12.30 pm to 2.30 pm) and 6 pm to 9 pm. Previously

pubs in the villages opened at 6 am and people walked out to them until Ripon opening hours.

June. The Aliens Restriction Act required all visitors or residents of Hotels, Boarding Houses or Apartment to sign a visitors' register stating their nationality.

Bishopton Hemp and Tow Spinning Mill, dating back to the 18th century, was completely destroyed by fire. It was built in 1792 at the same time as the theatre in Park Street and the residence known as *Green Royd*; although the fire was of such ferocity that it could not have been saved, the incident showed the total inadequacy of the Ripon manually-operated fire engine. It was suggested that the city should purchase a second-hand steam driven engine. The loss of the mill also meant the loss of 60 jobs, mostly those of women and girls. The following week the local newspaper carried an advertisement calling for flax and hemp workers in a Bristol mill.

Mr James P. Lee, a reporter on the *Gazette* for 40 years, died. His report of the Ripon Millenary Festival in 1886 was recognised as the most complete account of that event, and he assisted Mr W. Harrison with the *Ripon Millenary Record* of 1886. He was educated at Jepson's Hospital and Ripon Grammar School.

July. The Y.M.C.A. erected a hut with three billiard tables, games and refreshment counter and other facilities for soldiers at the camp near Whitcliffe Lane. It was officially opened by Lady Barran of Sawley Hall.

September. The Y.M.C.A. extended their premises in Water Skellgate to include an assembly room, a Post Office and cloakroom on the ground floor, and a writing room on the upper floor. There were also plans to provide a soldiers' and sailors' home. In addition to these facilities Ripon citizens made enormous efforts to provide leisure pursuits for the troops with a Union Jack Club in Kirkgate, a Soldiers' Club at the Mechanics Institute and institutes at all the Church halls.

Dean Freemantle retired after 20 years in Ripon. The Cathedral staff presented him with an illuminated address encased in a silver casket and Mrs Freemantle with a dispatch box containing £8, which she donated to the Red Cross. The civic presentation took place at the Town Hall where the Dean was given a silver rose bowl and a cheque, and Mrs Freemantle a diamond and gold watch bracelet inscribed with the City Arms.

1915-16. FREDERICK WILLIAM HARGRAVE, Timber Merchant and Saddletree Maker

Born in 1873 in Bondgate, which the inhabitants still regarded as a separate township. He joined, and later carried on, his father's business — the last of the Ripon saddletree makers — living at *East View* in Bondgate Green Lane next to his timber yard. He was elected to the Council in 1912 and retained his seat until his death in 1940. During that time he served on every committee of the Council and his long mayoralty spanned the most difficult years of World War I. He was a member of the Board of Guardians and held many other offices. A staunch Methodist,

Fred^k Wm Hargrave
MAYOR 1915 TO 1919

he was a pillar of the Zion Church in Blossomgate.
Rainfall in 1915 was 29.97 ins.

January. New Year's Day was observed by Scottish soldiers sitting down at the new Assembly Hall to a knife-and-fork tea and being entertained afterwards with a lantern slide show depicting the *Life of Christ*, slides interspersed with illustrated songs.

The City Council dealt with many cases brought under the new lighting order which laid down that no more than a dull subdued light could be visible outside premises of all descriptions. Vehicles were required to carry separate rear red lights in addition to white lights at the front.

Mr Firby of Ure Bank Terrace hooked and caught a pike weighing 9½ lbs, while roach-fishing in the River Ure with a light fly rod baited with maggots.

February. The West Riding Education Committee agreed that boys and girls between the ages of 12 and 14 should be allowed to work on farms or assist their mothers at home from 1 March to 1 November, or until the end of the war if this occurred earlier. One member, Lady Mabel Smith, urged farmers to overcome their prejudice against the use of female labour on the farms. This was very strong as shown by the abandonment of a meeting scheduled to discuss the question at the Assembly Rooms because not a single farmer would attend. To combat the antagonism Sir John Barran published in the *Gazette* the national appeal of Lord Selborne, President of the Board of Agriculture, calling on the women of England of every class to assist the farmers during the war.

Viscount French visited the Ripon Camp at the beginning of February. General Sir Bruce Hamilton, Officer Commanding the Ripon Military Training Centre, and his staff met the Field Marshal at the station where he inspected a guard of honour mounted by the Black Watch, before leaving for the Spa Hydro where he stayed the night. The next morning he inspected the North and South Camps, the Pioneers Battalion and the Officers' Training Corps.

A curious incident was reported from the works of Mrs Benson, saddletree maker, where a fortnight earlier a 10s Treasury note was missed. A thorough

search was made but it was not until a week later that it was found in a rat's nest in one of the workshops, torn into several pieces. The note was carefully put together and cashed.

The Military Cross was awarded to Lieutenant J. L. Jameson for an act of bravery during the German gas attack on the British lines at Ypres. Lieutenant Jameson was educated at Ripon Grammar School, where he gained a de Grey Scholarship to Leeds University.

The War Office complained that a rent of 30s per week for the use of the Council Chamber as a recruiting office was excessive. The Council agreed to waive the rent, provided the War Office paid all expenses for gas, coal, cleaning and repairs.

March. A grand Charity Ball was held at Wright's Assembly Rooms in aid of widows and orphans of soldiers and sailors of Ripon and district. Some 200 couples, soldiers and civilians, turned up to dance; many sought tickets in vain. Dancing continued until 3 am and included Scottish reels led by Highlanders from the camp.

The cinema, *The Picture Palladium*, was opened early in the month in Kirkgate and provided shows from 6 pm to 10.30 pm daily with matinées on Thursday and Saturday. Admission cost was 1s, 6d and 3d, with children half price. The *Gazette* reported that 'the interior appointments and tasteful decorations leave nothing to be desired' and an efficient ladies' orchestra played suitable music during the continuous performances.

The City Council made an order to fix the weekly half-day closing of shops on Wednesday or, at the option of the shopkeeper, Saturday.

The Finance and General Purposes Committee received complaints that the fees for interment of soldiers at the cemetery were too high. This arose from applying the by-laws which laid down double interment fees for non-residents as the upkeep of the cemetery was partly paid out of rates. The Committee felt unable to reduce the fees, as they were not asking soldiers' dependants to pay more than other non-residents.

A committee was set up to consider ways and means of providing an electricity supply in the city. A letter received from the Northern Counties Electricity Supply Company of Middlesbrough stated that they could not 'under the present national circumstances' consider a scheme for Ripon. The War Office stated that the plant laid down at the Camp was only sufficient for their own needs and Harrogate regretted that they could not help.

April. The death of Mr George Parker, a local poet, of *Kirkgate House*, was announced.

Admiral Milton, military representative, stated he had been instructed by the War Office to prepare a list of all men under 30 exempted from active service and that he must be very strict at Tribunals in applying the rules. This statement was made when the Mayor (Mr F. W. Hargrave, the last Saddletree Maker in Ripon) applied for exemption for three men in his employ: one was medically unfit and two were given conditional exemption. Admiral Milton said it would give a bad impression in the town when it was known the Mayor had got two of his men off.

The Medical Officer of Health estimated the Ripon population at 8,411 but that did not include the 3,000 workmen involved in the construction of the Camp or the large number of officers' and soldiers' wives and families billeted in the city. Many homes and cottages were overcrowded. The number of deaths was 215 for 1915 which included 63 persons over 65 years — the highest on record.

On Monday 24 April, a Military Tournament and Highland Display, the first of its kind to be held in England, was mounted on Ripon Racecourse. Members of the Highland Division gave demonstrations of the Highland Fling and the Seaforth Regiment danced the Highland Reel and the Reel of Tulloch. Large crowds from Ripon and district attended.

May. The Ripon City Tribunal for the hearing of cases for exemption from armed service announced that all applicants must appear in person. Much time was wasted when men were later found to be medically unfit, and it was urged that medical examinations should be carried out before the hearing.

The City Surveyor wrote to the owner of the *Wakeman's House* warning him not to let the premises because they were in a dangerous condition. There was divided opinion in the City Council as to the future of the building. Councillor Goldsworthy proposed that all the buildings at the corner of High Skellgate and the Market Square should be demolished. Councillor Kearsley was in favour of restoration and offered £100 towards its purchase, and it was agreed to negotiate with the owner, Mr Moss.

The new summertime was adopted in Ripon with very little disturbance.

Farmers could apply to the C.O. of the Camp for military labour to help in agriculture for a period not exceeding six working days.

The Electricity Committee resolved: 'That the Committee having ascertained that an electric lighting scheme can be established in the city for a sum of £4,000, it is resolved that the subject be considered at the termination of the war but the Committee cannot recommend the Council to relinquish any of its lighting powers.'

June. The Mayor appealed to Ripon citizens as loyal subjects of the King to comply with the Government's wishes to abandon the Whitsuntide holidays. In the event, the weekend brought unprecedentedly cold and stormy weather.

A captured German gun lent by the War Office was received by a detachment of the military at Ripon Station and escorted to the Market Square, where it was handed over to the Mayor and Corporation. It became a centre of attraction to the public.

July. The proposal for Ripon and District to acquire a motor fire engine had to be abandoned as the Ministry of Munitions refused its supply from the manufacturers, Messrs Merryweather, at a cost of £1,065. In the meantime the old manual engine was used for practice in the Camp, with the undertaking that it would be made available in the case of an outbreak of fire in the city.

August. Bugler Ellison of the Cameron Highlanders caused a mild sensation when he appeared in his kilted uniform at the Market Cross at curfew to blow the customary blast on the Wakeman's Horn. The City Hornblower had been taken ill; the civic authorities had found it difficult to find a substitute at short notice and so had appealed to the military authorities.

September. The Council fixed taxi fares at one shilling for the journey from the Railway Station to the Market Place, and a further shilling from the Market Place to Whitcliffe Lane.

October. There was a demonstration of an Emerson motor tractor at Nunwick Farm. The engine ran on paraffin but had to be started with petrol.

A new management scheme was adopted for the Hospitals of St Mary and St John in which the Master would be appointed by the Archbishop of York and the trustees, who would in future include three lady members, appointed by the Dean and Chapter, the City Council and the Poor Law Guardians.

A new Government order enforced the early closing of shops during winter months at 7 pm on weekdays and 9 pm on Saturdays. Most Ripon shops had already adopted 6 pm as the closing hour.

Susannah Corgan, Confectioner, sued George and John Blackburn, Motor Engineers, and the Palladium Picture House Company at Ripon County court for removing a baker's two-decker oven from premises in Kirkgate. The premises, prior to being partly demolished to make way for the new picture house, had been an old-established confectioner's business and the oven in dispute had been installed in 1897 by a previous tenant, Mr Daggett. The court found that the oven was a tenant's trade fixture and ordered the defendants to pay £25 damages.

Mr Thomas Wells, eldest son of the late Mr William Wells, Wine and Spirit Merchant, died on 26 October at the age of 53. Mr Wells had taken an active part in public life serving on the City Council for over a quarter of a century. He was well known in sporting circles and a director of the Ripon Racecourse Company. He was a member of the Board of Guardians, and for many years supplied a bottle of rum for the Christmas Day pudding sauce for inmates of the Workhouse.

Mr Robert Foster, one of the most prominent and highly respected farmers in the Riding, died at his residence, *Markenfield Hall*, aged 61. He took over from his father who had taken the lease on the 560-acre home farm from Lord Grantley 30 years before. Mr Foster had been concerned at the damage done to his land, which had been used as a manoeuvres area for troops from the Ripon Camp.

1916-17. FREDERICK WILLIAM HARGRAVE, Timber Merchant and Saddletree Maker

Rainfall in 1916 was 26.39 ins.

November. An ancient Horn, reputed to be one of the original Ripon Horns, left to the city by the

Fredk. Wm Hargrave

MAYOR 1915 TO 1919

late Mr R. C. de Grey Vyner, came into the possession of the Corporation and was placed on view in the City Museum.

At the Ripon City Court Mr Tom Williamson said there had been many complaints about late services at the Cathedral as it was such a distinct landmark for enemy airships. Late services had already been abandoned at York and Durham. Inspector Blacker said special arrangements had been made throughout the West Riding for representatives from particular places of worship to attend at the nearest Police Station during times of Divine Service; in case of an air raid warning, they would carry the message to the church. The method was allowed to continue but Mr Williamson thought it not very scientific.

The Dean in the course of his sermon on Mayor's Sunday spoke of the enormous increase in juvenile crime which in his opinion was due to the effects of the cinema, the number of shooting galleries and above all to the very great number of public houses in Ripon disproportionate to its size and need. This prompted a long letter in the *Gazette* from Mr Tom Williamson stating that the scenes described by the Dean as 'a disgrace to civilisation' had been seen neither by the Magistrates, police nor special constables. He agreed that a little disorder here and there was inevitable, but for the rest most exemplary and courteous conduct was shown by soldiers and civilians in daylight or in dark streets.

Lilian Banks (27), a widow of Ripon, was indicted for the wilful murder of her newly-born child. She already had three children and her husband had been killed in action in June 1915. The judge said she knew perfectly well what she was doing and sentenced her to three years' penal servitude.

December. Colonel Kearsley became the Chairman of the Recruiting Committee (Ripon Division) for the recruitment of men for the armed forces under Lord Derby's scheme. Each man of military age would receive a copy of Lord Derby's letter and be called upon individually by canvassers to ascertain whether he was willing to join the Colours or to obtain his reasons for not doing so. Those wishing to join at once could do so, the others would continue with their vocations and be called up when required. Two sets of 23 groups each according to age would be made and men would be called up in successive groups, the unmarried men to go first.

January. A brilliant display of the Aurora Borealis was seen in the early days of January and a description of the phenomenon written from the South Camp appeared in the *Yorkshire Post*.

A well-attended meeting held on 9 January at the Cathedral Hall resolved to set up a branch of the Mothers' Union for the Cathedral Parish.

The Board of Agriculture announced a scheme to encourage the rearing of pigs, poultry and rabbits by householders to increase the food supply. Local by-laws were relaxed to enable pigs to be kept and householders were asked to keep waste food suitable for pigs in receptacles separate from the usual ash put in refuse bins. It was also agreed that pig and poultry rearing on allotments would be allowed on Fishergreen and Aismunderby Road, but not on Kirkby Road.

A resolution was adopted at a meeting of the Ripon Diocesan Conference in favour of a separate See of Bradford. The Bishop of Ripon in supporting the motion said he was ready to surrender £500 per annum towards the establishment of the new bishopric.

Mr T. Ellis, a farmer of Ripon, paid £55 at York cattle market for an ordinary cow. This was probably a record price paid for a non-pedigree milk cow for the country.

February. The Town Clerk was instructed by the Council to write to the Post Master General concerning over-crowding and unhealthy conditions in the Post Office. Towards the evening the Military Police took control as large numbers of troops used it, and at times there were as many as 120 people in the Post Office. The young ladies behind the counter sometimes had to work from 10 am to 10 pm. The Post Master General was urged to open a sub-office in the Market Place.

On 15 February there appeared in the *Gazette* a big advertisement appealing for money to be invested in the Victory War Loan. It was announced that the total amount contributed by Ripon to the War Loan was nearly £400,000.

March. The Corporation agreed to take steps to purchase *Hugh Ripley's House* in the Market Place. The sale was completed in October at a cost of £1,200, the tenant continuing at a rent of £20 per annum. The premises which had been the Church Institute in High Skellgate were also purchased for £100, the books in its library being distributed among the Ripon elementary schools.

A correspondent in the *Yorkshire Post* pointed out that the majority of wounded soldiers in various stages of convalescence had to walk long distances from Ripon Station to the camp, and suggested that this was an opportunity for owners of private cars to show their appreciation.

The shortage of labour on local farms was temporarily relieved by soldiers from the York depot being released for at least a month. Those with previous experience would be paid 4s 9d per day, others 4s 3d per day; if living in with board and lodging provided by the farmer there would be a deduction of 2s per day.

The restoration of St Mary Magdalen was completed by the removal of the coarse rubble and brickwork blocking the windows and of the pig sties and hen runs abutting on the walls of the Chapel. Underpinning and fronting of foundations had been carried out and new purlins provided for the roof. The stripping of internal plaster had revealed a small piece of coloured fresco of a scroll design towards the east end of the north wall, and on the south side an early sculptured stone. The lead flashing of the roof and the brick floor had been put in order and all the plain diamond-paned windows reglazed using as far as possible the original glass. The 15th-century screen had been re-erected although much of the original was missing. Mr George Bland the architect supervised the restoration work which had been carried out by Messrs Coldbeck and Son, Builders of Ripon, but the lead window glazing had been done by Mr Pope of Leeds, well known for his restoration of windows in York Minster.

April. An outbreak of fire in the early hours of the morning of 3 April at the Spa Baths was got under control by the Ripon Fire Brigade in a couple of hours, but not before considerable damage was done. The Ladies' Wing was practically destroyed, the roof of the Pump Room burnt and other parts of the building damaged. The fire damage, thought to have been caused originally by faulty wiring, was estimated at £1,000. The fire was most regrettable as the Spa, after some years of struggle, was now doing well. During February of this year 2,070 baths had been taken. This incident was referred to at a meeting of the Fire Committee of the City Council when the Mayor informed the members that the Ripon manual fire engine had had to be dismantled, and so the city now had no appliance at all. The Committee had decided to purchase a motor fire engine, but the Local Government Board had refused permission to borrow the necessary finance; also the firm was too busy with other orders to be able to supply one. The City Council finally decided to purchase a second-hand steam fire engine at a cost of £180 (a new machine would have cost £600). A joint Fire Brigade Committee was formed with members from the City, the Ripon Rural District and the Wath Rural District Councils. The fire engine would be conveyed by motor or horses when necessary and the costs would be shared.

The Y.M.C.A. provided an amenity hut for Officers at the Ripon Camp, who had fewer facilities than other ranks for recreation in their leisure time. The hut included a billiard room with four tables, a lounge 60 ft. by 30 ft., furnished in club style, a quiet room for reading and writing, and a café which was expected to be self-supporting.

May. The Jacobean pulpit formerly used in the nave of Ripon Cathedral was converted into a cupboard and placed in the Chapter House of the Cathedral.

The Corporation sanctioned the establishment at *Thorpe Prebend House* of a collection of relics and curios brought home from the war by soldiers who might like to give them. Also a gift of antique china and glass was accepted for the museum from Mrs Isherwood.

A Food Saving Committee was set up in Ripon, and the Royal Proclamation designating Thursday 24 May as 'National Food Saving Day' was read at the Market Cross; a copy and an 'In Honour Bound' card was left at every house. The Government warned that because of the sinking of grain ships there could be actual starvation in 1918. In spite of travel difficulties, large numbers of visitors came to Ripon for the Whitsun Holiday. All the accommodation was full. However, the usual teas for school children and the Sunday School Demonstration were abandoned because of the food shortages.

June. As a result of a big reduction in the number of vagrants, the Local Government Board proposed to close the casual wards at Bedale, Leyburn, Great Ouseburn and Pateley Bridge. The ward at Thirsk was retained as it could be reached within the day by Ripon vagrants released at 10 am after doing two hours work, as could Knaresborough to the south.

The Military Sports were held on the Agricultural Show Ground on 16 June.

Driver Arthur Peacock of Ripon was charged with the wilful murder of driver Charles Thomas Yates in a field near Mackershaw Woods at Lindrick. Peacock, who cut his victim's throat, said a voice told him to do so and he obeyed. Evidence was brought to show that his father had died in an asylum and that he himself had been unbalanced for some time. A verdict of guilty but insane was returned, and Peacock was detained during His Majesty's pleasure.

A deputation headed by the Dean and the Canon-in-Residence and including the Chairman of the Board of Guardians, the Chairman of the Rural District Council, the headmistress of Skellfield School and other prominent citizens waited upon the Mayor and Corporation to express concern over the extent of poor housing in Ripon. The Dean expressed the views of the group attending from the Cathedral. He quoted from a Report of the Sanitary Inspector which highlighted the shortage of suitable homes for the working classes, the many homes which would be condemned as unfit to live in if alternatives could be found, and the fact that a number of houses had no running water and only an open yard shared by several tenants. The Dean said that he had himself visited some of the courts and houses in Bondgate, Blossomgate and Stammergate and could fully endorse the report. He urged that the Corporation should set up schemes to demolish condemned premises and build new on the site and acquire land for new building, adding that 'these should not be left to private philanthropists and speculative impulse'. In August a special meeting of the City Council was convened to consider housing schemes on sites in the vicinity of Trinity Church and the Grammar School and of Aismunderby and Bondgate for the accommodation of the working class. In October the Sanitary and Housing Committee recommended that a scheme be prepared to build 100 houses as soon as possible and a further 100 houses if the Ripon Camp should prove to be permanent, subject to satisfactory financial support from the Local Government Board.

July. The *Garrison Theatre*, the first of its kind in Northern Command, was opened on 16 July in the presence of a large audience. It was a wooden structure, standing at the junction of Galphay Lane and the Pateley Bridge Road, with a stage 21 ft. deep, seating 700 and standing room for an additional hundred. The first four rows had tip-up seats and the next 10 rows were of padded leather. A bar for other ranks was provided at the back of the theatre and an officers' lounge near the front seats.

August. A protest was lodged by the City Council against the closing of the footpath across the golf links at Ripon Parks from the riverside. It was maintained that this was a public footpath used within living memory for at least 50 years, and that the military authorities had no powers to close it.

The Ripon Reserve Centre held a vegetable show on the Ripon Cricket Field. All the exhibits had been grown in the camp and afterwards handed over to the military hospital.

The death of Miss Frances Mary Cross of *Coney Garth* was announced. Miss Cross and her sister were particularly remembered for their provision of the funds for the erection of the clock tower in North Road in celebration of Queen Victoria's Diamond Jubilee in 1897. Her will directed that she be buried in the family vault in the graveyard of Ripon Cathedral and that the funeral service be held in the choir, so that her body may rest before the altar 'which I love so well'. She left £1,000 to the Bishop of Ripon for work in the Diocese.

The Gas Committee decided to purchase and store 200 tons of coal to provide help for the very poor during the forthcoming winter.

September. A fund was set up to provide food parcels for Ripon men of the West Yorkshire Regiment who were prisoners of war in Germany. A house-to-house monthly collection of funds was organised.

October. The Ripon Agricultural Association considered the desirability of using the Ripon and Boroughbridge Canal to relieve the railways and the streets of Ripon from traffic carrying agricultural and general stores to the Camp.

As it might not be possible to obtain the necessary amount of tea for the inmates of the Workhouse, the Ripon Board of Guardians left it to the discretion of the Master to substitute coffee for breakfast on two or three mornings a week.

The Bishop of Ripon presided at a Consistory Court held at Ripon Cathedral when the former Vicar of Collingham (now a gunner with the Royal Garrison Artillery) was formally deprived of his vicarage and benefice on the grounds of gross moral misconduct.

1917-18.   FREDERICK WILLIAM HARGRAVE, Timber Merchant and Saddletree Maker

Mayor 1915-16-17-18

November. The Corporation received a communication from the Society for the Protection of Ancient Buildings about repairs needed on *Hugh Ripley's House*. The Finance and General Purposes Committee considered removing the front of the building and its reconstruction on another site, but decided to preserve the facade in position. After a full inspection in December, the Committee met Mr Moss who stated that he had given away the oak panelling, but would endeavour to get it back. The Surveyor was ordered to clean and repair the front of the building.

The Inspector of Police, who was the final authority on the extent of street lighting, gave permission for additional lamps to be lighted on North Bridge, Bondgate Bridge and Mawson Lane as soon as automatic regulators were fitted, so that they could be turned out within five minutes of receiving the warning of an air raid.

December. A cotton merchant from Harrogate was charged at the Ripon Court with committing an offence against the Defence of the Realm Act by 'taking photographs without permission of the competent military authority in an area for the time being specified as a prohibited area, to wit, Kirkgate'. He was taking photographs of the Cathedral with a Kodak camera. The charge was withdrawn on payment of costs.

Lieutenant-General Sir J. G. Maxwell presented medals for gallantry in the field at a military ceremony in the Market Square which was closed to all traffic with troops lining three sides.

January. The New Year was welcomed very quietly with no ringing of the Cathedral bells, no Watchnight Service and no band music in the Market Square. New Year's Day was a general holiday and many tradesmen also closed the following day.

The scarcity of food was becoming serious and stricter controls were introduced with suppliers of milk, and dealers in margarine and potatoes having to be licenced. The City Council confirmed the action of the Sanitary Committee in establishing a municipal piggery.

The Food Controller issued a notice stating that he had 'reason to believe that a number of persons had rendered themselves liable to the provisions of the Food Order by inadvertence' and were hoarding food. He asked for the voluntary surrender of such stocks for the public benefit. Proceeds from the sale of goods would go to the person who surrendered them, and no names would be disclosed.

Miss A. J. Darnborough, who made the gift of *Thorpe Prebend House* as a museum to the city, left an estate valued at £33,259. She bequeathed pictures to the National Portrait Gallery and the National Gallery. The residue of the estate was left to the Poor Benefices Fund of the Diocese of York.

The Ripon War Finance Committee published in a report that over 1,000 men out of a total population of 8,500 had joined the army from the city, of whom 109 had been killed or died of wounds. It was recommended that a list of the dead be prepared. There were 14 Ripon men prisoners of war in Germany. The Ripon Prisoners of War Fund sent six parcels of food and two of bread each month to each prisoner: a sum of £2 5s 6d per month was required to adopt one man.

The Dean of Ripon was present at the inauguration of a War Savings Association at Messrs R. Kearsley and Company. Fifty of the firm's employees were serving in the armed forces; 11 had been killed, many more had served and returned. The Dean said that all classes had been drawn together by suffering adversity and a feeling of joint responsibility. He trusted that the next months ahead would see victory despite the fact that now was a time of great crisis. He hoped that women workers would spend less on clothes and the men less on beer and tobacco so that the money saved could be put into War Savings.

A correspondent in the *Gazette* called attention to the very bad condition of the disused Dissenters' graveyard adjoining the old Temple in Allhallowgate and suggested the civic authorities should take it over and keep it in good order.

Public notice was given that occupiers of every house or building in the city were responsible by law to sweep and cleanse the causeway along and opposite the whole front of their respective building or become liable to a fine not exceeding £5.

The Corporation made application for the possession of one of seven German guns captured at the Front by a platoon composed of Ripon men under a Ripon Officer. The War Office intimated that it was not practicable to make any distribution of trophies at that time although the request was noted.

February. The Marchioness of Ripon left an unsettled estate of £107,634. She bequeathed £100 each to Corporal Harry Howland, late Grenadier Guards, who lost his legs in the War, and Driver L. Denyer who lost his feet; £1,000 to the Soldiers and Sailors Help Society; £1,000, her wardrobe, wearing apparel, laces, furs, the furniture in her bedroom and a picture of her black bulldog, Hippo, to her maid Marie Duyot and many other bequests to her family and friends.

There was concern that the old men who obtained their living by manual stone breaking would become redundant when the Council took delivery of a stone-crushing machine to provide material for repair of roads. Many of the roads in the city were unscheduled so that stone from the central store was not available for their repair. The new machine would be used for crushing local stone taken from the river bed.

A serious accident occurred at the station end of North Bridge. A pair of horses attached to an army transport wagon galloped out of the station yard, down the hill and ran into the east wall of the bridge. A portion of the wall collapsed and the horses and wagon, with its load of officers' kit, and the heavy stone work of the wall were hurled into the river which was in full flood. Both horses were killed, the wagon smashed up and the greater part of the kit swept away by the flood.

March. A Businessmen's Week was arranged to promote the sale of War Bonds to collect £20,000 to pay for eight aeroplanes which Ripon had been asked to provide. This was rather a large order but the Committee thought it could be accomplished. The Royal Flying Corps promised to fly over the city and district and drop literature and the Army would present a military display in the Market Square. The result was the raising of £65,000.

Mr Joseph Wray withdrew from the tenancy of the Bathing Pavilion and Boathouse up river from North Bridge and the Council accepted the application of Mr Duffield. The boathouse had always been popular with residents and visitors during the summer months, but of recent years the numbers had enormously increased: the ground in front of the boathouse often presented the appearance of a miniature seafront. The new tenant was also to have charge of the new bowling club on the site of the old water works. The use of the green was offered to the military provided they saw to its maintenance. An application to allow mixed bathing was not allowed, and the whole of Friday remained set apart for the use of ladies only.

The Council expressed concern at the delay in the completion of the King Street children's playground on land given by the Dean and Chapter. The Chairman of the Spa Committee said now that so many open spaces were occupied by the military and the traffic in the streets had so greatly increased, it was a matter of urgency that the children's playgrounds should receive attention.

April. Easter was overshadowed by a feeling of anxiety, associated with the great crisis through which the country was passing. The usual Lenten Oratorio was not sung this year in Ripon Cathedral because of the depleted choir and the absence of nearly every member of the chorus on active service. Mr C. H. Moody, who had recently pleaded for a return to a purer type of church music, played a group of motets as the main part of an organ recital which was given instead. On Good Friday, a parade of troops was mounted at the Zion Chapel for the service at 10.30 am. The annual tea was held in the afternoon for 160, which was followed by an anthem by the choir and an illustrated lecture by Mr Sunderland on 'Some personal impressions of Russia'.

Food rationing was introduced for everyone on 7 April after a successful trial run in London and the Home Counties.

May. The Ripon Women's Unionist Association was formed at a meeting held on 29 April. The speakers said that now women had the vote, it was hoped that they would use it.

The City Council voted in favour of a scheme to build a mortuary on the site of three old cottages in Hall Yard, Kirkgate. However, the Ecclesiastical Commissioners, who owned them, objected to the scheme and the Council agreed to an alternative plan to build at the Highways Depot, Skellbank.

The Whitsuntide weather proved to be brilliant throughout the weekend. There were numerous visitors to the city and the annual Sunday School Demonstration, which had been abandoned since the outbreak of war, was again held. The military band in the Spa Gardens drew a large crowd as did the military sports day on the cricket ground.

June. The Town Clerk reported a poor response to the appeal to the citizens to let rooms to married wounded officers who were hospitalised in Ripon. The military authorities had felt it would be a great advantage to these officers to be able to stay in the city with their wives. Only 10 offers had been received.

July. The County Council were the purchasers of three houses owned by the Charities Trustees in Coltsgate Hill for £1,040, to be used as a hostel by the Ripon High School for Girls.

A total of £30,740 was raised during War Weapons Week and arrangements were made to build an aeroplane to be named *Ripon and District*.

August. Under the Motor Car Act 1913 an order was made to impose a speed limit of 10 mph in the principal streets of the city.

Jane, Lady Furness presented to the Ripon Corporation a collection of foreign war implements and curios from the colonies. This collection was assembled by the late Lord Furness at a cost of £150. Councillor Hemsworth offered to catalogue the items and superintend their display on panels, which were to be placed round the staircase of the Town Hall.

A resolution was put to the City Council to allow boating on the Ure on Sunday afternoons from 1 to 4 pm for members of His Majesty's Forces (in uniform) and their lady friends, because as one councillor suggested 'troops parade the streets looking for some little excitement in our notoriously dull city and the boating might prevent the worst evils'. However, it was decided that it was very wrong to have Sunday boating in a Cathedral city and anyway the caretaker needed a day off.

The death was announced of Miss Joan Bickersteth, granddaughter of the late Bishop Bickersteth. A native of Ripon where most of her life was spent, she had been involved in many local activities. One of her hobbies was wood carving and she was one of a band of voluntary workers who carved the oak screen at the entrance to St Wilfrid's Chapel in the Cathedral. She was involved in forming a Ripon Voluntary Aid Detachment; she later took up nursing at the London Hospital and had been promoted to Sister a few months before her death.

Ripon farmers brought forward a resolution to the Wages Board for the minimum wage for farm workers doing harvesting to be 30s a week.

The City Surveyor produced a scheme for the utilisation of spare fruit by making jam at the Stall House in Blossomgate. This activity was urged by the Food Production Commission who allocated sugar denied to private individuals for this purpose. After lengthy discussion the City Council reluctantly agreed to go ahead with the scheme.

A special enquiry was ordered with reference to the appeals against conscription before the Armed Forces Committee, for a saddletree maker, a cart-tree maker and a saddletree plater. The Mayor said that Ripon was the only area where these articles, on which the railway companies and agriculturalists depended, were made north of Birmingham and Walsall.

October. Mr E. Parkin, who for five years had been parish clerk and Canon's verger at the Cathedral, was appointed headmaster of Jepson's School.

A special meeting of the City Council was called to consider the setting up of a National Kitchen on premises behind *Hugh Ripley's House*. Members of the Council had visited the successful kitchens at Otley and Leeds, all of which were financially successful and not dependent on the rates. Alderman Thirlway suggested a delay in view of the possibility of an early peace settlement and the fact that Ripon had no munitions factories. However, the Council agreed the scheme because Ripon was a discharge centre and would continue to have a floating population for at least two years after an armistice. In fact, the scheme was dropped after the armistice.

Among the victims of the Irish mailboat tragedy were a bride and bridegroom who had been married in Ripon on the previous Wednesday and were going on a visit to the bridegroom's home before his departure for the Front.

The death was announced of Dr Boyd Carpenter, Bishop of Ripon 1884-1911. He was born in Liverpool in 1841, became a scholar of St Catherine's College, Cambridge, and was ordained in 1865. He became a renowned preacher and was a great favourite of Queen Victoria, dating from his appointment as a canon of Windsor in 1882 and Chaplain to the Queen in 1884. Dr Carpenter was installed as Bishop of Ripon in the Cathedral on 9 September 1884. From the beginning he realised that the Diocese was too large and he was instrumental in the creation of the See of Wakefield in 1885 and the later appointment of the two suffragan bishops, when he suggested that his salary, then £4,200 per annum, should be reduced by £1,000 and the Bishop's Palace sold to provide the funding for the proposals. The Bishop took a very active part in the Millenary 1886 celebrations. In 1895 he was offered the See of Chichester but preferred to remain in Ripon. In 1900, he set up a Million Shilling Church Fund as a thank offering for the new century and in 1905 he was given the Freedom of the City of Ripon.

Sir Edward Ward, the organising secretary for the fund for providing comforts for troops at the Front, appealed to the Mayoress to continue to supply warm shirts, socks, mufflers, mittens, etc., which had been sent regularly by Ripon's Working Party as they would still be needed during the winter.

1918-19.   FREDERICK WILLIAM HARGRAVE, Timber Merchant and Saddletree Maker

Mayor 1915-16-17-18-19

November. The death took place at Falmouth of Lieutenant C. J. Gibson D.S.C., R.N.R., third son of Lieutenant-Commander and Mrs Gibson of Little-thorpe, at the age of 27. Mrs Gibson died two days later. Both were early victims of the influenza epidemic which spread throughout Europe in the following months. Lieutenant Gibson's body was buried with full Naval honours, being borne to the Cathedral on a gun carriage drawn by six black horses with officer outriders. The influenza epidemic continued over a period of weeks with a number of deaths from resulting pneumonia. Out of 11 soldiers at the camp who contracted the illness, six died and the deaths of two prominent local civilians, Sir Charles Nicholson (formerly of *Sawley Hall*) and Mr Cecil Bickersteth were announced.

On Armistice Day, 11 November, there were great rejoicings in the city. The Union Jack was hoisted at the Town Hall and from the balconies were displayed the American, French and Belgian colours: from one o'clock a general holiday was given and all the businesses were closed for the day. The troops were paraded at the Camp, when the National Anthem was played, after which the soldiers swept down into the city. Flags and banners appeared in the streets and the cheering of soldiers and civilians alike roused the old town as never before in its long history. The Cathedral bells rang and merry-making continued far into the night.

The first contingent of repatriated prisoners arrived in Ripon from Holland via Hull amidst great enthusiasm. Crowds thronged the streets eager to welcome the men to their first home camp. Altogether 1,700 arrived on 17 November and 2,500 on the next day. The large majority of the first comers were the Royal Naval Division, whereas most of the men in the second contingent had been captured on the retreat from Mons.

Arrangements were made so that boys of 12 years of age who had been pupils at Jepson's School for a minimum of two years could, if they wished, transfer to the Grammar School at an annual fee of six pounds.

The Council approved the layout of a scheme to erect 130 houses on the Aismunderby estate after purchasing the land from the Ecclesiastical Commissioners for £1,500.

December. The *Gazette*, now reduced to two pages per issue, carried several letters of opposition including one from Tom Williamson, against the wish of the Dean that the memorial to the men who died in the War, should take the form of a reredos in the Cathedral.

January. An outbreak of fire occurred at Newby Hall, the residence of Lady Alwyne Compton Vyner, causing considerable damage. The fire started in the floor of a servant's room over the principal staircase and was got under control by the estate fire brigade before the Ripon engine arrived on the scene.

The War Office gave notice that South Camp would continue to be occupied by troops during demobilisation and repatriation, probably until the end of 1919, when the City Corporation would be consulted as to its final use.

February. Arrangements were made with the War Office to clear the racecourse and grandstand so that race meetings could be held later in the year with a calendar similar to that of pre-war days.

The Mayor called a meeting to consider the erection of a War Memorial. No decision was taken except that any memorial must be non-sectarian and non-political.

The old Volunteer Drill Hall, which had become the Spa Garage in Park Street, was completely destroyed by fire with damage estimated at £3–4,000. The fire brigade managed to prevent any spread to the Ripon Co-operative next door.

March. It was decided to provide choir stalls and a pulpit in Holy Trinity Church as a War Memorial. The pulpit was to be dedicated to the memory of Ripon Grammar School former pupils who fell in the struggle.

At an auction in Ripon, Viscount Furness offered for sale Numbers 1 to 5 Market Place which consisted of Etherington, Drapers; the *Unicorn Hotel*; Harrisons, Printers and Stationers, and Croft and Blackburn's Garage. The *Unicorn* was sold for £8,000. The *Ripon Spa Hotel* which had 46 bedrooms, 7 bathrooms and 5 public rooms, was centrally heated and lighted by electricity, was also offered for sale but no bid was made.

The Ripon general rate was fixed for 1919 and was left unchanged at 2s 4d in the pound.

April. The City Council decided to make an application to the Board of Trade to authorise the supply of electricity, despite doubts expressed that once the troops had departed and Ripon reverted to being a small city there would not be much use for this form of energy.

The public were reminded that ration books would be required for some time in order to obtain meat, butter and sugar.

Ripon City Voluntary Association, which had been set up in August 1914 by the Mayoress, was officially disbanded having raised £470 to provide materials to make and dispatch to the troops, 1,216 pairs of mittens, 1,100 mufflers, and 525 pairs of socks as well as hundreds of other items.

Ripon City Golf Club presented a piece of silver plate to Mr T. F. Spence in recognition of his service as honorary secretary.

May. The Governors of Ripon Grammar School applied to the Board of Trade for authority to sell two houses in Kirkgate for the sum of £375.

Ripon City Football and Athletic Club held its first meeting since the beginning of the War.

The City Council accepted the estimates for the extension at the gas works with the provision of vertical retorts at a cost of £21,120.

New arrangements were made with Harrogate Corporation Water Sub-Committee for the supply of water after the expiry of the agreement between Ripon and Harrogate Councils and the War Office. Ripon asked for a maximum of 300,000 gallons per day, of which it was hoped 200,000 gallons could be supplied at no more than 4d per 1,000 gallons.

Changes were announced in the working of the Ripon General Post Office. The Office would be open from 8 am to 7 pm, afternoon deliveries would be resumed at Littlethorpe, Skelton and the nearby villages and three town deliveries would be made daily, the last one at 5.45 pm. Thus, local correspondence posted in that part of the rural area having a second collection would catch the third town delivery and enable correspondents to furnish replies for delivery on the following morning.

At Ripon Town Hall Major the Hon. E. F. L. Wood M.P. distributed the balance of the Ripon Prisoners of War Fund to 49 local prisoners of war, each man receiving six pounds.

June. A disturbance broke out at Ripon South Camp in the lines of the 23rd Canadian Reserve Battalion, when 150–200 men, who had been on picket duty, refused to go on a route march, broke into a canteen and took two barrels of beer. They were protesting against the postponement of their sailing back to Canada. The last battalion stationed in Ripon sailed on 28 June.

July. The City of Ripon was invited to raise £80,000 for the Victory Loan. The campaign was launched with a mass meeting in the Square. The total reached £193,303.

A hospital for disabled soldiers was founded at Roehampton in memory of the late Marchioness of Ripon and the work she did as President of the Fund of the King George Hospital.

Peace festivities were held in Ripon on 18 and 19 July. On Friday 19 July all school children were entertained to tea in their schools when each child received a new sixpence and new florins obtained from the Mint were provided as sports prizes. Afterwards the children were entertained at the various cinemas: Trinity Schools at the *Palladium*, Cathedral Schools at the *Electric*, while the remainder were accommodated at the *Spa Cinema*. On Saturday, the soldiers were served dinner in the Market Place, when Messrs Wells and Sons presented aerated waters and Hepworth and Company 100 gallons of beer. Mr W. H. Hutchinson and Captain Coates invited the men to a cinema performance at the *Electric Theatre*. Evening sports and dancing were held on the cricket field. In the afternoon 'old folks' over 60 were entertained to tea by the Mayor and Mayoress.

An appeal was launched on behalf of the Ripon Branch for Social Work amongst women and girls. During 1918, 65 girls in distress passed through the Home at 6, Skellbank, and most were found good situations.

The Mayor held a meeting with journalists to request the leading North Country newspapers to publicise the scheme formulated by the Corporation to use the site of the South Camp for industrial development. The business element of the city hoped to see this area become a centre for manufacturing and engineering. There was considerable opposition from those who wished the site to be restored to its former agricultural use.

Sir John Barran presided at the prize-giving at Ripon Grammar School. The Speech Day marked the retirement of the Headmaster, Mr C. C. S. Bland, after 24 years, during which time the school had expanded considerably from only 68 boys in 1902 to 110 in 1919. Mr Bland's first task was to provide much-needed laboratory accommodation without the funds to do it. As so often happened, the Marquess of Ripon came to the rescue with a donation of £500 and the new block was finished in 1907, followed by a new sanitorium in 1908. A swimming bath followed, largely by self-help, in 1913. The increase in numbers would have been greater had it not been for the competition from Jepson's Hospital which educated 40 boys up to the age of 14 for lower fees, £4 per annum in 1918 compared to £15 at the Grammar School. This had been the reason for transferring the Cathedral Choristers early in the century. Despite these problems, scholastic standards steadily improved with eight university scholarships in the decade leading to the war. The new Headmaster was Mr James William Dyson, M.A., a mathematician and formerly Headmaster of Boston Grammar School in Lincolnshire. Mr Dyson was one of a short-list of three from 158 applicants for the post at a salary of £450 per annum rising to £600 with house, coal, and so on. All three short-listed candidates withdrew, but eventually Mr Dyson retracted his withdrawal and accepted the post after the Governors had agreed to the abolition of cubicles in the boarding house.

The Governors of Ripon High School for Girls acquired the property known as *Hill Crest* on Coltsgate Hill to be used as a hostel for country girls attending the school. The total number of pupils had now reached 114.

Plans prepared by an Army Officer at the camp for the provision of a lake at High Cleugh were offered to the Council for twenty pounds. The military authorities had been willing to provide the labour if the city would find the materials. However, the Canadian troops left before the work could be done and the City Council decided not to proceed with the scheme.

August. The first post-war celebration of the Feast of St Wilfrid found the Market Place again converted into a fairground, though the shows were only a shadow of those before the War. However, the city was thronged with visitors in holiday mood.

A military sports day was held in a large field on the Bishop Monkton road under the auspices of the 55th Remount Squadron. For days gangs of soldiers prepared the large show ring and jumps and, despite the distance from the town centre, over 1,000 spectators attended.

On the site of the Catholic Women's League Hut at the corner of Studley Village Lane on the Pateley Bridge Road, a wayside cross was placed in memory of all the British and Canadian soldiers who passed through Ripon camp. The cross stands 17 ft. in height bearing a life-size figure of Christ. The rock at its base, weighing over four tons, was taken from the moors above Ripon and was the gift of the Marquess of Ripon.

At a meeting of the War Memorial Committee a site in the Spa Gardens was adopted together with a proposed design of a column in stone with a bronze figure at the top at a cost of £2,000. Other sites at Freemantle Terrace, St Wilfrid's Terrace, Courthouse Gardens, Borrage Bridge and the Market Square were considered but rejected for a number of reasons.

The two football clubs, Ripon City and Ripon United, decided to amalgamate.

September. At a sale held in London the Grantley and Brimham Rocks estate of Lord Furness were offered at auction but were withdrawn at £120,000.

October. Ripon Hall, Oxford, a memorial to the late Bishop Boyd Carpenter was opened. The Hall would continue the work of the Ripon Clergy College as a training centre on modern and liberal lines, for theological students desirous of entering the ministry.

It was reported that Ripon citizens had accepted a strike of railway workers calmly and philosophically. Industries in the city had been able to carry on despite being potentially cut off from the outside world, as the Ripon Canal was virtually not used and road transport had not yet been developed to any extent for long distance freight. Some citizens found themselves enjoying a late holiday stranded at various resorts. Demobilisation was stopped at Ripon Camp and workers coming in from the sur-

rounding district had either to cycle in or walk whilst many had to find lodgings within the city for the week.

The War Office informed the North Eastern Railway that although it intended to maintain the North Camp at Ripon for a Territorial Division, it would only be occupied for a short period annually and that future traffic would not justify the retention of the camp railway.

Miss Yates-Lee and Miss L. M. Bayley became the first women to put up for municipal election in Ripon and Bondgate, but were unsuccessful.

1919-20.　George Hotham Newton, Banker

Born in York where his father was a banker, he came to Ripon in 1896 to join the staff of the York City and County Bank. He was elected to the Council in 1911 and resigned in 1914 when he joined the Forces, becoming a Captain in the West Yorkshire Regiment. The Corporation had difficulty in finding a mayor in 1919; Newton stood for the municipal elections, came top of the poll and accepted the office. He was secretary of the Working Mens' Club and the Ripon Club. After the war he was a keen promoter of the Council's housing programme and his name was given to a development in Bondgate. In later years he left Ripon and when in 1957 his widow informed the Town Clerk of his death in Southend-on-Sea she asked the Corporation to accept and add to the city plate the gold key which had been presented to him at the opening of Newton Gardens.

November. In accordance with King George's proclamation, all business was suspended in Ripon for two minutes at eleven o'clock on the morning of the first anniversary of Armistice Day, 11 November. At five minutes to eleven, the City Hornblower, who was on duty at the Market Cross, sounded three blasts on the horn, when the camp buzzers were sounded. The Cathedral and other church bells were rung and short services were held. The police were on duty at the top of High Skellgate and other points and all traffic was stopped.

A curious situation arose with regard to the election of aldermen on 10 November. It transpired that aldermen who should have retired in 1916 had their terms of office extended by four years and therefore did not retire until 1920. Thus the elections which took place in Ripon and in 12 other boroughs were then void. The Town Clerk took legal opinion and was advised that aldermen in office on 10 November should continue. Thus Councillor Habgood had to revert to the rank of councillor and ex-Mayor Councillor F. W. Hargrave was left without a seat on the Council.

December. The City Council decided to hold up the housing programme for the time being and to convert a number of huts on South Camp into dwellings. A model of a house proposed in the scheme was put on view in the Council Chamber showing a parlour-type house with a living room measuring 19 ft. by 12 ft.

The City Council agreed to let the first floor of the warehouse adjoining the City Museum as a rehearsal room for the Ripon City Band at a nominal rent of £2 per annum.

The Bishop of Ripon, Dr Drury, accepted the Mastership of St Catherine's College, Cambridge, and a canonry at Norwich.

The Mayor of Ripon, accompanied by members of the Corporation and attended by the Sergeant-at-Mace, was present at Ripon Railway Station when the cadre of the 5th West Yorkshire Regiment arrived for demobilisation.

In a letter to the *Gazette*, Colonel Husband pointed out some of the factors which should be taken into account when considering the future of South Camp: the Corporation required land for housing and the camp could provide sites with made-up roads and sewers, together with laid-on water and electricity services; some Ripon citizens were asking for electric light and the Corporation was contemplating the purchase of land to erect a new city power station: the power station on South Camp was capable of supplying power to a town three to four times the size of Ripon; the Government was responsible for restoring land occupied by the camp to its original condition, the cost of which would be enormous and probably more than the land was worth. Colonel Husband suggested that the Corporation should approach the Government for financial help to retain the land, power station and railway for the building of a garden city.

January. The Ripon Carol Choir raised £80 for the entertainment of widows and orphans of local men who had fallen in the war. The children were entertained to tea, a Christmas tree and a party in the Y.M.C.A. The balance of the money was given in the form of tickets for goods for the children to be purchased from local tradesmen.

The W.R.C.C. divided the Ripon district into five areas for the purposes of a new scheme for District Nursing.

About this time, plans were complete or were being made to erect memorials to those who had died during World War I. The City War Memorial Committee announced that only £780 had been subscribed towards the £2,000 required for the erection of a Victory Column as a war memorial, and that this scheme would have to be abandoned in favour of the alternative cenotaph at a cost of £1,000. The final designs were prepared by Mr Wilcoxson, who had designed the memorial to the late Lord Ripon, and showed a pedestal of Standcliffe stone surmounted by a bronze bust. The finished work was unveiled on 5 October 1921. Two memorial windows were dedicated in June in Coltsgate Hill Wesleyan Chapel as a thanksgiving for peace, and in memory of the soldiers who frequented the Wesleyan Soldiers' Institute when in training at Ripon. A decision was made to erect a memorial in St Wilfrid's Roman Catholic Church to the soldiers from the parish and to all the four million British and Canadian soldiers who passed through the Camp. A memorial consisting of new choir stalls, pulpit and tablet was dedicated at Holy Trinity Church at a special service on 15 July. The Old Riponians instituted a scheme to raise £2,000 for a memorial to the 30 old boys of Ripon Grammar School who fell: over 250 old boys joined up. The Ripon Grammar School War Memorial, in the form of a brass tablet on the wall of the large schoolroom, was dedicated in December. The Mayor and Corporation attended a service in the Zion Chapel, Blossomgate when a stained glass window placed in the west front was dedicated on 2 September in memory of 15 members of the church. The estimated cost of the new reredos in the Cathedral rose to £4,500 due to increased rates in pay for skilled labour, and it was decided to carry out work to the value of the original estimate of £3,000, leaving many of the figures to be added later. The reredos was designed by Sir Ninian Comper and was dedicated in September 1922.

A Labour Battalion of 1,000 men arrived in Ripon to carry out the demolition of South Camp, but the work had to be delayed until the outcome was known of an interview that a deputation from the City Council had had with the Prime Minister and later with the Deputy Minister of Munitions, asking for an estimate of cost of returning the land to its original condition. Some of the huts on North Camp were converted into dwelling houses and the Housing, Sanitary and Industrial Committees jointly inspected these and later the empty huts on South Camp. Sixty huts on land belonging to Lord Ripon in Whitcliffe Lane were deemed suitable for temporary dwellings, as were a number on land belonging to the trustees of St John's Hospital. The Housing Commissioners gave permission for the use of wooden huts as temporary accommodation, with the proviso that there should be no stoppage of the building of permanent houses at Aismunderby. Most of the other huts were sold at about £80 each at three-day sales held monthly throughout the year; the horses and mules were also sold at special sales. Several of the huts were used on poultry farms. A Government decision was made at the end of February not to develop the South Camp area for industrial purposes and to encourage companies to build factories on Tyneside instead. At the same time the Ministry of Health approved the alternative housing scheme for the site. In September, The Unknown Players Film Company bought the North Camp Garrison Theatre for £1,110 at auction.

The future of North Camp was debated throughout the year. In September, a public meeting was held to discuss its possible take-over by a shipping company as a transit camp for emigrants. There would be about 2,500 people in the camp at any one time with individuals staying a few days or a week at the most. Opinion was divided, shopkeepers being in favour as they thought the emigrants might spend money in the town before their journey, whereas speakers at speech days at the Grammar School and the Girls' High School denounced the scheme on health grounds. In the meantime negotiations continued with the Government and later the Mayor announced that the Corporation had been successful in persuading the War Office to retain the North Camp and that part of it would be converted into married quarters to house 300 families expected to arrive in Ripon from March 1921.

February. On 5 February the death of Mr William Robertson of Palace Road, a blind poet, was announced. 'He had a love for beautiful expression and thought'. Some of his verse was published in book form as *Hymnal Echoes* and *Lays of Light*.

Escaped Russian trade union leaders gave lectures in the Co-operative Hall on their thrilling experiences and the horrors of Bolshevism.

In 1920 there were 44 licensed premises in the city. However, peacetime saw a dramatic reduction in the number of total convictions for liquor offences, 14 in 1919 as compared with 78 in 1915, whereas the figures for resident offenders were 10 and 13 respectively.

March. The Bishop of Ripon preached his farewell sermon in Ripon to a large congregation. Later in the year his work in the diocese was recognised at a presentation of a portrait in oils. The original was given to Dr Drury and a replica was made to hang in the Palace at Ripon.

The Annual Report for the Hospital was published showing that the total costs for 1919 were £1,116 4s 6d, which included £100 for surgeons' salaries, £185 15s 2d to pay the matron and nurses and £29 2s 9d for telephone calls and the horse ambulance. During the year 248 in-patients had been treated, and the accounts showed a deficit.

April. The West Riding Asylums Board increased the rate of maintenance for pauper lunatics to 29s 9d per week. The previous payment of 5s 0d per week was totally inadequate and had thrown a heavy burden on the local ratepayers.

Still another conference was held to discuss the desirability of re-opening the canal. A committee was formed to investigate the matter and report to the Industrial Committee of the Corporation.

The death was announced of Mr Matthew Kirkley who had been Ripon Town Clerk for the past 39 years. Mr J. H. Gough of Grantham was appointed to the post at a salary of £500 per annum.

J. HENRY GOUGH, F.C.I.S. A.S.AA.
TOWN CLERK.
1920-

May. Compared with Easter, when visitors to the city were less than usual, each day of the Whitsun holiday saw fresh crowds brought into town by charabancs and motor vehicles. On Monday afternoon visitors crowded the Market Place and lined the route for the annual Sunday School demonstrations.

June. The Revd Father Levick received from the Belgian Ambassador in London the Medaille du Roi Albert in recognition of his services to Belgian refugees during the war.

The Very Revd T. B. Strong C.B.E., D.D., Dean of Christ Church, Oxford, was appointed Bishop of Ripon. His consecration took place at York in September and on the following day he was enthroned in Ripon Cathedral.

The Grammar School found itself in severe financial difficulties and turned to the W.R.C.C. for assistance. The County Council undertook responsibility for its liabilities and the governing body was re-organised to include representatives of the local authorities and Leeds University. The City Council was asked to transfer to the Grammar School a grant of £160 previously made to the Girls' High School for evening technical classes.

The inmates of the Poor Law Institution had their annual summer outing to Fountains Abbey and for the first time the party was conveyed in motor vehicles.

July. A charge of 1s 0d imposed on motor charabancs unloading in the Market Place raised £44 in the first month.

The death occurred of Admiral Charles Lister Oxley at his Ripon home, *The Hall*, aged 79. He took a keen interest in the affairs of the city and was a magistrate for the West Riding and the Liberty of Ripon for many years.

The perennial controversy over the siting of the Fair in the Market Place for St Wilfrid's Feast continued. This year the Council sided with the show proprietors, ordering charabancs to park in Water Skellgate and not on the Market Place.

The annual report of the Comrades of the Great War, an organisation set up to work for the benefit of ex-servicemen, showed a membership of 412 in

15. *View from Somerset Row towards Water Skellgate (Gott)*

Ripon. A satisfactory settlement had been reached in 60 cases of non-payment or mistakes in War Pension awards. The Comrades undertook to care for the graves of soldiers buried in Ripon cemetery.

August. Speech day at the Girls' High School was a triumph for those who in 1908 had faced the strong opposition to the establishment of secondary education for girls in the town. The scholars now numbered 140 and speech day had to be held in the Ripon Training College as the school could no longer accommodate visitors as well as staff and pupils.

October. The *Gazette* published an account of the recollections of Mr George Marston of Salisbury Terrace, Bondgate Green, who had been born in Ripon in 1830. He said he could remember the town centre as being largely residential with no shops definitely in Blossomgate, and probably Westgate, only two in Kirkgate — a Grocer named Pimm and a Draper named Durham — and very few in the Market Place. He attended the laying of the foundation stone of the Bishop's Palace in 1837 and one of his early recollections was of St Wilfrid's procession led by two men, one with a tin whistle and the other with a drum.

The Temperance Hall in Duck Hill was re-opened after renovations. In the early part of the War it had been used by navvies building the camps and later by the Y.M.C.A. as a soldiers' institute.

Some train services were withdrawn and gas supplies were cut off because of the coal strike. However, in November a new plant at the gas works ensured a much-improved supply for the future.

1920-21. George Hotham Newton, Banker

Mayor 1919-20-21

November. The minimum stipend for clergy in the Ripon Diocese was increased to £220 per annum, a figure considered to be a fair salary. Discussions again took place concerning the site of the Bishop's residence, as there was a growing opinion in the Diocese that one of the larger towns such as Harrogate would be more suitable. Bishop Strong supported the view of most Riponians that the Palace should be in the neighbourhood of the Cathedral, and he installed a telephone to keep in touch with the wide area of his bishopric.

The Dean commented: 'I am bound to say that one thing which Riponians are very careless about is punctuality — if it could be agreed that the Post Office and Cathedral clocks said the same time, the other clocks at the Town Hall, Clock Tower and Station would join up and Ripon would be able to boast a definite time'.

December. The death took place at *Borrage House* of Tom Williamson, aged 60, Chairman of T. and R. Williamson Limited. He left his mark on the city in many directions, particularly as a magistrate and a town councillor. His Mayoralty in 1896 was well remembered for the installation of the Council offices at the Town Hall following the presentation of the building by the 1st Marquess of Ripon.

The Corporation decided to pursue an idea put forward by the Mayor that Ripon should be advertised with the showing of a specially-made film of the beauties of the city and the surrounding neighbourhood. This film was found in good condition among the city archives in 1982.

January. The death took place in his 86th year of Mr Leavens King. He had carried on business as a corn and flour dealer in the city for 50 years, was associated with the Wesleyan Church and was a staunch supporter of the Ripon Temperance Society.

The General Secretary of the Y.M.C.A. gave a lecture illustrated with slides on 'The graves of the fallen in France and Flanders', largely based on the work of the Imperial War Graves Commission. The large audience testified to the deep appeal which this subject had for many people.

February. The Council discussed the possibility of persuading the Carnegie Trust to finance a public library for the city. Councillor Goldsworthy had been informed by the Town Clerk of Harrogate that the Trust had vested its funding through the County Council, and that it depended upon the amount of energy the Corporation put into canvassing the matter whether Ripon or some other place got the library.

The Studley Royal and Ripon City Golf Clubs negotiated a reciprocal membership scheme, whereby members of each club could play on either course.

March. The death occurred of Viscountess Furness of *Grantley Hall* at the age of 38 on board the steam yacht *Sapphire* off Cadiz. The funeral took place at sea.

The Corporation had to consider taking over land on the north side of the cemetery as the cheaper portion of the Church of England burial ground was nearly full. The site of the proposed extension was in need of drainage, and as the cemetery was running at a loss the Corporation had to apply for borrowing powers in order to cover the cost.

The Corporation applied for permission to increase the tolls levied at the Ripon Market. The Ministry of Health instituted an enquiry after local retailers had brought up the old grievance against traders from other towns bringing their goods to market. As a result, it was proposed that the charge for stalls selling manufactured goods be raised from 3s 6d per day to 10s 0d per market day and £1 on fair days. No toll continued to be exacted from vendors of farm produce such as butter, eggs and chickens. One reason for the application was that only £1,094 had been paid from tolls towards the rates over the last nine years, whereas in the same period the Corporation had spent close on £4,000 on repairs to the Market Place. The new charges came into force on the first Thursday in November when the collector met with a flat refusal from indignant traders in drapery goods from Leeds and Knaresborough. An agreement was reached for that day but the traders stayed away on the following Thursday. The dispute was temporarily settled by changing the basis of charging for stalls to one depending on footage: 3d per ft. per day, 4½d each stall for poles per day, ground stands 3d per sq. yd. per day. In exchange the vendors of manufactured goods agreed to hire the stalls for six months and pay the charges in advance. They were well satisfied as the final charges worked out to be little more than before. Later in the year, the Council instituted parking charges on the Market Place at 1s 0d for cars and 6d for motor cycles.

The Vagrancy Committee of the Council became anxious for the spiritual welfare of those travellers of the road who occupied casual wards at the Workhouse at weekends. They recommended the Board of Guardians to provide special facilities, but the chaplains of the Ripon Poor Law Institution preferred to invite their visitors to join in the regular services arranged for other inmates. Mr C. Harker gave 18 extra prayer books.

A Women's Central Unionist Association was set up for the Ripon Division with local associations in each sub-area including one in Ripon city.

The Vicar of Holy Trinity Church, with the consent of the Bishop, was the first of the local clergy to follow the Lambeth Conference proposals to invite the ministers of the Free Churches to join in a united service on Easter Day.

The death was announced of William Henry Kearsley at the age of sixty-six. He had come to Ripon in 1867 to join his uncle, the late Robert Kearsley, at his varnish works where he became a director and secretary of the Company. He was elected to the City Council in 1886 where he served for 33 years, many times being asked to be Mayor. He was a J.P. for both the City and the Liberty and was an active worker in the United Methodist Church. A handsome stained glass window was placed in his memory in the south aisle of the Zion Chapel, Blossomgate.

Controversy broke out among ratepayers over the alternative schemes for working-class housing on the Aismunderby site: should new houses be built or existing reinforced concrete huts be converted at less expense? The City Surveyor estimated that conversion costs including roads and sewers would be £590 per dwelling. In the meantime, as an emergency measure, some of the shops in the Arcade were let as dwellings.

31 March was selected as Earl Haig Fund Day when entertainments took place in every town and village to raise funds to help ex-servicemen in distress. Mr C. H. Moody supervised the musical and dramatic events in Ripon, and the proceeds from these and from a fancy dress dance held later amounted to £184.

April. The German guns were at last placed in the grounds adjoining the Courthouse in Kirkgate Park. This was somewhat controversial. A comment in the *Gazette* stated 'Those who regard them as an emblem of the brave lives sacrificed will feel no more suitable spot could be found, but to those to whom they are only a reminder of the hundreds of brilliant young lives shattered by such engines of war will only regard them as a hideous blot on what should be a fair corner of the city'.

Ripon, in its peaceful aloofness from the industrial world, remained politically undisturbed by the coal miners' strike. The Royal Proclamation of the State of Emergency was posted at the Town Hall, the Market Cross and other prominent buildings and was read in all places of worship on Sunday. Citizens wishing to join the Defence Corps enlisted at the Town Hall. Tickets for coal rations were obtained from the Mayor's Parlour; the gas supply was cut off from 1.30 pm to 4.30 pm; public street lamps were lighted only at crossroads and near the Cathedral. However, the coal problem became more and more acute, and by the end of April not even a doctor's certificate could produce a permit as there was no coal to be had in the city although there remained a large dump of 1,000 tons of coal on the Camp. Twenty tons were released for the Workhouse and the Hospital. The Spa Baths were temporarily closed until the strike ended early in July. The local shortage caused a variation to be made at the usual tea following the

1887 — 1986   69

annual festival service for the Mothers' Union of Ripon Rural Deanery when lemonade and cakes were served.

May. The Venerable H. Armstrong, Archdeacon of Richmond, died. He was one of the four Residentiary Canons of the Cathedral from 1908-1911 and during the War was a familiar figure in the city as the Deputy-Assistant Chaplain-General of Northern Command in charge of training schools for chaplains at Ripon and Catterick, through which more than 200 clergymen passed before going overseas. The archdeacon was awarded the C.B.E. for this work.

Messrs T. and E. Cox, Photographers of Kirkgate, had two portraits hung at the P.P.A. Exhibition of professional portraiture and technical work held in the Royal Horticultural Hall, London.

June. The golden wedding of Colonel and Mrs Crompton of *Azerley Chase* was celebrated with a party for nearly 1,000 guests invited from the West Tanfield and Kirkby Malzeard areas. Motors, wagons, wagonettes and carts filled the roads leading to the Chase and the large numbers of sheds and stables proved very useful when the weather broke. One very long shed (which nowadays still contains the old family coaches dating from 1840) and an adjoining marquee were used to serve tea and for the performances of sword dances by a local team and music by the Kirkby Malzeard Musical Society. Fortunately, the weather cleared to allow the celebration to end with a dance on the lawn when Colonel and Mrs Crompton led off with 'Sir Roger de Coverley'.

Mr C. H. Moody, who was becoming famous as a guide at Fountains Abbey, wrote to the *Yorkshire Post* to express his disgust at the 'appalling' behaviour of some visitors to the Abbey. He suggested that Fountains was a place to be avoided on Saturday afternoons and Bank Holidays and asserted that to some of the ill-behaved visitors 'the solemn fabric was nowt but a . . . owd church wit' roof off . . .'.

Miss Lois Thirlway V.A.D., daughter of Alderman Thirlway, received the 1914-15 Star, the General Service Medal and the Victory Medal for her service with the B.E.F. in France.

July. The second annual pilgrimage organised by the Catholic Women's League was made to the Wayside Shrine erected at the end of Studley Lane on the site of their wartime hut and chapel. In all, some 450 to 500 people arrived from surrounding towns.

The return of the Fair to the Market Place for the August Bank Holiday meant that motor vehicles had to line the roadway causing traffic jams. The Council discussed alternative central sites for car parking so that the Market Place could be kept clear for use as a market.

August. Dr Lucius Smith, Bishop of Knaresborough, left Ripon to take up his residence as Rector of Methley. A presentation of a Pectoral Cross and a silver salver as farewell gifts was made at the Town Hall.

September. Ripon Rural District Council followed the general action of firms and public bodies in the matter of reducing bonuses and some wages paid to their officials. It was decided that the Medical Officer should receive a bonus of £13 instead of £26 per annum and the Surveyor £43 instead of £57 per annum. The wages of manual workers were reduced by 3d per day, a foreman by 4d per day and the driver of the steam roller by 8d per day. It was calculated that these reductions would still leave workmen with adequate wages to cope with the inflated prices.

A Ripon branch of the 'Middle Classes Union' was formed with the enrolment of 40 members. This body had been set up to enlarge the part played by the 'Middle Classes' in the government of the country.

1921-22. WALTER FENNELL

Mayor 1910-11-12-13, 1921-22

December. Major the Hon. Edward Wood, M.P. for Ripon, offered his Temple Newsam estate of 913 acres to the Leeds Corporation for the sum of £35,000.

The Corporation sent a telegram of congratulations to HRH Princess Mary and Viscount Lascelles on their engagement. The Lords Lieutenant of the North and East Ridings proposed to set up a subscription list (with a maximum of one guinea and the minimum the smallest coin of the realm) to fund an engagement present.

The Council objected to the erection of a petrol pump outside a local garage, as Ripon streets were too narrow to allow 'such things to be put up. They should be fixed inside the garage; after all they are not exactly ornaments'.

At the annual prize-giving at Jepson's Hospital, the Mayor made a strong appeal for more permanent support. He reminded citizens that the founder originally endowed the school with the idea of there always being 20 boys as foundation scholars, but owing to the conditions of recent years the number had had to be reduced to ten.

January. Members of all the denominations in the town assembled to the Town Hall for United Christian Fellowship. The Mayor presided and conducted the meeting.

February. Fears of an outbreak of foot-and-mouth disease proved justified when cases were confirmed at West Tanfield, Hutton Conyers, Wath and Lindrick.

The Auction Mart was closed until the next month when there was only a limited entry of animals for immediate slaughter.

March. County Councillor W. T. Moss, Alderman Lee and Alderman Thirlway were offered the Freedom of the City but declined the honour.

United Automobile Services Limited were granted a licence by the Council to run motor-bus services to the city. Two months later there were delays because of a lack of finance, but the Transport Manager said the company would respect the wishes of local people with regard to Sunday services, and hoped to run some late buses to the villages after cinema performances. In May a motor-bus service introduced to supplement the wagonette plying between the Market Place and the Railway Station was said to be 'gradually increasing in popularity.'

The Allotment Holders' Association wound up the limited company they had formed three years previously and joined forces with the Horticultural Society. Efforts were made to secure allotments for the inhabitants of Stonebridgegate and the Corporation advertised for land for the purpose.

Mr Harold Blackburn of Lickley Street was appointed Hornblower for a trial period of three months. Twelve guineas was allocated to purchase a uniform for the Town Hall Keeper, this to include two pairs of trousers.

With a view to relieving unemployment the Council applied to the Ministry of Health for £1,000 to carry out drainage work at the cemetery. The Bishop consecrated the additional ground in June.

April. At the first meeting of the newly-formed Photographic Society there was a lecture and discussion on the various types of cameras and their uses. At the second meeting the subject was 'exposures'.

May. For many years Ripon citizens had enjoyed free entry to Fountains Abbey on Bank Holidays, a privilege granted by the late Marquess: that the Spa Committee should have drawn the attention of the Railway Company to this fact was seen as 'an encroachment on the good nature of the owner of the abbey and grounds'.

The Ripon Traders' Association was re-formed and the Mayor called a meeting to decide whether to have Wednesday as early-closing day; a large majority voted to continue closing on Fridays.

A sign had recently appeared informing people entering Ripon that 'VEIHCLES' could be parked on adjacent ground; however, by nightfall this had been changed to 'VECHILES'.

A meeting of the Rural District Council criticised the maintenance of roads in the city, their vice-chairman having lost his windscreen after jolting over a pothole. In the town the mitigation of the dust nuisance and the more regular appearance of the water cart was called for.

June. Two labourers from Stonebridgegate and some women were summoned for damaging growing grass on the river bank belonging to the Beeches Farm. The defendants were each fined 5s 0d, 'as they

probably did not know what damage they were doing lying there and playing on the grass'.

A demonstration of wireless telephony by Mr Thompson and Mr Brady attracted a large company at the Assembly Rooms. Messages were heard from the Eiffel Tower and the Air Ministry, but arrangements to hear a concert by wireless broke down because of an accident to the transmitter at Wakefield.

July. During the month, 451 vagrants passed through Ripon compared with 517 in July 1921.

Because of a dispute with the Typographical Association the *Gazette* did not appear in its usual form for some weeks and there was no publication on 10 August.

August. The Corporation decided that the Mayoral procession could travel at a more rapid pace on official parade without loss of dignity. 'However, some think a breezy day might cause the flowing robes to flap about and make the City Fathers look like gigantic fowls hustling down the street'.

September. Much effort was put into organising a 'Ripon Shopping Week' at the end of September. There were window-dressing and lucky-number competitions with 250 prizes to be claimed in the various shop windows. In December the traders followed this with a concerted effort to make their shops more attractive for Christmas, in spite of high unemployment and general depression.

October. A Child Welfare Centre for army families was opened at North Camp. Staffed by volunteer helpers, the facilities included a rest room for mothers and an inspection room and a nursery for the children.

1922-23. WILLIAM HEMSWORTH, Antique Dealer

Born in 1867, he came to Ripon at the age of four, was educated at the Grammar School and apprenticed to J. G. Metcalfe, Cabinet Maker of Kirkgate. He excelled in his craft, particularly in wood-carving, and acquired an encyclopaedic knowledge of antiques. His business in Fishergate became famous and was patronised by Queen Mary on her visits to Yorkshire. He was a keen sportsman and became an enthusiastic motorist. Co-opted to the Council during the war, he was elected in 1920. He was active in the expansion of council housing and the creation of Southgate, and the acquisition and layout of the Spa Park. He was devoted to the collection and study of objects and documents of the past, many of which he donated to the city. His memorial is *Hugh Ripley's House* which in 1924 he was determined the city should own and care for as one of its most important buildings — *The Wakeman's House*. He died in 1946.

November. The Chairman of the Gas Committee attributed losses during the year to the extraordinary expenditure during the coal strike. He said that the heating properties of Ripon gas were excellent but a little more 'candle-power' would be appreciated. There had been complaints about the street lighting and the manager had promised that the main thoroughfares would be illuminated during the winter months.

December. Mr J. Hainsworth, a shopkeeper in the Market Place, was fined 4s 0d for using a car, the colour of which had been changed without notifying the authorities.

The Council agreed to extend the bowling green and to construct two all-weather hard tennis courts at the Spa at a cost of £225.

The Mayor presented an antique oak chair for the use of future Mayors of Ripon when attending services in the nave of the Cathedral.

January. The Mayor called a public meeting at the request of 40 ratepayers to discuss ways in which work could be provided for the 400 unemployed in the city. The War Department had found six weeks' work for 200 men employing them to remove the water pipes serving South Camp. The pay was 9d per hour as they were only allowed to pay 75 per cent of a labourer's wage which at that time was 1s 0d per hour. On the other hand, following the re-arrangement of office accommodation in the Town Hall and the re-allocation of officers, clerks and other workers, it was found that Ripon Corporation was employing more staff than some towns with a population of 20,000 inhabitants. The Mayor thought that this was irresponsible and decided that drastic changes would have to be made.

The ceremony of Blessing the War Memorial took place at St Wilfrid's Catholic Church. The memorial, which had been erected outside the north wall of the church, takes the form of a Pieta, representing the dead body of Our Lord taken down from the Cross and resting on the knees of His Blessed Mother.

The meet of the Bedale Hunt in Ripon Market Place, considered by Ripon citizens to be one of the most interesting sights of the year, was cancelled as a mark of respect to Miss Madge Verelst of *Melmerby Hall*, a member of the Hunt, who had died in India.

February. A successful start was made in the collection of linen by the Hospital Linen Guild which had been formed in connection with the Ripon Cottage Hospital. The favourite form of gift was towels and pillow cases and by May 450 articles had been sent in.

During the severe weather at the end of February, the soup kitchen was opened in the market stall house, Blossomgate.

March. In proportion to its size, Ripon had a large number of charitable institutions: one of the most deserving but probably one of the least known was the Nina Convalescent Fund, which for over 20 years had carried on beneficent work for the sick poor of the city. The Fund made no systematic appeals to the public but relied on private subscriptions for support.

The Revd W. J. Limmer Shepherd, Vicar of Holy Trinity, finished a new book, *Great Hymns and Their Stories*, which was published by the Religious Tract Society. Miss Florence Bone, the authoress, came to live in the city and one of her books, *The Lavender Hedge*, had its plot laid in Ripon.

The Ripon City Council co-operated with the Ripon Rural District Council on the improvement of the bridge leading over the Ripon Canal from the Boroughbridge Road to Littlethorpe.

The Mayor, Alderman Hemsworth, took a great interest in the restoration of *Hugh Ripley's House*, from then on known as the *Wakeman's House*, which was in appalling condition after years of neglect. He laid a scheme before the Council to put the building into a state which would reflect credit on the city. Some of his fellow members gave lukewarm support as they feared the financial responsibility involved in repair and decoration, but in May they voted £50 towards the cost of renovation. By August, the exterior of the house had assumed a respectable appearance and Alderman Hemsworth turned his attention to the restoration of the interior. In a letter to the *Gazette*, he explained that the old balustrade staircase and musicians' gallery would be restored, the linen-fold panelling which had been displayed in the *Thorpe Prebend Museum* would be re-hung and dog-grates inserted in place of the modern ranges. He appealed for gifts of suitable pieces of furniture appropriate to the time when Hugh Ripley had lived in the house. Amongst the items given were: a tinder box and steel, one of the earliest English specimens; three old Ripon spurs from Mr Dixon's house in Kirkgate; an oak-panelled half-door, an oak wall-cupboard and two antique rush light-holders. Mr T. R. Mountain presented a series of old guild banners which had been used in the 1886 Millenary celebrations; Mr C. Parker of Kirkgate gave an oil painting by John Morris of Ripon, the only known picture of the old Bedern House; the Smithson family of North Street presented the period door, believed to be the original door to *Hugh Ripley's House* for reinstatement. Gifts continued to be made so that by the time the work was complete and the restored building was formally opened by the Mayoress in July 1924 it had become a store of local antiquities. An important addition was the 'greate chiste' which had been traced to Keighley in private ownership and acquired for the city. This large oak chest, originally used as the store place for the Corporation plate, had been missing from Ripon for many years. There was reference to it in 1680 when it had passed from one Mayor to the next. A number of paintings had been presented including one of

Byland Abbey by Julius Caesar Ibbotson, 1757; a painting of *Fountains Abbey* (showing Mr and Mrs Aislabie directing operations in the Abbey grounds) painted in 1815 by a local artist, Mr R. Dunning and one by the same artist of *Hackfall*. Mr Walter J. Kaye of Harrogate presented to the city a painting of Ripon *c.* 1600. Readers of *Jock o'Rippon* by Mr C. C. S. Bland would recognise the ford into which the Wakeman was rolled in a barrel down Bedern Bank by the young 'bloods' of Studley. Scales and Weights of Ripon, stamped W. BELL, Esq., Mayor, 1784-5 had been discovered by the Mayor and placed in the *Wakeman's House.*

Mrs Haxby of Allhallowgate presented a set of spurs to the Corporation which had been made by her husband, Albert Haxby, a craftsman who had won prizes for his work at various local and national exhibitions. Shortly before he died in 1921, he expressed a wish to his wife that 'if ever Billy Hemsworth gets to be Mayor of Ripon ask him to accept my spurs and add them to the regalia'.

An interesting addition to the Ripon City Museum was the original bull ring and stone to which the bull was chained in the cruel days of bull-baiting by dogs in the Old Market Place or Bull Square. The relic had been photographed in 1906 by Sir Benjamin Store before it was removed with the cobbled paving of the Square. The ring and stone was preserved by Mr William Harrison in the yard behind his printing works in the Market Place, but was afterwards lost until Alderman Hemsworth re-discovered it

languishing in a rockery, and had it placed on the lawn in front of *Thorpe Prebend House*. It is recorded that in 1676 the bull ring had been repaired at a cost of 4s 0d.

March. Strenuous efforts were made to encourage visitors and to develop Ripon as a holiday centre and health resort. The latest move to direct tourists to the city was the erection of two signposts at the Kirkby Hill corner of the Great North Road (now A1) and at Baldersby Lane end.

April. The death took place at the age of 84 of William Walls, a partner in the Ripon and Claro Varnish Company. He was a member of the Ripon Liberal Club and was elected in 1906 to the City Council, on which he served for six years. For a number of years he was one of the overseers for the city.

The Primitive Methodist Synod was held in Ripon for the first time and provided an unique occasion in the history of the city: a Bishop of Ripon preached in a Methodist Church for the first time.

May. Lord Ripon informed the Ripon Industrial Committee that he would not lease or sell any of the North Camp land for any purpose that would encourage the retention of the camp buildings.

The death occurred at Worthing of Harry Kearsley J.P., aged 63, the only son of Robert Kearsley of *Highfield* and grandson of George Kearsley, Coal and Iron Merchant, who erected the varnish works which later became R. Kearsley and Company Limited. When his will was proved in September, it was shown

16. *Old Queen Street and Middle Street from the north (Fossick)*

that he had left £37,624 with legacies to many friends 'left in the hope that they may in some small degree repay the legatees for many little acts of kindness, and afford them, at any rate, a few pleasant moments'. These included £500 to William Hanley Hutchinson and £100 each to the others: he also left provision for the children of his late partner, Henry Cecil Bickersteth. He also directed that a duly qualified medical man should open one of his main arteries before his funeral to make sure he was dead, and receive a fee of £25 for so doing.

A novel event in the Whitsun weekend celebrations was a motor-cycle meet in the Market Place on Whit Sunday. On Monday, the city was crowded: the first event of the day was a fancy-dress parade of motorists and later a gymkhana was held on the football ground.

Empire Day was celebrated in the Ripon Elementary Schools. The Mayor and Mayoress and members of the Education Committee visited each of the schools in turn, where patriotic songs were sung, questions put to the children from the Empire Catechism and the school Roll of Honour and the Union Jack saluted. A special feature was playing of the gramophone recording of their Majesties' messages to the children of the Elementary Schools of the Empire.

June. The City Council discussed the funding for the purchase for £1,450 of two pieces of land situated at the corner of Park Street and Church Lane. Usually money for municipal land purchases came from the district rates, and the Ministry of Health held an inquiry. In this case, the Council decided to use insurance money which had been paid to the Spa Committee following a fire at the Spa Baths. A deputation headed by the Revd G. Hooper suggested that the land should be used to provide playing fields for children at that end of the town who had nowhere to play. This paved the way for the development of the Spa Park. However, this suggestion was not without opposition as at the November Council meeting there were unsuccessful attempts made to secure the ground as a building site or for allotments or, as far as the opponents were concerned, for any purpose other than a children's playground. There was further argument in February 1924 over the official wording and names carved on the newly-erected gate-posts to the park. It was suggested that the wrong committee had been given credit, and later that week the lettering was obliterated by being smeared over with tar.

After an interval of ten years, Ripon Industrial Society held an exhibition of arts and crafts with 628 entires and 93 competitive classes, and an exceptionally good loan exhibition. Since their last exhibition there had been a gap of ten years with a World War, which meant that the approach to arts and crafts had changed significantly. The attendance figures over three days were 2,060, but the financial result was disappointing with a loss of £18.

July. The Agricultural Show was well-favoured this year, as it fell in one of the finest weeks. There was a good average attendance, but the entrance fee of 2s 0d was considered high. There was a large number of motor cars which came in at the Bishopton entrance to the field and which easily outnumbered the horse-drawn vehicles.

The death occurred of Miss Elizabeth Florence Bickersteth, only daughter of the late Bishop Bickersteth. On the death of her brother, Mr H. C. Bickersteth, Mayor of Ripon 1883-4, Miss Bickersteth took charge of his family of four sons and two daughters and filled for them the place of parents they had so early lost. She would be long remembered for her acts of kindly charity, but it was chiefly to the work of Prevention and Rescue that she devoted her warmest attention. The Refuge for Girls in Skellbank was carried on through her support.

August. The St Wilfrid Feast of 1923 was regarded as one of the most successful on record. The procession was headed by the police, followed by the City Band, then 'Knobsticks' or special constables, followed by the City Bellman and the Hornblower; 'St Wilfrid' with his attendant and monks mounted on horseback; and behind these 'King Alfred' carrying the charter. The costumes were hired from Leeds.

HM Queen Mary made an informal visit to the Cathedral while she was staying with Princess Mary at Goldsborough Hall.

Ripon again justified the title of 'Mecca of the Motorist', for there was a 'Rally of Raleigh Riders' in the Market Place, and a few days later it was the starting point of the Auto Cycle Union's six-day reliability run.

October. The sudden death on a grouse moor at the age of 71 of the Marquess of Ripon, without issue, raised interesting speculation as to the future of Studley Royal estate. A London paper circulated the rumour that Lord Ripon had left Fountains Abbey as a gift to the nation, but this was finally contradicted by his lordship's solicitors. In November it was stated that under the terms of his will the estate was to be sold. The announcement in December that the estate had been bought by another branch of the family was received with general satisfaction. Mr Clare Vyner, the new owner, was a son of Lady Alwyne Compton-Vyner; he married Lady Doris Gordon-Lennox, a daughter of the Earl of March and granddaughter of the Duke of Richmond and Gordon. It was stated that the new owner would grant the same privileges which had been enjoyed by the public for so long.

1923-24. WILLIAM HEMSWORTH, Antique Dealer

November. A census of vehicles in High Skellgate, from 14 to 20 August, showed a total of 18,508 vehicles of which 93 per cent were mechanically propelled. Nowadays the same number of vehicles passes through Ripon each day.

December. The famous Alexander Marsh and Carrie Baillie Shakespearian Company appeared at the Victoria Hall during Christmas week. The repertoire of plays included *The Merchant of Venice*, *A Midsummer Night's Dream*, *Twelfth Night*, *The Taming of the*

Ald. William Hemsworth. Thrice Mayor 1922-23-24-25

Mayor 1922-23-24-25

Shrew and for the Saturday matinée, *The Tempest*.

The Christmas festivity was quietly observed in Ripon. Through the kindness of Captain and Mrs Prior Wandesforde, the unemployed of the city, with their wives and children, numbering about 500, were entertained on Christmas Day to dinner, tea and an entertainment, with the help of 40 willing helpers from the British Legion and the City Football Club. Dinner and tea were at the *Lawrence Rooms* and later they enjoyed a Christmas tree in the Y.M.C.A. Hall with sweets and crackers for the children.

February. Two lectures given during the month were intended to educate women to a proper sense of their newly acquired privileges and responsibilities. Miss Kitson J.P., spoke on 'The work of women magistrates', and Dr Clara Stewart M.B., B.Sc., dealt with the recent Parliamentary Bills and Acts relating to women and children.

The Council approved the layout of the land at Mallorie Park Drive (purchased in 1923 for £1,150) for the erection of houses at rents ranging from £30 to £40 per annum. The work was to be carried out by the unemployed and when completed the plots would be sold at a cost to cover the outlay. The Corporation would not accept responsibility beyond the laying of sewers and gas mains and the making of roads. Later in the year a scheme was approved for the erection of 32 houses on the Bondgate Grange site. Ripon Hockey Club was disbanded owing to the lack of playing members. This had been one of the most successful of local sports clubs, but it was now the policy of schools to give premier place to football.

March. Any hopes of North Camp becoming a valuable suburb of Ripon, either as factories or as bungalow settlements, were ended by a decision in the Railway and Canal Commission Court that it must be cleared by 1 March 1925.

At the Milnes-Gaskell library sale in London a 1760 copy of the *Book of Common Prayer* with a fore-edge painting of Fountains Abbey realised £21.

At the annual meeting of the Joint Cricket and Tennis Club one of the lady members put in a plea for Sunday tennis, on the grounds that the golf links were open for play on Sunday, but the suggestion

was ruled out. A copy of the rules and regulations of the Ripon Cricket Club in 1852 was discovered in the papers of the late Mr Samuel Darnborough of *High Berrys*. The rules were framed and presented to the Ripon Cricket and Athletic Club.

April. The Master of the Poor Law Institution appealed in vain for the gift of a pram or pushcarriage for the Institution so that the small children could be wheeled in the fresh air. Perambulators were regarded as a luxury and not included in the regular equipment of the Workhouse.

A large crowd gathered in the Market Place on 23 April to hear the broadcast of the King's speech when he opened the British Empire Exhibition at Wembley. This was heard from the *Gazette* office, then situated behind the Café Victoria.

May The announcement of the death of Father de Vacht was received with real regret in Ripon where his pastorate of the Catholic Church was still remembered. He was beloved of the people irrespective of their religious beliefs, his kindly nature being tolerant to all: many claimed him as their friend.

At a meeting presided over by the Mayoress it was decided that Women's Institutes should be formed in as many villages as possible with Ripon as the centre.

The Medical Officer of Health in issuing his Annual Report said that the general death rate, as well as the tuberculosis mortality and infant mortality, were all lower than at any time in his 13 years of records. Effort was still much needed to improve housing conditions and educate the people in healthier ways of living. The population in 1921 was 8,321; inhabited houses 2,077. There were four varnish and paint manufacturers, two engineering firms and three saw mills. People engaged in industrial work averaged 400, the district being more residential than industrial.

At the instigation of the Mayoress, the women of Ripon appealed for funds to clear off the debt on the War Memorial in the Spa Gardens; although it was some time since the erection of the memorial, the sum required for inscribing the names of the men commemorated had never been raised.

June. The Mayor presented to the city regalia, in commemoration of his silver wedding, the only known specimen of 'a Ripon wrought spur' made of fine steel and inlaid with finely chased silver about 1600. It had been purchased by Alderman Hemsworth himself some years ago from the Heslington collection.

An offer by a syndicate formed by Dr T. Waterhouse to take over the Victoria Hall was accepted by the Ripon Public Rooms Company Limited. This meant the citizens of Ripon were certain of having a good-sized hall in which entertainments could be held. While the Territorials were in camp in July, the Hall was in use every evening for dancing.

July. The Corporation joined with the two Rural Districts in the purchase of a motor fire-engine which was temporarily housed at the Stall House in Blossomgate.

Ripon Rural District Council expressed strong

---

opposition to the proposal to widen the Harrogate-Ripon road throughout its entire length. It was argued that such a road would only increase the dangers of travelling but the main opposition was on the grounds of cost, even as a measure for finding work for the unemployed. The W.R.C.C. Highways Committee later adopted the proposal and recommended that 25,000 tons of hard core and other material should be obtained at a cost of £8,750 from the Ripon Military Camp.

August. The Territorial Camp, which had been established on the outskirts of the city for over two months, came to an end with the departure of the Durham Light Infantry Brigade. The military parades, sports and the concerts of the military bands in the Spa Gardens had attracted much attention.

Ripon was honoured with distinguished visitors when two parties of American bankers broke their tour to the North of Scotland. They arrived in a handsome fleet of Armstrong-Siddeley cars and were welcomed at the Town Hall by the Mayor.

October. The announcement that the Mayor had accepted a third year of office was not allowed to go unchallenged. At the meeting from which the invitation was given five members refrained from voting. Those who on different occasions had had cause to complain of the manner in which business had been transacted were not deterred by any thought of the finer feelings of others but went straight to the point, demanded the production of the minutes (which had not been published), and plainly told the Mayor he had 'lingered on the stage too long'.

The sudden dissolution of Parliament largely overshadowed all other events and there was a good deal of conjecture as to the possibility of a contest in the Ripon Division. Considerable excitement prevailed when Mr Ramsay MacDonald and his party arrived at the *Unicorn Hotel*. The Premier, who was looking tired, delighted the waiting maid by writing his signature on the corner of her apron at her request.

At the meeting of the Board of Guardians an application from the Master and Matron for an increase in salary was granted, on the grounds that both had shown themselves efficient, and that the Ripon Institution was much below other institutions of a similar size in the matter of salaries. The Master's pay was increased from £60 to £80, and Mrs Millard's from £40 to £65 per annum. At Settle, where the workhouse was of similar size to Ripon, the Guardians were advertising for a Master at a starting salary of £200.

The Victoria Opera House was re-opened with a ball under the distinguished patronage of Lady Doris Vyner. The renovation and redecoration gave Ripon a better equipped hall than it had ever possessed. A *café chantant*, with an attractive programme of dances, music recitations, and sketches on one evening, and a whist drive on another, were all part of the re-opening celebrations.

1924-25. WILLIAM HEMSWORTH, Antique Dealer

Mayor 1922-23-24-25

November. The work of providing suitable memorials for marking the graves of soldiers and sailors who died in the War continued and the Imperial War Graves Commission erected 150 gravestones in Ripon Cemetery.

The Martinmas Fair was advertised for four days with the usual attractions, including some novel ones from Wembley, but nothing appeared on the Market Place and it was a very dull fair.

The new Ripon Musical Society, formed for the provision of high-class chamber, orchestral, and ballad concerts, gave a chamber concert by the well-known Edward Maude String Quartet in the Assembly Rooms.

December. The annual concert in aid of the Christmas parcels fund was held in the Coltsgate Hill schoolroom. The primary object of the fund was the visitation of the sick, lonely and poor, and each Christmas there was a distribution of parcels. A whist drive was held in aid of Mr Moss's fund for providing boots for poor school children. At the December meeting of the Board of Guardians, Mr Moss moved that the usual Christmas extra be given to those receiving out-relief — 4s 0d to adults and 2s 0d to children. The late Canon Waugh's gift of 1s 0d to each adult and 6d to each child in receipt of out-relief was also continued. The offer of a barrel of beer from Messrs Hepworth's brewery was accepted, but only after a good deal of argument.

January. The Council discussed sanitation and agreed to the substitution of dustbins for ashpits.

February. Dispensary and Cottage Hospital: 161 in-patients and 115 out-patients were treated in 1924; there had been six deaths and 165 operations were performed. There was a need for funds for modernisation and additional accommodation. Two girls, aged 11 and 13, were charged with stealing a hospital collection box containing £1 4s 11d from Calvert's paint shop in North Street. Fund-raising continued throughout the year with a Sunday demonstration in June in aid of plans for three wards for men, women and children with a connecting nurses' room.

The Ripon Branch of the National Farmers' Union unanimously passed a resolution urging that the gathering of plovers' eggs should be prohibited.

Pictures, including portraits by Hoppner, Lawrence and Romney, belonging to the late Marquess of Ripon, were sold in London. Queen Mary was so keenly interested that she paid a private visit to the collection. The first day's sale realised over £4,000.

March. The 1864 Horn, which was in regular use by the Hornblower, required repair to the mouthpiece and re-plating; when it was taken to Leeds by the Mayor for this purpose, the name of the maker 'Lundy, Leeds' was found incised on a small plate.

The Ripon Sunday School Union reported the numbers of scholars on its roll: Congregational (North Street) 52, Primitive Methodists (Allhallowgate) 125, Wesleyan Methodists (Coltsgate Hill) 149, Wesleyan Mission (Water Skellgate) 119, United Methodists (Blossomgate) 89, making a total of 534 with an average attendance of 401.

The death occurred of Thomas Richard Mountain, aged 92, coach and omnibus proprietor, and former Councillor and Alderman. His premises in Fishergate were taken over by the Westminster Bank, but his sign, a coach-and-four, carved in stone at the top of the corner pillar of the building, remained there until Woolworths remodelled the frontage in the 1960s.

April. Parts of the Market Square were relaid after complaints about the uneven surface and pools of water remaining after rain.

T. and R. Williamson Limited issued for public information correspondence with the Feoffes of Jepson's Hospital concerning an attempt to purchase a portion of the school garden which separated their properties. The Feoffes, though the hospital was in financial difficulties, refused to sell and the expanding firm reluctantly agreed to lease a strip of land along the river bank. The dispute is commemorated by the *Pons Asinorum* plaque, designed by Mr Crossley Eccles, on the wall of the walkway constructed on the side of the Skell.

May. Some students of the Training College reflected discreditably on the institution to which they belonged when they overstepped the bounds of good behaviour in their zeal to take photographs of the Duke and Duchess of York in Studley Park. The Duchess was a friend of Lady Doris Vyner.

The Mayor, Mayoress and Corporation attended a formal inauguration of the Council's housing scheme in Bondgate. A tender of £5,320 for 12 houses had been accepted and the Council had drawn up terms of tenancy and fixed rents of 5s 6d and 6s 3d for two-bedroomed houses and 8s 0d for three-bedroomed houses. In December there were 105 applications for these dwellings, and accusations of favouritism at the allocations were levelled at the Corporation.

August. John Burns of Bradford and George Jarmen of Manchester were each fined £2 for playing the three-card trick on the racecourse.

The public weighbridge at the end of North Street near the Old Market Place collapsed under the weight of a steam traction engine drawing fairground equipment.

September. The Corporation presented to the town of Ripon, Wisconsin, U.S.A., a pair of Spode plates, made in 1785 and bearing the crest of the City of Ripon, to symbolise the friendship existing between the two Ripons.

October. The Mayor had placed in his window a copy of a Council Meeting Agenda which included a grant to the Mayor as a subject for discussion. Councillor Spence referred to the courtesy of the Mayor in breaking through all previous custom to bring the matter of his expenses before the public. A motion to pay the Mayor was defeated.

Mr J. B. Firth retired after 40 years as organist and choirmaster at Holy Trinity Church. He was presented with a cheque for £101 12s 6d and an illuminated album.

An Allhallowgate man, summoned for setting snares in Sharow Hall grounds, was asked by the Chairman of the Bench if he were married and replied 'No, that's all the luck I had'.

1925-26. CHARLES HARKER, Printer and Bookseller

Born 1875, a member of an old Dales family. Came to Ripon and set up business as a printer in Westgate. In 1921 he took over the long-standing business of William Harrisons in the Market Square. Harrisons had printed the *Ripon Millenary Record* and Charles Harker carried on the tradition of the firm, publishing much local material and producing *The Wakeman*, a monthly miscellany about Ripon past and present, from 1947-58. He was a member of the Council from 1923-45. Housing was one of his chief interests and he was a founder member of the Ripon Housing Improvement Trust. A sportsman in his youth, he gave a silver cup to be competed for in the Tennis Tournament and was prominent in raising funds to purchase the Cricket Ground. He was a founder member of the Rotary Club and a churchwarden at the Cathedral, and served as a special constable in both World Wars. The Freedom of the City was conferred upon him in 1958. He died in 1965.

November. A bronze signet thumb-ring, dug up in the garden of the gasworks manager's house, was identified by the Mayor, Alderman Hemsworth, as the signet ring of Thomas Dowgill, Wakeman in 1592.

Poor housing conditions continued to concern the Council and Councillor T. F. Spence suggested a course of action: absentee landlords should have their responsibilities pointed out to them, local owners should be compelled to carry out repairs with a scheme of deferred payments arranged through the Council, owners of cottage property should give preference to the most needy cases and there should be an exhaustive enquiry into the means of providing cheap housing.

Alderman H. M. Thirlway was presented with a Victorian silver salver on completing 42 years on the City Council.

December. Tradesmen made a generous response to an appeal to provide a soup kitchen on Saturdays during the severe weather. At the opening the Mayor and Mayoress served 250 customers.

Parliamentary By-Election: Major J. W. Hills, Conservative 16,433 votes; Mr J. Murray, Liberal 11,422. The vacancy was caused by the appointment of the member for Ripon, the Hon. Edward Wood, Minister of Agriculture and Fisheries, as Viceroy of India. He took the title of Lord Irwin and later succeeded his father as Earl of Halifax.

January. The Midland Bank opened new and commodious premises at the corner of Westgate and High Skellgate.

A petition from the unemployed of the city was presented to a special meeting of the City Council. The occasion lent itself to a display of much oratory to little purpose, as nothing constructive was done.

In February two men were before the Bench for not paying maintenance to their families from their dole money.

The Faraday Medal was awarded to Colonel R. E. B. Crompton of *Azerley Chase* in recognition of his work as one of the pioneers of electrical engineering and the outstanding part he had played in the development of the electricity supply in this country.

February. Dr A. E. Burroughs, formerly Dean of Bristol, was enthroned as Bishop of Ripon.

A possible increase in the rates was blamed on the famous scheme for widening Quarry Moor Lane. 'The only satisfaction ratepayers can find is that it will probably have the effect of making some members of the Council stop to think before launching out into foolish schemes of unnecessary extravagance'.

March. The British Fascists held an 'Important Meeting and Smoking Concert' at the *Unicorn Hotel*. A meagre audience heard that the 'Red Idea' was to reduce the viability of Empire and then, when it had no heart to fight, swamp it and wipe it out.

April. After a 69-year-old man had died of starvation in the Poor Law Infirmary, £94 8s 0d was found in a bedroom at his cottage at Sawley.

Entirely due to the foresight of the Mayor, property in Queen Street and the cottages behind was bought for £2,400 to make provision for a car park. 'Visitors will be able to park with the smallest margin of inconvenience. Payment will come out of income and will be no charge upon the rates, a matter of no small importance'.

May. The effects of the General Strike were felt in Ripon. No trains ran, special bus services were organised and there was considerable traffic through the town including two armoured cars. Limits were set on the amount of coal which could be bought and flour mills were asked to conserve supplies. Special constables were enrolled and the May race meeting was cancelled. A Thanksgiving Service for the end of the General Strike was held on 20 May, but the coal strike continued for months, and in an early cold spell in October there was concern as householders were limited to one cwt. of coal per fortnight. Permits were required for coke for domestic and industrial purposes and display lighting was forbidden. The local press declared that 'Ripon as a loyal Conservative centre stood by the Government and the Conservative Association set up a committee composed entirely of working men to meet, discuss and report back to the Divisional Executive, refuting the claim that only the Labour Party represented working men, and declaring the strike to be a useless weapon'.

The tennis courts and surrounding walls of the Spa Park were completed: this improvement had certainly provided employment but some ratepayers questioned the expense. The Atco Company demonstrated one of their machines for the Council and Councillor Metcalfe asked whether they had a man who could work a motor mower if they purchased one.

June. The old Tithe Barn in the school playing field in Priest Lane was pulled down as the roof had fallen in and it was unsafe. The Tithe Barn, thought to be one of the last in the Diocese, had a door at each side so that farmers could enter, unload their tithes and proceed through. It had lately been used as a garage.

July. The Hospital extension, three wards and a nurses' room, was completed after great efforts to raise money and the new buildings were opened by Princess Mary.

September. The City Council was granted permission by the Ministry of Health to borrow £19,500 for the purchase of 987 acres of land at Ripon Parks and Ure Bank, and £3,000 for buildings thereon, for the purpose of establishing a training ground for Territorial Forces.

The Council received a report from a consulting engineer on the feasibility of providing an electricity supply for Ripon and District. The matter had first come before the Council in 1896, and in November 1927 the application by the Corporations of Harrogate and Ripon to supply electricity to the Ripon area was at last approved by the Electricity Commissioners.

The Council decided by nine votes to six that the City should be divided into four wards: up till then councillors had been elected to represent the whole City.

October. An old glass seal bearing the initials 'N' and 'WK' and dated '1671' was found by a workman riddling gravel at Robinson's Quarry in Dallamires Lane. Alderman Hemsworth identified it as the seal of William Kirkby, Mayor of Ripon in 1674-5, and his wife Norah. The seal was placed in the *Wakeman's House*.

Mr C. H. Moody gave an opening recital on the Cathedral organ which had been extensively restored at a cost of £1,500 raised by public subscription. The attendance was disappointing and it was suggested that the popularity of jazz might be killing finer tastes. During this rebuilding the wing cases of the organ had been removed from above the screen and their pipes re-sited behind the choir stalls.

1926-27. CHARLES HARKER, Printer and Bookseller

Mayor 1925-26-27

December. Jepson's Hospital had been in financial difficulties for some time, and the Board of Education made a scheme under which the charity was absorbed into the Grammar School Charities and the boys transferred there. The end of the 'Bluecoat School' was sad news, and there were protests about the loss to citizens and accusations of collusion in high places.

Councillor Eden proposed that the Council should build a swimming bath, but met with strong opposition. Councillor Spence had never known such 'a period of mad spending' by Ripon Corporation.

Christmas prices in the market: chickens 5s 6d, 'good looking' hens 3s 9d to 4s 6d, geese 1s 0d per pound, rabbits 2s 3d to 2s 6d.

Report of the Medical Officer of Health for 1926: death rate 11.90 per 1,000; infant mortality rate 21.12 per 1,000 births. There had been an epidemic of scarlet fever though the disease was of a mild type,

and 74 houses in the town were declared to be unfit for human habitation.

January. *West Mount* in Kirkby Road was purchased to replace the premises of the Ripon Home for Girls in Bondgate. The Home was intended to train girls for domestic service, and the Dean commented that the domestic comforts of residents in Ripon had been greatly promoted by the efficient help they had received from girls trained by the Home.

Plans were received for the proposed widening of the Ripon-Harrogate road between Borrage Bridge and the Harrogate Gas Works. This was to include a by-pass for Ripley. In March 1928, the City Council approved the scheme as they were responsible for the cost of only a furlong of the length of road to be improved.

Interviews were held to give details of the assisted emigration schemes of particular interest to the unemployed: for £2 a passage to Canada was available with guaranteed employment for farm and domestic workers. A Canadian representative came again in November to offer assisted passages, help with family settlement and to stress the opportunities for farmers with capital of £200 to £500. Prospective emigrants were interviewed.

February. The finances of the Hospital continued to cause concern, and Dr Husband proposed that all householders whose income did not exceed £5 per week should contribute a small regular sum and receive free treatment in return.

March. The Ripon Board of Guardians adopted a resolution 'That this Board is very concerned and distressed to find so many male applicants for relief who have fought and been maimed and disabled in the Great War, and the country, after all the promises made on its behalf, has failed to stand by them and prevent their becoming chargeable to the Poor Law'. The Board struggled with a big increase in vagrants for which adequate accommodation was not available. In July the number rose to 419, almost double the total for 1926.

April. The Ripon Fire Brigade demonstrated the new Davy Automatic Fire Engine at the Market Cross, the *Unicorn Hotel* and the Town Hall. The spectacle was enjoyed but there was some disappointment that the City dignitaries did not themselves make any practical test of the apparatus.

May. Two records were made in summary justice: at their normal sitting the magistrates of the City Police Court dealt with 19 cases in 42 minutes, and on the two days of the May race meeting 'so well did the police do their duty that it was not necessary for the court to sit'.

June. The Mechanics' Institute, that venerable institution which had done such good service to the City for many years, quietly faded away. Its building in Finkle Street is now the Post Office. The 1880 school buildings of Jepson's Hospital, which had been purchased by T. and R. Williamson Limited, were resold to the Ripon Citizen's Social Club. The club arose from the demise of the

Mechanics Institute and became the Ripon City Club at the end of the year.

August. Alderman Hemsworth complained of bias in the press reports of City Council meetings; proceedings were either suppressed or so altered as to convey a wrong impression in the interests of a favoured few.

Extremely high flood water in the Skell swept away the Rustic Bridge and caused flooding in Firs Avenue. T. and R. Williamson Limited fixed bronze tablets on the river wall of their office bearing the words 'Flood Level August 8th 1927'. The summer weather was disastrous. The Executive of the N.F.U. meeting in Ripon in June bemoaned the bad condition of Yorkshire agriculture. The Ure and Skell were in flood in early July; it was still raining in September when the Bishop wrote 'The weather has been, and still is as I write, a national tragedy in the fullest sense of the word. One is not surprised to hear of murmuring against God's Providence'. In the middle of the months crops stood in the fields still ungathered.

September. There was good cheer at the *Golden Lion* where Mr L. Beaumont urged 'Give us a call' to sample his Best Mild and Finest Bitter at 6d per pint and Best Old Beer at 8d.

A pavilion removed from the back of the former Mechanics' Institute to the Highways Yard was erected in the Spa Gardens as the cheapest way of providing shelter there.

October. The Rotary Club of Ripon received its Charter. The Club was sponsored by the Rotary Club of Leeds and had been inaugurated in May. The first President was Dr C. H. Greenwood and the luncheon meetings took place at the Lawrence Café owned by Mr J. Grice, a founder member, now the offices of the Halifax Building Society.

The Royal Repertory Company opened for a six-month season at the Opera House which after a most propitious opening in 1924 had been closed for some time.

1927-28. THOMAS FOWLER SPENCE, Varnish Manufacturer

Born 1878, the son of Frederick Spence of Messrs Wells and Sons. He joined T. and R. Williamson Limited on leaving the Grammar School and was for some years their sales representative in Lancashire. Returned to Ripon in 1910 and was elected to the Council in 1914. He had been secretary of the Ripon Harriers and Swimming Clubs and for many years was secretary of the Golf Club which owed much to his enthusiasm. Managing Director of T. and R. Williamson Limited in 1918, he became Chairman in 1921 (the fine office block facing Borrage Bridge was completed in 1926) and he was President of the National Association of Paint, Colour and Varnish Manufacturers in 1932. He was a Liberal and was a member of the National Liberal Club, but did not let this enter local politics. He was elected to the West Riding County Council, was one of the founders of the Housing Improvement Trust, was chairman of the Governors of the Grammar School and held many other offices. In 1945 he bought Quarry Moor and presented it to the city 'to be kept for Ripon children for all time'. He died at his home, *Redhills*, Palace Road, in 1949.

November. Holy Trinity Church celebrated its centenary with a parochial gathering and the publication of a commemorative booklet. The Mayor and Corporation attended the commemoration service.

The families from the cottages in Yorkshire Hussar Yard, demolished as an entry to the car park, had been found better accommodation, but 150 houses in Ripon, 30 of which had been condemned for many years, were scheduled as unfit for human habitation.

December. Progress in sanitation was made; the City Council agreed to bear the cost of £1,220 for converting to a water-carriage system 122 pail closets and half the cost of £1,400 to replace privy middens.

The Tallow Factory in Fishergate was demolished. The building, in poor repair, was purchased by Mr W. Gibson when the late Marquess of Ripon's property was sold. It was built in 1807 and an extensive trade in tallow candles for household use was established by Mr Vant and carried on by Mr B. P. Ascomb who was four times Mayor of Ripon. The fitments, including a jenny for spinning wicks, were placed in the *Wakeman's House*.

A boy convicted of stealing toys and causing damage in North Road was sentenced to three strokes of the birch, his accomplices were put on probation and their parents ordered to pay costs of 7s 6d and 3s 9d.

January. A Women's Institute, first mooted in 1924, was inaugurated in Ripon. It was one of the first Institutes in the district and it was hoped that it would encourage the movement in the neighbouring villages. One of the Institute's first moves was to voice the public demand for a swimming bath in Ripon. The Corporation, already handicapped with other schemes, thought a bath would be a luxury as the river had a continual supply of fresh water which could be enjoyed in the open air; however, 'if the ladies could find means of raising the money . . .'.

February. After several attempts to establish a proper library in the city, W.R.C.C. placed a collection of books in the Town Hall and Miss Ingram was appointed as Hon. Librarian.

March. Several members were gravely concerned at the wisdom, siting and cost of the Corporation's housing schemes — 'there always will be slums'. By a majority of one it was decided to proceed with the building of 38 houses on the Aismunderby site, a decision which later induced nostalgia in the press — 'it was a glorious meadow bordering on an English country lane . . . now, with Bondgate Back lane gone forever and transformed into Southgate, who can claim that the old city never changes?'.

Mr E. Brady, 26 Market Place, a wireless enthusiast, established communication with an amateur in Australia. In August, a Ripon man was summoned for having an apparatus without a licence; the Bench imposed a small fine of 5s in the hope that this first case might be a warning to others. A public subscription to provide wireless in the Cottage Hospital raised the money in less than a month.

April. The new parking ground proved its worth with many motor cars and charabancs using it instead of the square. The high road through the town was 'of a tortuous nature and very awkward to negotiate' and some of the city authorities proposed a new road through on the eastern side.

June. The Council accepted the tender of the Power Lines Construction Company to lay electricity distribution cables for £10,210. Earlier in the year the Cleveland and Durham Electric Power Company sought permission to supply electricity to Ripon and District, but this was opposed by the Ripon and Harrogate Councils, as Ripon was committed to taking electricity from Harrogate. In November the Council confirmed its Electricity Committee's proposal to connect small houses for £2 18s 11d and larger houses for £5 14s9d plus meter fixing and rental. Councillor Grice rightly predicted the exit of the small consumer; there was a general outcry against the cost and requests that installation should be free. The Electricity Committee agreed to this, but the Council ruled them out of order though it was later agreed that connections up to 33 ft. should be free of charge. The cable laying was almost completed by the end of the year.

July. Mr Clare Vyner decided to sell the Cricket Field giving the club the first option at £1,200, the decision to be made by the end of the month. A speedily organised appeal raised £900 and the sale was completed, the Cricket Club taking out a mortgage for £400.

Father Levick was severely criticised by fellow members of the Board of Guardians for saying that the casual wards at the Workhouse were 'an illustration of the treatment meted out by justice as compared with that of charity'. The Guardians had come under criticism for refusing a request by the Vagrancy Committee that casuals should be admitted to Sunday services in the company of other inmates of the Workhouse.

The water cart made its appearance to the great relief of people harassed by dust in many parts of the town. Needless to say, rain fell within a short time of the cart having completed its rounds.

August. In a letter to the press Alderman Lavin accused the Corporation of irregularities in the acceptance of tenders. The Council was invited by the Ministry of Health to comment on the allegations. Argument continued about the placing of electricity contracts and it was decided to hold an inquiry before replying to the Ministry.

October. Debates in the Council Chamber remained acrimonious and Alderman Spence initially refused to stand as Mayor for a second term because 'It becomes increasingly evident that the conduct of the City's business . . . is seriously hampered by the undercurrent of personal antagonism which persists year after year'. Alderman Spence ultimately accepted office.

1928-29. THOMAS FOWLER SPENCE, Varnish Manufacturer

Mayor 1927-28-29

November. In the municipal elections Miss Gertrude Wells of Blossomgate was elected as the first woman member of the Corporation.

December. The Town Clerk sought finance: 'Why go elsewhere? Invest your spare cash in your own city. A fair rate of interest, £25 and upwards received at any time. Mortgage deeds prepared free. J. Henry Gough, Town Clerk'.

Food prices in the town were estimated to be 65 per cent above 1914 levels: beef 1s 5d lb., mutton 1s 7d lb., bacon 1s 3¾d lb., bread 9¼d lb., flour 1s 4d lb., potatoes 10½d 14 lbs., butter 1s 10¼d lb., milk 5½d qt., eggs 1½d each.

January. The Ripon Board of Guardians received a request from Harrogate Infirmary for increased support from Ripon where only 10 subscribers contributed seventeen pounds. It was suggested that a charge of three guineas per week for in-patients and 1s 6d for out-patients' visits might have to be made. The Guardians maintained their own subscription of three guineas, but commented that most local people preferred to support the recently extended Ripon Cottage Hospital.

February. Ninety miners, a contingent in a party of 1,000 unemployed men marching to London, who should have stayed in the Workhouse at Thirsk, found it impossible to conform to the rules there and appealed to the Mayor of Ripon for help. He agreed to receive them and found willing supporters in the Constitutional Club, and with the assistance of many helpers the marchers were given a few hours' comfortable rest. A similar situation arose in April 1930 when a party of unemployed from Tyneside arrived in Ripon en route for London carrying a banner and collecting boxes for funds to help them on their way. They had had a long march as the only accommodation available to them in Thirsk was at the Workhouse which would have meant detention and treatment as 'casuals'. They were given shelter at the Y.M.C.A. and provided with supper and breakfast.

March. At a meeting between the Corporation and the Directors of the Victoria Opera House the Council was offered the first option of buying the building. It was said it would be a disaster if the City's only large public hall were to be used for other purposes; however the Corporation did not respond and in July the Wellington Film Company took a 20-year lease and the Opera House opened as a cinema in the autumn.

The City Council set a rate of 3s 5d (the County Rate was 5s 7d) and economised by reducing their staff by four. The foreman was offered a post as storekeeper and horse-feeder at a reduced wage of £2 per week; a younger man with a knowledge of road construction and repair was advertised for at a wage of £3 10s per week.

May. Councillor Briscombe reported that a footpath at Hellwath had been obstructed by a fence and asked the Council to take action — 'those with whom this walk is a favourite will be indebted to the Corporation for making their way easier'.

A joint Gas and Electricity showroom was opened at 2 North Street after work on the premises had been completed at a cost of £650.

Miss Bessie Hardisty of Low Skellgate, who had been successful in several other competitions, was one of seven finalists in the *Sunday News* Beauty Queen contest. She received a prize of £25.

A party of Kensitite preachers visited Ripon and conducted a vigorous open-air campaign. Nightly addresses in the Market Place were designed to refute from the Protestant viewpoint doctrines which had been put forward by a recent Roman Catholic mission.

The Archdeacon of Richmond, the Ven. A. H. Watson, advocated emigration by young people as a cure for unemployment. He said it was not banishment but pioneer work. They must be sent out with the conviction that they were not only English men and women but Christian men and women, each one being just as much a missionary as any clergyman who entered the mission field.

The members of the Ripon Divisional Labour Party closed their meeting by listening to Mr Philip Snowden, Chancellor of the Exchequer, broadcasting from Station 2LO. They held a Saturday evening May Day Demonstration on the Market Place.

The Northern Counties Otter Hounds held their first meet in Ripon. In September they met again at the North Bridge and hunted upstream.

Sir Alan Cobham visited the racecourse with his aeroplane *Youth of Britain*. A large crowd gathered, and he was continuously employed in taking passengers over and around the city. The Mayor and other dignitaries were invited to 'fly with him over the area they control', and Sir Alan was particularly considerate to school children, far exceeding the number of free flights which had been arranged.

June. The L.N.E.R. *Walk and Ride* tickets were advertised as a summer attraction; 26 routes were available from Ripon, for instance by rail to Arthington, walk 8.5 miles to Collingham Bridge and return to Ripon by train for 2s 9d. Meanwhile Ripon householders were informed that thousands of Londoners wanted holiday apartments — 'for 2s 0d you can let your rooms advertising in the special holiday columns of nine London newspapers'.

In the Parliamentary Election Major J. W. Hills, Conservative (23,173 votes) increased his majority over Captain F. Boult, Liberal (14,542) and Mr A. Godfrey, Socialist (4,339). Major Hills was made a Privy Councillor in the Birthday Honours List and the Cathedral bells were rung in celebration.

A boy of 10, summoned for stealing, was placed on probation for 12 months and ordered to receive six strokes of the birch rod. His companion, a year older, was committed to an industrial school in Birmingham until he was 16.

Complaints of traffic congestion revived old disputes about the provision of new roads and alternative routes. Blockages were said to be almost a daily occurrence in Kirkgate — 'future generations will find it difficult to understand why this narrow twisting road was so long kept as the main road into the Market Place'.

The St John's Ambulance Brigade acquired a motor ambulance which quickly justified its introduction, although there were objections to so large an outlay of money. The Council offered to contribute towards the upkeep of the vehicle and two councillors were appointed as City representatives on the Committee.

The Bishop, Dr E. A. Burroughs, held a service for cyclists and welcomed them in his palace grounds. For some years these annual services, which attracted great numbers of cyclists, were notable events. On this occasion Mr A. W. Hemsworth was in charge of marshalling and stewarding; 'informal dress is to be regarded as the most suitable wear but any kit will do'. A story was told that the Dean, Dr C. Mansfield Owen, seeing the Bishop amid the scantily-clad throng outside the Cathedral, said 'I'm glad to see that you at least are properly dressed'. 'Only the outward man I fear, Mr Dean', replied Dr Burroughs, lifting his purple cassock to reveal a pair of shorts.

August. The public electricity supply was switched on by the Mayoress and the taunts of those who had criticised the long delay fell a little flat. The event was celebrated by a dinner for the Corporation and guests at the *Spa Hotel* where the menu included 'Beans à la Molyneux' in tribute to the City Engineer, and 'Crompton Tarts with Transformer Cream'.

Ripon traders expressed their alarm at the amount of shopping now done out of Ripon. It was approaching the dimensions of a scandal — 'so long as there are shopping centres within easy ride by bus or train the feminine mind will yield to the temptation of a day out'. The problem was how to bring home to the keepers of the purse the unfairness and injustice of this.

October. The Council passed a well-merited vote of appreciation to the City Gardener for the beautifully-kept public gardens and the fine display of flowers he had maintained throughout the year. They were concerned at the amount of vandalism: Corporation property in the Spa Gardens had suffered much damage and the aid of the police was sought. Blame was placed on the lack of proper discipline and parental control.

The Council's housing schemes proceeded and names were chosen for the extensions on the Aismunderby Estate: Curfew Road and Wakeman Road.

The on-going problem of the Mayor's expenses was settled when a resolution proposed by Alderman Spence that the Mayor should receive an allowance of £125 per annum was carried by six votes to four; Alderman Hemsworth protested that there was no need for the Mayor to spend more than £10 per year. In December the Council decided that the mace should be placed on the table and the mayoral chain worn at the ordinary monthly meeting of the Corporation: the custom had been allowed to lapse for two years.

October. The ruins of St Anne's Chapel in Agnesgate were scheduled for protection as a historic building by the Commissioners of Works.

The fountain erected at the junction of North Road and Magdalen Road by John Fevers in 1875 was moved to the Spa Park. The Spa Committee complained that it was no longer fulfilling the donor's intended purpose of providing refreshment for man and beast.

A peal of 'Stedman Caters', 5,079 changes taking 3 hrs 35 mins, was rung with the Cathedral bells half-muffled in recognition of the day of mourning for the victims of the R101 airship disaster.

1929-30. SIDNEY GEORGE MOSS, Grocer and Provision Merchant

The son of W. B. Moss of Hitchin; educated at Kent College, Canterbury. Came to Ripon in 1899 as manager of the Ripon Branch of W. B. Moss and Sons Limited. The shop stood in Queen Street at the entrance to Moss's Arcade which ran alongside the road to the Bus Station, and there were other branches in the town. The business, of which he was principal, was sold in 1961. He accepted the mayoralty in his first year on the City Council: he did not otherwise seek public office except in his work for Methodism. He was organist and choir-

master at the Central Methodist Church, Circuit Steward and a Lay-Preacher. He lived at *North Lodge* and died in 1968.

December. The death occurred of Mr Francis Blackburn, the last family member of the firm of Croft and Blackburn, which traced its establishment back to 1742. He had joined the late Mr Samuel Croft in the coachbuilding business, which was completely reconstructed with the advent of the motor car.

Ripon Farmers' Union joined protests from the North Riding at the shilling per week increase in land-workers' pay. They maintained that produce prices could not stand it and 'the earning capacity of any worker must depend on the extent to which his work is capable of being sold in the market'.

The Zion United Methodist Chapel in Blossomgate re-opened after repairs and decorations as the first church in the town with electric light. Santa's Grotto at D. G. Brown's store in Kirkgate was more elaborate than usual and for the first time featured a 'highly coloured electrified Christmas Tree and Fairy Glen'.

Rainfall in 1929 was 25.37 ins., as recorded by Mr T. F. Adamson at *High Berrys*; 26.30 ins. as recorded by Mr F. D. Wise at *Red House*.

January. A collection to relieve distress in the coalfields raised £106 17s 4d.

A decision by the City Council to spend £17,000 on house building at Aismunderby met with some opposition. It was contended that many occupants of council dwellings were well able to provide for themselves and the houses from which some had been moved were not undesirable. According to the press the poor ratepayer was reaching the limit of endurance. At that time Mr J. Atkinson was advertising south-facing semi-detached three-bedroom houses in Whitcliffe Lane at a price of £550.

Mr L. A. Fraser, formerly of Bondgate, who had emigrated with his family to Canada, reported that he was doing well. He was earning £5 per week on a hay-pressing outfit and had a cottage with an acre of land and a stable for one dollar a week. He wrote 'There are knocks for everybody and those willing to stand them will succeed'.

There were eight Hemsworths at the Ripon Motor Club's annual dinner. Mr and Mrs W. Hemsworth had entered the competition for Moss's Cup; despite a breakdown at Skipton they arrived at Keswick dead on time and sent a telegram to say so. It was delivered at Ripon 'Arrived Keswick dead'.

At an exhibition mounted in London by the Midland Bank, deeds, notes and a pair of pistols which had belonged in the 18th century to the Ripon bank of Farrer, Williamson and Company, were on display. The pistols were said to have been carried by bank officials transferring specie between York and Ripon.

February. 'Talking pictures' came to Ripon. Members of the Corporation were invited to attend the first showing of *The Broadway Melody* at the Opera House. To the embarrassment of the management and the annoyance of a full house, the electricity supply failed. On the next day the Council sent a deputation to Harrogate to demand an explanation and were informed that there had been a breakdown just outside Ripley. The Palladium was closed for redecoration and the installation of Western Electric Talking Apparatus. It re-opened in March with *Fox Movietone Follies* and admission prices of 1s 3d, 9d and 6d.

X-ray apparatus was installed at Ripon Hospital: hitherto patients had had to travel to Harrogate for examination. The full cost had not been met but there was confidence that the sympathetic generosity of the public would supply the funds for this sheer necessity.

The L.N.E.R. advertised spring excursions from Ripon: to Darlington for 3s 0d, Harrogate 1s 6d, Leeds 2s 6d and London, Kings Cross (return the same day) 16s 6d.

Mr Leavens King was appointed headmaster of the Cathedral Boys School in succession to Mr J. W. Caruth, who retired after 46 years in teaching.

Twenty-four palliasses and pillows and a hot bath were provided for casuals passing through Ripon Workhouse. 'Tramps in clover — soft slumber and a hot bath' said the *Gazette*. Two vegetables were ordered to be served to the inmates when these items were on the dietary.

March. The County Library service housed in the Town Hall now had 700 borrowers and urgently needed more spacious accommodation. The Council recorded its appreciation of the work done by the Honorary Librarian, Miss Ingram, and her colleagues.

The Council budgeted for a 6s 8d rate, a drop of 1s 2d in four years, and sought economies. Despite recriminations, an Albion lorry for the Gas Committee was purchased from a non-Ripon source for £370, whereas the local price was £410. A suggestion that the Surveyor's office should be lighted by electricity raised immediate alarm as 'the thin edge of the wedge'. In the end the rate had to be increased to 7s 2d.

Ingram's Place, a court of 10 houses at the bottom of Stonebridgegate, was acquired by the Ripon Housing Improvement Trust for alteration and reconditioning. The Trust had been formed as a Public Utility Society with the object of improving the standard of working class housing and keeping rents at an economic level. It was claimed that with Corporation assistance the Trust's scheme could be operated at not more than a halfpenny rate and the aim was to let dwellings at 5s 6d per week. Thirteen per cent of Ripon's housing was below standard.

Alderman T. F. Spence chaired a meeting of the League of Nations Association in the Town Hall, where the speaker was Mr A. Duff Cooper.

An outbreak of scarlet fever which had started in February continued for several weeks, and at one time there were 13 patients in the fever hospital in Princess Road.

The Ripon Board of Guardians met for the last time; its duties passed to the County Council and a Public Assistance Committee was established. It was feared that the passing of the Board would reduce the incentive to local public service in the future.

April. Chapman's Travelling Zoo paid a one-day visit to the Market Place and gave three performances. There were lions, bears, a leopard, a puma and a llama, and two monkeys which caused endless amusement. The kindly treatment meted out to the animals was commented on.

Mrs Tom Williamson presented to the city the land on the bank of the Skell between Borrage Bridge and Borrage Green Lane. It was given with the object of 'preserving for the citizens a tree-shaded oasis in an old city that has lost so much of its sylvan beauty in recent years'.

May. Reluctantly, but acknowledging that they had very little option since electricity had now become a necessity of modern life, the Council sought to borrow £2,000 to fund assisted schemes for electric wiring and £1,000 for showroom appliances.

June. The Unemployment Grants Committee approved expenditure of £25,000 for the extension of the catchwater supply at Leighton Reservoir. Initially it was intended that all jobs should be recruited from the unemployed in Ripon, but later it was decided to give work to men living nearer the site. The work involved a 47-hour week at 1s 0d per hour, transport from Ripon at 7s 6d weekly and the cost of the National Insurance stamp 1s 4d, leaving 38s 2d net per week.

The Ripon Agricultural and Canine Show attracted 1,293 entries including: 27 farm horses, 27 'hunters', 16 'leapers' and 446 dogs.

The bases of two large circular columns were discovered when the paving was removed beneath the central tower of the Cathedral. They were considered to be remains of a Norman or pre-Conquest church. One of these circular blocks was removed and was for many years in the Consistory Court in the north aisle of the nave: it now serves as an altar stone in the Chapel of the Resurrection in the undercroft.

July. The annual tradesmen's holiday took the form of an excursion to Liverpool and more than 300 people travelled for the day out on a special train. Later in the month the Bishop's car was found in Liverpool: it had been stolen from outside Ripon Cathedral by two young army absentees.

September. Miss Eva Lett succeeded Canon I. A. Smith when the latter retired after 22 years as Principal of Ripon Training College.

The County Council published recommendations for the future structure of education in Ripon and the surrounding villages. All children should be provided with secondary education in Ripon itself, either at the Grammar School or the High School for Girls, or at a new Senior School to be built for 720 pupils aged 11 to 14. The Coltsgate Hill School was to be closed and village children were to be brought into Ripon by bus or provided with bicycles.

1930-31. JOHN PROUDFOOT, Station Master

Born at Eastgate in County Durham, he started work for the North Eastern Railway Company when he was 14. He was appointed as Station Master at Haverton Hill in 1918 and served on the parish and rural district councils there. Transferred to Ripon in 1925, he was on the Sharow Church Council and Superintendent of the St John Ambulance Brigade. He was appointed Station Master at Malton in 1940 and at the time of his death in 1950 was Chairman of the Norton Urban District Council and a governor of the Grammar School. He was a Freemason and a Rotarian.

December Unemployment in Ripon reached its highest figure for four years with a total of 484 men out of work.

January. The Ripon to Masham railway line was closed. Mr E. Bland of Princess Road, who had seen the first train arrive 55 years before, was there to see the last.

The Council applied to the Unemployment Grants Committee for funds to provide work for the unemployed, and schemes to improve Borrage Meadow and widen Quarry Moor Lane were authorised. Rent-free allotments were made available in Kirkby Road.

At a Rotary Club dance held to raise funds, Sir William Aykroyd spoke of the aims of the Ripon Housing Trust Limited. To clear Ripon of slums would require the demolition of 50 dwellings and the improvement of a further one hundred and fifty. Some houses had already been reconditioned and the Trust hoped to provide dwellings for tenants from condemned housing; £8,000 to £10,000 would be required.

Dr C. H. Moody's Amateur Operatic Company, rehearsing for *Merrie England*, applied to the court for permission to use the balcony at the Opera House. This was refused and future productions were thought to be unlikely.

February. Alderman Briscombe reported a poisonous gas scare in St Marygate. The occupants of one house had to go to the Pictures because the fumes were so bad and he himself had hardly dared to go in. The only benefit he could see would be for the Gas Committee to take out a patent so that they could supply the best poison gas in the next war. (There had been a breakdown in one of the retorts.)

The Council approved payment of an extra 2s per case to the workman who fumigated houses where infectious diseases had occurred — 'the work was not of the nicest nature'.

March. Demolition prior to the rebuilding of the Yorkshire Penny Bank in the Market Place uncovered timber framing and wattle-and-daub infill from a building contemporary with the *Wakeman's House*.

April. After long discussion, the W.R.C.C. decided because of the prevailing economic situation not to proceed with a proposed relief road from Harrogate Road, down Quarry Moor Lane and Bondgate, up Bedern Bank and through the parking ground.

May. The date '1765' in large iron figures was revealed on the gable end of the former *Blue Bird Café* at the top of Kirkgate when the building was removed to make way for the new Westminster Bank.

June. The *Ripon Observer* was purchased from Mrs M. E. Marks by Messrs R. Ackrill Ltd., and incorporated in the *Ripon Gazette*. After supporting two local papers since 1885, Ripon now saw the first issue of the *Ripon Gazette and Observer*.

Gas lighting in the Cathedral was replaced by electricity with floodlights at clerestory level. The change over made possible the removal of much unsightly piping which had been installed as a temporary measure during the war.

Sixteen cars were burnt out in a very severe blaze at Glover's Borrage Bridge Garage. Exploding oxy-acetylene cylinders increased the damage, the whole roof collapsed and the rear part of the premises was completely gutted.

Corporation employees were alleged to have abused their privilege of taking time off for funerals and the Council decided to allow only four hours' paid leave, and this solely in respect of the burial of the employee's wife or child, or of one of his permanent fellow workmen in the department.

It was reported to the Health and Sanitation Committee that only seven ashpits remained in the city; over the last 10 years, 833 ashpits and middens had been done away with.

The Aismunderby Estate was nearing completion and when finished 234 houses would accommodate

1,200 people. There was little evidence of over-crowding and it appeared that the majority of families in very poor housing could not afford a rent of 8s 0d per week. However, 160 houses still had no internal water supply.

July. Registered workshops in Ripon totalled 88: 14 Bakehouses, seven Boot and Shoe repairers, one Basket Maker, 10 Cabinet makers and Joiners, four Dressmakers, three Laundries, six Milliners, eight Motor repairers, one Monumental Mason, six Printers, seven Plumbers, three Smiths, seven Tailors, one Engineer, one Wheelwright and four Outworkers.

August. It was decided to celebrate the Faraday Centenary by an Electrical Week. The Cathedral, Town Hall, Market Cross, *Wakeman's House* and *Thorpe Prebend Museum* were floodlit and the Spa Gardens illuminated with fairy lights.

The L.N.E.R. closed the canal for repairs after an accident at Ox Close Lock when a lock gate burst and only superhuman efforts prevented a yacht and a motor cruiser from being swept in. The owner of one of the boats wrote to the press saying he and many others would use the canal basin if the weeds which clogged the waterway were cleared. A Motor Boat Club was formed in the hope of obtaining permission to use wharf and storage facilities from the Railway Company.

October. Parliamentary election: Major J. W. Hills (National Conserative) had a majority of 32,773 over his Socialist opponent, Mr R. J. Hall, who forfeited his deposit.

A meeting was held in the Town Hall to promote a 'Save the Pound League'. The objective, as outlined by Miss Addy, was to organise in one supreme national effort the many sporadic movements that had been made to relieve the National Debt.

1931-32. JOHN PROUDFOOT, Station Master

Mayor 1930-31-32

The Population Statistics for 1931 were: birth rate 15.6 per 1,000; death rate 14.47 per 1,000; infant mortality 60 per 1,000.

Rainfall for 1931: at *Red House*, the gauge registered 39.05 ins.; the wettest month was September (4.79 ins.), the driest March (1.16 ins.).

December. A special meeting of the City Council was called to resolve the conflicting opinions on the financial difficulties of extending the electricity supply to the surrounding villages. It was decided to apply for a loan to supply power to Sawley, Grantley, Galphay, Winksley, Kirkby Malzeard, Grewelthorpe, Azerley, Wath, Melmerby and Skelton-on-Ure.

January. The first meeting of the Ripon Week of Prayer was held at the Town Hall. The Mayor presided at the event, organised by the World Evangelical Alliance, to follow the National Day of Prayer.

Miss Marion E. White of *Highfield* bequeathed £1,000 to Ripon Cottage Hospital and £5,000 to the Cathedral.

Canon Levick was presented with a cope to mark his 25 years of service as priest-in-charge of St Wilfrid's Roman Catholic Church. The ceremony took place at the Lawrence Restaurant.

Councillor G. H. Newton, Mayor 1920-21, resigned after long service from the City Council on leaving the district.

February. The decline of Ripon's Market threatened to affect the prosperity of the city. Market tolls fell from £781 7s 3d in 1928 to £569 2s 6d in 1931. The loss in revenue to the city was variously attributed to national depression in trade, the development of motor transport, restricted space on the Market Square, and lack of covered accommodation there. The suggestion that high tolls might be responsible met with some resistance.

The Chamber of Trade at its annual meeting on 14 February discussed the serious position of the market. One view was that the decline was related to the general economic depression in the country. Others held that the city was gaining in custom attracting more trade from outside the city but this growth was spread throughout the week. Profits from motor-car parking went to the Corporation, whereas that from horses and traps had gone to local hotels. Approval was given to the Corporation's proposed experiment to set up one portable shelter towards the end of March.

The Ripon Agricultural Association was wound up because of lack of support: only 16 members attended the A.G.M. on 4 February. This meant the loss to Ripon of the annual agricultural show, but the money from the sale of the association's assets was left in the care of trustees to benefit any future similar society.

The Ripon Amateur Operatic Society presented *Les Cloches de Corneville* at the Victoria Opera House.

England's lady billiards champion, Miss Joyce Gardiner of Gloucester, visited the Constitutional Club in Ripon when she played matches with the members. A collection was taken for the Cottage Hospital.

A young soldier stole a car from the Market Place on Saturday night, 20 February, and was sentenced to hard labour (other similar offences were reported at Harrogate and Leeds). The car was found at Catterick and the offender had slept in it.

March. A fire at the Yorkshire Varnish Works gutted the boiler house but valuable stock in the adjoining rooms was saved. The fire was put out within an hour with the help of the Ripon Fire Brigade.

The City Council criticised the electricity committee chairman (Councillor Hargrave) for failing to consult his committee members about the high price he had agreed to pay farmers to grant wayleaves for the erection of electricity poles in the Ripon/Galphay area. The criticism was rejected by a majority and the minutes confirmed.

A Ripon branch of the new political party, the Agricultural Party, was formed at a meeting held in the *Unicorn Hotel*. Mr C. V. Redwood, chief organiser of the party, addressed the meeting.

The recently formed West of Yore Hunt met in Ripon Market Place, the first meet there for 10 years. A collection was made for the Cottage Hospital.

April. About 50 members attended a course in English Church Music at the *Spa Hotel*, held by the School of English Church Music and the Church Music Society.

Works of two local artists were accepted by the Royal Academy for inclusion in the annual summer exhibition: one, *St Agnesgate from the Cathedral*, by a Riponian, an old boy of the Grammar School, Mr J. H. Harwood, and the other a study, *The Painter's Mother*, by Miss Mary Ethel Hunter.

The rates fell by 1s in the £ for a full year, but the City Council passed on only part of this when it reduced its rate by 4d in the £ for a half year.

May. Improvements noted in the racecourse were a new wooden stand and a new car park on the Boroughbridge side of the course.

June. Resentment was expressed in the City Council over what was termed the County's interference in urging action over housing in Ripon as a result of the Medical Officer of Health's report.

A *Gazette* editorial and the Chamber of Trade criticised the City Council for letting the Market Place too frequently for amusement fairs. It was felt that this should be restricted to the period of St Wilfrid's Feast.

Wireless was installed in the Poor Law Institution with a formal ceremony by the Mayor and Mayoress on 7 June.

Tenders were accepted for extending electricity supplies to the areas of Wath, Melmerby and Skelton-on-Ure at the special meeting of the City Council.

To celebrate a national aviation day at Ripon on 22 June, Sir Alan Cobham brought aerobatic displays, parachute descents, and so on, to the Ripon racecourse. He urged the Mayor to improve the racecourse for an aerodrome.

July. The Cathedral belfry needed to be reconstructed and the bells recast. Miss J. White of Highfield offered to cover the whole cost as a memorial to her parents, brothers and sisters. On 5 July a temporary bell arrived at the Cathedral to do duty while the Ripon bells were recast at Loughborough.

The eighth centenary of the founding of Fountains Abbey in 1132 was celebrated on Sunday 14 August. A service there was attended by the Duke and Duchess of York, the future King George VI and Queen Elizabeth, and by representatives of the Anglican and Nonconformist churches. The abbey was floodlit during the following week and special buses laid on. The Roman Catholics declined to join in the services and strong complaints were made when they were refused permission to have their own services.

The City Council finally approved a contract for the transport of coal to the gasworks by road rather than by rail as in the past.

An eel, 6 lbs in weight and 42 ins in length, was landed by Mr Bell, a Harrogate angler, at Middle Parks, Ripon. It was said to be a record catch.

September. The new East Wing of the Diocesan Training College was formally opened by Earl Grey to replace the old wing, demolished as unsafe on the advice of Sir Giles Gilbert Scott. A service in the Cathedral preceded the ceremony.

The first annual meeting of the Northern Counties Archery Society was held on Ripon Cricket Ground. On 17 September the shoot for the famous Scorton Silver Arrow which last took place in Ripon in 1886 was won by a Yorkshire-born archer, Mr T. R. Salterthwaite.

In spite of arguments that tenants could not afford the higher rents of other properties, the City Council agreed by a majority to demolish 12 houses deemed insanitary.

October. Hunger marchers passed through Ripon on their way from Tyneside to London. They were given accommodation for the night in the former Girls' Home in Bondgate by permission of Councillor F. W. Hargrave.

A rest or recreation room for the unemployed was opened by the Mayor in the Temperance Hall. It was provided by the Committee of the National Council of Social Service and the appeal for funds for the room brought in £100 in the last week of September.

At the annual dinner of the Ripon Chamber of Trade in the Café Victoria, the Mayor attacked the apathy of Ripon ratepayers: only one ward was interested in the council elections. However, aldermanic appointments made by-elections necessary, and considerable interest was shown with four contestants for two seats.

The City congratulated Dean Owen on his 80th birthday. Subscriptions raised were used to purchase a grand piano which the Dean presented to the Diocesan Training College along with a substantial donation of his own.

To assist the provision of electricity to Sawley, Grantley and Galphay, the City Council borrowed £1,210 to make the supply extension possible.

At Wakefield the proposal of the W.R.C.C. that Clotherholme, Littlethorpe, Sharow and Studley should be incorporated with the boundaries of Ripon City was dropped because of opposition by the Ripon City Council, the Rural District Council and representation of the parishes concerned.

The Union of the three Methodist Churches of Ripon was celebrated by a social gathering in the Zion Schoolroom, followed by a short service in the Market Place on Sunday 30 October. After the service there was a procession to Coltsgate Hill Church where a Union Celebration Service was held.

Ripon Horticultural Society held its first Chrysanthemum and Autumn Show in the Y.M.C.A. Hall.

1932-33. RICHARD THORPE, Removal Contractor

Son of John Thorpe, Carter, of North Road, he was educated at the Wesleyan School on Coltsgate Hill and first worked in warehouses in Leeds. His removal and storage business in North Road was established in 1897, and was much involved in the building of the South Camp in World War I. He was a founder member of the British Association of International Furniture Removers. He captained the Fire Brigade in 1914-18 and was a special constable in both wars. He was elected to Council in 1911 and gave much time to problems of unemployment; he went to Canada in 1927 to study and report for the Overseas Settlement Association and was on the council of the Fountains Abbey Settlers' Society. He was a governor of the Grammar School and Jepson's Hospital School and a committee member of the Mechanics Institute, active when it was transformed into the City Club. He died in 1940.

Population statistics for 1932: birth rate 16.87 per 1,000, death rate 15.20 per 1,000, infant mortality 20.97 per 1,000.

December. The City Council applied to the Ministry of Health for sanction to borrow £4,266 to cover the cost of reconstructing the plant at the Gas Works which was now worn out and therefore uneconomical.

Miss Dorothy Una Ratcliffe, the well-known authoress and poet, was married at the Ripon Registry Office.

Food for the unemployed had been of major concern. The Committee headed by the Mayor decided they would withdraw the scheme based on purchase of supplies from allotment holders, the gardens of large houses and local farmers, provided

that local tradespeople formed a suitable scheme themselves. The Chamber of Trade criticised this idea as impractical. However, its delegates met the Committee on 16 December and agreed to draw up a scheme of their own for consideration. Meanwhile Ripon butchers planned to provide meat at low cost with a subsidy through gifts from the public in cases of special need. In March 1932 the unemployed figure rose to 650, but over the year was on average between 550 and 600. At the end of April 1933 the scheme for the distribution of free food for the unemployed was wound up. The distribution had included 715 lbs of fresh meat, 160 rabbits, 6 tons of coal. In addition, 4,448 lbs of fresh meat at half price and 4 tons of potatoes had been sold at subsidised prices.

Mr J. M. Wray, a highly-respected Ripon trader in the shoe and boot business, died aged ninety-four. His son had taken over the business 23 years earlier.

January. An appeal fund launched for repairs to the Cathedral Clock. By 9 February this had reached more than its target and on 24 April the City Council decided to pay for the illumination of the clock subject to the approval of the Dean and Chapter.

At 8.30 am on 14 January an earth tremor which affected much of northern England was felt in Ripon, but no damage was reported.

Mr W. D. Row of Row and Sons, Jewellers and Opticians, died. He was the first optician to introduce modern scientific methods of sight-testing in Ripon.

February. Ripon Corporation schemes to cope with the problems of unemployment included levelling the car park, preparing for a bus station and tidying the Temple graveyard.

The Council resolved to amend the by-laws to permit the building of steel-framed houses despite opposition to the measure on the grounds of lowering standards of housing in the city.

Woolworths advertised in the *Gazette* the opening of their magnificent 3d and 6d store at 15 Fishergate, Ripon, on Saturday 18 February.

A failure of electricity on Sunday 12 February caused evening services in the Cathedral and other places of worship to be held by candlelight and gas. The Dean's text was Revelation Ch. XXII, Verse 5, beginning 'And there shall be no night there; and they need no candle neither the light of the sun'.

The Ripon Amateur Operatic and Dramatic Society broke its long tradition of nearly 30 years of operatic production by performing a play, Ian Hay's *The Sport of Kings*.

The Ripon Chamber of Trade decided at its annual meeting to suspend activities for 12 months owing to lack of support. Only 12 out of a possible 70 members attended the meeting and most of the work was being done by ten members.

A heavy snow storm with drifts four to six feet deep caused much damage to property and disrupted communications by road, rail and telephone. The city's electricity supply was quickly restored, however, despite the blizzard.

March. Allhallowgate Methodist Church members attended the formal opening of the extension to the schoolroom. The opening ceremony was performed by Mr Tennant of Northallerton on behalf of the Misses Stout.

At the annual meeting of the City Golf Club the secretary included in his report a reference to damage done to the course by 'marauding youths'.

A week of motor accidents amounting to an 'epidemic' was reported, one in High Skellgate, another in the Market Place, a third in Minster Road and a fourth in North Road. Fortunately no one was seriously injured.

The income of the Spa Baths for 1932 was only £85 as against an expenditure of £1,590 showing neglect of the facilities by both residents and visitors. There was, however, an increasing local demand for a public swimming bath.

Commander Clare Vyner of Studley Royal co-operated in several schemes to provide work for the unemployed. He was a Governor of the Management Council of the Fountains Abbey Settlers' Society, which had been founded to train and settle unemployed persons on the land. A training camp for youths was opened on the Studley estate where an improvement scheme at Fountains Abbey was carried out involving the removal of nearly 2,000 tons of silt from the River Skell. He also offered four acres of land on the banks of the Laver at Bishopton at a nominal rent to a Co-operative Garden Society formed by the Ripon Social Service Centre. The Society intended to employ a qualified gardener as instructor and it was expected that there would be work for 60 to 100 men.

April. The Cathedral bells were heard for the first time since their return from recasting at Loughborough on 14 March. The dedication service took place in the Cathedral on 8 April and the bells rang officially for the first time at 5 pm at the close of the service.

The *Ripon Gazette* and the *Pateley Bridge Herald* announced their special rail excursion to Skegness, departing from Ripon at 6 am and returning at midnight. The return fare for an adult was 16s 6d. On Wednesday 5 July, 200 people went on this outing and many Ripon shops were closed that day.

Rumours were gathering about the state of the city finances. The *Gazette* editorial affirmed that these reports, including stories of losses of thousands of pounds, were exaggerated by the Council's secrecy. On 10 April a special Council meeting was held. The public attendance was so large that the doors of the Council Chamber had to be left open to allow those on the stairs to hear the proceedings. After much argument it was resolved to separate the offices of Town Clerk and City Accountant. Resolutions, which might have led to the resignation of the Town Clerk and which sought to have more detailed minutes of the matter in hand, were rejected.

On 20 April the *Gazette* published a letter from the Chairman of the Finance Committee, Councillor Spence, stating that discrepancies in the cash department of the Rate Office were suspected. This led to the enforced resignation of a junior clerk and the chaos became such that accountants were called in. Although lack of supervision was revealed, no serious financial losses were discovered; but investigations continued.

At the Council Meeting on 24 April there was considerable altercation about Councillor Spence's letter. Councillor McHenry was accused of passing on confidential information to the Council, but eventually the unconfirmed Minutes of the Financial Committee Meeting of 10 April were accepted. In the following month a second special meeting of the City Council again drew a large attendance of ratepayers. To dispel rumours the Council decided to issue a draft statement of the situation, maintaining that criticisms were 'eyewash'. They admitted 'gross errors of arithmetic' due to inadequate supervision but prophesied that financial losses would be only slight. Time was needed to sort out the confusion and the new accountant would introduce new methods.

The auditors' Interim Report on the city finances became available for the year ending 31 March 1932. The Report revealed a loss of £146 1s 11d, attributed to inefficient management. The need for further investigation of the records was emphasised and criticism was made of the Town Clerk who as part of his duties had prepared the accounts. The Council agreed that he should be allowed to make his defence.

Dr C. H. Moody, organist and choirmaster of Ripon Cathedral, and Mr John Firth, for 40 years organist of Holy Trinity Parish Church, were offered Honorary Membership of the Royal College of Music to commemorate the College's Jubilee in May.

At a meeting of the Ripon Amateur Operatic Society there were complaints about the 'power of the conductor and the disloyalty and lack of commitment of some members'. Doubt as to the availability of funds for an operatic production in the 1933-34 season were expressed and at the September meeting the decision not to produce an opera was finally made.

It was announced that a one-way traffic system would operate on the east and west sides of the Market Place, and that experiments would be made with signals at the junction of High Skellgate and Westgate as advised by the Highways Committee.

May. The death of Ripon's oldest tradesman was announced. Mr John Ogle had carried on business as a grocer in Blossomgate until shortly before his death at the age of 90. He entered the trade as an errand boy. Mr Ogle was known as 'the Tea-man' and the sign of a tea canister hung above his shop.

Dr William Temple, Archbishop of York, made his first visit to Ripon. He preached in the Cathedral to a congregation which included the Mayor, members of the Corporation and civic officials.

June. It was reported that the hot, sunny Whitsuntide holiday had been marred by an accident, the drowning of a Middlesborough boy visiting a friend in Ripon, in the River Ure near Fishergreen. A week later there was a second report of a near-fatality in the same place.

Ripon Angling Club held their centenary dinner at the *Unicorn Hotel*.

Mr William Steel celebrated his 90th birthday. He entered the service of the late Mr Samuel Wise, Clerk to the Magistrates, on 12 January 1857 and was with the same firm of solicitors for 70 years.

July. At a special meeting of the City Council it was decided to draw up a Town Planning Scheme for Ripon under the terms of the Town and Country Planning Act 1932.

Friendly Societies celebrated their Golden Jubilee Hospital Sunday with a procession from the Market Place to the Spa Gardens headed by the City Band and the Mayor and members of the Corporation.

Miss M. E. Rudd of Ripon was selected to play tennis for England against Wales. She won the ladies' singles, the ladies' doubles and the mixed doubles in the Yorkshire Lawn Tennis Tournament at Scarborough.

Harry Anderson, aged six years, won the Challenge Trophy of the Ripon Piscatorial Association by catching 107 minnows during the annual fishing match for boys.

A radio relay service was switched on by the deputy Mayor, Alderman Briscombe, at the premises of Mr C. R. Pinchbeck in Fishergate.

August. The Hornblower complained of an attempt by soldiers from the camp to interfere with the horn-blowing ceremony. The Mayor looked upon this incident as horseplay but said it must not be repeated.

The last swimming club had been disbanded in 1923 and a gala sponsored by a small group of Ripon sportsmen who had revived the City Swimming Club was held at the bathing pavilion on the River Ure.

September. Allegations of gambling at the Social Service Centre were made at the second annual meeting. It was proposed that a paid supervisor should be appointed so that 'the wrong type of man' might not keep 'decent artisans away' and a new committee was formed to find suitable entertainment. On 13 October the Mayor reopened the club.

Ripon residents deplored the loss of the late mail service which had been provided by a bus to York at 8.30 pm and now was discontinued. The service was restored in July 1934.

A giant marrow, 30 lbs in weight, was grown by Mr G. Leatham.

October. Farm workers met in the Co-operative Assembly Rooms to protest against the West Riding Farmers' proposals to cut wages by 5 per cent.

A clearance scheme for the Stonebridgegate area was adopted by the City Council. The arrangement between the Council and the Ripon Housing Improvement Trust had been approved by the Ministry of Health. An inquiry opened at the Town Hall into the Corporation's proposal to make the Queen's Head Yard a slum clearance area.

The Ghyll, a new play by the Ripon artist and playwright Mr George Jackson was performed at the Lawrence Rooms.

It was reported that two Ripon schoolboys had been charged with throwing missiles which damaged trains travelling between Harrogate and Ripon. The boys were bound over.

1933-34. RICHARD THORPE, Removal Contractor

Mayor 1932-33-34

Population statistics for 1933: birth rate 14.07 per 1,000, death rate 15.85 per 1,000, infant mortality rate 25.63 per 1,000. Rainfall in 1933 was 26.49 ins; wettest month February, 4.89 ins; driest month August, 0.21 ins.

November. The appointment of a manager/caretaker by the Spa Baths Committee was accepted, despite the storm of protest in the City Council that the Council had not been given the opportunity to object to the position being given to a man who was not local.

Dramatic results were obtained in the municipal election. Three retiring councillors were defeated. One of the successful candidates, Mr A. D. Henderson, was the first Labour councillor for 20 years. It was suggested that this upheaval in local politics was due to the crisis in the municipal accounts and the attitude of some councillors to housing schemes.

The decline in the voluntary income of the Hospital was causing concern: £486 in 1928 to £365 in 1932. Increases in the Contributory Fund and patients' fees had so far enabled the Hospital to balance its accounts.

Another Council uproar occurred, this time spoiling the proceedings following the Mayoral election. Alderman Dixon and others attempted to get Councillor Hargrave replaced on the Health and Housing Committee by Councillor Moss, on the grounds that the Councillor had opposed the housing policy of the Council and had himself offended against the health regulations. Four out of six members of the new committee were said to be opposed to the housing policies of the previous committee. Councillor Hargrave put up a detailed defence, and at the Council meeting next day the original appointments were confirmed.

The one-ward system in municipal elections was to be restored after a trial of a four-ward system for seven years. The City Council felt that to have several wards promoted division, that the new system had not encouraged more people to vote and Ripon was sufficiently small for all the councillors to be known by its residents.

The first open pigeon show of the Ripon Homing Society was organised at the *Saracen's Head*.

January. Mr T. F. Spence, defeated in the poll in November 1932, was returned unopposed in the municipal by-election.

Littlethorpe, the race-horse trained by the Ripon trainer, R. Renton, had its fourth successive win.

February. According to the Clerk of the Privy Council, there was no procedure for restoring a borough divided into wards to the status of an undivided borough. Therefore an appeal was to be made by the City Council to the Ripon M.P., Major Hills.

Unemployed hunger marchers from Tyneside passed through Ripon on their way from Thirsk to Harrogate. An advance party arrived by car to prepare a meal in the Market Place. Before the marchers arrived, onlookers were addressed by the Leeds District Secretary of the Economic League, who accused the marchers of being Communist-inspired and intent on fomenting unrest.

A production of *The Farmer's Wife* was given at the Victoria Opera House by Dr Tom Waterhouse's company of amateurs, on their first visit to Ripon for five years.

Dr S. W. Hughes, General Secretary of the Free Church Council, visited Ripon to address the annual meeting of the local council and preach at Zion Church.

The Ripon Chamber of Trade decided at an annual meeting at the *City Café* to resume its activities, suspended last year, despite the continued small attendance.

At the annual meeting of subscribers, it was decided to change the name of the Ripon Dispensary and Cottage Hospital to the Ripon and District Hospital.

March. The Labour Councillor, Mr R. J. Hall, was defeated by a large majority by Councillor T. F. Spence in the County Council election.

Colonel Gethin, J.P., of *Cayton Hall*, South Stainley, died. He had been involved since his retirement from the Army in Conservative and Church affairs and in Scouting. He was an amateur painter of some distinction.

The first broadcast of music from Ripon Cathedral took place. A programme of motets and organ music was presented.

Many cases of failure to comply with one-way signs in Ripon were reported. The usual reason given was that the signs were not clear. The Magistrates at the City Court criticised the signs on this account.

May. The new covered stands at the Ripon racecourse were reported to be completed.

The Council decided after considerable argument to repudiate the bill sent in by Messrs Blackburns, Coates and Company for their investigation of the city accounts. It was however agreed to call the firm in again when the new City Accountant had made the books ready for audit with the help of two temporary assistants. A final settlement was agreed in March 1935.

Ripon became the first city in England to send a civic greeting across the Atlantic by radio. A short service from the Cathedral was also broadcast. On the same day Ripon Diocese also became the first to have a service broadcast from its Cathedral in which the Bishop spoke to all the churches of the diocese.

The Ripon Nursing Division of the St John Ambulance Association became runner-up in the national competition, thus winning the Corbet Fletcher Trophy. An appeal for funds to buy a new ambulance met with a large response.

The new oak chancel screen carved by Messrs Abbott and Company for Holy Trinity Church was dedicated on 27 May.

June. Seven thousand pigeons were released from Ripon Station for the West of England Federation race, the largest number ever released in Ripon.

An old Grammar School boy, Maurice William Brayshay, was knighted. Sir Maurice had had a brilliant career in engineering, mainly on the Indian railways.

July. A 'disarming' incident occurred. The two German guns in front of the Court House were handed over for scrap: the Russian gun nearby was retained.

Ripon Cathedral's campaign on behalf of the National Cathedral Pilgrimage to raise money for the unemployed by special services, organ recitals and guided tours had disappointing financial results.

A petition for a swimming bath, which was supported by the Dean of Ripon and head teachers in the City, resulted in the decision of the City Council to provide a public swimming bath at the Spa Baths. A Ministry of Health Inquiry was held in October.

Ripon's first lady Magistrates, Mrs Hemsworth, Mrs Harker and Miss J. Pratt, were appointed to sit on the Ripon City Bench.

August. The death at the age of 51 was announced of Dr E. A. Burroughs, Bishop of Ripon for over eight years. At his appointment he was the youngest member of the Episcopal Bench.

HM Queen Mary and The Princess Royal passed through Ripon on their way to take tea with Captain and Mrs Compton at *Newby Hall*. They made purchases at Mr Hemsworth's antique shop in Fishergate and were presented with a basket made by boys from the Social Services Centre.

September. Alderman W. R. Dixon accepted the invitation to be the next Mayor of Ripon. The election was opposed by Alderman McHenry because of the manner in which the election was made. The formal election took place on 9 November.

The Ripon City Electricity Undertaking was transferred to the Harrogate Corporation. Final approval was given in January 1935 and formal transfer was made at a ceremony in the Town Hall in June.

Another school, the Coltsgate Hill Council School, which had been on the condemned list for some time, was to be closed.

The West Riding Education Committee gave its approval to a scheme for the reorganisation of Ripon schools. A new senior school with modern equipment and teaching facilities was to be built.

A Ministry of Transport Inquiry was held into the Corporation's proposal to make the general parking area off Queen Street and Victoria Grove into a bus station. The congestion of streets and inconvenience to customers were the reasons given for the proposal but the Chamber of Trade and bus companies objected.

October. The funeral service of Mr John Fisher Wilson was held in the Cathedral on 24 October. He was 82 years of age and was the last survivor of the original City Band formed in 1867.

The appointment was announced of Canon G. C. L. Lunt as Bishop of Ripon. Canon Lunt was vicar of Portsea and an Honorary Canon of Portsmouth Cathedral.

1934-35. WILLIAM RUSSELL DIXON, Paint Manufacturer

WILLIAM RUSSELL DIXON
MAYOR
1934-5-6,
1942,
1945-6-7.

He was to be Mayor June to October 1942 after the death of Margaret Sara Steven and also in 1945-46-47. Born in 1886 and educated at the Grammar School, he was apprenticed to an ironmonger in Lincolnshire. Went to India in 1909 and returned to Ripon in 1922 to join the family business of W. E. Dixon, Iron-mongers, in Kirkgate. He was appointed sales manager of T. and R. Williamson Limited in 1926, and later moved to Wm Moss and Sons' Varnish Works, where he became general manager and director in 1936. Elected to Council in 1923, retired, and was again elected in 1929. Alderman 1932. He was presented with a silver salver after 25 years' service in 1951 and received the O.B.E. in 1956. His chief interests in local government were housing (his name was given to Russell Dixon Square, the sheltered development in Harrogate Road) and education; he was chairman of the Governors of the Modern School and Governor of the Grammar School. He was an active Methodist, a member of the Coltsgate Hill Church and a lay preacher. Chairman of Ripon Charities for many years. He was a keen golfer. He died in 1970.

Population statistics for 1934: birth rate 15.4 per 1,000, death rate 13.52 per 1,000, infant mortality rate 23.07 per 1,000.

November. An evening play centre was established at the Cathedral Girls' School, on the initiative of the Ripon Training College, making the city the first place

in the West Riding to have such a centre.

A sitting of the Ripon Liberty Court had to be adjourned because no magistrates turned up.

It was reported that only one ward was contested in the Municipal Elections. Miss Wells, the retiring councillor, retained her seat.

A drought had continued from March until November. Heavy rain on 10 March slightly eased the situation, which became serious again in October when water had to be drawn at heavy cost from the Harrogate supply. The drought broke at last in November so that the Harrogate supply was turned off on 7 November.

Alderman J. B. Briscombe died on 12 November. He had been a member of the City Council from 1897-1900 and 1920-1934. He had had to decline the position of mayor because of ill-health. Alderman Briscombe had been associated with many local activities such as the Early Closing Movement, the Oddfellows Friendly Society, the Cricket Club and the Bowling Club.

The Ripon Ratepayers' Association was formally launched under the chairmanship of Dr P. A. Steven.

The footpath between Hackfall Villas and Lark Lane had been the subject of argument in Council and com-mittee meetings: the question at issue was whether owners of property there should be obliged to restore the path. It was decided to have a meeting of the par-ties involved with a view to making application to the Quarter Sessions for the diversion of the footpath.

The Town Hall Keeper and Sergeant-at-Mace, Mr T. Hammonds, was suspended and asked to resign because of suspicion of fraud in his other capacity as collector of market tolls. He was found guilty of embezzlement and fraudulent conversion and was sentenced to three months' imprisonment without hard labour in June 1935.

The Northern Agricultural, Bacteriological and Pathological Laboratory in the Arcade, Ripon, announced that it was now equipped and ready to carry out the necessary tests and deal with all pro-blems affecting the health of poultry.

January. Parents of school children were invited to have them immunised against diphtheria in view of epidemics in other parts of the country.

A branch of N.A.L.G.O. was formed in Ripon with an inaugural dinner at the *Lawrence Café*.

Mr Fred Denby Moore, J.P., of *Mowbray House*, Kirkby Malzeard, near Ripon, received a knighthood in the New Year Honours List. He was a member of the Bench of Ripon Liberty court and a Governor of the Training College.

February. A Sunny Homes Exhibition was opened by the Mayor in the *Lawrence Café*. It remained open for a week and all the latest domestic appliances were displayed.

The new Bishop of Ripon, the Rt Revd G. C. L. Lunt, was consecrated in York Minster and later enthroned in Ripon Cathedral in the presence of HRH The Princess Royal and a large congregation.

The W.R.C.C.'s boundary proposals suggested the inclusion of Clotherholme, Littlethorpe, Sharow and

Studley Roger in Ripon City, and the creation of two wards instead of four. At a Ministry of Health Inquiry these proposals were attacked and rejected by the Minister in October a year later.

Becky's Café and some of the old houses in Bedern Bank were demolished.

March. Ripon Ratepayers' Association censured Ripon Corporation's administration of financial matters and demanded more information.

A portrait of John Aislabie of Studley Royal was offered to the City Council. Money was raised for its purchase by subscription and the Council received the portrait on 13 December.

Mr E. Shinwell, ex-Minister of Mines, addressed the Ripon Divisional Labour Party in the Assembly Rooms.

Miss Ruth Harrison, the English professional Women's Billiards Champion, played at Ripon City and Constitutional Clubs.

At the A.G.M. of the Ripon Housing Improvement Trust it was reported that the first building scheme under the 1930 Act had been completed. This consisted of 12 units named Alma Gardens; two blocks of four bungalows for aged persons and two blocks of three-bedroomed houses.

April. The first offender to be caught exceeding the new 30 mph speed limit in Ripon appeared before the Ripon Liberty court and fined £1.

Gipsy Smith, the famous evangelist, preached at Coltsgate Hill Methodist Church. The congregation was so large that arrangements were made to relay services to the schoolroom.

May. It was reported that the Ministry of Health had sanctioned the City Council's application to borrow £7,500 for the building of a new swimming bath and work would begin at once. Attempts to stop the scheme in Council failed.

King George V's Silver Jubilee was celebrated with a service in the Cathedral and later with an air display at the racecourse. Jubilee medals were awarded to eight Ripon residents including the Mayor, Town Clerk and City Surveyor. The Silver Jubilee was commemorated by a fund to provide for the development of the Victoria Nursing Institution, but there were arguments over the plans.

There was a Civic Reception for the synod of York and Whitby District of the Methodist Church which met in Ripon and was attended by about seventy ministers and 129 lay delegates.

The Salvation Army returned to Ripon in new band quarters at the Temperance Hall which were declared open by the Mayor. The following year the Army moved to premises vacated by the Girls' Club in Water Skellgate.

The new St John Ambulance Station was built at a cost of £1,000 in North Road. It was opened by Lady Aykroyd and dedicated by the Dean.

Reference was made in the *Gazette* to the forthcoming demolition of the old Bath House in Skellbank, the first point to which the Aldfield sulphur water was brought in Ripon.

It was reported that the City Council was considering the Ministry of Transport's scheme for a relief road for Ripon, to take the form of a ring road from Quarry Moor Lane to North Road, via Bondgate Green Lane, Bedern Bank and Victoria Grove. The Chamber of Trade expressed strong opposition to the plan as harmful to business interests. Alternative schemes were suggested but the Council resolved in favour of the Ministry scheme. The W.R.C.C. approved the scheme on 17 March 1937.

June. The Training College held its first open day — a new departure — and received 400 visitors.

The annual choral and folk dancing festival of the Yorkshire Federation of Women's Institutes was held at Grantley Hall and attracted 5,000 women.

July. Canon G. W. Garrod, the senior Residentiary Canon of Ripon Cathedral and principal of the Training College, received the honorary degree of Doctor of Philosophy at the University of Leeds.

It was reported that Mr W. J. Strachan, M.A., had been selected from 185 applicants to succeed Mr J. W. Dyson as Headmaster of Ripon Grammar School.

The Revd Hedley Hodkin, minister of Coltsgate Hill Methodist Church, left Ripon on his resignation from the Methodist ministry. He was ordained as a priest of the Church of England and took up a curacy in Morpeth.

The Duke of Gloucester was in camp at Ripon with the Lancers.

The League of Nations Union organised a Ripon Peace Pageant in the grounds of the Training College.

Thorpe Prebend House Museum in St Agnesgate was reopened after extensive repairs to the building and rearrangement of the contents.

August. The secretary of the Ripon City Football Club reported that the club would have to close next season unless support increased. After 12 years in the York and District League, the Club was changing back to the Allertonshire League in the hope of improving the gates.

An appeal for £8,500 for the repair of the Cathedral roof was launched. The roof was suffering from an invasion of death watch beetle.

A policy of more active slum clearance was proposed for the coming year. The Stonebridgegate clearance orders had been approved and four more orders were recommended by the Council.

The British Legion Club in High Skellgate severed its connections with the British Legion, and became the Victory Club because it was unable to continue purely on the subscriptions raised by Legion members. The British Legion made a fresh start in Ripon with 6d in hand.

September. A Committee was formed to organise the 1,050th anniversary of the first Charter to the City in 1936. Miss Naomi Jacob agreed to write the book of the pageant free of charge. However, the scheme was abandoned because the City Council refused to guarantee the event.

General Evangeline Booth of the Salvation Army visited Ripon during her 1,000-mile motor tour of England. She was received by the Mayor and Mayoress in pouring rain and later addressed a meeting in the Spa Gardens.

The Ripon Archers Club, re-formed in the previous year, had a triumphant success at the Northern Counties Championship Archery Meeting at Buxton, when one of the members, Mrs Buchanan, won the St Wilfrid's Challenge Badge at her first public archery meeting and her daughter Mary also did well.

October. Messrs Blackburns, Coates and Company's report on the city finances 1931-32 and 1932-33 was published in two parts.

Plans of the proposed new senior school were published. It was likely to cost £24,450 and nine acres of land on Clotherholme Road had been purchased for the site.

The sixtieth anniversary of the Ripon Cricket Club was celebrated with a dinner at the *Unicorn Hotel*.

The candidates representing the Ripon Ratepayers' Association had a notable success in the municipal elections, when all the retiring candidates seeking re-election were defeated.

Forty-six choirs with 600 voices took part in the Ripon Diocesan Choir Festival in the Cathedral.

The death occurred of Mr Oliver Wright, for 53 years a newsagent in the city and for 29 years the City Bellman.

A 100-mph gale struck the city but comparatively little damage was caused. Trees were blown down, tiles blown off and hay and straw stacks damaged.

Major J. W. Hills (Conservative) retained his seat by a massive majority (30,804 to 9,116) in the General Election, defeating his rival Mr R. J. Hall in a straight fight.

The *Palladium Cinema* was reopened by the Mayor. Substantial improvements included modern ventilation and heating, a stage and extra seating and the introduction of the latest Western Electric Sound Apparatus.

The seventy-fifth anniversary celebration of Ripon Training College took place. Mr F. D. Wise, aged 94, who had attended the laying of the foundation stone in 1860, was present at the event.

A runaway bus moved off with 30 passengers, no driver and no conductor, from the stop outside the company's Market Place Offices. The traffic island at the top of Kirkgate halted its progress and no one was hurt.

1935-36. WILLIAM RUSSELL DIXON, Paint Manufacturer

Rainfall in 1935 was 32.55 ins. The driest month was July with 0.41 ins., the wettest September with 5.44 ins. Population statistics: birth rate 16.1 per 1,000, death rate 12.06 per 1,000, infant mortality 43.79 per 1,000.

January. Lieutenant-Colonel J. C. R. Husband, who had been deputy coroner and coroner for Ripon and Kirkby Malzeard district for 50 years, resigned. He was succeeded by Mr W. H. Coverdale.

Ripon mourned the death of King George on 20 January and King Edward VIII was proclaimed by the Mayor.

February. A Ministry of Health Inquiry was made

Mayor 1934-35

into Ripon City's application to amend the Market Place tolls. In spite of the objections of the stallholders, Parliament passed the necessary Act.

A choir of 23 clergy sang at the consecration service of the nave altar in the Cathedral in memory of Dr Lucius Smith, formerly Canon Residentiary of the Cathedral and late Bishop of Knaresborough. Dr Smith was the author of *The Story of Ripon Minster*, published in 1914.

April. The Swimming Bath was opened by Sir Percy Jackson, Chairman of the W.R.C.C., with a grand swimming gala.

A play, *Hunger*, written by Mrs Percival Smith, Honorary Secretary of the Ripon Women's Institute, won them the banner for 'The most original play' at the Drama Festival of the Yorkshire County Federation of Women's Institutes, held at Tadcaster.

A car travelling along the disused military road between Galphay Lane and Clotherholme found the bridge over the Laver was unable to stand up to its weight and fell into the river. None of the occupants were injured.

The Mayor welcomed the Sparkhill Citadel Salvation Army Band on its weekend visit to Ripon. On the same Saturday the Ripon Harmonica Band gave its first public performance at the *Palladium*.

A booklet was published by the Ripon printing and stationery firm of Messrs William Harrison and Sons to celebrate their centenary, 1836-1936.

A Ripon branch of the International Contacts Bureau was formed to arrange visits between Ripon and German schoolboys.

May. The President of Ripon College, Wisconsin, U.S.A., was received by the Mayor.

June. Mr William Steel, for 75 years a solicitors clerk with Messrs Hutchinson and Buchanan and for 63 years assistant diocesan registrar, died.

An agreement proposed by the Harrogate and District Town Planning Joint Committee to check ribbon development was signed by Ripon and several other authorities.

July. Mrs R. W. Buchanan of the Ripon Archery Club continued her successful career by winning the Associated Club's prize with the highest score at the

Grand National Archery meeting at Oxford; she was competing for the first time. The success of the Archery Club continued at the Northern Counties meeting at Scarborough, when prize winners included Lieutenant-Colonel D. L. Selby-Bigge, Mrs R. W. Buchanan, and Miss Hillborn. The Ripon Ladies won the Silver Challenge Shield for inter-club competition.

August. Miss Sheila Lunt, only daughter of the Bishop, was married in the Cathedral to the Revd S. Harvie Clarke, Rector of Jarrow-on-Tyne.

September. The invested property and funds of the Ripon Home for Girls at *West Mount*, Kirkby Road, were transferred to Dr Barnado's Homes and *West Mount* was opened as a Dr Barnado's Home in July 1937.

The deaths occurred of two Ripon artists, Miss M. E. Hunter and Mrs K. E. Hill, the latter a miniature painter of some distinction.

October. Ripon Railway Station won a first-class prize in the L.N.E.R. (N.E. Area) competition for the best-kept station.

Unemployment was so far reduced at Ripon that at the annual meeting of the Social Services Committee it was resolved that its activities should be suspended and the tenancy of the Temperance Hall terminated.

Ripon Drama Club gave its first public performance, a production of St John Ervine's *The First Mrs Frazer*.

The Jarrow Crusade, consisting of about two hundred men, reached Ripon and were billeted in the former Coltsgate Hill Council School. They were received by Bishop Lunt, the father-in-law of the rector of Jarrow. A meeting in the Market Place gave them a vote of support and they were entertained at the *Palladium Cinema*. They attended a special service in the Cathedral and left for Harrogate on Monday 12 October. A group of 185 Scottish Means Test Marchers later entered Ripon headed by a drum and fife band. Public assistance was refused unless they conformed to the customary three days in the Workhouse as casuals but, after a night in the Drill Hall and the intervention of the Mayor and the Labour candidate for Ripon, they were allowed to receive meals throughout the West Riding.

1936-37. JOHN IRELAND McHENRY, Tobacconist

Born in Kirkcudbrightshire, he came to Ripon in 1886. Elected to the Council in 1924, he sat until 1946 and served at some time on every committee. He was proud of his Scottish ancestry but became devoted to his adopted town. He saw Ripon as a 'Garden City' and was enthusiastically involved in the improvement of parks and gardens and planting schemes. His tobacconist's shop in North Street was an acknowledged venue for the exchange and discussion of Ripon's affairs. He died in 1946.

Rainfall in 1936 was 37.34 ins. Population statistics for 1936: birth rate 14.7 per 1,000, death rate 15.53 per 1,000, infant mortality 56.45 per 1,000.

November. The Council voted to reaffirm the agreement with the W.R.C.C. to proceed with the relief road

scheme under the Five Year Plan. The W.R.C.C. had intended that, should the plan be rejected, they might draw up a scheme for a complete bypass.

The Co-operative Society opened a new bakery at its Park Street premises.

The Diocesan Centenary celebrations began with a Rally in the Palace grounds in July, attended by an estimated 2,500 people. In November, services were held in Leeds and Harrogate and there was a Choir Festival in the Cathedral. The Centenary was also celebrated by a Pilgrimage of Youth, a Mothers' Union service, a Missionary Festival and a Commemoration Service which was broadcast; 3,000 people heard the Archbishop of York preach and gifts were received from the parishes in the diocese. The closing event was a service in the Cathedral where the Bishop of Ely, formerly Vicar of Leeds, preached.

At the instigation of the Rotary Club, bulbs were planted on the side of the Harrogate Road to mark the forthcoming Coronation.

December. Although the numbers of unemployed had fallen, the Mayor made his usual appeal for his Relief Fund for the winter months.

The Cathedral suffered two losses in this month with the deaths of Canon Garrod, senior Canon Residentiary and formerly Principal of the Training College, and of Mr E. W. Winser, a verger at the Cathedral for 50 years.

The Mayor proclaimed George VI on Tuesday 15 December, following the abdication of Edward VIII.

Throughout the year there were several slum clearance orders referring to buildings in Allhallowgate, Skellgarths and various courts. The W.R.C.C. Medical Officer reported 360 houses in Ripon unfit for habitation. Council house building plans included 88 houses on the site of Quarry Moor Lane.

January. Canon Battersby Harford, D.D., who died on 6 January was Principal of the Ripon Clergy College from 1902 until 1912, and Canon Residentiary of Ripon from 1911 until his death.

The New County Library in Skellgate was opened by the Bishop on 13 January. Alderman Mrs Unwin of the W.R.C.C. handed over the care of the new library to the local library committee. By 28 January nearly one thousand tickets had been taken out.

The R.A.F. Aerodrome at Dishforth began its official career with the arrival of Bomber Squadrons 10 and 78.

A break with ancient custom was made when Miss Mary Blackburn, the daughter of the Ripon Horn-blower, became the first woman to set the watch. Her father and his deputy were both ill on the evening of 26 January.

February. The death occurred of Mr H. M. Thirlway, Mayor of Ripon 1888-89 and 1913-14, aged 86.

The first pedestrian crossing was introduced in Ripon.

The new Ripon Employment Offices opened in the former Girls' Club premises in Water Skellgate, formerly in restricted quarters in the Arcade.

March. Mr T. F. Spence, the retiring County Councillor, won the County Council election, defeating the Independent candidate, Mrs M. I. G. Garner and the Labour candidate Mr Edward Hartley.

Ripon's permanent memorial to the coronation of George VI took the form of tree-planting at High Cleugh. The Mayor and six ex-mayors were present to plant the trees.

April. The merger of the Ripon and Pateley Bridge Rural District Councils by order of the Ministry of Health took effect from 1 April.

The death was reported of Mr J. G. Kearsley, J.P. Mr Kearsley was the head of the firm of Kearsley and Company, Agricultural Implement Makers and the inventor of a grass-cutter and other experimental machines.

Mr E. Benson, a well-known Ripon zoologist, died. He had been a schoolmaster, Fellow of the Zoological Society, and was noted as the designer of the Mappin Terrace for bears at the London Zoo.

The Ministry of Health approved the purchase of the Alma Estate at a cost of £4,000 by the City Council.

May. The City Council put out a number of orders as part of its slum clearance scheme, the areas being affected being Lands Court, High Skellgate, Coltsgate Hill and Johnson's Court. It also used compulsory purchase orders for house building in Bondgate, Stonebridgegate and Church Lane.

The coronation of George VI was celebrated in Ripon with a civic procession, religious services, historical tableaux and a torchlight procession along with other festivities. Coronation medals were awarded to six Ripon citizens.

Frank Orton had a remarkably successful season with the Ripon Cricket Club: 107 not out v. Stockeld Park; five wickets for two runs v. Burley Lawn; 118 not out v. The Stags.

June. The death was announced of Mr Francis Lowley of the Ripon firm of Undertakers. Mr Lowley had made scenery for many theatical productions in the city and had helped his father to construct pieces for the Millenary Festival of 1886.

July. The vacancy caused by Councillor Spence becoming an Alderman resulted in a County Council by-election in which Mr S. Brayshay defeated Mrs M. I. G. Garner.

Miss M. E. Rudd, the Yorkshire Tennis Champion, married Mr M. J. Wood in Ripon Cathedral. A large crowd attended the ceremony. The following month she and her partner Miss Burrows won the Yorkshire Ladies Doubles Championship for the third time (Mrs Wood for the sixth time) and became joint owners of the Challenge Cup.

September. An archaeological dig at Ailcey Hill unearthed skeletons, probably Anglo-Saxon burials of the 5th or 6th centuries.

October. Mr Arthur Kitson, the Ripon-born inventor of the Kitson incandescent light, died. He had worked with Edison and Graham Bell.

As part of an Army recruiting drive, soldiers of the 2nd Battalion West Yorkshire Regiment marched through Ripon and gave a demonstration in the Market Place.

1937-38.   JOHN IRELAND McHENRY, Tobacconist

Mayor 1936-37-38

Statistics for 1937: birth rate 15.9 per 1,000; death rate 13.47 per 1,000; infant mortality 58.8 per 1,000.

November. Ripon and District Boy Scouts Association acquired the Temperance Hall in Duck Hill for their headquarters and training centre.

At the municipal elections all the retiring councillors were returned unopposed.

Tim, the horse ridden by 'St Wilfrid' for many years, dropped dead at the top of Skellgate; he was 34 years of age.

The City Council opposed the War Office's proposal to relinquish the Ripon Army Camp as too small for their needs, and offered to contact local landowners with a view to extending the site. No decision was reached.

The President of the Ripon Chamber of Trade formally opened the city's first milk bar at 41 Market Place.

December. The Mayor officially opened the illuminated shopping week by switching on the lights. The scheme was initiated by the Chamber of Trade.

A pigeon owned by Messrs J. W. Turkington and Son of the Ripon Social and Flying Club won in the Club's first season the British Government's trophy and gold medal, awarded annually to encourage the breeding of homing pigeons.

Montague Burton opened their new store at 28/29 Market Place.

January. Continuing their house building schemes, the Council announced plans to purchase the Highfield Estate and land at Gallows Hill. The Training College and local residents strongly opposed the purchase of the former, and when the Ministry of Health gave approval and the Council confirmed the purchase, the residents of College Road lodged a successful appeal to the High Court.

The introduction of congregational singing into the Sunday evening services at the Cathedral caused some controversy.

February. The Ripon Women's Luncheon Club held its first luncheon at the *Spa Hotel* under the presidency of Mrs Grotian of *North Stainley Hall*. The club had a membership of 100. The speaker at the luncheon was Lieutenant-Colonel Stewart Roddie, C.V.O., who lectured on 'The maelstrom of Europe'.

A new by-law was passed by the City Council to protect the plants in the area.

A League of Helpers for Ripon and District Hospital was formed.

March. It was announced that all the essential repair work to the roof of the Cathedral had been completed, but that £2,000 was needed to meet the full cost of £10,000.

April. Improvements to Ripon Racecourse included a new weighing room block, the enlargement of the paddock and the car park, and a new champagne bar.

A spring drought was recorded for March and April: the gauge at the Grammar School registering only 0.12 ins. for the two months. A measurable quantity of rain fell on only three days in each month.

May. The bicentenary of John Wesley's conversion was commemorated by a joint service in Coltsgate Hill Chapel.

June. The proposed purchase of a new fire engine was accepted by the Ripon City Council and the Ripon and Pateley Bridge Rural District Councils.

July. A privately-built air-raid shelter, the first in Ripon, was inspected by the Mayor at No. 8 Harrogate Road.

The stable at Messrs Hepworth and Company's brewery in Bondgate was damaged by fire.

A weekend of military exercise was centred upon Ripon with feigned bandit attacks on a city garrison, which later counter-attacked to capture the bandit camp.

Two events made news at Holy Trinity Parish Church. The Vicar sat in the church porch all day to receive gifts which amounted to £127 12s 3d, and ten days later the oak doors, a memorial to Mr H. M. Thirlway, were dedicated.

September. Air Raid Precautions were begun in the city: trenches were dug in the Magdalen Recreation Ground; lists of first-aid posts were published; 500 volunteers were needed for the A.R.P. services. In April the use of gas masks was demonstrated in Princess Road and in September when supplies of gas masks arrived the population were fitted at rooms allocated at the new bus station.

A special service was held in Ripon Cathedral at the time of the Munich meeting between the Prime Minister, Mr Chamberlain, and Adolf Hitler.

October. The first section of the Ripon Relief Road from Bedern Bank to North Bridge was approved by the Ministry of Transport.

An editorial in the *Gazette* referred to the closure of Coltsgate Hill School because the buildings did not comply with the required standards of education authorities. An appeal was launched for the improvement of church schools to avoid further such closures.

1938-39.   Frederick Isaac Trees, Builder

FREDERICK I. TREES.
MAYOR 1938-1939.
MAYOR 1939-1940.
MAYOR 1940-1941

Born 1881, the son of Abel Trees, of a family long-established as builders in Ripon. Educated at the Grammar School. Took over his father-in-law's business as a wool merchant in Wellington Street, but later passed this to his elder son, returned to building, and developed the Lark Hill Estate. Elected to Council in 1929, was an alderman for 11 years. In his mayoralty during the war years he organised relationships with the services, hospitality for troops, Civil Defence, evacuee accommodation and war savings, and had a strong sense of his responsibility as chief magistrate. He was a keen sportsman and supporter of the Cricket and Football Clubs. A gifted speaker and entertainer, he was active in the Debating Society. President of the Olde Tyme Dance Club and a member of the Rotary Club. He died in 1949.

November. It was announced that Major J. W. Hills had decided not to contest the Ripon division, which he had represented since 1925, at the next election. Mr Christopher York was selected as the prospective Conservative Candidate. Major Hills died on 24 December and Mr York was elected at the by-election held in March 1939 with a majority of 13,000.

The *Old Ship Inn* in Bondgate was demolished to make way for a new hotel which kept the same name.

December. The West Riding Public Assistance Committee proposed to close Ripon's Poor Law Institution and Infirmary along with others and to send the inmates to institutions elsewhere.

January. A notice appeared in the local press advising those A.R.P. volunteers who had already

17. The Old Ship, *Bondgate (Gott)*

attended First Aid Classes that they should now undergo anti-gas training.

Conflicting opinions in the Corporation continued to delay local housing projects. Doubts were expressed over the proposed site of Gallows Hill; it was too far from the life of the city, the shopping centre and other amenities; many would leave when housing conditions became easier; the cost would be expensive because the site was too small. It was decided to go ahead when the Ministry of Health agreed to the borrowing of £1,250 for the land. The poor condition of many houses in the city made it imperative that building should commence as soon as possible. A new scheme was passed to build 16 flats to replace property already improved by the Ripon Housing Improvement Trust in Stonebridge-gate. The Trust later complained that only the site value had been given in compensation. The Trust still owned the Alma Flats and hoped to be able to retrieve some of the loss sustained on the Stonebridgegate property.

Lady Doris Vyner lent flowers and plants for a most successful Ripon Hospital Ball at the *Spa Hotel*, an occasion enlivened by the pink coats of the huntsmen.

The Estates' Committee agreed to the erection of a new greenhouse at the cemetery at a cost of £85 as those already there were fast approaching dissolution. A councillor commented 'They are in the cemetery, why worry?'.

The Mayor asked for the co-operation of house-

holders in a forthcoming survey of the available accommodation in each house for children and/or mothers and teachers, in the event of a national emergency. The Government would pay 10s 6d for the board and lodging of one child, 8s 6d where more were accepted. For lodging only the rate would be 5s for each adult, 3s for each child. Supplies of food to shopkeepers would be increased. In May it was announced that in the event of war the city of Ripon would receive 2,000 evacuees from Leeds; Ripon rural area was scheduled for 1,215 and the former Pateley area 1,220.

The Bishop of Ripon, the Rt Revd G. C. L. Lunt, was awarded the honorary degree of Doctor of Divinity by the University of Leeds.

Notice was given that every household would receive an official booklet on National Service with instructions on how to volunteer. Committees would be set up to advise the public on this so that, in the event of war, industry and essential services would have sufficient people to enable these to carry on without dislocation.

February. The Highways Committee decided to increase the wages of Corporation workers from 1s 0d per hour to 1s 0½d per hour.

The City Engineer was asked to clean and take samples from the water tank in the Market Place to ascertain that in a state of emergency the water would be fit for human consumption.

Air Raid Warning sirens were sounded in the Town Hall, Kearsley's Works, and at Ripon Steel Works as practice for the efficiency of the Air Raid Warden's corps. A hostel for 30 refugees was to open in the Fountains Hall estate. Over thirty acres of land was to be cleared and replanted and the refugees were to study afforestation and all branches of farming.

March. It was reported that the Grammar School had a record number of boys on the register (231); Speech Day would be moved from Summer to the Lent Term; a moratorium would be imposed on carrying out proposed building extensions due to 'national financial stringency'; and a section of the Air Defence Cadet Corps would be formed at the school.

The cost of Air Raid Precautions was blamed for the proposed increase in the rates from 3d to 8d in the pound.

April. New demands were made by the Board of Education on the managers of the Cathedral Boys' and Girls' Schools to expend £5,500 on renovations and extensions. Unless the buildings were brought up to standard, a new council school would have to be provided from the rates at a cost of £25,000.

May. It was announced that Mr W. Garbutt, at present headmaster of Kingsley Senior School, Hemsworth, had been appointed headmaster of the new Senior School to be opened in Ripon on 1 September.

Proposals by the War Office to build another large camp on the same site as the north World War I Camp for the new militia and to continue using the Ure Bank site for Territorial training met with a mixed reception. Many local people disapproved of the threatened influx of troops to the city and landowners were dismayed at the prospect of losing good farming land. However, by the end of June Ripon had recaptured (albeit in smaller measure) the atmosphere of World War I, with the largest unit in the Territorial Army, the Tyne Electrical R.E. (some 1,800 strong) undergoing a two-month training course at Ripon and the construction of the permanent camp which amounted to a small town. The work was carried out by a force of 3,000 at the peak period with 800 men accommodated on site. The two camps, (Clotherholme for R.E.s and Ure Bank for Infantry) were each self-contained, except for a common reception station and hospital and a single camp hall seating 1,000 and equipped as a cinema. The barrack blocks were self-contained and connected to an ablution building by covered corridors, each combined unit having its own central heating system. There were 11 football pitches, 14 tennis courts and four cricket pitches. At the end of June, a conference was held to discuss the enormous increase in drunkenness and disorderly conduct in the city which the police blamed not on the camp workers, but on the camp followers, who had flocked to Ripon. It was felt that publicans could be more helpful in reducing the number of cases and avoid the need for police court proceedings.

Ripon Motor Boat Club's new slipway at Littlethorpe was opened by the Mayor at a very colourful ceremony with most of the boats dressed for the occasion. Since its beginning in 1931 with four members and four craft, the Club had flourished; there were now over 250 members and 104 craft.

Defects in the masonry of the central tower of Ripon Cathedral were causing anxiety to the Dean and Chapter. The two western pinnacles and the whole of the western parapet, an area restored in 1864, were taken down. The roof was reported to be in need of £1,000 for repair. Meanwhile services usually held in the nave had been transferred to the choir.

June. The Mayor of Ripon opened a local appeal in support of the Lord Mayor of London's national appeal for the benefit of the dependents of the men lost in the submarine *Thetis* disaster.

At the Ripon Rotary Club's Ladies Day, the guest speaker was Miss Naomi Jacob, who gave an address on 'Life under a Dictator'. She described conditions in Italy under Mussolini.

Colonel R. E. B. Crompton of *Azerley Chase* celebrated his 94th birthday. He was best known for his pioneering work in the electric light industry to which he had contributed some 200 inventions. As a young man in 1861 he made a motor car which had rubber tyres, a forerunner of the limousine of today. As a boy of eleven he was signed on as a naval cadet in HMS *Dragon* in the Crimean War when he was a guest of an uncle, who was an admiral of the Fleet. He also spent six weeks in the trenches outside Sebastopol, becoming eligible for the Crimean War Medal and the Sebastopol Clasp. Colonel Crompton died in February 1940, and a film of his life and work was made at a London film studio in 1943.

The W.R.C.C. announced that the contract for the completion of the Air Raid Precaution trenches in the Spa Park had been let and that they would grant a licence to retain them for use by the inhabitants of the area.

Miss Yates-Lee retired after 30 years' service as headmistress of Skellfield School. The school, formerly housed in Ripon, was now a public school at Baldersby Park with a Board of Governors. In October 1940, it was moved to Nidd Hall for the duration of the war.

July. Yorkshire archaeologists met in Ripon; the first day took them to the Cathedral, Ailcey Hill, Kirby Hill Church, Aldborough Church and the Roman wall and pavements at Aldborough. They visited *Markenfield Hall*, Fountains Abbey and *Fountains Hall*. Professor Hamilton Thompson acted as leader and Mr T. S. Gowland was responsible for the local arrangements.

A Garden Fête was held at *Newby Hall* by permission of Captain and Mrs E. R. F. Compton to help to fund the Ripon and District Scouts' new headquarters recently opened in the old Temperance Hall on Duck Hill.

The week saw the end of an era in the educational life of Ripon. The Church Schools were to be adapted to meet the new requirements for junior schools and the new Senior School would be occupied next term. As part of the new regime the elementary school at Coltsgate Hill had been closed.

August. Women's cricket was now well established in England. Miss Barbara Wood opened the bowling for the Rest in a match against the English Women's team which was to tour Australia. Miss Wood had played cricket for Yorkshire for three seasons and was the only Yorkshire representative.

Large crowds attended the summer Bank Holiday 'St Wilfrid' celebrations in Ripon. The procession was led by the Ripon City Prize Band and the Feast officially opened with the traditional jam tarts. The Leeds R.A.S.C. and the Tyne Electrical Engineers, both of the Territorial Army, joined the Sunday Parade to the Cathedral and a march-past took place in front of the Town Hall. Part of the fair had been moved from the Market Place to a site near the Clock Tower and the residents in the North Road area complained bitterly of the noise created.

The first sandbags to be brought into use in Ripon as a precautionary measure were seen at Ripon Railway Station, one of the first in the north to put this form of protection into use.

A comprehensive scheme of evacuation was planned. The children would be from Lawnswood High School, Leeds Grammar School and from Junior, Technical and Elementary Schools, a maximum of 1,000 children. These would arrive in the course of a two-day operation, with their teachers and leaders, and on the second day a maximum of 800 mothers and their children would arrive. The city was divided into 20 districts with the headquarters at the old Coltsgate Hill School. It was expected that less than the allocated 1,800 evacuees would arrive and in fact only 650 children and 80 mothers and children came at the beginning of September. However, there were already some people appealing against billeting on the grounds of ill-health or insufficient domestic help. The local authority made it clear that if necessary it would use its compulsory powers, though it hoped to be able to carry out the scheme on a voluntary basis.

The new Modern School was opened by the Chairman of the County Council, Sir Percy Jackson. He stressed Ripon's good fortune in having the first school of its type to be built by the County Council. In the opening term, 480 children of 11 years of age upwards were enrolled.

September. On Sunday 3 September, the news was given on the radio by the Prime Minister, the Rt Hon. Neville Chamberlain, that Britain was at war with Germany. The first air raid warning was sounded in the city because of unidentified aircraft over the Midlands and Eastern Counties. The A.R.P. manned their posts. Gas masks for babies and small children had not yet been received and there was reported to be a shortage of cartons for gas masks. Coltsgate Hill Methodist Sunday School had been adapted as a first-aid post. The Dean and Chapter announced that from 17 September the evening service would be at 3 pm instead of 6.30 pm and the curfew would be rung at 5 pm instead of 9 pm. The Wakeman's Horn would be blown at 6 pm. Some of the most ancient and valuable glass in the Cathedral was removed to a place of safety. Commander Vyner, who had rejoined the Navy, and Lady Doris Vyner placed *Studley Royal* at the disposal of Queen Ethelburga's School, Harrogate. Viscount and Viscountess Swinton were accommodating Harrogate College at *Swinton Castle*, Masham.

By the end of September, with evacuees, forces in training, and workers at the camp, the population had nearly doubled, with an increase of about 7,000 bringing the inevitable problems. War-time restrictions were already beginning to be felt, with reductions of 50 per cent in the bus services caused by petrol rationing and a more severe curtailment of trains from Ripon Station (47 to 16 trains a day). Postal services were cut down to fewer deliveries per day.

The death occurred suddenly at his residence of Canon Claud Cyprian Thornton, for the past two years Archdeacon of Richmond and formerly Vicar of Christ Church, Harrogate. He was 61. One of his last activities had been the preparation in Ripon of a club-room for soldiers. He took a keen interest in the children recently evacuated from Leeds to Ripon and provided special services for them on Sunday afternoons; he was popular with all classes of the community. He twice preached before the King at Buckingham Palace and at Sandringham.

Ripon Y.M.C.A. reverted to its war-time services for the Forces. The reading and writing room, billiards, table tennis, etc., and the refreshment centre were all in steady demand seven nights a week and on three afternoons. The penny cup of tea never lost its popularity. Hot baths were provided for troops who could not get them at the camp.

While the majority of residents in Ripon and District gave a hospitable reception to evacuees, there were those unwilling to offer accommodation. It was recognised that cases of hardship were inevitable, that the allowance paid by the Government was inadequate, and that some parents who could well afford it refused to contribute. It was forecast that there would soon be a means-test. A serious problem was the dirty and verminous condition of some of the children. At a meeting in the Town Hall early in October to discuss the problems which had arisen, the need for finding means of filling leisure time for both children and adults was stressed. Clothing and boots were needed for the minority of children from poor homes. The Reception Officer described the difficulties which had arisen from the uncooperative attitude of some of the better-off residents. On 21 October, the Minister of Health notified all local authorities that in pursuance of an evacuation plan any person lodged in particular premises had to be provided with the accommodation specified. Parents of evacuees who wanted to visit their children were told to use the cafés in Ripon and not to expect meals from their children's hosts; also that if they could afford it they should arrange for laundry to be done in their own homes.

October. The Chamber of Trade recommended shop closing hours of 6 pm on Monday to Friday and 8 pm on Saturday, which was amended to 7.30 pm in November.

Efforts were being made to provide recreation for the troops in the city. A new Services Club had 'spacious and comfortable' accommodation, including a canteen, writing facilities, games, a gramophone and a piano. Ripon Y.M.C.A. again threw open its doors with a willing band of helpers on duty each evening. A hearty welcome was offered by the Ladies' Committee, Toc H, the Cathedral and other local churches. Coltsgate Hill Methodist Church members provided a social evening after the service, with music and community singing. The Zion Methodist Church provided a similar social scene each evening and members of the Allhallowgate Methodist Church, who had been deprived of their school, supported this effort. An appeal was made for donations to the Services Club formed by the late Archdeacon Thornton. It was delightfully accommodated in the Montague Burton building, had cost £60 to set up and needed £280 to maintain it for its first year. The club was always full and much appreciated by the Forces stationed in the district.

The first summons under the Light Restrictions Act was heard in Ripon. It was reported that Special Constables were getting some abuse when pointing out to Ripon householders that lights were showing, and in November several cases were before the Court for obscene language connected with lighting.

The price of petrol was raised by twopence a gallon to 1s 8d.

Mr George Bell of City Square, Leeds, opened a branch of his civil and military tailoring business at 32 Kirkgate, Ripon. He was a member of a family of distinguished tailors, the fifth of nine sons, six of whom entered the tailoring trade. Mr Bell founded his business in Leeds in 1907. After the War he moved to premises next door to the Wakeman's House in the Market Place where Mr Whiteley Nelson had carried on a tailoring business.

Many complaints had been made because there were as yet no air-raid shelters in Ripon for the public, although shelters had been provided for staff in the Town Hall, the Highways Yard and the Gas Works. The County Council had carried out a census of cellars in the city and steps were being taken to convert some of these into refuges. The work was not carried out as Government grants were only given for surface shelters and early in 1940 shelters were provided on the Market Square and in Blossomgate.

1939-40.   FREDERICK ISAAC TREES, Builder

Mayor 1938-39-40-41

November. Alderman F. I. Trees was elected Mayor for a second term; it was announced that owing to the War there would be no banquet at the Mayor-making.

Dr C. H. Moody offered to arrange Sunday evening entertainments in the form of community singing, which he would conduct personally at the Opera House from 8 pm to 9 pm. While the entertainments were primarily for the troops, the public would be admitted.

Instructions were given for the removal of the most valuable paintings in the Council Chamber and Mayor's Parlour to a suitable place in the basement at the rear of the Town Hall.

There was general anxiety in the city about the much-increased population and the much-reduced food supply. Food rationing had not yet been introduced and the Ministry of Food, though holding large stocks, placed the onus on local grocers, who complained of reduced supplies from their wholesalers and the necessity of rationing their customers from meagre supplies. Ripon householders protested about the small amount of butter, bacon and sugar available.

A Committee was formed to administer the Ripon Fund for Christmas parcels for the local men in the forces, but there was now a limited time to accumulate funds and get the parcels away. One hundred and

twenty-six pounds was donated so that 232 parcels were able to be sent costing 10s each and containing Christmas cake, chocolate, cigarettes, razor blades and a writing compendium.

December. The death was announced of Alderman Gertrude Wells, Ripon's first woman Councillor and Alderman. She was succeeded by Councillor Margaret Sara Steven.

January. No mention of current weather conditions was permitted in wartime but the *Gazette* did report a funeral at Dallowgill where the coffin was conveyed to the church across the fields by sledge. It was learned later that the temperature recorded on 3 January, 12°F of frost, was the lowest recorded and that the snow which started to fall on 16 January had reached a depth of 14 ins. by the end of the month.

An application was granted by the Justices for an extension of permitted hours from 10 pm to 11.30 pm at the *Spa Hotel* each Saturday evening for dinner dances. The clientele would be select and either uniform or evening dress would be worn. It was suggested that as the entrance fee would be 4s no one would attend 'just for a drink'. The licence would be reviewed at the end of March.

The death occurred at the age of 88 of Miss Caroline Cornelia Van Cortlantt Bower, born at *Elmscroft*, now the centre block of the Ripon *Spa Hotel*. She was a great outdoor enthusiast and carried out work with children, providing a cot named 'The Ripon Cot' at the Children's Hospital, Chelsea. Miss Bower was a member of a famous family, one brother (Mr Herbert Bower, M.A.) was Mayor of the City 1907-8-9; another brother (Professor F. Orpen Bower) was Regius Professor of Botany at Glasgow for 40 years; her uncle (Francis Orpen Morris) was one of Yorkshire's most distinguished naturalists, who wrote *A History of British Birds* in six beautifully-illustrated volumes.

Lady Graham, Chairman of the West Riding organisation, spoke of the work of the Women's Land Army at a meeting of the Ripon Branch of the National Farmers' Union. She spoke of the prejudices, especially in the north, against women on the land and warned that it might well become a choice not between a man and a woman but between a woman and mutton. The minimum pay for a trained girl over 18 was 28s per week, with overtime at 7d per hour.

Ripon had three air-raid sirens, located at the Grammar School, the Police Station and the Surveyor's house, Whitcliffe Lane and there were three Wardens' posts, at 12 Queen Street, in the cellars of 22 Fountains Terrace, North Street and at 2 South Crescent. There were as yet no public shelters and it was estimated that shelter would be required for 600 people.

The Venerable D. M. M. Bartlett, Archdeacon of Leeds and Vicar of St Wilfrid's, Harrogate, was appointed Residentiary Canon of Ripon Cathedral and Archdeacon of Richmond in succession to the late Archdeacon C. C. Thornton.

Sir William and Lady Aykroyd of *Grantley Hall* celebrated their golden wedding. They had lived there since 1926 when Jane Lady Furness left. Sir William was a prominent West Riding industrialist and in 1926 was High Sheriff of Yorkshire.

Men aged 23 had to register for National Service in February and it was estimated that this would affect 250,000 men over the whole country. Twenty-four-year-olds would register a month later.

Bad weather was affecting the distribution of meat and prices rose accordingly. Those housewives who could afford it bought turkeys, chickens, guinea fowl, geese, duckling and rabbit.

The usual controversy followed the application of the military authorities for the opening of Ripon cinemas on Sundays. The Ripon City Cricket Club allowed soldiers to use their ground on Saturday and Sunday afternoons.

Many evacuees had returned home to Leeds for Christmas and, as Lawnswood Girls' School and Leeds Technical School were re-opening, a number of the children would not be coming back to Ripon. Their billets had been kept open and some householders had drawn the allowance. The Ministry of Health demanded repayment which was considered unfair, as the military were clamouring for accommodation and would have taken up the billets if they had been available. In February it was announced that no more evacuees would be sent to the Ripon area. This prompted the closure of the Evacuation Welfare Office.

March. The death of Colonel J. C. R. Husband was announced, at the age of 83. After qualifying as a doctor he had joined his father, Dr Charles Husband, in his Ripon practice and in 1936 he was appointed coroner for Ripon City and Liberty. From 1909-1912 he had been Commanding Officer of the 6th Battalion of the West Yorkshire Regiment.

April. It was announced that the Bishop of Ripon was leaving the Palace to take up residence at *High Berrys*, now *Bishop Mount,* and that Dr Barnado's organisation would take over the Palace.

The Dean and Chapter expressed concern at the cost of maintaining the fabric of the Cathedral; the roof timbers had some death watch beetle infestation and the stonework of the central tower needed attention. It was important if possible to retain the services of a skilled craftsman. Steel ladders on the exterior of the building and steel pipes alongside these were required to guard against the danger of fire from incendiary bombs.

May. The Bishop invited the people of Ripon to join him in the National Day of Prayer on Sunday 26 May.

The Ripon Study Group formed a Ripon Branch of the W.E.A. to be run in conjunction with the University of Leeds at an annual subscription of 3s.

The Bank Holiday was cancelled by a sudden order to remain at work. However, many shops in Ripon remained closed and there were many visitors about and, surprisingly, quite a few cars on the roads.

Mr Anthony Eden's appeal for men on the Home Front to join a force to be known as the Local Defence Volunteers (and later as the Home Guard) met with an immediate response with over 200 men registering in the Ripon Police area; this included the city, Aldfield, Copt Hewick, Kirkby Malzeard and North Stainley. The age of the recruits ranged from 17 to 65 and most had some experience in the use of firearms. Numbers reached 500 men by the end of June. The Mayor's appeal for volunteers for air-raid wardens, however, was disappointing.

The local Y.M.C.A. War Service Fund collected £1,214 for a mobile canteen.

Many people mourned the death of Father Levick, priest of St Wilfrid's Roman Catholic Church from 1907; he had succeeded Father de Vacht as chaplain to the 1st Marquess of Ripon who bequeathed many of the beautiful furnishings from the private chapel at Studley Royal to enrich St Wilfrid's. During World War I, Canon Levick did wonderful work among the soldiers in the Ripon camp and was untiring in the help he gave to Belgian refugees who found a temporary home in Ripon. He was an authority on Fountains Abbey. When he became Canon of Leeds in 1929 he was given £50 from the people of Ripon.

June. The death was announced of Sir Reginald Guy Graham of *Norton Conyers Hall* at the age of 67. He was the ninth holder of the title, succeeding in 1920. He served in the Boer War and World War I, was closely connected with the Ripon Choral Society and served on many official bodies. The new baronet, Sir Richard Bellingham Graham, was a Pilot Officer in the R.A.F. and connected with banking.

The City Council decided to remove the sandbags from the front doorway to the Town Hall and to have the front windows bricked up.

Men of the B.E.F. who had returned from the evacuation of Dunkirk and the Channel Ports were entertained in Ripon and District; 50 men were entertained to tea at the *Café Victoria* by the Dean and Chapter; the Y.M.C.A. took 50 to Fountains Abbey and gave them tea in the grounds; two other parties of 100 each were invited to *Grantley Hall* by Mr Aykroyd and to *Mowbray House,* Kirkby Malzeard, by Sir Fred Moore.

Sunday services were, in future, to be held in the nave of the Cathedral as the chapter-house, choir vestry and the undercroft had been prepared for use as shelters in the event of an air-raid during services.

July. There were complaints concerning a delay in the collection of scrap iron and it was pointed out that there were still many sets of railings which had not been removed. A depot set up by the W.V.S. in Park Street following an appeal broadcast by Lady Reading for scrap aluminium was bombarded with pans of every description, water bottles, shoe trees, moulds and even a portion of a World War I zeppelin. In November the Town Clerk announced that it had been decided not to remove the railings at the cemetery and the Spa Gardens; however, in the same month the Chapter announced that iron railings and sundry ironwork around those graves in the Cathedral graveyard, the ownership of which was not known, would be sent for the service of the country. The Council also decided not to dispose of the drinking fountain in the Spa Gardens presented to the city in 1873 by Captain J. William Patterson.

August. The Feast of St Wilfrid was celebrated and

there was much consternation expressed about illuminated stalls in the Market Place which remained open until midnight.

September. The County and City Councils agreed to release employees for limited duties as Special Constables, Home Guard, A.R.P. wardens and First Aid Workers, without loss of pay, and appealed to other employers to follow suit.

Racing was reinstated throughout the country and Ripon racecourse was chosen by the Jockey Club for the first meeting. The L.N.E.R. ran a special race train and the attendance was 10 per cent above that of a peacetime September meeting.

Ripon made a spontaneous and united effort during Spitfire Fund Week when £1,509 was collected from the churches, the pubs, the young and the old. In November efforts were again activated by the bombing of Coventry and a second cheque for £1,000 was sent.

October. An appeal was made for knitters to provide woollen garments for the Forces during the winter and the Committee of the Ripon Christmas Parcel Fund asked for donations of money for the work so that parcels could be despatched to all Ripon men in the Forces abroad before Christmas. In all, 552 parcels were sent and in most cases letters of thanks were received in the New Year.

The Minister of Home Security approved in principle the basement of Messrs Burton's premises in the Market Place being prepared as a public shelter. School shelters were to be provided and the crypt of Holy Trinity Church could now be used. The Council were asked to take steps to prevent the public shelters from being used for purposes for which they were not intended.

A letter in the *Gazette* from the Mayor spoke of the plight of some refugees from the bombed areas, many related to men serving in the Forces, who had arrived in the city to become victims of some people who let rooms at exhorbitant rates. He hoped that the Council would not have to resort to law to check such extortion. More and more people were evacuated from vulnerable areas and by December the population of Ripon had increased by 5,000. Some houses were overcrowded and there were complaints that some of the larger houses were providing little or no accommodation; the Mayor had again to threaten to use his compulsory billeting powers if people did not make sacrifices to help the less fortunate.

Mr H. Metcalfe of Messrs Metcalfe and Company, Furnishers, gave an American organ for use in the chapel at the cemetery.

Ripon's United Effort week closed with a parade of Regular and Voluntary troops, an exhibition of physical training in the Market Place and a fire-fighting exercise by the Ripon Fire Service at the Cathedral. Mr Bernard Newman, the well-known writer, gave a lecture in the Lawrence Hall on 'Espionage and Fifth Columnists'.

1940-41. FREDERICK ISAAC TREES, Builder

November. The death of the Dean of Ripon, Dr Charles Mansfield Owen, was announced. He was 88

FREDERICK I. TREES.
MAYOR 1938-1939.
MAYOR 1939-1940.
MAYOR 1940-1941

Mayor 1938-39-40-41

and active up to his last day. Dr Owen, the son of a barrister, graduated at Oxford and his first and only curacy was in a poor Southampton dock area. He came to Ripon in 1915 and was a familiar figure during World War I on the platform of Ripon Station, welcoming and saying farewell to troops. In World War II he showed an equal interest in the men of the Forces as far as his strength permitted. He had a genius for raising money, particularly for the Cathedral, and was generous in his own giving. Dr Owen was very much part of Ripon, enjoying the link between City and Cathedral, especially the presence of the Mayor and Corporation at public worship. His love of everyone and his particular fondness of cats, his cheerful greeting and his feeling for the City endeared him to all.

The Government was prepared to assist in the provision of Air Raid Shelters to those whose income did not exceed £250 per annum. The City Engineer sent out forms asking for information about the provision of shelters and suggested that the onus was on each householder to improve his own shelter accommodation.

The people of Ripon watched with genuine regret if not dismay the disappearance of the pinnacles on the western towers of the Cathedral. They were modern by comparison with the rest of the fabric, being erected in 1797 by Dean Waddilove, along with the battlements which replaced those damaged in the gale of 1714.

By order of the Secretary of State all shops had to close at 6 pm except those selling tobacco or newspapers, with early closing on Wednesday at 1 pm and late night closing on Saturday 7.30 pm.

December. Ten Christmas trees arrived at the Cathedral, five from Major Compton of *Newby Hall* and five from Lady Doris Vyner of *Studley Royal*. They were placed between the pillars of the nave and festooned with small bags to receive gifts for war charities.

January. The year began very quietly with no music in the Market Square, where the activities of the City Band were greatly missed.

The Salvation Army Hut in Water Skellgate was

becoming very popular with the Forces and there was an appeal for more helpers to cook and serve the light meals so much in demand — eggs, sausages, chips and sandwiches — from 10 am to 10 pm.

Married women became eligible for all Council appointments and the Council rescinded a 1935 resolution which forced women employees to relinquish appointments on marriage.

Photographs were taken of the City's Charters which were then sent together with the Corporation plate to the strongroom of the Midland Bank. The Corporation's valuable glass, china and paintings were also removed to a place of safety for the duration of the war.

A Red Cross Penny-a-Week Fund was inaugurated and collected by volunteers to provide the society with money to send food, tobacco, cigarettes and clothing to Prisoners-of-War.

Appeals were made for men to join the Ripon Company of the Home Guard, as numbers had been reduced by members joining the other Services or leaving the district to take up war jobs elsewhere. The Chapter asked for volunteers to undertake fire watching at the Cathedral, as at least 42 fire fighters per week were needed. In some parts of the city, the organisation of fire watchers and fire fighters had been completed with nearly 60 parties trained to deal with incendiary bombs. Many people still were unwilling to co-operate on a voluntary basis, so the Minister made it obligatory for occupiers of business premises to watch their property and for employees to take duty of 48 hours per month without remuneration.

Lieutenant J. D. Grice, R.E., son of Mr and Mrs J. Grice of the *Lawrence Restaurant*, was believed to be the first Ripon man to be mentioned in dispatches for distinguished service in the field.

Councillor T. F. Spence was elected Alderman in place of the late Alderman Hargrave, and Mr F. Lowley was made a co-opted member of the Council.

Temporary permission was given for the Hornblower's elder daughter, Mrs Mary Storey, to act as his substitute on those occasions when other duties prevented him from blowing the Horn at 6 pm. When Mr Blackburn broadcast with Mary from Manchester in the *Northern Lights* feature programme, his younger daughter Muriel, aged 13, sounded the Horn in the Market Square. The Hornblower in what was his eighth broadcast related the story of the Ripon custom of setting the watch.

February. The Council circulated a questionnaire to all householders in the city to determine those who had refugees billeted with them and the amount of accommodation which was still available.

March. Canon Godwin Birchenough was appointed Dean of Ripon to succeed the late Dr Mansfield Owen. The new Dean would live in the Residence in St Marygate and not at the Deanery.

The first instalment of child refugees from London arrived and were billeted at St Margaret's Lodge, College Road. The group would ultimately number 24 children aged between two and four. Mrs Lunt, the

Bishop's wife, thanked those who had provided money and necessities and asked for gifts of summer clothes and lengths of material as the children had brought only woollen garments.

April. An appeal was made by the Mayor for young local women to come forward and register for munitions work in the Midlands, where many thousands were needed.

May. A day nursery was set up for evacuated mothers and babies in the old Liberal Club in Kirkgate, where mothers could leave their babies between 10.30 am and 5.30 pm. Arrangements were made for them to do their washing and give the babies a bath.

Ripon's oldest tradesman, Mr Thomas Appleton, founder of the Pork Butchers of that name, died aged 93.

June. The Minister of Food required all consumers to register under the egg-rationing scheme and warned that during the winter only two or three eggs would be available per person per week. Every householder able to do so should keep a small number of hens. Corporation house tenants were allowed to keep up to six hens but no cockerels were permitted.

July. Dean Birchenough made his first financial appeal to provide the premium for insurance of 'movable goods' in the Cathedral against war risk; any damage to the fabric would be the responsibility of the Government. The organ was insured for £500, the bells for £500, and the choir stalls, seats, the nave stalls and both altars for £150 each.

The City Engineer was instructed to demolish the premises known as the *Railway Inn* in Stonebridgegate and other property in Ingram's Row.

Mr T. J. Hawley was appointed as Hornblower on the retirement of Mr H. Blackburn after 22 years service.

To ease congestion, an extension of the one-way traffic circuit was submitted to the Ministry of Transport. It was suggested that outward traffic westwards to Kirkby Malzeard should leave Ripon by way of Kirkby Road and the inward journey be made by way of College Road. Traffic towards Boroughbridge would leave by way of Kirkgate and Bedern Bank and enter the city by Water Skellgate and High Skellgate, with the suggestion that Thirlway's corner at the top of High Skellgate be demolished.

September. As elsewhere, men resident in Ripon between the ages of 18 and 60 registered for Civil Defence duties.

The clergy of Ripon Cathedral wore scarlet cassocks for the first time on Sunday 7 September, said to be a privilege granted only to Cathedrals of Royal foundation. The lay clerks and choristers had worn the scarlet cassock since 1909 but the clergy had retained their black cassocks.

The Corporation advertised for a chef or cook manager for a *British Restaurant* in Ripon at a salary of £240 per annum. The restaurant opened in Priest Lane in November on a cash-and-carry basis. A large crowd of customers was attracted by a good meal for a shilling — the first menu was celery soup and bread (2d), meat, potatoes, swede and gravy (7d), currant pudding and sauce (2d), and a cup of tea (1d). In January, when the cafeteria was opened in the Methodist Mission schoolroom, Allhallowgate, it was furnished with green-topped tables, each seating six, with a total of 200. The Priest Lane premises were retained as a cooking centre. It was named the *Wakeman Restaurant* and was run by the W.V.S.

October. The Ripon Christmas Parcels Fund Committee suspended its operations owing to the impossibility of obtaining suitable articles this year. It was decided instead to send Postal Orders and greetings and in December ten-shilling Postal Orders were sent to 672 Ripon men serving in the Forces.

The Council decided that the Horn should be blown at the start of blackout if this occurred earlier than 9 o'clock.

The sale of property, chiefly 52 dwelling houses in Bondgate, ordered by the executors of the late Alderman Frederick William Hargrave, attracted a large attendance.

1941-42. MARGARET SARA STEVEN

The first (and only) woman Mayor of Ripon. Born in Buckinghamshire, the daughter of the Revd J. Tarver, she and her mother came to Ripon after his death. In 1908 she married Dr P. A. Steven of Park Street. She was trained as a social worker and after her marriage was active in the work of Ripon Girls' Club and with mothers and children. She was elected to the Council in 1933 and was much concerned with housing and public health. After the outbreak of war she organised the Women's Voluntary Service and hospitality in Ripon homes for troops stationed at the camp. She was elected an alderman in 1940 and died in the May following her election as Mayor.

November. Miss Kay retired after 33 years on the staff of Holy Trinity School, where she had been headmistress since 1917.

At the inaugural meeting of the Friends of Ripon Cathedral, it was announced that The Princess Royal had consented to be the first Friend and Patron. It had been suggested earlier in the year that the Friends should supervise the preparation of the memorial to Dean Charles Mansfield Owen which was to take the form of three figures to be placed in niches over the entrance to the south choir aisle. Mr Esmond Burton, then considered to be one of the greatest sculptors in medieval design in the country, was asked to carry out the work. A plaster cast of the central figure was on view at the meeting and it was announced that due to the generosity of Sir Fred Moore, it had been possible to fill the niches on either side at an estimated cost of £330, towards which £215 had already been subscribed.

December. The *Gazette* asked for photographs of men and women serving in the Forces for publication in the paper. To date 509 photographs had been received and 472 had been published, but it was known that 692 Ripon men were serving. No photographs of women serving in the Forces had been sent despite previous appeals.

Ripon had a very quiet Christmas. Market Day was busy and there was brisk business on Christmas Eve. Buses and trains were heavily laden with people going home if possible and, in spite of the war, the spirit of Christmas was abroad. The Ripon mummers performed their old-time burlesque on Boxing Day.

It was estimated that there was still 20 to 30 miles of iron railings in place in the city; owners would be informed if the railings were *not* to be taken and all the rest were ordered to be removed.

January. The annual distribution under two old Ripon charities took place in January. Coal was distributed to widows residing between Allhallowgate and the Old Malt Kilns, North Street, in accordance with the will of Ann Kettlewell, dated 16 December 1857, and grants were given as stipulated in the will of Ann Day of Bishopton, dated 3 April 1707.

HMS *Burdock*, a corvette costing £120,000, was allocated to Ripon and district as their target for Warship Week to be held in March. The week was a great success with the raising of £166,171, virtually all from small investors.

The Council decided to send 36 statute books, rate books and ledgers dated prior to 1800 to be shredded for salvage, and a chandelier lying unused in the cellar of the Town Hall for scrap.

February. Stories and pictures appeared in the press describing the severe weather in January. The River Ure froze from bank to bank and although the ice soon broke up, for days afterwards blocks floated down river.

The Dean Owen Memorial in Ripon Cathedral was dedicated by the Bishop of Ripon in the presence of the Deputy Mayor, Councillor W. R. Dixon, members of the Corporation and a large congregation. The memorial consists of coloured figures of Our Lady flanked on the left by Archbishop Roger de Pont l'Eveque and on the right by Archbishop Walter de Grey.

March. During Warship Week, there was a march through the city of troops stationed in the area and as the detachment of W.A.A.F. and A.T.S. marching at the end of the procession turned off down Kirkgate, a horse and cart joined the proceedings and 'decorously paced along in time to the music of the military band'.

Members of the Women's Land Army stationed on local farms who were short of work during the snowstorms in January and February realised that the Corporation could not cope with snow clearance because of lack of manpower. They volunteered their services and soon had the streets clear.

The death of Mr William Folliott Powell of Sharow Hall occurred at the age of 97. He had been a considerable public figure in the district, having sat on the Ripon Rural Council, the Board of Guardians and the Bench of the Ripon Liberty. Mr Powell had also been chairman of the Income Tax Commissioners for Ripon.

April. The Revd Father Cyril Earnshaw was appointed Priest-in-Charge of St Wilfrid's Catholic Church, following the death of Father Bernard McAdam in March after only a short time in Ripon.

The duration of Double Summer Time was to be extended by one month, i.e., from 4 April to 8 August. This presented special problems for farm workers, and arrangements were made for milk collections by road and rail to be re-timed.

May. Mrs Margaret Steven, the first woman to be Mayor of Ripon, died while in office. She had spent a life of devoted service in the city and was greatly missed. At a special meeting of the Ripon City Council, Councillor W. Russell Dixon was unanimously elected Mayor for the remaining months of the municipal year.

June. Mrs Garner was elected Alderman in place of Alderman Mrs Steven, and Mr Reginald Petty of Ripon Grammar School was made a co-opted councillor.

Mr Roy Gilyard-Beer, third son of the late Mr T. Gilyard-Beer of 5 Bedern Bank, was admitted a Fellow of the Society of Antiquaries. The last Riponian by birth to be so honoured was John Richard Walbran who was born in Allhallowgate in 1817 and elected Fellow in 1854. Mr Gilyard-Beer had been a pupil at Ripon Grammar School and was then serving in the Intelligence Corps. Mr T. S. Gowland, another Riponian, became an F.S.A. in April 1943.

The second groyne or breakwater in the River Laver near Mallorie Park Drive had become undermined and had to be demolished. The bank of the River Skell near the Rustic Bridge had started to crumble and was strengthened by planting willows.

Elizabeth Vyner, aged 18, only daughter of Commander and Lady Doris Vyner of *Studley Royal*, died while on service with the W.R.N.S. She had been named Elizabeth after the Queen who was a close friend of Lady Doris and had often stayed at *Studley Royal*.

An appeal was made for medical herbs to be collected to replace those herbs usually imported from abroad. Ripon responded well to the call and under the auspices of the W.V.S., the Girl Guides and Boy Scouts, a collecting centre was opened in Bodega Chambers in Queen Street with a drying shed at Holmfield. The scheme was launched at a meeting where Professor F. O. Bower lectured on medicinal herbs.

Mr K. D. Hanna was appointed Town Clerk at a salary of £400 per annum. He succeeded Mr J. Henry Gough who had retired through ill-health after 22 years' service.

The Sanitary Inspector reported on his inspection of 40 houses in Priest Lane that four houses were definitely verminous and one was possibly so. Three sprayings of vermicides made at 10-day intervals were required. There was also infestation with rats in some premises and notices were served to owners of the properties to deal with nuisances. Orders were given for periodic inspection to be made of all Corporation property.

The *British Restaurant* had been running at a loss of £500 per year which would be met by the Ministry of Food. Two open ranges were converted to gas heating at a cost of £100.

The Chief Constable of the West Riding asked the Council to provide suitable condemned property for a demonstration of fire-fighting and life-saving. As no such property was available he asked for a temporary building to be erected. The Mayor condemned the project as a sheer waste of money and a useless experiment, a performance in no way comparable to what would happen in reality. Councillor Harker suggested the Police Station and the Mayor the Court House as possible venues.

August. The necessity for economy much reduced the annual St Wilfrid's Fair in the Market Place and the 'Saint' made his pilgrimage through the city without music.

A farm in Lark Lane harvested a crop of flax with a yield of 50 cwt. per acre. The fibre was sent for manufacture into linen and the seeds provided linseed oil and feed cake for cattle.

Mr George Jackson of North Cottage had two portraits accepted for an exhibition of works by artists of the Northern Counties in the Laing Art Gallery, Newcastle upon Tyne.

September. At 11.30 am on the anniversary of the outbreak of war, a National Day of Prayer, the Mayor spoke from the Town Hall balcony inviting the people in the market, stallholders, farmers and dealers, to go with him to the Cathedral for 15 minutes of prayer.

Professor Bower presented an oak chair to the Chapter made of wood taken from the Cathedral at the time of Sir Gilbert Scott's restoration about 1861.

October. A scheme was presented at the Friends of Ripon Cathedral's annual meeting to provide figures to fill the vacant niches of the choir screen. It was reported that the misericords had been removed from the choir and several pieces of early glass from the windows had been dispersed for greater safety.

1942-43. ARTHUR NETTLETON, Brewer

ALD A NETTLETON

MAYOR

1942-1943
1943-1944

Born 1886 at Oulton near Leeds, where he went to school. Entered the brewing trade at Selby. In World War I he served for three-and-a-half years in the Royal Fusiliers and was wounded and taken prisoner. He was appointed manager of Hepworth and Company's Ripon Brewery in 1923. Elected to the Council in 1929, Alderman 1935. He was a member of the local Education Committee, a Trustee of the Hospital Charities (St John's and St Mary's) and a governor of the Girls' High School. He loved music and sang for 20 years with the Choral and Operatic Societies and in the voluntary choir at the Cathedral. He died at his home in The Crescent in 1963.

January. There was considerable controversy over the decision to remove the ornamental gates of the Spa Gardens and to replace them by a wooden gate. By July 1944, 13,806 yds of iron railings and 584 gates, weighing in all 231 tons, had been requisitioned. One gate in North Road was retained on the grounds of artistic merit. There had been 18 claims for compensation, resulting in a total payment of £23 1s 5d.

March. At the Annual Meeting of the Ripon Cricket Club it was announced that because of the War the club ground would not be available for play this season. Evening and Saturday matches would be arranged on the Grammar School Cricket Ground.

April. The Council increased the rates by 4d in the £ to 7s 6d in the £ for the next half year. This increase was due to expenditure on the Joint Isolation Hospital and the making of Victoria Grove Road. One councillor commented on the 'very magnificent effort' that had been made to keep the finances of the cemetery in surplus. Alderman T. F. Spence wondered if the customers would agree.

May. Lieutenant-Colonel Wilberforce, owner of the Markington Hall estate and a descendant of William Wilberforce, the anti-slave campaigner, and Captain Patrick Graham, the third son of Katharine Lady Graham of *Norton Conyers*, were killed in action in North Africa.

Ripon 'Wings for Victory' campaign opened with a target of £150,000.

A performance of the *Yeomen of the Guard* by the

Ripon Amateur Dramatic Society created a happy diversion from the War. One hundred pounds was raised for the Ripon and District Hospital.

July. The Council considered a scheme for post-war housing in Ripon to alleviate the present overcrowding and to allow for very necessary slum clearance and general development. It was estimated that 517 new houses would be needed. The difficulty would be choosing suitable sites; the only virgin land available was the Gallows Hill area which had room for 86 houses.

A decision to initiate a scheme to provide elementary school children with midday meals was taken at a joint conference between members of the Local Education Committee, Head Teachers and officials of the W.R.C.C.

To mark his 80th birthday and 'in slight appreciation of his comparatively good health during a long life', Sir Fred Moore sent a cheque for £1,000 to endow a bed in Ripon Hospital.

August. War-time austerity was revealed in the appeal in the Cathedral Parish Magazine for 95 clothing coupons to provide choristers with new cassocks and surplices, worn out with 28 years of use. No one imputed extravagance to the Chapter, but there was doubt concerning the legality of the gift. This was resolved happily by the Board of Trade who agreed that loose coupons could be collected by the congregation and exchanged for a voucher, which in turn would be exchanged for the goods.

A unique art exhibition at the Town Hall was mounted by members of the Forces varying in rank from sapper to brigadier. The majority of exhibitors were professional artists in civilian life, among whom were Dennis Flanders, R.A., and Ernest Greenwood, a portrait painter of distinction.

September. Ripon Books for Salvage campaign attempted to double its original target of 15,000 books. Nearly 25,000 books were collected out of which 3,500 were sent to the Forces and 250 to blitzed libraries. Members of the W.V.S. sorting the books brought to light some valuable items, for instance the book commemorating the presentation of the Town Hall to the city by the Marquess of Ripon and two volumes of the 2nd edition of Johnson's Dictionary of 1786.

A record of 360 masons' marks in the Cathedral was completed by Mr J. P. Hill, the Cathedral mason, probably the first record of its kind to be made in Ripon.

Iron doors from the cells of the first floor of the cell-block of the Ripon Police Station were sent for salvage. These cells were rarely used and it was not envisaged that there would be any great increase in crime. These doors were originally made in Ripon when the Liberty Prison was built in 1816 and the West Riding Constabulary retained one door as a museum piece. In 1983 when the Ripon Museum Trust was preparing the cell-block for the opening of the Ripon Prison and Police Museum, the West Yorkshire Police returned this old door and it was rehung in its original position.

A serious fire at the *Victoria Opera House* burnt out almost the complete interior of the building. Fire watchers had been on duty until 6 pm and the Ripon N.F.S. was called out half an hour later. The main structure and the adjoining buildings were saved. The *Opera House* re-opened to the public in March 1944 with new seating.

The death was announced of Dr Samuel Hey at the age of 73. Dr Hey had come to Ripon 41 years previously as partner to the late Dr J. C. R. Husband.

October. A children's Clothing Exchange was set up by the W.V.S. in Kirkgate to help to overcome the difficulty of clothing coupons.

1943-44. ARTHUR NETTLETON, Brewer

Mayor 1942-43-44

Rainfall in 1943 was 24.52 ins, a very low figure. Population statistics: estimated population 9,368; inhabited houses 2,525; number of births, legitimate 154, illegitimate 20; deaths 93.

December. The Revd H. R. Williams, Precentor of the Cathedral, was presented with a silver salver by the parishioners in grateful remembrance of his ministry from 1917 to 1943.

A very quiet Christmas was recorded in Ripon, a festival spent chiefly at home, parties of carol singers visiting houses in the evenings. The Christmas Market was notable for the fantastically high prices paid to producers for their stock of poultry.

January. Studley Park, once the home of herds of deer, came under the plough and the herd was but a remnant of pre-war years. There were formerly between two and three hundred head but by 1944 only 20 fallow and 20 red deer remained. Even these would be thinned out to provide venison as an addition to the meat ration.

February. Considerable structural damage was done to the premises of Messrs Row and Son, Jewellers, Market Place, when an empty bus invaded their shop after coasting down the east side of the Square of its own volition.

March. The Ministry of Food arranged a nationwide drive to exterminate millions of rats which were destroying costly and scarce foodstuffs. In Ripon, people were asked to notify the Sanitary Inspector of any known infestations in the city.

Elders of Allhallowgate Methodist Church burnt the

deeds, relating to the debts accumulated during the extensions of the school premises and now paid off, as a symbol of freedom.

April. Mr Strachan, headmaster of Ripon Grammar School, reported at the School Speech Day that the school had 250 boys and no more could be taken. The boarding side was also full, with 55 boarders. He referred to the new Education Act which provided for three types of Secondary School, Grammar, Modern and Technical, and said he hoped the result would not be three separate compartments. He himself would like to see the three types of school under a single administration if not one roof. This last idea was not taken up and the two secondary schools on each side of Clotherholme Road remained separate. This had been feared by the Chairman of the West Riding Education Committee, who expressed in a speech given in the following April his dissatisfaction at Ripon's insistence in keeping a policy which divided the community into two classes and which he described as 'muddle-headed and fundamentally uneducational'.

Canon Cunningham gave a full exposition of the new Education Bill, particularly as it affected the Cathedral Schools, at the Cathedral Parish Annual Meeting. The cost of bringing the church schools in the Diocese up to the standards laid down by the new Bill had been estimated at £120,000.

Mr P. R. Pfaff, alto lay clerk of Ripon Cathedral, left to become organist and choirmaster of Tiverton Parish Church in his native county after 30 years with the Cathedral choir. He had been organist at Holy Trinity Church, a music teacher in the city and had taught at Jepson's School.

At a property sale, five houses in Brewster Terrace were bought for £1,400; two houses and shops (Nos. 54 and 55) and nine cottages (Nos. 45-53) made in all £750. In September £545 was paid at auction for two properties in Westgate: No. 8 occupied as a grocer's shop by Mr Norman Lee and No. 9 by Messrs H. Bake and Sons, Saddlers.

Ripon and District Salute the Soldier Week raised £177,510 as compared with Wings for Victory in 1943 at £156,000 and Warship Week in 1942 at £166,000.

June. The Ripon Library ordered the *Yorkshire Post*, its first daily newspaper, for an experimental period of six months. If there was evidence that Ripon people wished to read it, the paper would continue to be available.

The death was announced of the Rt Revd Thomas Banks Strong, K.B.E., M.A., D.D., Bishop of Ripon from 1920-1925, and later of Oxford.

July. The Trustees of the Underwood Trust decided that the Underwood Scholarship should in future be held by a girl at the Ripon Girls' High School. In 1657, Alderman William Underwood of London had left all his estate 'situate at or near the Horse Fair end in the town of Ripon to pay the rents and profits thereof to ten poor widows of good conversation £5 yearly, that is to say 10 shillings apiece. The residue to put poor children to school at 10 shillings apiece'. For some years the money had provided a scholarship for boys at Ripon Grammar School but the Trustees felt it was time for girls to benefit from the Trust.

Evacuees from flying bombs continued to arrive in Ripon from the south. The Zion schoolroom in Blossomgate was used as a Rest Centre, a few found temporary quarters in the city by private arrangement, but the majority were found billets in the rural areas.

August. The fair at the St Wilfrid Festival was much smaller than in pre-war days, occupying only half the Square. The Canadian R.C.A.F. band led the procession.

In July a Ripon woman Alderman was sentenced to six months in the Second Divison at Leeds Assizes for corruptly receiving sums of money as rewards for failing to carry out her duties as an Enforcement Officer of the Board of Trade. This created a vacancy on the City Council because an Alderman who had been convicted under the Prevention of Corruption Acts was disqualified from being a member of the Council. At a special meeting of the City Council, Councillor Fothergill was elected an Alderman and Sir Maurice Brayshay, K.B.E., J.P., was co-opted to take his place as a councillor.

September. Ripon was one of the first towns to escape from the blackout. Under new Government restrictions, the streets could be dimly illuminated and the first light to be restored was the Mayor's lamp outside his house in Skellfield Terrace.

An exhibition of work by artists from the School of Military Engineers was mounted in the Town Hall in aid of the Merchant Navy Fund, including *Thursday Market, Ripon* by Sapper Dennis Flanders, R.A.

October. The sixth, and it was hoped the last appeal, was made for the Ripon Christmas Parcels Fund. As in previous years postal orders for ten shillings were sent to men and women from Ripon in the Forces (1,035).

1944-45. LEAVENS MARSON KING, Schoolmaster

Born 1889. The King family had settled in Ripon in 1860 and became prominent in the commercial and public life of the city. Educated at Coltsgate Hill School

and the Grammar School. He was firstly an apprentice teacher at Coltsgate Hill School, then appointed junior assistant at the Cathedral Boys' School in 1907 and became headmaster there in 1930. Elected to Council 1932-35 and co-opted in 1940. He pressed for the construction of the swimming baths, and was later chairman of the Finance and General Purposes Committee for many years. Awarded an M.B.E. for his work as chairman of the Festival of Britain Committee in 1951. Secretary of the Ripon Branch N.U.T. and President of the West Riding Teachers' Association, member of the Diocesan Education Committee. He was a manager of Trinity School and a feoffee of Jepson's Hospital. As secretary and treasurer he served the Football Club for many years and was secretary of the Cricket Club and, for more than 50 years, an umpire. He was a churchwarden at the Cathedral. He died in 1983.

December. A farewell parade service for the 6th West Riding Battalion Home Guard in Ripon Cathedral was one of the many held throughout the country to mark the Stand Down Order disbanding the Home Guard.

January. Wintry conditions set in at the beginning of the year. Market Days were very poorly attended and tobogganing and skating enjoyed. Twenty-four degrees of frost were recorded.

The Appreciation Fund was founded to show the City's gratitude for the services of Ripon men and women in the Forces: as the Mayor said in raising his appeal for funds 'our city had been spared the major horrors of war. Let us make a thank-offering for this'. The fund was to be used to buy personal gifts for ex-service personnel and relatives of those who had fallen, and to assist those in need.

February. The local Youth Club wanted the *Old Deanery* as its centre, as it was no longer occupied by the Forces. The Dean and Chapter were sympathetic but the County Youth Committee urged the Council to consider only the Modern School for the purpose.

The British Restaurant and Communal Feeding Kitchen were to be closed at the end of March, because the Council considered there were not sufficient customers to make these paying propositions.

Mendelssohn's *Elijah* was sung in Coltsgate Hill Methodist Church by the choir, augmented by the Harrogate Air Ministry Choir and other singers.

Answering an enquiry on the proposed relief road from Bedern Bank to the Parking Ground, the Clerk to the County Council replied that work on the relief road would begin as and when funds were available for this first section of the undertaking, and when the Ministry of War Transport indicated a satisfactory grant.

Gifts from Ripon did not reach the standard set by other West Riding towns in response to the Ripon W.V.S. appeal for household items to help to replace those lost in 'V' bomb attacks. The boroughs adopted by the West Riding were Fulham, Chelsea, North Kensington, Westminster and part of Hampstead.

A dispute over the music for services in Ripon

Cathedral came before Mr Justice Uthwatt in the Chancery Division, in the form of an action by the Royal College of Organists, represented by the Attorney-General, against the Dean and Chapter as defendants. The prosecution contended it was the duty of the latter to maintain and hold full choral services every Sunday morning and evening. The action was dismissed with costs.

March. A complaint was made to the Council by letter on behalf of the men and women serving in the Forces concerning German prisoners being exercised in the streets of Ripon when they could be paraded in the open lanes. No action was taken because the Council had no jurisdiction in the matter.

A presentation was made to Miss H. Kay who was retiring for health reasons from her post as Headmistress of Ripon Cathedral Infants' School. She had joined the staff in 1918 and became headmistress in 1932.

April. Nos. 1, 3 and 5 Stonebridgegate were given by Mr J. Rayner as a gift to the Corporation; one of the houses had been the first Temperance Hotel in Ripon, started by members of the Williamson family.

May. An experimental demonstration of demolishing air-raid surface shelters was given by the Royal Engineers in the Market Place. Officials of the Ministry of Home Security were present to judge the suitability of the method employed in Ripon for similar demolition work in other parts of the country.

Victory in Europe was celebrated on V.E. Day, Tuesday 7 May, and on the following day. Flags, bunting and streamers decorated the streets; Mr Churchill's announcement was broadcast from the Town Hall and the Mayor asked people to join in a short service in the Cathedral. In the evening there were services in all places of worship and next day there was an assembly at Ripon Cemetery where a short service of 'Remembrance, Thanksgiving and Resolve' was held. A Service of Thanksgiving for Victory in Ripon Cathedral was attended by hundreds of people. Members of the Forces and many organisations paraded including the Royal Engineers, A.T.S., R.C.A.F., the Home Guard, the British Legion, the National Fire Service, the Civil Defence Service, St John's Ambulance, Scouts and Guides, and a detachment of the West Riding Constabulary and Special Constables. Many street parties were held to celebrate Victory in Europe, amongst them Lickley Street, Canal Row, Curfew Road, St Marygate, Aismunderby Road, Quarry Moor Lane and Stonebridgegate Flats. Within a few days Commander Clare and Lady Doris Vyner received official information that their son Charles de Grey Vyner, Sub-Lieutenant R.N.V.R., had been killed on active service. He was a nephew of Major E. R. F. Compton of *Newby Hall*. Three years previously the Vyners' only daughter Elizabeth had died while serving with the W.R.N.S.

County Alderman T. F. Spence presented land at Quarry Moor to be kept for the use and enjoyment of Ripon children for all time. The Moor had been used as a training ground for troops in the war years, but now the Chancellor of the Duchy of Lancaster

agreed to sell it to the Corporation for £200.

June. The Ripon and Skelldale Group of Women's Institutes met at *The Hall* by kind permission of Mr and Miss Oxley. After a business meeting, tea was provided in the Scout Hall on Duck Hill and afterwards there were games and competitions in the gardens. Miss Florence Bone, the President, spoke of the way in which the Group had justified its existence during the war.

Five schoolboys aged 10 to 13 were charged with breaking and entering a shop, from which they stole various items and money, and with the theft of bows and arrows from the Ripon Archery Club. Four of the boys asked for previous cases of stealing to be taken into account, ranging from 10 to 16 offences. The chairman of the Ripon City Court warned them that birching would be considered for any future offence since probation or committal to a remand home seemed to be taken as a laughing matter.

At the General Election, the first held since the beginning of the War, Major York retained his seat with a substantial majority. He had served as M.P. for Ripon for six years. The voting results were: Mrs M. Cowley (Liberal) 6,122, Mr R. Hartley (Labour) 12,599, Major York (Conservative) 29,674. The results of this election were not declared until three weeks after the polls, so that votes of service personnel overseas could be included. The ballot boxes were held in custody during this period at Harrogate police station.

At the instigation of Councillors Spence and Harker, a special victory celebration was held for Riponians aged 70 and over. A hundred and seventy older citizens had tea in the *Lawrence Restaurant* and emerged 'hot, but happy' after a 'right good do', according to comments overheard as the guests left.

July. There was a large attendance from all parts of the Diocese at the Annual Meeting of the Friends of Ripon Cathedral. The Dean reported that the misericords were back in place after their war-time exile, that the ancient manuscript books had been returned to the Library and that it was hoped very soon to replace the medieval glass in the window near the font. At Choral Evensong, the *Magnificat* and the *Nunc Dimittis* were sung to settings composed by Dr Moody for the 800th anniversary of the founding of Fountains Abbey in 1132.

The Home Office announced that sanction would be given for the removal of human remains from the vaults in the undercroft of Ripon Cathdral and for their reinterment in the Cathedral churchyard, provided the necessary consent was obtained. The particulars given in the Public Notice referred to:

William Williamson (1818) and Ann his wife (1814)
John Williamson of *Hollings* (1835); Dorothy his wife (1855)
James Lucas (1814)
William Weddell of *Newby Hall* (1792) and Elizabeth his wife (1831)
A.H.D.W. (1797)
T.D.W. (1799)
Richard Wood of *Hollin Close Hall* (1797)

Elizabeth Wood (1797), Henry Wood of *Hollin Hall* (1844), Richard William Wood, his son (1813) Richard Wood of *Hollin Hall* (1815) and Della his wife (1819)

Brian Leckenby, aged 12, was drowned in the Skell paddling near Alma Bridge. His younger brother David attempted to save him but was almost drowned himself.

August. The Dean and Chapter announced that when the Cathedral Choir reassembled in September the Sunday morning service would be restored to the status quo, and settings would replace the chants introduced two years earlier. Dr Moody hailed this as 'a historic phase in the record of Cathedral music'. During the choir holiday, the choir of St Michael's, Headingley, sang Evensong one Saturday, an innovation which the Dean hoped would be a precedent so that choirs competent to do so would sing the services in holiday times.

The Volunteer Car Pool came to an end. It had proved a most useful organisation during the past three years after the basic petrol ration was abolished in July 1942 and all private cars came off the road. The V.C.P. met this situation by offering something like a taxi service for Government Departments, Local Authorities and Hospitals.

The County Council decided to accept a tender of £27 17s 6d for repairs to the Court House and £70 10s for re-arrangement of the heating apparatus, provided the City Council was willing to bear half the cost. If this was agreed the County Council were willing to pay for repairs to the approach road to the Court House.

Steps were taken to prepare the Gallows Hill site for housing as soon as possible, and application made to the Ministry for sanction to borrow £250 for the purchase of this site.

The houses in Belle Vue Yard off Somerset Row included in the Clearance Order of 1938 were now in such a dangerous condition that the owner was given notice to clear the site. Failing this, the Corporation would carry out the work.

Normally the City Band leads the way for 'St Wilfrid' on his white horse, but this year the saint proceeded silently and unannounced because no musical accompaniment could be found. Many old citizens were disappointed to find 'St Wilfrid' had already passed by before they were aware of his coming. The fair on the Market Place was almost up to pre-war standards.

The surrender of Japan and prospects of world peace were celebrated by a public holiday on V.J. Day with thanksgiving services and celebrations. There was a torchlight procession from the city centre to Gallows Hill, ending in a bonfire and fireworks. Large congregations attended the Sunday Services of Thanksgiving in the Cathedral, churches and chapels, and collections were taken for the Ripon Appreciation Fund.

The full statement of the housing situation in Ripon was given by Dr C. H. Greenwood, the Medical Officer of Health, and the chairman of the Health and Housing Committee, to a meeting organised by the Ripon Standing Conference of Women's Organisations. Between 1919 and 1939 the local authority had built 442 houses in Ripon to replace 215 which had come under slum clearance schemes, and 227 which had been demolished or closed for various reasons. Private housing had accounted for 285 new houses in the same period. Dr Greenwood referred to the time when new housing was an unpopular subject, and many people refused to know how bad conditions were in the old courts. In 1933 he had put forward a programme for 156 houses needing to be condemned, but it took him three years to persuade the Council to take action. When he succeeded, the Council added another 230 houses to his scheme. At the outbreak of war in 1939, 176 houses remained to be dealt with and still remained. The Housing Committee had now approved a building programme of 500-600 houses of which 176 would complete the unfinished pre-war slum clearance, 200 would replace houses which had become unfit during the war, 25 were to reduce overcrowding and 120 were to cater for the increased population. Dr Greenwood felt that the Women's Organisations were asking for too high a standard for new housing.

The Resettlement Survey Committee posted 1,000 questionnaires to Ripon men and women in the Forces, but only 635 were returned. These showed that 118 did not intend to return to settle in Ripon, 259 were entitled to reinstatement in their former employment, 34 had secured jobs and 224 had no prospects of employment. Of the 472 forms sent out to proprietors of businesses in Ripon, professional men and householders, only 152 were returned. Many householders failed to send back the forms, indicating that the changed conditions had reduced the demand for domestic staff.

The announcement of the retirement of Miss Eva Lett owing to ill-health as Principal of Ripon Training College was received with very great regret. During the 15 years Miss Lett had held office, the number of students at the College had increased considerably, a new wing had been added and other improvements made to the buildings.

September. A B.B.C. programme, *Roundabout*, featured the ancient ceremony of blowing the Horn at Ripon Market Cross. The old time of 9 pm had been recently re-established. The history of the custom was briefly described on the programme and Mr T. Hawley blew the Horn.

1945-46. WILLIAM RUSSELL DIXON, Paint Manufacturer

January. Among the entries in the New Year Honours List was the conferment of the O.B.E. (Military Division) on Wing Commander Sir Richard Bellingham Graham of *Norton Conyers*. He was a Chief Intelligence Officer.

Mr John Brocklebank, organiser for the northern part of the West Riding for the National Union of Agricultural Workers, was appointed a magistrate for the North Riding.

Mayor June-October 1942 after the death of Margaret Sara Steven; 1934-35, 1945-46-47

Mr and Mrs J. Vincent Hodgson of *West Grange* received confirmation of the death on active service of their daughter, Sister Marjorie Aizlewood Hodgson, Q.A.I.M.N.S. She had been presumed killed with other nursing personnel while nursing the wounded aboard the SS *Kuala* after the evacuation of a hospital in Singapore in 1942. The ship was bombed and sunk by the Japanese.

The Health and Housing Committee invited tenders for the demolition of the former Girls' Home in Bondgate and for the building of eight houses on the site. The home had been requisitioned by the War Department during the war.

February. The Working Men's Club in Priest Lane was closed down because of lack of support. The Club, a non-political and non-sectarian body, had started life more than 50 years before as the Young Men's Society, meeting in a room above the Priest Lane Mission Hall, originally the Primitive Methodist Chapel. It had been open every week-night, offering games and other facilities, but did not serve alcohol or permit gambling.

March. The Ripon Cricket Club's decision to play Sunday matches came in for criticism from the Ripon Methodist Circuit Youth Council.

The Ripon School of Military Engineering (S.M.E.) established at Claro Barracks had its first official open day; visitors included Senior Engineering Officers not only from British Forces in Germany and Italy but also Polish and Greek officers.

The death was announced at the age of 75 of Mr William Hemsworth. He had been Mayor 1922-25 and for many years was one of the most active City Councillors. Both Queen Mary and The Princess Royal had visited his antique shop in Fishergate and it was he who was chiefly instrumental in securing the *Wakeman's House* for the City Council.

The Ripon Junior Youth Council was established to provide leisure facilities for girls and boys at the Y.M.C.A. premises, which were to be brought up to date. Mr C. Hawthornthwaite was elected as the first Chairman.

April. The post-war future of education in Ripon was much discussed. Mr F. Ward, Headmaster of the Ripon Modern School, addressed the Ripon Rotary Club on 'Links in Education'; Miss Johnson, Headmistress of the Ripon Girls' High School, spoke on secondary education to the Business and Professional Women's Club, and Mr W. J. Strachan, Headmaster of the Grammar School, discussed 'The future of Grammar Schools' on Speech Day. Mr Strachan condemned the practice of allowing children to do work out of school hours. 'Some farmers seem to think that their boys can be taken away from school at any time when labour is short on the farm'.

Captain W. J. Coates, D.L., J.P., O.B.E., resigned as County Commissioner for Boy Scouts for the North Riding of Yorkshire. He said that his decision had not been taken in a hurry but felt it was time to retire now he had reached the age of ninety.

On the night of 12 April a disastrous fire swept through *Studley Royal* leaving the mansion a smoking ruin. The walls remained standing but, with the exception of the entrance at the north-east corner, they formed an empty shell. Two weeks previously Queen Ethelburga's School, which had been evacuated from Harrogate during the war and housed in the mansion, had dispersed for the Easter holidays to reassemble in their own premises after the vacation. The school equipment and furnishings had been packed ready for removal. The Caretaker, Mr Percy Hudson, discovered the fire just after 10 pm and the siren was sounded at Ripon Fire Station at 10.30 pm. Within ten minutes the brigade was at the fire to be faced with the problem of pumping water from the lake three-quarters of a mile away. Reinforcements for the fire brigade were called from as far away as Leeds but it was a losing battle as a westerly breeze was blowing and the fire had started in the west wing. The rapidity with which the fire swept through the building allowed only a small number of the valuable pictures and tapestries to be saved, and practically all the school equipment was lost. Some oil paintings and valuable documents locked in the strong room survived the fire. The ruins were later removed; the Georgian stable block converted into a residence for the Vyner family. The *Studley Royal* estate had passed successively from the de Aleman family in the 12th century to the Tempests; to the Mallories of *Hutton Conyers* when William Mallorie married Dionisia Tempest in 1451; and to the Aislabies after Mary Mallorie married George Aislabie, the Principal Registrar to the Archiepiscopal Court at York early in the reign of Charles II. The Mallories built a fine house on the estate, which together with the grounds were developed and beautified by the Aislabies, particularly by John Aislabie, who restored the house after it was partially destroyed by fire on Christmas Day 1716. The Aislabies of *Studley Royal* and the Robinsons of *Baldersby Park* and their successors, a complex inter-related family group of Robinsons, Weddells, Allansons, Lawrences and Vyners, dominated 18th- and 19th-century Ripon and in turn each family owned *Studley Royal* or *Newby Hall*. The last of this group to own *Studley* by inheritance was the second Marquess of Ripon, who died without issue in 1922. In 1923, Commander Clare Vyner, a great-nephew of the first Marchioness of Ripon, had purchased the property.

Miss Juliana White, recently deceased, left a half share of her house, *Highfield*, to the Bishop of Ripon and the Archdeacons of Richmond and Leeds, to be used for the benefit of the Clergy of the diocese. Other bequests included £5,000 to Ripon Cathedral and £1,000 to the Ripon and District Hospital. *Highfield House* was sold to the Training College in September to house 25 students and the money was invested for the benefit of the clergy.

May. Through trains from Ripon to Kings Cross were back on the timetable, and there were additional ones from Harrogate with connections from Ripon.

The Palace of the Bishops of Ripon was sold to Dr Barnardo's Homes by the Ecclesiastical Commissioners.

The new Principal of the Training College, Miss Valentine N. Hall, took up her appointment at the beginning of the term after the acting-Principal Miss N. C. Buysman retired.

Mr K. D. Hanna, who had been Town Clerk of Ripon since August 1942, was appointed Town Clerk of Retford. Mr J. R. Nicholson, assistant solicitor of the County Borough of Ipswich, took up the appointment in July at a salary of £600 per annum.

The Housing Committee suggested four sites for housing: Allhallowgate Hill for five old-persons' bungalows; Camp Close, Bondgate, which could include shops as well as houses; four and a half acres on the Holmfield estate at the edge of *The Grove* and *Grove House* properties, and land on the south side of Lead Lane.

June. 8 June was declared a public holiday and was celebrated as Victory Day. There was no official programme of festivities as it was generally thought that in a hungry and storm-tossed world, jollification and revelry would be out of place. It was felt there should instead be thanksgiving for deliverance.

A Committee was set up by the City Council to direct attention to the precautions which must be taken to mitigate the effects of world food shortages. Europe's last wheat harvest was only 23 million tons as compared with a pre-war figure of 42 million tons; the failure of the monsoon in India meant the failure of rice crops and thus Asian countries, normally rice consumers, were asking for supplies of wheat.

The death took place at Meopham, Kent, of Mr Sidney Brayshay, the third son of the late Mr William Brayshay, solicitor of Palace Road, Ripon. He was one of four brothers who all brought distinction to Ripon Grammar School by their success at university and in their later careers. Sidney Brayshay after leaving Cambridge entered the Public Works Department of the Federated Malay States whither he returned after distinguished service in the Royal Engineers in World War I.

July. The City Council agreed that the Press would be admitted in future to the Committee Meetings of the Council.

18. Allhallowgate (Gott)

The first race meeting at Ripon since the war was enjoyed by a large crowd.

The Ripon and District Branch of the United Nations Association was formed at a meeting held in the Town Hall.

A petition was launched for the Ripon franchise area to be divided into east and west wards instead of into the existing four because of the wide disparities in the number of electors in each ward. The Privy Council approved the division into east and west wards which was to come into effect from 1 November.

The City Council passed a resolution for the introduction of light industries in the Ripon area. This followed the Resettlement Survey Report based on 875 replies from a questionnaire sent to each of the returned 1,070 Ripon men and women who had served or were still serving in HM Forces. Of these, 273 people had no prospect of employment, and besides these there would be a much greater number of civilians released from war-time occupations.

An old document, which proved to be a draft Charter of Philip and Mary restoring certain privileges to the Archbishops of York of which they had been deprived by Henry VIII, was found in the Town Hall during a paper salvage drive. It was given to Mr T. S. Gowland to be added to the Liberty Records.

The Bishop of Ripon, Dr Geoffrey Charles Lester Lunt, was confirmed as Bishop of Salisbury, the diocese in which he had been educated. He had been Bishp of Ripon for eleven years. King George nominated Canon George Armitage Chase, M.C., M.A., Master of Selwyn College, Cambridge, and Honorary Canon of Ely Cathedral, for election by the Dean and Chapter as the new Bishop of Ripon. Dr Chase was consecrated in York Minster on 30 October and enthroned in Ripon Cathedral on 13 November before a packed congregation which included The Princess Royal, the Earl of Harewood, and many Yorkshire mayors and mayoresses.

The Bread Rationing Scheme was introduced in Ripon with little inconvenience, owing to the efficient work of the staff at the Food Office.

August. Miss E. M. Walker of Ripon, Honorary Secretary of Yorkshire Archaeological Society, was one of a team excavating the site of a Roman villa at Wath, under the direction of Major Gilyard-Beer, who was on demobilisation leave.

Ripon and District Young Farmers' Club made a brave bid to revive the old Ripon Show. There was a surprisingly good attendance despite the appalling weather which made gas-capes, mackintoshes, umbrellas and gum boots the order of the day.

At the opening of a National Recruiting Campaign meeting in the Market Place, the Mayor quoted the First Lord of the Admiralty: 'No one hates war as much as the soldier who has to fight it'. Major W. M. Robson of the War Office said 100,000 men were needed to bring the Regular Army up to strength. Rates of pay would be comparable with other trades at 28s per week all found.

Negotiations were in progress to restore the ruins of Fountains Abbey as a Benedictine monastery, to be a memorial to all members of the Roman Catholic Church who fell in the two World Wars.

September. F. W. Coulson and Company was one of the new firms which were set up in Ripon. The firm manufactured fairground equipment in the old Wesleyan School premises in Coltsgate Hill. In September there were 20 employees, including five women, and it was hoped this number would increase to between 70 and 80 before the end of the year.

A. B. Trees, the old-established Ripon builders, completed the first two houses to be built since 1939. They were on the site of the Low Mill, the last working cornmill, which had been demolished in 1938. They had been constructed to conform to Government restrictions which limited the floor space to 1,000 sq. ft. and the selling price to a maximum of £2,000. There were 517 applicants in Ripon for new homes in the public sector and the Corporation proposed to build 500 houses which would be constructed by Ripon firms. They hoped to meet the requirements in the face of restrictions, in particular a shortage of skilled labour.

19. The old Low Mill: the last working cornmill (Fossick)

The British Legion announced that it proposed to take over *Lucan House*, Sharow, from the military authorities as a home for approximately 80 aged and infirm ex-servicemen.

October. Dr C. H. Greenwood retired from the office of Medical Officer of Health for the city, and from the practice he shared with Drs A. C. Brown and R. M. H. Anning. He came to Ripon in 1907 as partner to the late Dr G. R. Green and 20 years later was appointed as M.O.H. It was largely due to his efforts that the extremely bad conditions in some of the old courts were brought to light, although it was years before he got the backing of the City Council. By then he had taken a major part in forming the Ripon Housing Improvement Trust, a voluntary Housing Society, the first of its kind in the country.

1946-47. WILLIAM RUSSELL DIXON, Paint Manufacturer

Mayor 1934-35; June-October 1942; 1945-46-47

Rainfall in 1946 was 33.4 ins. Recordings at Ripon Grammar School showed that the driest month was March, the wettest November.

November. Thirlways shop at the top of High Skellgate was demolished to improve the south-west entrance to the Market Place with a grant from the Ministry of Transport for £871 and a total cost of £1,191.

The Inland Revenue authorities warned the Corporation that, if the plans for the erection of hutments on North Road to provide office space for their local staff were not passed, they would use an alternative site which had been offered them in Northallerton. The tax authorities later occupied the waiting rooms at the bus station as offices until they were required by the Corporation.

Mr C. Doubtfire of Kirkgate won £10,000 as second prize in the Irish Sweepstake.

After a long illness the death took place of Mr John Rogers Park of Kirkgate. He was an art dealer and a member of the Fine Arts Trade Guild. In 1929 he became Art Master at Ripon Grammar School and his success in his work was shown by the number of Old Boys who rose to hold responsible positions in the art world.

20. Thirlway's Corner (Gott)

December. Mr and Mrs H. A. Green of Blossomgate received the bar to the D.F.C. awarded to their son Squadron Leader R. J. E. Green of No. 139 Squadron, R.A.F., at an investiture. The bar had been awarded in December 1944 and he died in action during the following month at the age of 24.

January. The Ripon Health and Housing Committee recommended the appointment of a full-time Medical Officer of Health for Ripon City and the Ripon and Pateley Bridge Rural District, and also the establishment of a Divisional Health Office.

Ripon was zoned as an industrial authority. This aroused much controversy and it was suggested that the local council would have to pay higher wages to its employees.

The purchase of Holmfield Estate by Ripon Corporation had been completed in December 1946 and the Committee now approved the layout for new housing.

February. A heavy snowfall in January caused no dislocation in the city, although many hamlets in Wensleydale were cut off. In February heavier falls of snow again isolated country districts, and on 25 February the city was virtually snowed up; bus services, except those to Harrogate, were withdrawn and milk deliveries disrupted. The worst snow storm occurred on 22 February. By 13 March, 50 nights of frost and seven weeks of snow on the ground had been recorded.

Fuel saving became an urgent necessity and severe cuts in street lighting were ordered. Because of low coal stocks, gas consumers were 'put on their honour' to economise. Services in the Cathedral were held in the choir and the Methodists worshipped at united services. The Swimming Baths were temporarily closed. Coke sales from Ripon Gas Works were restricted and queuing for coke supplies was reported. The Ministry of Fuel and Power asked for a 10 per cent cut in consumption but difficulties with supply continued in March.

The first consignment of food and clothes for 'Starving Europe' left Ripon.

March. It was announced that the City Rate for the half-year ending in September would go up by 11d in the pound.

The relief road scheme was once again postponed due to doubts expressed by the Ministry of Transport about the road passing the west front of the Cathedral. No representative of Ripon City Council was invited to be present at the planning committee in October when the decision was reached, an omission said to be due to an oversight.

April. The West Riding Education Committee suggested a multilateral school for Ripon. Despite some criticism expressed by local representatives, a conference in the Town Hall accepted a resolution to request governing bodies of the Modern and Grammar Schools to discuss the project.

The first annual clay-pigeon shoot on behalf of Ripon Hospital was held at Skelton-on-Ure.

The death was announced of Sir William Aykroyd of *Grantley Hall*. He was chairman of Ripon Housing Improvement Trust, President of the Ripon Branch of the Y.M.C.A., of Ripon St Johns Ambulance Brigade Association and of Ripon City Cricket Club.

In September the West Riding Education Committee decided to purchase *Grantley Hall* for use as a residential adult college which was opened on 6 May 1949. The agricultural and sporting estate was sold separately in lots at an auction in the Lawrence Ballroom in December.

During April, two brilliant displays of the 'Northern Lights' were seen in Ripon.

May. Mr John Frederick Rowse reached his 100th birthday on 7 May. Although Mr Rowse had lived in Littlethorpe for only ten years, Ripon claimed him as their third centenarian since 1704, according to the records. The occasion was marked by a visit from the Mayor and a special peal of the Cathedral bells. Mr Rowse died in June 1948.

A Council proposal to buy a refuse destructor had to be abandoned as the manufacturer could not make delivery because of the shortage of steel. There had been difficulties in finding suitable land for tipping refuse which were overcome by making arrangements with a neighbouring authority to accept Ripon's refuse.

The first 'Eisteddfod' of the Ripon Methodist Youth Council, held in the Zion Church, attracted many entries.

A committee was set up to produce a scheme for the newly-formed Skelldale Housing Society to provide a residential hostel or service flatlets for elderly people. In March 1948 the Society purchased *Borrage House* from the executors of Mrs T. R. Williamson, who had died in the previous December.

At the end of the month, after a heat-wave, severe thunderstorms damaged footpaths and roofs. More thunderstorms followed in mid-July with damage to trees in Sharow Park.

June. After much debate and discussion, a poll showed a majority in favour of opening Ripon cinemas on Sundays by 1,174 votes to two hundred and thirty-one.

The Traffic Commissioners authorised the use of the Bus Station with entrance and exit into Queen Street for an experimental period. In April 1948 privately-owned vehicles were excluded from the area where buses unloaded. Employees of the United Bus Company were against the scheme and staged a one-day strike on Saturday 21 June. The plan to provide an entry to the station from Bedern Bank was abandoned.

The Princess Royal unveiled the Cathedral Choir Screen on 28 June. The new figures were the work of the sculptor Esmond Burton.

21. Ripon Cathedral Organ and Screen (Gott)

The delays since March which had affected the council housing programme were said to have been caused by bad weather and the shortage and poor quality of materials; for example, the surveyor condemned nearly all the windows received for the new houses in Bondgate.

July. Ripon City Council, meeting in Committee, rejected the proposal that they should apply for transfer from the West to the North Riding when the forthcoming review of local authorities took place. Feeling was summed up in the words that it would be 'like leaving the Brigade of Guards to join the Boy Scouts'.

At a special service in the Cathedral, the Archbishop of York received £108,703 towards the target of £275,000 set by the Ripon Diocesan Challenge Fund. The money was to be used for the endowment of new parishes, the training of new clergy and the repair of war-damaged churches.

August. HM Queen Elizabeth spent three nights as the guest of Commander and Lady Doris Vyner at *Studley Royal*. She was welcomed at Ripon Station and on the following day she attended Minden Day celebrations at York and later visited Fountains Abbey. During the weekend there was a drive and picnic in the Dales, and the Queen attended Sunday morning service in Ripon Cathedral.

A man charged at Ripon Court with being drunk and disorderly and with breaking a window in the Welfare Institution in Allhallowgate, claimed he was trying to get a bed. 'I always thought you could get into the workhouse if you had nowhere to go for the night.'

September. The first four houses on the new corporation estate at Gallows Hill were occupied at a rent of £1 a week including rates. They were the first of 76 similar houses to be built. While digging foundations for one of the houses, workmen found the remains of four skeletons, probably of persons hanged on the gallows which stood there in the 16th and 17th centuries.

The Dean of Ripon dedicated gifts including a crucifix and a Bible to the Chapel of St Mary Magdalen, a ceremony which marked the end of the programme to redecorate and re-light the church. The seating was renewed as part of the process of refurbishment.

October. The conversion of *Holmfield House* into four flats was completed and five flats in *Yoredale House* would be ready for occupation later in the month.

A building which had once been a Salvation Army Canteen near the Railway Station was re-erected in Quarry Moor Lane as a Glad Tidings Hall by the Ripon branch of the Assemblies of God.

1947-48. WILLIAM H. CLAYDEN

Born in Hessay and went to school in Carlton Minniott. He started work with the L.N.E.R. in Tyneside and was transferred to the Railway Company's staff in Ripon in 1929. He was an active member of the N.U.R. and secretary of the union's Friendly Society. He was a director of the Ripon

Co-operative Society and supported the Football Club, and also a sidesman and church councillor at the Cathedral. Co-opted to the City Council in 1943, he was appointed to the Liberty Bench in 1944 and did much work for the Police Court Mission. In 1949 be became Secretary of the N.E.R. Cottage Homes and Benefit Funds; his work took him away from Ripon and he died in retirement at Halifax in 1977.

Rainfall in 1947 was 28.50 ins. August was the driest month with 0.5 ins., March the wettest with 5.11 ins. Population statistics: birth rate 21 per 1,000, death rate 12.2 per 1,000.

November. Field-Marshal Viscount Montgomery visited Deverall Barracks on 3 November.

The tragic death of Mrs T. R. Williamson occurred, caused by burns from falling on a fire. She had wholeheartedly supported her husband Tom Williamson in his adherence to the Liberal Party and she was chairman of the Ripon Women's Liberal Association for many years. In her younger years she appeared on the stage in Ripon in many amateur dramatic and musical performances, and with her husband produced the Plantagenet epoch pageant 'Boadicea to Victoria' for the Diamond Jubilee. During World War I she gave practical help in the work for the Belgian refugees. After her husband's death in 1920 she compiled a history of the Williamson family for private circulation. When the Women's Institute movement was started in Ripon she was the first president, and did much to establish it in its successful career.

Mr James Metcalfe retired aged 75 after 60 years' employment at the Yorkshire Varnish Works.

A report on the ancient buildings of Ripon by the Society for the Protection of Ancient Monuments was received by the Corporation. This formed the basis for the first list of buildings of architectural and historic interest in the city.

December. Two young German prisoners-of-war died in a collision with a van on the Harrogate Road.

The Boundary Commission proposed a new Ripon constituency made up of the City of Ripon, the urban districts of Ilkley and Otley and the rural districts of Ripon and Pateley Bridge and Wharfedale.

Colonel Malcolm Stoddart-Scott, M.P. for the

existing Pudsey and Otley Division, was adopted as Conservative candidate for the new Ripon Division. The existing Ripon M.P., Mr Christopher York, was adopted for the Harrogate Division.

January. Christmas 1947 was more than ever a 'fireside festival' because of the abolition of the basic petrol allowances and shortages generally. Later in 1948 there were complaints about the poor quality of coal and meat.

An exhibition of painting and fine arts by German prisoners-of-war detained at the Ure Bank Camp was opened in the Town Hall by the Bishop of Ripon.

J. S. Lowley and Sons, Painters and Decorators, of Low Skellgate, celebrated their 100th year of trading in Ripon with a dinner.

22. Low Skellgate (Gott)

Concern was caused by a proposal made by the W.R.C.C. to initiate Parliamentary legislation which would give it wider powers over highways and the acquisition of land.

February. Miss Maria Jane Flowers celebrated her 100th birthday on 14 February.

March. The city rate was reduced by 2s 1d in the pound.

The annual takings from the Ripon Spa were less than those of one day at the Harrogate Spa. In view of this low income it was recommended that no further expense should be incurred in repairing broken pipes, and that the Spa should be abandoned.

April The Ministry of Health gave the Council permission to build eight or possible 12 houses on the Holmfield Estate.

The Conservative College was opened at Swinton Park when Mr R. A. Butler gave the inaugural lecture.

The Dean and Chapter announced that they proposed to use *The English Hymnal* instead of *Hymns*

Ancient and Modern in the Cathedral.

The Ministry of Transport queried the approval given by the City Council to purchase 7,500 sq. yds. of the Deanery Fields for private car-parking.

Professor William Orpen Bower, one of the most distinguished members of a notable Ripon family, died aged ninety-two. He was born at *Elmscroft*, and educated at Repton, Trinity College, Cambridge, and at Wurzburg and Strasbourg. Regius Professor of Botany at Glasgow University from 1885 to 1925, he was one of the outstanding botanists of his time, and received many honours including doctorates from seven universities. He was a Fellow of the Royal Society and in 1930 President of the British Association. He published many books and articles, the last being *Sixty Years of Botany in Britain* which appeared in 1938. Professor Bower retired to Ripon and took a keen interest in the affairs of the city and the Grammar School. He lived latterly at the *Old Deanery Hotel*.

To mark his 50 years of residence in the city, Alderman James Eden gave land adjoining Grove Lane to the Corporation for use as a children's playground. His previous offer to purchase land on the Gallows Hill estate had been rejected by the Council.

The Ripon and District Horticultural Society, which had been inactive since 1940, voted unanimously to disband and to present its assets to the Young Farmers' Club.

The Edward Room in the Opera House was opened as the National Insurance Office for the Ripon area.

Holy Trinity Church celebrated the completion of its £5,000 restoration programme with a thanksgiving service on Sunday 25 April. In his sermon the Bishop of Ripon warned against 'dry rot in pulpit and pew'.

Ripon City Education Sub-Committee discussed the West Riding County Colleges Scheme, and approved a suggestion for the establishment of a Juvenile Employment Service to be attached to the proposed County College.

May. A new out-patient building at the Ripon Hospital was opened by Dr P. A. Steven. This extension was made necessary by the increase in attendance from 6,615 in 1945 to 13,255 in 1947. A wooden building was erected because of the shortage of bricks, at a cost of £2,750.

June. The City Council accepted the offer of the gift of Camp Close as a playing field from the Deputy Mayor, County Councillor C. T. Wade of *The Mount*, Littlethorpe.

Ripon Hospital Linen Guild was closed after 25 years of service because the hospital had come under state control and ownership.

July. It was announced that gypsum might be quarried on Ripon Parks Farm.

The Ripon and District Art Group was established in its new headquarters in the *Unicorn Hotel* Yard. It was opened by Mr Charles Harker; an exhibition of work by local artists was on view.

A second outbreak of food poisoning in Ripon schools served by the school canteen in Bondgate Green was blamed on the use of infected utensils there. Teachers, canteen helpers and over ninety children were affected.

Ripon City 1st XI was re-admitted to the Allerton-shire Football League, in which they had played for most of the time between the Wars.

William Wood Smithson of Ripon won the Romany Society's cup and medal for the best Romany essay. Mr Smithson took as his subject 'A walk up the Skell valley to Fountains Abbey'.

August. Mr Tom Beckwith retired after 55 years service as assistant to the magistrates' clerk at Ripon City Court and the West Riding Court.

A police 'pillar' system of telephones was established in Ripon.

September. Mrs Lillian Rainford, F.R.G.S., of Ripon, was installed as President of the English Section of the Theosophical Society in a ceremony at the Y.M.C.A. in Ripon.

Mr J. A. Berry succeeded Mr J. R. Nicholson as Town Clerk.

The final annual meeting of the subscribers and governors of the Ripon and District Hospital was held. The possibility of forming a League of Friends of Ripon Hospital was envisaged, so that help could still be given although the hospital itself was now under state control.

Ripon Hall at Oxford celebrated its Golden Jubilee. As the Ripon Clergy College it was founded in Ripon in 1898 by Bishop Boyd Carpenter and moved to Oxford in 1919.

October. Local protests were made to the proposal of the W.R.C.C. in their Schools Development Plan that Ripon Grammar School and Ripon Girls' High School should be closed and the Modern School converted into a mixed multilateral school.

The Cathedral War Memorial to the men and women of Ripon who gave their lives in World War II was unveiled by Lady Doris Vyner who had lost a son and daughter. The ceremony of dedication was performed by the Dean.

The Ripon City Women's Hockey Club, which had ceased activities just before the outbreak of war, was re-formed by unanimous agreement at a meeting held in the Lawrence Rooms.

The new ambulance of the Ripon Division of the St John Ambulance Brigade was dedicated by the Bishop in the Market Place.

1948-49.   WILLIAM H. CLAYDEN

November. A new dramatic society named The Rowel Players was formed, with Mrs M. Alderson, who had directed a recent production of *Dear Octopus* at the Garrison Theatre, as Honorary Secretary.

Councillor W. M. Clayden was asked to remain as mayor until 1 May 1949, as a result of a change in the date of mayoral elections laid down in the new Local Government Act.

Seven baby girls were christened on Sunday 5 November, the largest number christened at one time in Ripon Cathedral in living memory.

The cost of an extension to the Gas Works was estimated at £25,700, an undertaking necessitated by increased demand.

Mayor 1947-48-49 (November-May)

The Ripon Council Health Committee commissioned the purchase of a 'mechanical horse' to collect refuse. It was estimated that the machine would do the work in half the time taken by the present system of using horse and cart and borrowed haulage.

Allegations were made of squalor in Ripon houses in which rooms were let to army families. The War Department had failed to provide accommodation, although plans existed to build 70 army houses in Clotherholme Road.

To meet the national shortage of plant for generating electricity, the police notified the public of details of load-shedding between 8 am and 12 noon and between 4 pm and 5.30 pm.

December. Although final sanction would be needed from the County Council, the City Council approved a trial one-way clockwise system for traffic round the Market Place, despite doubts expressed about the efficiency of the system on the south side of the square.

Dr G. C. L. Lunt, Bishop of Ripon from 1935-1946 and later Bishop of Salisbury, died in *Bishop's House*, Salisbury, on 17 December. The memorial service in Ripon Cathedral was attended by The Princess Royal.

Ripon and District Association Football League celebrated its 21st birthday at a dinner in *Studley Royal Hotel*, when Mr A. Smith of Bishop Monkton received a presentation to mark his 20 years presidency.

Miss M. W. Johnson retired after 33 years as head-mistress of Ripon Girls' High School.

March. The death was announced of Miss Constance Cross of *Coney Garth*, the last of the sisters who had donated the Clock Tower to Ripon to commemorate Queen Victoria's Jubilee in 1897. Miss Cross was a skilled needlewoman and wood-carver and a generous benefactor to the Cathedral.

Vandalism on the Holmfield housing estate was reported, where trees had been wantonly destroyed.

The death was announced of Alderman T. F. Spence, managing director of the firm of T. and R. Williamson Limited and Mayor from 1927-29. Alderman Spence was particularly noted for his keen interest in sport.

April. Major E. B. Eccles (Conservative) defeated Mr C. T. Wade (Independent), a retiring councillor, in the new Ripon County Divison.

23. Old Market Place (Jackson)

The year was distinguished by the hottest and sunniest Easter on record.

In the last week of the month sweets went off the ration, but no big rush to buy greater supplies was reported.

Seven horse riders passed through Ripon on a ride from Lands End to John-o-Groats which was intended to draw attention to the alleged trade in horse flesh.

China Sun, the race-horse owned by Mrs M. Wells, wife of Councillor W. N. Wells, won the Ripon City Handicap at the Spring Meeting on 30 April.

1949-50. FRANCIS CHARLES LOWLEY, Joiner and Undertaker

Born 1903. Son of Francis Lowley, to whose business in Low Skellgate he succeeded. Educated Trinity School and Jepson's Hospital as a chorister at the Cathedral. Co-opted to Council in World War II. A bachelor, Councillor Mrs I. E. L. Oakley acted as his mayoress. Conferred the Freedom of the City on the Royal Engineers and Dr C. H. Moody, and was much involved in the Festival of Britain celebrations. His main interest on the Council was housing, and he supported the efforts to provide a public hall in Ripon. He worked for youth, particularly the Scouts, and the Cricket Club, and founded the Friends of Ripon Hospital. A lay clerk at

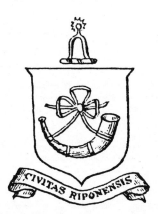

the Cathedral, he was much involved with musical and dramatic activities, and for many years was producer for the Amateur Operatic Society. He died in 1980.

May. The City Council confirmed the minutes of the Gas Committee for the last time: Ripon Gas Works had passed into national ownership on the last day of April.

The contents of an entire farm including livestock, machinery and household furniture arrived in Ripon by rail on 4 May at 7.30 am. The consignment was the property of Mr R. S. Bosomworth who had taken over Sycamore Grange Farm at Copt Hewick. It had left Devon at 6.45 pm the previous evening.

The re-introduction of party politics into municipal elections after the war resulted in victory for three Conservatives and one Independent, who was supported by the Conservatives.

Miss Barbara Wood of *Caxton Lodge* returned from a tour of Australia with the England Women's Cricket Team.

An 8-ft bomb was found in the River Ure below Ox Close. However, the fuse had been removed and the army concluded it had been used for practice by bomb disposal squads.

June. A very dry summer caused a drought which lasted until the autumn. At the end of August, the position was so serious that the public were asked to cut consumption by 10 per cent and only an emergency supply from Harrogate saved the situation: there was only 10 days' supply left in the Lumley Moor reservoir.

July. The Chapel of All Souls in the Norman undercroft of the Cathedral was dedicated by Bishop Chase. It was to be used as a mortuary chapel.

A ceremony was held on 27 July in the Market Square to honour the Corps of Royal Engineers, whose School of Military Engineering had been stationed at Ripon since 1940. A composite detachment of 250 men marched from Deverell Barracks and formed up on the Market Square to music played by the band of the Corps of Engineers. A fanfare of trumpets was sounded on the arrival of the Mayoral party, and the Union Jack and the R.E. flag were broken. The Mayor, Alderman F. C. Lowley, in company with the Chief Royal Engineer, Lieutenant-General Sir Guy C. Williams, K.C.B., C.M.G., D.S.O.; the Commandant, School of Military Engineering, Brigadier B. C. Davey, C.B.E.; and the Commandant, Ripon Wing School of Military Engineering, Colonel C. E. A. Browning, M.C., inspected first the Guard of Honour and then the whole parade. After the Mayor's address, the Town Clerk read the Deed of the Freedom of the City to be presented.

CITY OF RIPON

To the Chief Royal Engineer the Officers and Other Ranks of the Corps of Royal Engineers.

GREETINGS
Whereas We the Mayor Aldermen and Citizens of the City of Ripon in the West Riding of the County of York being sensible to the great record and glorious traditions created by your distinguished Corps over many years of loyal and devoted service to our beloved King and Country and being desirous of recognising and fostering the intimate association existing between us have this day conferred on you the Freedom of our City.

NOW WE DO BY THESE PRESENTS grant you the privilege honour and distinction of marching through the streets of the City of Ripon on all ceremonial occasions with bayonets fixed colours flying and bands playing.

IN WITNESS whereof we have caused our Corporate Common Seal to be hereunto affixed this Twenty Seventh day of July, One thousand, Nine hundred and Forty-nine.

Signed:
F. C. Lowley, Mayor
J. A. Berry, Town Clerk

The Mayor presented the Deed to the Chief Royal Engineer who then signed the Roll of Honour on behalf of the Royal Engineers and made a speech of acknowledgement. The C.O. of the parade advanced to the Mayor: 'Sir, may I march through your City with Bayonets fixed and Bands playing?' After permission was given, the parade party mounted the saluting base on the east side of the Square and after the trumpeters sounded a fanfare, the parade, headed by the band, marched round the Square past the Mayor, who took the salute, and then down North Street to the Clock Tower, right down Princess Road and thence along Stonebridgegate, St Marygate, Minster Road, Kirkgate, Westgate, Blossomgate and Kirkby Road back to the Barracks. The Framed Scroll giving the Freedom of the City to the Royal Engineers was hung in the Mallorie Chapel in the Cathedral after a short dedication during the morning service on the Sunday following the presentation ceremony. The scroll itself was prepared and illuminated by the artist Mr J. Porteus Wood.

August. A mass radiography unit made its first visit to Ripon for personal health checks on lung and heart conditions.

A party of Norwegians spent a fortnight with Ripon hosts and hostesses under the auspices of the 'World Friends' organisation.

The death of Mrs Elizabeth Harnet Hartland, daughter of the late Mr and Mrs Robert Williamson, marked the end of the association of the Williamsons with Ripon, which had begun in 1775 when the family's paint and varnish works was established. Mrs Hartland took part in the Ripon Millenary Festival of 1886 and the Ripon Pageant ten years later. Her home, *Grove House*, was the subject of a compulsory purchase order by the Ministry of Health because the land was required to complete the Holmfield estate.

September. The Revd W. Watson completed 50 years in the Methodist ministry. Although he had retired, Mr Watson was still in charge at the Allhallowgate Chapel.

A scheme for the sale of corporation houses to occupiers, first mooted in June, was recommended to the City Council after consideration by the Housing Committee. Later the Ministry of Health refused to approve the scheme.

October. The 1949 drought continued with a rainfall seven inches below average for the nine months up to the end of September. The Army made arrangements to draw water supplies from the river Ure. By November the water situation was reported to be

24. *Junction of Park Street and Blossomgate (Jackson)*

improving as the rainfall increased. By the middle of the month Ripon had 76 days' supply and there was no need for extra water from Harrogate.

The Ripon Isolation Hospital in Princess Road was reserved for the care of those suffering from chronic illnesses; patients with infectious diseases would in future be treated at Thistle Hill Hospital in Knaresborough. This reorganisation was made because few cases now required isolation and the change was possible because hospitals were now under regional control.

A proposal to build a new secondary school on the football ground in Mallorie Park Drive created uproar among local sports enthusiasts and brought opposition from the education sub-committee of the Ripon Council.

Four firms tendered for a contract to build six additional houses on the Holmfield estate and the Council decided to choose the contractor by drawing a name 'out of a hat'. The winner was the firm A. B. Trees, who agreed to stand down when the next contract was offered.

The first trade union rally ever to be held in Ripon met in the Assembly Rooms and the National Union of Agricultural Workers was addressed by the Mayor.

November. Mr F. I. Trees, a former Mayor who had been on the Council for 20 years, died on 12 November. His mayoralty from 1938-41 covered the early years of the war.

Harrogate and District Football Association celebrated its Golden Jubilee. Ripon United was one of the 15 original affiliated clubs.

Vandals pulled up the 350 wallflower plants at the junction between Quarry Moor Lane and Southgate. They were quickly replaced but the new plants suffered the same fate.

Mr H. W. Hill, conductor of the Ripon City Prize Band, was awarded the certificate and badge of the National Brass Band Club and made a life member.

The population of Ripon was 9,669, according to the annual report of the Medical Officer of Health for 1948.

The Royal Engineers presented a silver George IV inkstand and engraved desk-pad to the City at a ceremony in the Lawrence Ballroom. The Ripon Wing S.M.E. returned to Chatham in March: it had been stationed in Ripon since 1939.

Television signals were received in Ripon by Mr Arthur Yates from the new Birmingham station. The sound was clear but the vision faint; however, Ripon had been believed to be completely out of range.

The Justices of the Peace Bill, then before Parliament, threatened the existence of Ripon's Quarter Sessions although there was a slight possibility of saving the Court by an amendment which permitted the Lord Chancellor some discretion.

Three hundred European voluntary workers began clearing Dallowgill Moor of unexploded mines and shells under the direction of the Dangerous Area Clearance Unit.

February. The Council's housing plans made real progress during 1950. In February Ripon secured a further allocation of 50 council houses as a result of a deputation to the Regional Office of the Ministry of Health. The compulsory purchase order of *Grove House* was confirmed. The 100th post-war house to be built in Ripon was completed on the Holmfield Estate and received an official opening in April. However, despite the provision of 18 houses in 1947, 39 in 1948, 32 in 1949 and 45 in 1950, there was still a waiting list of 100 families at the end of the year. In April the Housing Committee decided to change the energy supply in 70 Corporation houses from gas to electricity and in June the Council approved the purchase of land near Lead Lane for a housing site of 23 acres.

Ripon Caledonian Society held its first Burn's Night celebration with a dinner at the *Old Deanery Hotel* on 25 January.

Serious flooding occurred in Ripon when the River Ure reached its highest level since 1932. Lickley Street was badly affected and Sharow Road and Magdalen Road were also flooded.

Two candidates were nominated for the General Election which took place on 23 February: Mr W. S. Hill (Labour) and Colonel M. Stoddart-Scott (Conservative). The latter was returned as M.P. for Ripon.

March. The final parade of the S.M.E. before their return to Chatham after ten years in Ripon took place on Sunday 5 March. The following day Riponians turned out to cheer the departing troops as they marched to the station.

The proposal to use Paddy's Park for Council building came to nothing when a borehole test revealed its unsuitability as a housing site.

'Freebooter', the horse owned by Mrs Brotherton and trained by Mr Bob Renton of Ox Close, Littlethorpe, won the Grand National. Mr Renton presented a silver rosebowl to the City.

1950-51. FRANCIS CHARLES LOWLEY, Joiner and Undertaker

Mayor 1949-50-51

May. St Clare's Home, Ripon, for mothers and babies, which was owned by the Archdeaconery of Richmond Moral Welfare Association, had to be closed because of the cost of bringing it up to Home Office requirements.

The new by-laws for the hygienic distribution of food were adopted by the City Council subject to confirmation by the Ministry of Food.

An Old People's Welfare Committee was established to help the elderly in Ripon and to co-ordinate the work of voluntary organisations.

A dancing school was set up in Ripon by Gillian Wright and Eric Irving.

Mr W. Booth, who retired after 50 years as superintendent of the St John Ambulance Brigade, was presented with an armchair.

There were six candidates for four seats on the Ripon City Council. Mr J. B. Briscombe topped the East Ward poll at his first attempt, unseating Councillor G. W. Spence.

Alderman F. C. Lowley accepted nomination for a second year of office as mayor and was formally re-elected, with Councillor Mrs Oakley as his mayoress; the customary mayor-making ceremony was attended by Nigerian administrators including Inspectors of Schools and Factories who were visiting Ripon at the time. They later sent a letter of thanks to 'a city which stands supreme in our minds compared with other places'.

Quarry Moor was de-requisitioned by the Army and a sub-committee was set up to take charge of the area.

June. The Lord Chancellor regretted that he could not comply with the request made by the City Council to retain Quarter Sessions in Ripon. This meant that the city and district would have only one court of Summary Jurisdiction which would operate under the name of the Ripon Liberty Court thus preserving the title of the ancient Liberty. The Mayor presided over the City Bench for the last time on 20 December. From 1 January 1951 by the terms of the Justices of the Peace Act the Mayor would no longer automatically be the chief magistrate of the city. The last Quarter Sessions were held in Ripon on 28 September 1951.

The Cathedral organ was rededicated after being away for five months in the hands of organ builders. The sum of £4,500 out of the £5,000 required for the repairs had been received.

Mr W. H. Moss, a nephew of a former mayor and a member of a well-known Ripon family, was killed in the King's Cup Air Race.

Although the Spa and Estates Committee refused to allow Jehovah's Witnesses to hold Gospel meetings in either the Spa Gardens or the Spa Park, the City Council gave permission for such meetings to take place in the latter.

Mr Douglas Turnbull of Copt Hewick, a Jehovah's Witness preacher who was a conscientious objector to conscription, was gaoled by Ripon Magistrates for failing to undertake work specified by the Ministry of Labour and National Service.

July. A series of fires occurred in Ripon during the

second weekend of the month, including one at T. and R. Williamson Limited, Varnish Works, which damaged a dry colour room and the boiler house.

Only seven volunteers applied to join the new Civil Defence force.

The Camp Close playing field presented to Ripon by Councillor and Mrs Wade was officially opened by the Mayor.

August. To mark the jubilee of horse-racing on the existing course, the Ripon Race Course Company presented a silver bowl to the winner of the St Wilfrid Handicap on August Bank Holiday Monday.

The revived Ripon Tennis Tournament attracted 100 entries. An editorial in the *Gazette* criticised the organisation of the tournament, but supporters defended it.

At a ceremony attended by over 6,000 members, The Princess Royal opened *Lister House* as a British Legion Home.

September. The union of the Zion and Coltsgate Hill Methodist Churches, approved in July at the Methodist quarterly meeting, was confirmed by the York and District Synod.

The Bishop of Ripon dedicated the new St John Ambulance, expressing the hope that he would not be the first to need its services, a plight which had befallen one of his predecessors on a similar occasion.

October. The Princess Royal visited Ripon to lay the foundation stone of an extension to the Training College. She walked along Princess Royal Road on the Holmfield Housing Estate and visited three houses there.

Ripon Cricket Club became the champions of the York and District Senior League: their final opponents had been unable to raise a side and so points went to Ripon.

A parade by 200 officers and cadets of the Air Training Corps from Ripon and other areas marked the opening of a new Headquarters for the Ripon Flight Air Training Corps. The new HQ was behind the Inland Revenue office in North Road.

The Nondescripts Hockey Team renamed themselves the Ripon Men's Hockey Club and acquired the use of a new ground. The Ripon Ladies' Hockey Club at last acquired a home ground in a field adjoining the cricket field with entrance from Mallorie Park Drive.

The Ripon Camera Club was formed with a ten-shilling annual subscription.

Because there were two prematurely-born babies in the Hospital, a long power cut was diverted from Ripon to other areas.

November. A council house in Southgate was scheduled for demolition as unsafe because it had been built on peaty ground. This was the fourth council house to be demolished in 12 years. A lively debate ensued and the City Council confirmed the recommendation of the Housing Committee to use part of the Holmfield open space for building.

The Mayor unveiled the War Memorial to the 82 men and women of Ripon who gave their lives in World War II. Their names were added to the Cenotaph in the Spa Gardens.

The death was announced of Alderman Eden of *Kingstonia*, the head of James Eden and Company Limited, the wholesale and retail fruit merchants. He had been a member of the City Council from 1924-27 and again from 1938 until his death.

Mr Boynton of Whitcliffe Lane gave 12,000 tulip and daffodil bulbs to be planted on the side of the canal along the Boroughbridge road.

The Medical Officer reported that 95 houses which had been declared unfit for habitation before the outbreak of war in 1939 were still occupied.

December. Suggestions that the proposed new sun parlour for the Spa Gardens should be built by direct labour were challenged, and the Council decided to put the work out to tender.

An otter was killed by a bus on Hutton Bank.

There was much criticism of a B.B.C. programme on Ripon for overseas listeners because the Cathedral was hardly mentioned.

Corporal P. H. Bell of the R.A.F., a Ripon man, was killed in riots in Singapore.

January. Miss Marion Sedman of the Ripon Ladies' Hockey Club was selected as captain of the North side against the Midlands and as reserve right-back for England.

A motor cyclist being chased by the police through Ripon reached a speed of 65 mph in Mallorie Park Drive.

A campaign was begun to recruit more Civil Defence volunteers as there were still only 22 recruits.

The first big table-tennis event to be staged in Ripon took place: Yorkshire beat Cumberland.

February. Ripon and District Photographic Society planned to make a photographic survey of the city to celebrate Festival year.

Not one case of drunkenness had been heard in Ripon Liberty Courts over the previous two years and there had been no proceedings against licensees, but there were two cases of driving while under the influence of drink in 1949.

Mrs A. J. Hall received a presentation on her resignation as Honorary Secretary of the Ripon Methodist Mission Sunday School after 52 years' service.

Ripon was visited by Richard Dimbleby for the *Down Your Way* radio programme.

The Ripon Group of Women's Institutes held an exhibition of local treasures to celebrate the 1951 Festival of Britain Year. A selection of these was later on view at the County Exhibition at York.

The Council approved the proposal of the Spa and Estates Committee to demolish the bathing pavilion because of the cost of repair and supervision. Part of the rear wall was to be left as a windbreak and seats placed along the river bank.

March. At a West Riding Standing Joint Committee it was revealed that a new police station was to be built on North Road. The proposal to build a new Court House was dropped and improvements were to be made to the old one.

The Over 60's Club, sponsored by the Old People's Welfare Committee and later renamed the *Friendship*

Club, was inaugurated in the Bondgate Mission Hall.

A swan was injured in collision with a car at Low Mill and died in the Police Station. A letter to the *Gazette* called attention to the sad isolation of the mate but in April a new swan of unknown origin arrived on the canal and eventually mated with the survivor.

The weather at Easter was the worst in living memory. There was a snowstorm on 26 March, Easter Monday, and many acres of spring wheat remained unsown in the Ripon area.

April. Ripon Housing Improvement Trust Limited considered selling their property, *Alma House,* with a view to winding up the Trust.

The bus station, built 15 years earlier but never used as such, was to be brought into operation for a three-month trial period beginning on 20 May. New parking and one-way regulations were to be introduced at the same time.

The Post Office found confusion in the numbering of some Ripon streets and asked the Council to renumber houses in Mallorie Park Drive, Kirkby Road and Clotherholme Road.

The Ripon Circuit Methodist Youth Council held a two-day Eisteddfod in the Zion schoolroom, followed by a procession of witness led by the City Band to the Market Place where the gathering was addressed by the Mayor.

The Guard of Honour for George VI at the opening of the Festival of Britain Exhibition on the South Bank on 4 May was provided by the 3rd Army Engineer Regiment, then stationed at Ripon.

The year 1951 marked the Jubilee of the Nina Convalescent Fund founded in 1901 in the name of Mrs Husband, first wife of the late Dr J. C. R. Husband. On 20 April the Mayor sponsored the League of Friends of Ripon Hospitals to provide 'extras' for the hospitals.

1951-52. FRANCIS CHARLES LOWLEY, Joiner and Undertaker

Mayor 1949-50-51-52

Population statistics for 1950: birth rate 18.32 per 1,000; death rate 122.68 per 1,000.

May. *Newby Hall* was opened to the public for the first time with an admission charge of 2s 6d, thus becoming one of the 'half-crown houses'.

The Festival of Britain opened with a service in St Paul's Cathedral in the presence of King George and Queen Elizabeth. The Mayor and Mayoress were fortunate in being selected to join the congregation and the Council gave permission for them to be accompanied by the Sergeant-at-Mace carrying the City Mace and wearing the Baldric.

The Ripon celebrations began on Sunday 6 May with a service in the Cathedral. Miss Kathleen Atkinson was chosen from ten candidates as Ripon's Festival Queen and was crowned by the Mayoress at a ceremony on the Market Square on 14 May. Later in the month, 15 members of the Girls' High School Choir took part in a performance of Vaughan Williams' *The Sons of Light* sung in the Albert Hall and conducted by Sir Adrian Boult. In June a display was mounted at the Training College on the theme of 'Ripon through the Ages'. Exhibitions were mounted of art, antique furniture, needlework, and other crafts in the Assembly Rooms; the Cathedral treasures in the Cathedral and the City treasures in the Town Hall were also on show. Events in the Festival celebrations continued in August although the month experienced a record rainfall of 5.68 ins. as compared with 2.81 ins. in 1950; on 4 August Ripon Festival Cricket Week began; the Dagenham Girl Pipers performed in the Spa Gardens to a gathering of over 1,000 spectators, and the Festival of Britain Motor display given by the Royal Signals National Display Team and a Gymkhana organised by the Ripon Motor and Cycle Club at Ripon Racecourse attracted about 1,500 people. In September, a 'Festival of Music, Elocution, Drama and Literature' was held in the Central Methodist Church and School, but the number of entries was disappointing. Ripon's contribution to the Festival of Britain ended with fairy lights, fireworks, a bonfire, and a torchlight procession from the Town Hall to Quarry Moor.

Rainfall in May was 7.5 ins., compared with 1.69 ins. in 1950.

Cheshire County Members of the British Legion presented a bus costing £1,000 to Lister House.

The City Council approved a scheme to build 20 flats behind Freemantle Terrace in North Road.

The Mayor and Mayoress attended the ceremonial opening of the first York Festival at a gathering which included The Princess Royal and the Prime Minister.

June. On Saturday 2 June about 900 'Z men' arrived in Ripon to do their initial 15-day training as Royal Engineers. On the same day more than 600 ex-students attended their Triennial Reunion at the Training College. The city was full to overflowing. The army courses were scheduled to run until mid-October, and complaints were received especially from residents in Ure Bank, College Road, and Clotherholme Road of the noisy behaviour of these men returning to camp between 10.30 pm and 1 am. The Commanding Officer apologised and promised to do all he could to deal with the matter, but in

September, the 'Z men' again distressed Ripon citizens. A discolouration of the city's water supply was the cause of much concern and was due to the disturbance of natural mineral deposits in the pipes, resulting from greatly increased consumption by the army camps.

The Health Committee received a report that Ripon had 300 houses which could never be brought up to modern standards. The City Council approved in principle to build that number of houses on a 24-acre site in Lead Lane and other houses on a site at Barefoot Street. Later in the year a notice appeared in the *Gazette* concerning the compulsory purchase of land in Lead Lane.

The first fatal accident in the history of T. and R. Williamson Limited's paint factory, founded in 1775, occurred when Walter Wood, aged 35, fell into a horizontal mixer. At the inquest a verdict of accidental death was recorded and the Coroner stressed there was no question of negligence.

A Police Safety Officer stated that nine out of the ten road traffic accidents reported in Ripon in the previous month involved military vehicles in the charge of 'L' drivers.

It was reported that the stonework of the Cathedral was in urgent need of repair. Weathering and damage caused by corrosion of iron clamps inserted in the 1850s had affected the stonework of the south-west tower, the north-east buttress of the central tower, the clerestory windows on the south side and the central tower windows.

The sum of £327 was stolen from a suitcase containing British, Armenian, Argentinian and Uruguayan currency, left in a bedroom in the *Spa Hotel* by a guest, Mr A. M. C. Butterfield, who was visiting his mother at Tanfield.

July. Four hundred 'Old Contemptibles' from the North-Eastern area held their annual rally for the first time in Ripon. They assembled in the Market Place and marched to the Cathedral for a service.

The Ripon Motor Club was revived after being in abeyance for three years.

The Council rejected as too expensive the offer of the Executive of the Docks and Inland Waterways to sell the canal to the city. Suggestions for its use had included a possible lido, a boating pool or a fish hatchery.

On 16 July the first television test pictures were received in Ripon from the station at Holme Moss. Television dealers found the reception excellent and in October the station opened for regular transmission. Mr Arthur Yates claimed that his new indoor extension aerial made the 'H'-type TV aerial unnecessary.

The Mayor inaugurated Ripon Cricket Club's new scoreboard.

On 31 July the Dean of Ripon, the Very Revd G. Birchenough, retired. He had presented the Cathedral with a cope to celebrate his 70th birthday. The Dean had been given the title of Dean Emeritus.

August. There were complaints of traffic jams in Ripon during the holiday season.

September. The *Queen of Scots* Pullman, the London-Glasgow express, made an unscheduled stop at Ripon station because derailed wagons had blocked the line at Melmerby. Local services were disrupted but the line was soon cleared.

The returns of the 1952 census showed a population in Ripon of 9,464, an increase of 873 over the 1931 figure.

For the first time in Ripon there was a Battle of Britain commemoration ceremony. An A.T.C. flag flew over the Town Hall for a week. On the last day a cadet standing on the roof of the Town Hall lowered the flag, bugles beat a retreat and the A.T.C., marshalled in the Market Square, presented arms.

The Chamber of Trade organised a Festival of Britain Shopping Week at the end of the month. Features included a window numbers competition, a knitting contest and a balloon race. The event was not a success. The Carnival Ball had to be cancelled because of lack of support, and the organisers ran out of gas for the balloons.

October. At the General Election, Colonel Malcolm Stoddart-Scott (Conservative) retained his seat as M.P. for Ripon against Mr S. I. Andrews (Socialist).

The death occurred of Sir Fred Moore of *Mowbray House*, Kirkby Malzeard. He was well known as a J.P. and a local benefactor; he left bequests to Ripon Cathedral and the Diocesan Board of Finance.

The winning balloon in the Chamber of Trade race travelled about 730 miles to Norway. The second and third balloons reached Denmark and Germany.

Reginald Foot, the popular B.B.C. organist, gave a recital at the Central Methodist Church in Coltsgate Hill.

Caxton's 1479 printing of the *Epitome of the Pearl of Eloquence* was rediscovered by Mrs R. S. Mortimer of Leeds during her cataloguing of the Cathedral Library. The book was sent for authentication to the British Museum. The volume was in poor condition and there was debate about the expense of repair and whether it should be sold. The estimated value was £20,000 and through the generosity of Alderman Horace Hird of Bradford the book was beautifully restored and was returned to the Library in August 1952. Dr Moody suggested it should be sold to provide funds for other work. This proposal raised much controversy at the time and it was not acted upon until 1961, when the *Epitome* was sold to the Brotherton Library of the University of Leeds to provide funds for the Choir School Foundation.

November. On 28 November the Revd Frederick Llewellyn Hughes was installed as Dean of Ripon. The Princess Royal and many church and lay dignitaries attended the service.

December. British Legion Headquarters held an inquiry into the affairs of Lister House. There had been complaints reported in the press that the residents were treated like children and dissatisfaction had been expressed with the diet and medical care.

The former foundry of J. Kearsley and Company, situated behind the Post Office in North Street and

25. *The east side of the Market Place (Jackson)*

famous for its manufacture of agricultural implements, was demolished. This allowed an exit to be made into Allhallowgate for the Post Office, relieving congestion in North Street. The Electricity Board was to have a new sub-station built on the Kearsley Site. In January demolition workers felled the 100-foot chimney of the foundry, a well-known Ripon landmark.

A taxi-driver was fined for breaking a by-law. He had failed 'to conduct himself in an orderly manner and with civility and propriety towards a person seeking hire'.

Discussion took place in Council about the state of the Baldric, which needed to be repaired and strengthened. The practice of each mayor adding a medallion had been discontinued in 1942, but, if this custom were to be revived, some medallions would need to be removed and stored to give space. The Baldric was by now very heavy to wear. A sub-committee was appointed. In October 1952 the Council agreed that the Baldric should be repaired and a second Baldric provided.

A demand for a public hall in Ripon was led by Mrs Alderson of the Rowel Players who had lost money on their production in the Garrison Theatre. Other organisations were approached and a public meeting in the Town Hall supported the demand: the idea of temporary flooring in the Spa Baths during winter months was rejected.

The Mayor took the initiative in organising carol singing in the Market Square on Christmas Eve.

January. Alderman King was awarded the M.B.E. in the New Year Honours List in recognition of his work during the Festival of Britain.

Mr D. Gordon Darnton of *Ashley House*, Ure Bank Terrace, a consultant physicist, published details of his electronic magnetic device for use in examining steel and other ferrous materials.

General regret was expressed at the decision of the Ripon Agricultural Show Committee to cancel the show in 1952 because of the lack of support in 1951 and the consequent loss of £300.

Dr Moody was presented with the Freedom of the City at a ceremony which took place in the Lawrence Ballroom. He received the Freedom Scroll inscribed by a local artist, Mr J. Porteus Wood, and a bracket clock. The B.B.C. recording of the occasion was so faulty that they promised to make a second tape. On the same evening, the Cathedral congregation and friends gave Dr Moody a cheque for £800.

A record total of 130 tons of paper salvage was collected in Ripon during 1951: £10,000 had been raised from this source since 1946.

February. The Mayor sent Ripon's sympathy to the Royal Family on the death of King George VI and a special wreath depicting the Ripon Horn was made by Kingstonia Nurseries for Ripon Corporation's tribute to be sent to Windsor. On Saturday 9 February Queen Elizabeth II was proclaimed in the Market Place and at the west door of the Cathedral by the Mayor, and loyal greetings were sent to the new Sovereign. On 15 February more than 2,300 people attended the memorial service in the Cathedral for the late King.

Mr Charles Harker, Mayor 1925-26-27, gave a silver whistling tankard to the Corporation to commemorate the Festival of Britain.

Ripon Fire Station in Blossomgate was renovated. The improvements included central heating, offices, a recreation room and a shower bath.

March. The Highways Committee discussed the possibility of removing the Clock Tower to facilitate the flow of traffic, but 300 people signed a petition and the Council decided against the removal.

The Public Inquiry into the compulsory purchase order on the Lead Lane site stressed three objections: the depreciation of property values, the loss of land for food production and the loss of livelihood. The Council declared, however, that this was the only suitable large site for a housing estate. The Housing Committee rejected the plans for seven-storey blocks of flats put forward in May and in August building plans were approved for 279 houses at a cost of £400,000.

Steps were taken to re-establish the pre-war local Association of Girl Guides.

The Ripon and District Chamber of Trade was dissolved after more than 27 years of intermittent existence. The reason given was lack of support; 'The only asset we have is the president's badge'. The Chamber was to be revived in July 1954.

Major E. Bruce Eccles was unopposed at the W.R.C.C. elections.

April. Zebra crossings which at last appeared in Ripon were not at first at all well received.

Ringlands Circus came to town. 'Salt' and 'Sauce', the elephants, were great favourites with children. A trapeze artist, Miss Shirley De-Vel, fell 40 feet into the circus ring during a performance but was fortunately not seriously injured.

1952-53. WILLIAM MAYLOTT ECCLES, Solicitor

Born 1910 in Ripon, son of Joseph Maylott Eccles, Company Secretary. Educated Coltsgate Hill School and Ripon Grammar School. Entered the office of Stanley Brayshay with whom he subsequently

26. 18th-century cottages, Blossomgate (Jackson)

served his articles, qualifying as a solicitor in 1937. Served in the Royal Artillery 1942-45, leaving with the rank of Captain. Elected to Council 1946, retired 1961, served on every committee and for many years Chairman of Finance and General Purposes. Mayor in Coronation year, when he and the Council were active in arranging celebrations in the city. Attended the Coronation Service in Westminster Abbey by Royal Summons — one of the few mayors to be so honoured. Conferred the Freedom of the City on HRH The Princess Royal, after which he and the Mayoress entertained HRH to tea. Received Queen Elizabeth the Queen Mother on her visit to Studley Royal. Hosted a lunch for the Council and guests to meet Field Marshal Viscount Montgomery on his visit to Ripon. Played hockey; goal-keeper for the Yorkshire Colts, Captain Ripon City Cricket Club and Ripon City Golf Club, founder President of the District Badminton Union and President of the Harrogate District Union of Golf Clubs. A Rotarian and legal adviser to many organisations in the city. Also Mayor 1953-54.

Rainfall in 1952 was 38.64 ins., the highest recorded for over 20 years.

May. The W.R.C.C. allocated £4,500 for repairs to Trinity School.

After an absence of 25 years a former Riponian, Mrs Lynn Cole of California, said 'Ripon's much the same'.

June. The Ripon Rowel Players were in financial difficulties, having made a profit of only £39 in 1951, but members decided to organise a Coronation Drama Festival in 1953, an event which would take the place of their third production of the year.

Skellfield School celebrated its 75th anniversary.

A recorded session of *Gardeners' Question Time* made by the B.B.C. in Ripon in May was broadcast.

Between January and June, 17 cases of drunkenness in the city were reported, nearly all involving non-residents. Only five cases had been heard in the whole of 1951.

July. A Ripon schoolboy, Derrick Hunt, won the Yorkshire Schools' County Championship javelin-throwing competition and represented the county in the National Championship.

The funeral took place on 17 July of Sir John Barran of *Sawley Hall*, for 25 years chairman of the Governors of Ripon Grammar School.

Improvements were made to the Harrogate Road between Quarry Moor and Borrage Bridge to produce a uniform width, with better sight lines and better provision for pedestrians.

The new screen for Holy Trinity Church, made by Mr J. R. Thorpe, was on view for the first time at the Church fête.

August. Although stallholders in the market place complained about poor custom, the *Gazette* stated that St Wilfrid's weekend had broken many records and crowds had thronged the city. A skittle and coconut stall was destroyed by fire during the fair and two others were badly damaged.

An anonymous donor gave a stone-cutter worth £350 to the Cathedral, a gift that was to save hours of hard labour.

A meteorological report stated that 1 July was an exceptional day, the hottest and wettest of the month with a temperature of 80°F and 0.58 ins. of rain, half the total for the month.

Ripon Golf Club planned to offer free golf to six local young people to encourage the sport among the younger generation.

The will of Miss J. F. Bittleston of 7 The Crescent, Ripon, contained bequests to many good causes in the locality and elsewhere, including £500 to Ripon Cathedral.

September. Three Ripon men were among the crews of the aircraft which dropped supplies to the British North Greenland Expedition. From Ripon and District gifts including spirits and cigarettes were sent to members of the expedition stranded on the ice. One of the aircraft crashed and later, in November, the pilot, Flight Lieutenant Clancy, who was unhurt, talked to the Ripon A.T.C. in connection with recruiting.

October. Sodium discharge lights replaced gas lamps on the Harrogate Road.

The new premises for the Girls' Section of Ripon Y.M.C.A. opened. This was in effect a revival of the former Girls' Club, using part of their premises.

Over 2,000 people attended the service in the Cathedral on 11 October when The Princess Royal presented the new County Girl Guides' Standard to the County Commissioner for the north-eastern district of the West Riding.

On 31 October, Holy Trinity celebrated the 125th anniversary of its consecration. The Dean preached at a special service on 26 October, the Vicar kept vigil to receive gifts on 31 October and there was a birthday party that evening.

November. The Rowel Players performed Noel Coward's *Blithe Spirit* in the Garrison Theatre.

December. A dramatised version of the novel *Love Across the Cobbles* by the local writer Miss Florence Bone was given in the Modern School Hall by the Ripon Evening Institute Players under the guidance of Mrs Manuel.

The Corporation was given a medal struck 120 years before in celebration of the first reform election in Ripon in 1832 after the passing of the Electoral Reform Act.

February. The whole Ripon area was badly affected by a severe blizzard; when the Bellman opened the market on 12 February only four stalls had been set out.

Houses in Finkle Street were declared to be dangerous, unhealthy, and due for demolition. The matter dragged on until October when the Ministry of Health was reported to be delaying the scheme. In December there was a Public Inquiry into the proposed clearance.

Large numbers of crocus bulbs were taken by vandals from the Harrogate Road where two displays had been planted.

Ripon Young Farmers' Agricultural Show Committee decided to disband due to lack of interest in the show.

A new prefabricated classroom annexe at Ripon Girls' High School cost £2,250.

The Ripon Girl Guide HQ in Water Skellgate was opened.

The floods in Lincolnshire were declared a national disaster. Troops from Ripon were rushed to the scene and an ambulance left for a week's duty in Lincolnshire, where a Ripon couple had managed to escape from a flooded bungalow. Nearly £2,000 was raised and there were awards for Ripon men in connection with the floods.

March. Ripon Fire Brigade was called to Ripon Railway Station when two trucks carrying liquid ammonia caught fire.

The death of the Very Revd G. Birchenough, Dean of Ripon 1941-51, in Cobham, Surrey, was announced. On 21 March, his ashes were buried in All Souls' Chapel in the Cathedral at a memorial service.

The Council decided to discontinue work on the caravan site on the river bank near the boathouse.

On 24 March the city mourned the death of Queen Mary who had been a frequent visitor to Ripon. A memorial service was held in the Cathedral on 31 March.

W. M. Abbott and Company, the well-known firm of cabinet makers, celebrated their centenary.

April. Ripon rates increased by 4s 6d to a record of 25s 2d in the pound.

Ripon and District Royal Naval Association held its first annual dance. In May the Dean dedicated its standard.

Queen Elizabeth the Queen Mother visited *Studley Royal* to unveil the memorial to Elizabeth and Charles de Grey Vyner in Fountains Hall. *The Queen of Scots* Pullman train made a special stop at Ripon Station where the Queen Mother was greeted by the Mayor.

A police report referred to 20 cases of 'breaking and entering' in the city in the past few months.

Work began on road repairs in the city centre, scheduled to last until October and including Borrage Bridge, Skellgate, the Market Place, North Street and Kirkgate. There were many complaints about the effect of this on trade.

The Bishop dedicated the screen in Holy Trinity Church in memory of the former precentor, the late Revd Ranald McPherson.

27. *Kirkgate (Jackson)*

1953-54. WILLIAM MAYLOTT ECCLES, Solicitor

Mayor 1952-53-54

Population statistics for 1952 showed the lowest death rate since 1935: 10.61 per 1,000. The birth rate was 18.96 per 1,000.

May/June. During the fifth race of the day, the Newby Plate, at Ripon races, three jockeys were injured and a horse killed.

Local hoteliers planned to run a 'Pickwickian' horse-drawn coach from the *Unicorn Hotel* to Fountains Abbey starting on 1 June. This was part of a wide range of events to celebrate the crowning of Queen Elizabeth II on 2 June. The day itself was marked by a united church service in the Cathedral, followed by a parade when the salute was taken by the Deputy Mayor, as the Mayor was in London for the Coronation ceremony. Rain caused the postponement of the evening celebrations until Saturday 6 June, when there was a torchlight procession and fireworks. A coronation bonfire was lighted and the market place was the scene of dancing and community singing: many street parties were held. On 10 June, the Yorkshire Symphony Orchestra played in Ripon Cathedral, the first occasion on which a full orchestra had given a concert there. Coronation medals were awarded to a number of Ripon people including the Mayor, the Town Clerk and the city's M.P. Two new cups were given for Ripon Children's Sports Day by anonymous donors to commemorate the Coronation. Lickley Street was voted the best decorated street during the Coronation and a plaque was put up to commemorate this.

The only fatal accident to have occurred at the Spa Baths since their opening took place when Mr J. C. Knowles was found dead in the slipper baths. Mr Knowles was 80 years of age and death was due to shock caused by extensive burns.

July. The Ministry of Housing and Local Government issued a permit for only half the number of houses the Council had planned to build in 1954 on the Lead Lane site. The foundations for the first six houses were laid during July.

Ripon Rugby Club acquired the use of a field adjoining the cricket and soccer fields. The new ground was opened with a special evening 'friendly' match in September 1955.

Ripon was reported to be using more water per head than Leeds. It was essential to stop waste and a big reduction in consumption was achieved by mending a serious leak of water in Fishergate. The Army was asked to use the borehole earlier in the season and the City Engineer was instructed to obtain equipment to test for leakages.

Mrs McGrigor Phillips (the poetess Dorothy Una Ratcliffe) withdrew the paintings she had loaned to the Corporation because of the poor conditions in which they were being shown in the *Thorpe Prebend House*.

The Mayor opened the scented garden for the blind at *Thorpe Prebend House*, a coronation gift from the Corporation.

August. There were complaints about the new higher kerbs in High Skellgate where the street was too narrow for large vehicles to pass each other and it was impossible for them to mount the pavement. One suggested solution was to create a one-way traffic system.

An appeal made to all Ripon householders to support the Public Hall Trust, set up with Alderman Lowley as chairman, brought a disappointing response.

A man lost not his shirt, but his shoes at Ripon races. He went to sleep after the races and awoke to find old shoes substituted for his own.

Café proprietors in Ripon complained of having the 'poorest summer for years'. They blamed traffic hold-ups caused by road repairs, but the City Engineer doubted this. The police reported more accidents than usual in the city during the last two months (fortunately not serious) and these were also attributed to the road repairs. A West Riding report showed that Ripon had had the greatest number of accidents per head of population in the county in 1952, one to every 80 people as against an average of one per hundred.

September. The Battle of Britain Week Exhibition opened in the Assembly Rooms, where various kinds of equipment were displayed and Mr Arthur Yates operated a radio transmitter.

Ripon's water supply remained so unsatisfactory that the Water Committee resolved to call in a consultant engineer to report on the general situation, and in particular to advise on the cost of a scheme to reduce wastage at the army borehole. Harrogate Council stated it would be unable to provide extra water to Ripon.

The W.R.C.C. reported the need to spend £10,000 on repairs to Ripon's two Cathedral schools. The Education Sub-Committee suggested it might be better to build new schools rather than patch up the old ones, but this was regarded as unlikely in view of the county's building commitments elsewhere.

October. The Government allocated 50 extra houses to the city and it was hoped that Ripon building firms would be able to obtain work on these. Disappointment was expressed that work on the first phase of the development had been given to a firm outside the city.

The Princess Royal received the Honorary Freedom of the City of Ripon at a ceremony in the Palladium Cinema after the Princess had inspected a guard of honour mounted by the Royal Engineers in the Market Place.

November. Mr H. W. Hill retired after 20 years as a bandmaster and conductor of the Ripon City Prize Band. He had joined the band at the age of ten, and at the age of 67 Mr Hill was made an honorary life member.

The former Congregational Church in North Street was leased to Mr W. N. Dixon to be used as a poultry processing factory. By New Year 1954 the output was expected to be 1,000 chickens a day.

December. A Royal Signals combat vehicle was marooned in the river Ure near North Bridge during routine tests. The driver was hauled ashore by rope and the vehicle was eventually recovered.

The Army released the land requisitioned at Quarry Moor. Miss M. Spence formally presented to Ripon Corporation the deeds of this land which had been the gift of her father Alderman Spence to the city.

Colonel M. Stoddart-Scott, M.P. for Ripon, intro-duced a private member's bill to the House providing for the exchange of medical certificates between couples proposing to marry. He believed the measure was unlikely to get far but it would call attention to a problem which had led to legislation in Scandinavian countries.

Miss Barbara Holland, P.E. teacher at Ripon Girls' High School, accepted the invitation to be a member of the All England Women's Hockey team due to tour South Africa in the summer of 1954. She was to be selected again for the Australian tour of 1956.

The Dean appealed for £4,000 to repair the south-east wall of the Cathedral where the foundations were slipping.

Ripon's accident rate still caused concern, although again the accidents were not serious. The figure for November 1953 was nearly double that for the same month in the previous year, despite all the propaganda for road safety.

January. The traditional way of welcoming in the New Year, when 600 people assembled in the Market Place, had changed little since 1904.

28. Market Day (Jackson)

Field-Marshal Viscount Montgomery again visited Ripon as the guest of the Dean, the Very Revd F. Ll. Hughes. He was given an informal lunch at the Town Hall, read a lesson at Matins in the Cathedral and later talked to Ripon schoolchildren.

The first snowfall of the year halted traffic for about an hour on the Harrogate Road. The cost of clearing the snow in Ripon was £920, about £400 above the estimate.

February. Attention was drawn to the research work being carried out by the Red Hand Works in Ripon to prevent corrosion on the bottoms of ships by barnacles and weeds. The firm was established in Ripon during the war when the London factory was bombed.

Dr C. H. Moody retired as Cathedral Organist after 52 years. His successor, Mr Lionel Dakers, took office on 1 August. Later in the year Dr Moody was given the Lady Maud Warrender Award of Merit for his services to the Church and Music, and in December he was presented with two cheques, the first for £1,233 by the Mayor collected by public subscription and including donations from abroad, and the second for £1,105 by the Dean on behalf of the Cathedral.

Improvements to the Racecourse included an extension of Tattersalls to give increased capacity, a new snack bar and alterations of the entrances to speed up the flow of racegoers.

The first school traffic wardens started work at Trinity School and on the Boroughbridge Road on 11 February.

March. Door-to-door canvassing of Ripon houses in support of the appeal for a Public Hall was carried out.

The City Council voted to sell the Fire Station in Blossomgate to the W.R.C.C. instead of leasing it to them.

April. All except one of the staff of the Princess Road hospital for the chronic sick resigned in protest against the 'consistent neglect of the hospital's needs', although their resignations were delayed out of respect for the impending retirement of the matron. The chief complaints concerned lack of central heating and a lift, and the poor quality of the beds supplied. Volunteer staff from other hospitals took over. Improvements were not started until early 1956 and after a year's closure the hospital was re-opened in May 1957, when structural alterations and redecoration had been carried out, central heating installed and a new day-room provided. A hoist was provided as it had proved impossible to find room for a lift.

The County Education Committee inquired into the question of paid work being done by Grammar School boys as reported by the headmaster at Speech Day. This contravened county by-laws which prohibited paid work by boys under 14.

Councillor Constantine stated that the occupied houses in Lickley Street were liable to imminent collapse and stressed the need for immediate rehousing. At the beginning of May the first five houses of the Lead Lane estate were occupied and one of these was taken by a Lickley Street tenant. Later there were reports that this new estate was not popular because of its distance from the town centre. Also in May, the Ministry approved the compulsory purchase of property in Allhallowgate and Finkle Street.

1954-55. CHARLES AUGUSTUS FEARN, Bank Manager

Born 1892. Came to Ripon in 1938 as Manager of the National Provincial Bank and retired 1952. Elected to Council by a by-election, 1952. Served 1914-18 in the King's Own Yorkshire Light Infantry with the rank of Captain, awarded the M.C. at Cambrai. 1939-45 served in the Home Guard. Member of the Ripon Branch of the British Legion and on the committee of Lister House, the British Legion Home. Member of the Cricket, Golf and Rugby Clubs, and a founder and life member of the Craven Gentlemen's Cricket Club. Also Mayor in 1955-56 and 1962-63. He died in 1977.

Rainfall in 1954 was 29.96 ins. Population statistics: birth rate 17.58 per 1,000; infant mortality (10.98 per 1,000) was the lowest on record for the city (the national rate was 25.5 per 1,000).

May. The new village hall at Littlethorpe to replace the building burned down in 1945 was opened by Mrs Ingham.

The N.F.U. wished to take over Ripon's slaughter house when meat rationing ended but the City Council asked the Ministry of Food to assign the lease of the slaughterhouse to them.

Miss Florence Horsbrough, Minister of Education, opened the Training College extension at the rear of the main building which provided a dining-hall and kitchens, study-bedrooms, a sick bay and common room. The ceremony was preceded by a service in the Cathedral at which the Archbishop of York preached.

Freebooter, the former Grand National winner, went into full retirement at his home, *Ox Close*, Ripon.

The Yorkshire Cricket 2nd XI defeated Cumberland and Westmorland with five minutes to spare at a Minor Counties Cricket match at the Ripon Cricket ground, the first match of such importance played there since World War I.

Arrangements were made to revive the Ripon W.V.S. at a meeting held at the Town Hall.

The *Wakeman's House* was to be let to the antique dealer, Mr A. Edwards, who would use the front part as a shop and supervise the city's museum collection in the back room.

June. Boundary changes were announced for Ripon Magistrates' Court, but the name *Liberty* was to be retained.

A party of West African journalists was received by the Mayor during a visit to the city.

Owlets in the Cathedral roof were rescued by one of the masons.

A spell of bad weather began. A Bondgate woman was struck in the face by a telephone when she used the instrument during a violent thunderstorm. Toward the end of the month, gales caused widespread minor damage, especially to trees.

A Conservative Rally on the racecourse addressed by the Home Secretary, Sir David Maxwell Fyfe, attracted about 7,000 people.

A civic exhibition was mounted in celebration of the granting of James I's charter in 1604 to the City. A special service on 27 June in the Cathedral commemorated the City Charter and the refoundation charter of Ripon Minster given by the King in the same year. This event was attended by The Princess Royal and many ecclesiastical and civic dignitaries. On the same day, traffic was diverted for nearly an hour when a bus and a lorry jammed in High Skellgate.

Controls on the sale of fat stock were lifted after 14 years. High prices were made at the first free auction at the Ripon Farmers' Livestock Mart.

Member of the British Legion from 12 counties were present when Earl Haig opened a British Legion Fête and Rally at Lister House.

The Council purchased a new type of refuse vehicle to cope with the city's narrow streets.

During renovations at the *Black Swan* in Westgate, three old flues were discovered and later in the year more of Abbot Huby's wall was found behind the *Unicorn* when the old stables were demolished.

August. The Princess Royal attended Ripon races and saw her horse *Swallow Dive* win the Mallorie Handicap.

Mr P. Rodford won the cup for the best puppy and novice at the Yorkshire Collie Club's show at Wakefield.

The one-way traffic system was adopted for an experimental period, northbound traffic via High Skellgate, southbound via Kirkgate, Duck Hill and Water Skellgate. Much comment ensued: the Highways Committee discussed the problems during the next month but decided to retain the system.

September. The sale by auction of the house used as the convent on Coltsgate Hill was called off because of the last-minute interest shown in the property by the West Riding Education Committee who eventually acquired the building for incorporation in Holy Trinity School. The nuns, Sisters of Charity of St Paul the Apostle, moved to a house in Crescent Parade.

After 10 years' of existence, the Ripon and District Pig Club was disbanded. The narrow margin of profit made in the sale of pigs was not worth the labour involved.

A three-day Road Safety Exhibition, of special significance in view of the recent increase in accidents in the city, was held in the Assembly Rooms.

Jimmy Jewell and Ben Wariss, the celebrated comedians, appeared at a midnight matinée in the Palladium to raise funds during the Battle of Britain Week. The cinema was packed.

An amplifying system was tried in the Cathedral for the first time during the Battle of Britain service and, after more tests, was to become permanent.

Mr Tom Hawley retired from his duties as Ripon Hornblower. He had served the city in this official capacity for 15 years, but claimed to have first blown the Horn 60 years before. The Council made a presentation to him in December.

October. The possibility of 'twinning' Ripon with the French town of Foix was discussed and more information was sought. The Mayor of Foix visited Ripon in June 1955 and in June 1957 Alderman Wells visited the French town for twinning ceremonies. Part of the Foix celebrations was a banquet which last four hours.

Comment continued on the road regulations in the city. Ripon traders still objected to the 'no parking' proposals for North Street. The Education Sub-Committee discussed the provision of zebra crossing and school-crossing patrols. The Minister of Transport was reported as saying there were more road signs to the square mile in Ripon than anywhere else in Britain, and one defendant in court claimed he saw nine road signs at one junction.

November. Despite complaints of vandalism on Council housing estates, the idea of a tenants' committee to try to prevent damage did not find favour with the tenants.

The Finance and General Purposes Committee discussed the problems associated with St Wilfrid's Fair; the noise, traffic, fire hazards and the procession itself 'in appearance like a conglomeration of scrap vehicles'.

Ripon Toc H marked its 25th anniversary with a service in the Cathedral.

December. The Princess Royal agreed to be the Patron of the Ripon Choral Society.

The argument about the possible experimental ban on parking in North Street continued unabated, and in consequence the Highways Committee postponed its decision on the matter for a month, by which time the new Road Traffic Act might have come into force.

A new housing allocation was announced by which 70 per cent of the new houses would be assigned to slum tenants and only 30 per cent to those heading the 'points' list.

Lumley Moor reservoir was reported to have been full for a record 55 days, but water consumption was still considered to be much too high.

The W.R.C.C. lodged a petition against the closure of part of the Ripon canal proposed in the British Transport Bill, which was then under construction.

29. North Street (Jackson)

February. Plans to build permanent barrack accommodation at the Army Camp delighted Ripon traders. However, in November, the Army made it clear that the rebuilding would be a long-term project and would not begin for a few years.

The West Riding Education Committee announced that the first peripatetic music teacher to be appointed would be assigned to the Ripon district.

As part of the programme of events marking the 400th anniversary of the refounding of the Grammar School, a Literary 'Brains Trust' was broadcast. Speech Day was on 29 April when the Minister of Education should have attended but was unable to do so because of an accident. An exhibition of school archives was mounted in the Town Hall in July and the celebrations culminated with a commemoration service held in the Cathedral later in July.

The construction began of a new stall-house in the car park near the bus station.

A complete replacement of gas street-lighting by electricity was approved in principle. In April plans were speeded up and in December the final stages of the changeover were approved by the Finance Committee.

As part of the national scheme, preparations were made for the innoculation of Ripon 13-year-olds against tuberculosis.

March. Mallorie Park Tennis Club joined the new Harrogate and District Tennis League and Mr F. Collinson of Ripon became the first president of the League.

The City Council made headlines in the national press when the Finance Committee voted to provide a cushion for a typist to save her nylon stockings.

A Sikh soldier who had been absent from the army for two-and-a-half years without leave was court-martialled at Ripon Barracks and given a sentence of six months' detention: however, the man was discharged because of the difficulty of meeting his religious requirements in the army, a situation responsible for his desertion in the first place.

The premises in Finkle Street occupied by the Customs and Excise Department were to be vacated in about a year's time, when the Ripon Post Office would move from North Street into the building.

Holy Trinity School Orchestra won first place in the

school orchestra class at the Harrogate Musical Festival and in the next month were awarded the highest number of points in their class at the Horsforth Musical Festival.

The Bondgate Compulsory Purchase Order for slum clearance was confirmed by the Ministry of Health. In December, a Public Inquiry into the King Street clearance had brought a lament from one protestor about the loss of old buildings but the Chairman of the Public Health Committee defended the demolition. By the end of 1955, the Council were beginning to think that the post-war housing problems were nearly solved. A notable success had been the building of nearly 100 houses on the Lead Lane Estate. However, the satisfaction felt over the Lead Lane scheme was temporarily clouded by the appearance in March 1956 of faults in some of the houses, such as the lack of outside stores, the warping of interior doors so that some could not be closed, larders heated by neighbouring fireplaces, and smoking chimneys. In reply, the Council offered permission for tenants to put up their own sheds, as the Government refused to authorise loans for building brick sheds; warped doors would be replaced; new larders would be provided or, if tenants paid 2s 0d a week extra rent, refrigerators would be installed; fallen mortar would be removed from chimneys and experiments made with cowls.

Prefabricated classrooms were erected at Holy Trinity School.

April. The official charter was presented to the new branch of the National Association of Round Tables of Great Britain and Ireland formed in Ripon in 1954.

On Good Friday the reconstructed Hell Wath bridge was opened. Funds for the work on the new bridge were raised by Toc H when the old structure was washed away in the floods of November 1951. Easter sunshine brought crowds to the city and bumper trade to the hotels.

The Transport Commission accepted the Survey Board's suggestion that Ripon Canal should be closed because of lack of use. The Ripon Motor Club considered forming a company to take over the canal.

Hammonds' Bakeries Limited of Magdalen Road, Ripon, the largest bakery in the area, closed due to high overhead costs and the price of flour. The bakery was established in 1917 as the N.C.B. Bakery and had served most of the local Army and R.A.F. camps.

At a choral festival held at the Modern School of the Yorkshire County Federation of Women's Institutes, the Ripon W.I. choir won two trophies.

1955-56. CHARLES AUGUSTUS FEARN, Bank Manager

May. A new members' grandstand was built at Ripon racecourse; other improvements included remodelling the dining and refreshment rooms, a low concrete stand and additional seating in the club stand.

The courts of Ripon City, Ripon Liberty and Kirkby Malzeard Petty Sessions were combined in one Ripon Liberty Division. The new court sat for the first time on 4 May.

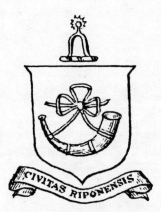

Mayor 1954-55-56

Sir Robert Fosset's Mammoth Jungle Circus visited Ripon.

Mr and Mrs C. Crabtree of Harrogate presented a sound system costing £700 to the Cathedral.

Lord Swinton received an Earldom and was henceforth styled Baron Masham of Ellington and Earl of Swinton.

Colonel Malcolm Stoddart-Scott was re-elected M.P. for the Ripon division with a majority of 12,000 in a straight fight with his Labour opponent, Councillor Eric Brierley.

June. The Trustees of the Studley Estate were unwilling to allow trial tests to find out whether 15 acres of their land would be suitable for a cemetery. The Corporation considered compulsory purchase, but the tests when eventually made proved that the land was unsuitable.

The first diocesan choral festival since before the war was held in the Cathedral.

New communion furniture was given to Ripon Central Methodist Church in memory of the late Miss Letitia King.

Two Labour candidates, Mr N. W. Pollard and Mr W. J. Baily, became the first Labour councillors in Ripon by their victory in by-elections. In May, Conservatives had made a clean sweep at the local elections, winning every seat.

July. Susan Ellis of Ripon won not only the Girls' Open Singles in the Harrogate Tennis Tournament but all the five events for which she entered, including the Ladies' Singles.

Local shop-owners complained that the selling of bacon in Ripon Market was undermining their trade. The stallholder, a man of 80 who claimed to have sold bacon there for most of his life, admitted his business was increasing.

The City employed a second Hornblower, the two men to officiate alternately, a month at a time, since it was considered that the job was too demanding for one person.

The newly-installed photo-finish camera at Ripon racecourse was used for the first time at the finish of the Masham handicap.

Ripon and district experienced a heatwave: on all

but four days in the month the temperature was over 70°F, there was no rain for 29 days but it was not the driest July on record. A good harvest was predicted.

August. The Inspectorate of the Ancient Monuments Commission organised an archaeological dig in the grounds of the Old Deanery, in the hope of finding the remains of the medieval Ladykirk, traces of the Celtic monastery or the remains of Romano-British origin. After completion of this dig, bungalows were to be built on the site. Excavation revealed a graveyard, the remains of a building which might have been the Ladykirk, and Saxon combs.

The Anthroposophical Society held their annual conference at the Training College. More than two hundred members attended and visitors from other European countries were present.

A 'mystery disease' affected cattle in the Ripon area with symptoms similar to those of myxomatosis in rabbits. It was diagnosed as contagious ophthalmia, a disease more common in the south of England.

A fire at Whitakers' Station Garage in North Road apparently started in the early hours of the morning in the office. Guests were roused in the nearby *Station Hotel* and firemen fought the blaze for more than two-and-a-half hours.

Eight French children whose parents had assisted Allied airmen to escape during the war paid a fortnight's visit to Ripon.

It was estimated that the sewage works extension scheme would cost about £28,000.

Local members of the Harrogate Sub-Aqua Club discovered old timbers in the Ure near North Bridge which had almost certainly formed part of the medieval bridge.

September. The first diesel trains were scheduled to run from Ripon to Bradford and Harrogate, one each way per day.

During demoliton work in Allhallowgate the remains of a clay-pipe manufacturing site were discovered.

The season of high temperatures and low rainfall was emphasised in the report of Mr W. Clough of Burton Leonard: 62 days in the previous five months of temperatures over 70°F compared with an average of 28 and there had been only five-and-a-half inches of rain in the previous four months instead of the usual 11 or 12 inches. The drought thus caused brought threats of prosecution of water-wasters and the fear of the introduction of standpipes. Increased supplies were brought from Harrogate, with the realisation that every week meant an extra halfpenny on the rates. The army planned to pump water from the river Ure. Lumley Moor reservoir was down to only 18 days' supply at the end of September and the water supply had to be cut off in some places on the first Monday morning in October because of the extra consumption on washday. During that month the situation eased; the public economised and there was a little rain but not enough, it was emphasised, to fill a reservoir. In November it was hoped that with increased wet weather pressure would soon be back to normal. Although the public had responded to earlier appeals,

the year saw the highest water consumption figures ever recorded in Ripon.

October. Mrs A. M. Wilkinson published her new book, *Wilfrid of Ripon*. Her next work, *The Fountains Story*, published by the Wakeman Press, appeared in October 1957.

Council plans for a new bowls pavilion which had been approved in principle in February were shelved to save funds.

No. 36 Corps Royal Engineer Regiment left Ripon for Germany. There was a march past in the Market Place with fixed bayonets and the Regiment then proceeded to the railway station.

November. After protracted negotiations for land purchase, the work of widening and making up Lead Lane was expected to be put in hand. The three-year delay meant costs had risen.

The Revd H. Filby presented an early printed book to Ripon Cathedral Library, a collection of poetry, music, religious essays and sermons written by Johannes Gerson in 1489.

The Hospital Management Committee decided to move Ripon's male geriatric patients, then accommodated at Knaresborough Hospital, to Bedale, but agreed to discuss the possibility of extending the provision at Princess Road for female geriatric patients to include facilities for males.

An outbreak of hooliganism resulted in extensive damage to street lamps caused by youths with catapults. An 'unbreakable' street lamp in Grove Lane received its ninth replacement. In March four schoolboys were brought before the Ripon Juvenile Court charged with taking lead from Council houses to make catapult pellets.

December. A suggestion made by the Housing Committee of 'no frills' houses for problem tenants caused an outcry and reached the national press. The Chairman spoke of the Press distorting the facts.

At a Public Inquiry into a Corporation plan to sink a borehole and make a reservoir near Kirkby Road, two objectors raised their fears that their private water supplies might be affected, but this was stated by the Town Clerk to be a remote contingency. The Minister of Health deferred the making of a decision on the borehole until every alternative had been explored. He considered the success of the undertaking uncertain, because it was likely that the water so provided would be too hard and suggested that the solution might lie in an approach to the Harrogate Corporation for a permanent bulk supply.

At an inquest on the death of a seven-year-old boy accidentally killed in Clotherholme Road by a military vehicle, the driver was exonerated. Safety measures were worked out by the police and military authorities to meet complaints about the behaviour of children coming out of school at the end of the day.

A failure in Ripon's electrical supply occurred for the second time within just over a month. Temperatures were below freezing and the fault lay in the main 11,000-volt cable between Harrogate and Ripon.

The new valuation lists showed that the total

rateable value of the City had increased by 51.5 per cent from £72,481 to £109,848. In general, the increases were steeper for business premises than for dwellings, most householders finding their rateable value had increased by less than 40 per cent. Many traders protested about 'gross injustices'. As a result of the new valuation, the City's rates were reduced by 1s 0d in the pound in March 1956, but this was put back the following year.

The Army proposed to make a lake for training purposes on the bend of the Ure between North Lees and Hutton Conyers, subject to agreement with the Area Planning Officer.

December. Mr J. A. Berry, Town Clerk of the City for the last seven years, resigned to take up a similar post in Kisumu in Kenya.

January. Alderman Russell Dixon received the O.B.E. in the New Year Honours List in recognition of his 30 years of service on Ripon Council.

Five hundred officers and men of the 35th Field Engineer Regiment arrived at the camp from operations in Cyprus.

T. and R. Williamson Limited, paint and varnish manufacturers, introduced a £10,000 synthetic resin plant which it was estimated would double the firm's productive capacity in this field.

An American press report gleefully ascribed the Army's decision to introduce a one-way traffic system in Coltsgate Hill to the need to avoid paying frequent compensation for the damage done to the awning of Mrs Burrell's corner sweetshop.

The Council decided to seek loans from the public at 5 per cent interest for periods of from three to five years.

Ian Eccles of Ripon reached the finals of the mixed doubles in the All-England Junior Badminton Championship at Wimbledon; he was competing for the first time.

February. The severe cold spell which began at the close of the previous year continued, an ill wind which blew good to the Lumley Moor Reservoir where 14 ins. of snow and 4.12 ins. of rain brought it nearly to full capacity. March was ushered in with hurricane winds of up to 90 mph causing widespread damage. In July, a freak storm, when more than two-thirds of an inch of rain fell in 20 minutes, severely damaged *Markenfield Hall*.

March. The Council accepted the draft of a Town Map after a number of amendments had been made which were concerned for the most part with the failure to earmark sites for any particular use. The public were invited to make objections.

Ripon responded well to the polio vaccination scheme offered to all children born between 1947 and 1954 by the Ministry of Health.

Major F. R. Ingham of *Bellwood Hall*, Ripon, was selected as High Sheriff of Yorkshire for 1956.

Refuse collectors removed three carpets left outside the Girls' High School for cleaning by the caretaker; two of the carpets were eventually rescued from the tip.

April. The Corporation Finance Committee rejected a suggestion that the canal should be drained and used for tipping. The locks on the canal were to be filled up and it was planned that cascades should replace the locks.

1956-57. WILLIAM NORMAN WELLS, Wine Merchant

Born 1896. Son of Arthur Wells, mayor 1898-99, and grandson of William Wells, mayor 1869-70, and followed them in the old-established Wine and Spirit business in North Street. Educated at the Grammar School. Joined the Army from school in 1914, invalided home in 1917 and later an instructor on the reserve list; West Yorkshire Regiment in 1939-45, attained the rank of Major. Elected to Council in 1946. President of the Ripon Divisonal Conservative Association; awarded the C.B.E. for political and public services. President of the Ripon Branch British Legion. Governor of the Grammar School and a director of the Racecourse Company. Member of the Rugby Club, had played for the Harrogate Old Boys team. He died in 1984.

May. The Labour party lost one of the two seats gained on the City Council in the previous year's by-election.

The Royal Engineers constructed a 200-foot heavy girder bridge across the Ure at Bridge Hewick, the first in this country of a new type developed by the Army.

The Princess Royal attended a performance of Haydn's *Creation* in the Cathedral.

During a service in the Cathedral on 13 May the Archdeacon announced that the central tower was unsafe. Within a week an appeal for £100,000 to repair Ripon Cathedral was launched at Leeds Town Hall and before the end of the month £42,000 was raised. The first stage of the restoration work was completed by October.

Alderman W. Norman Wells was elected Mayor. Both his father and grandfather had held office as Mayors of Ripon.

Mr J. Garbutt launched a prototype fibreglass pleasure boat on the Ure, which he hoped might result in building up a new light industry in Ripon.

Sir Mortimer Wheeler, the distinguished archaeologist and TV personality, spoke to the Harrogate and Ripon Branch of the English-Speaking Union at the *Spa Hotel*, Ripon.

A 15,400-ton ore-carrier was launched in Glasgow and named M.V. *Ripon*. A painting of the city was commissioned for the ship's saloon and Ripon provided a plaque.

June. To mark the 40th anniversary of its opening, the Palladium Cinema screened *The Lumière Show of 1898*. The British Film Institute lent this collection of some of the first films ever made.

The *Black Dog* darts team from Ripon ended a very successful season. The team won the Yorkshire Darts Championship, but were defeated in the quarter-finals of the Northern Counties Championship by the eventual winners of the competition.

July. The Council rejected the fluoridation of the city's supply of drinking water for the present.

To ease the drainage problem which had led to flooding and backing-up of sewage, a new 12-inch sewer was to be laid along Clotherholme Road at an estimated cost of £5,250.

Very heavy rain turned Ripon streets into torrents. The Grammar School records showed that 1.14 ins. fell within four hours.

The *Wakeman's House* and *Thorpe Prebend House* were found to be in need of extensive repairs, estimated at £13,000. It was hoped that a grant might be made from the Ministry of Works. In October, the *Wakeman's House* was temporarily shored up.

The W.R.C.C. decided to make the one-way traffic system throughout the city permanent. A temporary roundabout was constructed at the bottom of Bedern Bank, but the W.R.C.C. maintained that this would not be a permanent feature because of the proposed relief road.

The new Post Office in Finkle Street was opened. The old Post Office in North Street, built 50 years earlier, continued to be used as a sorting office.

August. Bank Holiday crowds watched the 1,250th anniversary celebration of 'St Wilfrid's' return from exile to his own city and on the Monday a record crowd of 24,000 at the Ripon races saw the St Wilfrid Handicap.

The first part of the scheme to improve the city's electricity supply was completed when an 11,000-volt cable was laid from the south under the River Skell. Heavy rain had hindered the work, as the river had had to be partially dammed in very difficult circumstances.

An unusual military event took place when 350 gunners of the 429 (Antrim) Coast Regiment (T.A.) arrived in Ripon to be converted into a Field Engineer's Regiment of the Royal Engineers. A plaque was put up in commemoration in the Town Hall.

September. The Yorkshire Varnish Company Limited, one of five similar concerns in Ripon, announced that production would shortly cease in Ripon and would be moved to Felling-on-Tyne. Fourteen employees would be made redundant, but the office staff would remain in Ripon as sales would continue there.

There was much improved support for the Ripon Rowel Players with their presentation of *Love in a Mist* at the Opera House.

The Cathedral Chapter House was re-opened and re-dedicated after being closed for 18 months for repairs.

Councillors had experienced concern about plans for the three-storey development in Allhallowgate, one storey for old people's flats and two-storey maisonettes above, but a model of the proposed block put on view allayed their doubts. In September the plan was accepted in principle by one vote.

An appeal for £25,000 was launched to build the new Methodist Church in Harrogate Road.

October. The Ripon Corporation Finance Committee set up a sub-committee to look into the question of the preservation of the city's archives, a move prompted by the discovery of a picture damaged by damp.

Ripon Amateur Operatic Society secured a permanent home at last, the lease of premises formerly occupied by the girls' section of Ripon Y.M.C.A. in Water Skellgate. Members worked hard to get the rooms ready for use and early in the following month presented *Miss Hook of Holland* at the Opera House nearby when it was hoped that the public would give much more support than to the spring production of *No, No, Nanette*. The producer had warned that, unless this extra support was forthcoming, the Society would have to be wound up.

A taxi stampede occurred regularly on Monday mornings when several hundred troops returning from weekend leave tried to get transport from Ripon Station to the camp. The bus hired by the Army had been withdrawn because soldiers would not buy tickets in advance.

The Mayor suggested that all local ex-servicemen's organisations should centre round the British Legion. The Royal Naval Association rejected the idea, but some members of the R.A.F.A. felt it might be useful in view of their declining numbers.

November. In January, the North Street parking ban had been approved by the W.R.C.C. When this was enforced a loud outcry from local traders ensued. They argued they would lose trade because customers were not willing to walk further. In the *Gazette* the Bellringer's column commented, 'In the middle of a grave international crisis, we're worried about walking 200 yards to the shops'. Further prohibitions were also proposed in Kirkgate and Westgate. The protests continued but all three schemes were put into force over the next 18 months.

Independent Television became available: reception varied from excellent to non-existent.

Miss Marie Hartley and Miss Joan Ingilby visited Ripon to autograph copies of their book *The Yorkshire Dales*.

The Mayor proposed that the Corporation should apply to Parliament for the restoration of the title *Wakeman* to replace that of *Mayor*. The M.P. was told by the government that the change would run counter to standardisation policy and a private bill would be required.

The Ripon Labour Party opened its new head-quarters at 26b Market Place.

The Council complimented workmen on the recovery of lead valued at £3,400 from the old Spa pipe track.

December. The Suez Crisis made petrol rationing necessary, but shopkeepers found the restrictions did not prevent record Christmas shopping.

It was proposed to carry out urgent repair work at the Spa Baths. The slipper baths were reported to be in an appalling condition, but the suggestion that £300 should be spent on refitting was rejected on the grounds that their use was diminishing as more and more people had their own baths.

Citizens complained of the rowdyism and violence of off-duty troops. The town patrol of the Military Police was augmented and trouble declined in the city centre but increased in Clotherholme Road. Incidents reaching the Courts included the beating-up of Ripon civilians by a group of soldiers and the smashing of windows in 16 Ripon premises after a 'demob' party.

January. Several hundred Riponians 'danced in' the New Year in the Market Place.

Electric lighting was to be installed in the Court House at last. This would obviate the necessity of stopping court proceedings while a policeman climbed up to light the gas.

During the previous month the Gas Manager had complained about the failure of the water supply when a gas boiler had almost blown up. The Water Committee decided to lay new mains but urged the gas works to put in a new water storage tank for emergencies.

Collections in the city for the Hungarian Relief Fund totalled £1,460.

Sir Len Hutton attended a Sports Forum at the Garrison Theatre, organised by the *Daily Express*, and returned to Ripon in the autumn to open a fête in aid of funds for the Ripon Cricket Club, at which £450 was raised.

Ripon Cathedral was chosen for the annual Gordon Memorial Service. The Princess Royal took the salute in the Market Place from Gordon Memorial School boys and troops of the Ripon Garrison.

Five Ripon schoolboys were carried to safety from an island in the swollen waters of the River Ure at Ripon Parks. The police and firemen responsible for the rescue were presented with Royal Humane Society Life-Saving Awards.

February. After earlier successes in the season, Ripon Rugby Club's hopes of winning the Yorkshire Cup were dashed when the team was defeated at Mallorie Park by the Old Crossleyans.

The Princess Royal was present at the service held in the Cathedral in memory of Lord Baden-Powell, attended by more than 1,500 Boy Scouts.

March. The Ripon Branch of the R.A.F.A. open-ed their new headquarters at the *Turk's Head* in Low Skellgate.

The Nina Convalescent Fund, founded to provide holidays for convalescents, no longer attracted suf-ficient support to function as an independent organisation. From the following January, the Old People's Welfare Association would administer its funds.

The Ure Bank Bobbin Mill closed. Wooden bobbins had been made for the textile industry on the site from 1883, but an output of 130-140 gross a week in 1944 had fallen to 200 gross in a year in 1954, a decline due to industrial change and the use of metal or plastic bobbins; the number of employees had dropped from 15 to one. The Scottish firm who owned the mill put the premises up for auction and in the summer it was taken over by a Ripon firm, Allton's Structural Steel Limited, to be used for light steel structural work, much of which was imported. This last relic of Ripon's medieval economy was thus replaced by a section of the light engineering industry.

A new font was presented to Holy Trinity Church in memory of Mr W. J. Young, a churchwarden for many years.

The net loss of revenues on commercial premises caused by the recent rating valuation was estimated at £7,000, but the Ripon M.P. refused to vote against the Government on this issue.

During the previous year Littlethorpe Church had been licensed for the solemnisation of marriages. On 23 March the first marriage took place since the opening of the church 80 years before, when Miss D. Mitchell of Littlethorpe was married to Mr J. Dunnington.

Mr W. A. Brown was chosen to succeed Mr F. Ward in July as headmaster of Ripon County Modern School.

April. The Ripon-born footballer Derek Kevan played for England against Scotland. His selection and performance were criticised despite his scoring an equalising goal. Kevan was selected again in October.

Mr Fred Collinson made his 21st appearance in a principal role for the Ripon Amateur Operatic Society during the Company's performance of *Rio Rita* at the Opera House.

The last of the city's five grain mills, in Duck Hill, was put up for auction but later the property was withdrawn. It had been hoped to sell it as a going concern producing cattle and poultry feeding stuffs. Negotiations for a private sale were reported to be in progress.

The Ripon and District Motor Cycle Club, which was in existence from 1908-1954, was now re-formed.

William Wells and Sons, wine merchants of North Street, won two gold medals for ginger beer and pineapple juice in a soft drinks competition held by the British Bottlers Institution in London. 'We just sent them in for fun really' commented Alderman Norman Wells.

The Corporation bought the premises of the Yorkshire Varnish Works Company Limited in Low Mill Road to use as a highways depot. This would involve moving a 20-ton weighbridge, sinking tanks for petrol and diesel fuel in the floor and many other alterations. The old depot in Skellbank was sold.

A 20-year-old jockey, Edward Hide, won four out of five races before a large crowd at Ripon racecourse.

30. Old Duck Hill Mill (Fossick)

1957-58. WILLIAM DAVIES TOULMAN, **Garage Proprietor**

Born in 1908 in Ripon. Educated at the Cathedral Boys' School and the Grammar School, to which he won a de Grey scholarship. Apprenticed to motor engineering with Croft and Blackburn Limited; later acquired Walker and Barker's Garage in Water Skellgate. Mayor 1957-58-59. An active member of Ripon Friendly Societies; a Foundation Governor of the Grammar School; and a member of the Rugby Club and the City Club. His hobby was gardening. He died in 1985.

May. A pulpit reading desk of silver was dedicated in the Cathedral in memory of Dean Birchenough.

A total eclipse of the moon was clearly visible in Ripon on Monday 18 May.

Good support for the Revival and Divine Healing Crusade held in the Assembly Rooms for two weeks encouraged the organisers to continue the Crusade for a longer period.

The Ripon Sailing Club was formed, a separate organisation from the Motor Boat Club, and arranged its first competition on Whit Monday.

June. The N.A.A.F.I. canteen at the Harper Barracks was gutted by fire, with the loss of thousands of pounds worth of equipment. Residents in the area said the exploding asbestos made it sound like an army exercise.

After initial protest, Ripon agreed to join the new Water Board, later known as the Claro Board, made up of Harrogate, Wetherby, Knaresborough, Pateley Bridge and Nidderdale. The alternative had been to join Leeds, but it was felt that, although water rates might rise due to the cost involved in levelling, the supply would be more secure.

The Bishop dedicated a new window designed by Sir Albert Richardson in the Mallorie Chapel of Ripon Cathedral, donated by Mr Charles Crabtree in memory of his mother.

The 'Repair Ripon Cathedral Fund' appealed for an increase of 50 per cent to £150,000 because more serious damage to the fabric had been discovered than anticipated. The response was immediate. Many people living in the area, for instance in Sharow, Masham, Well and Swinton, organised fêtes and divided the proceeds between their parish churches and the Cathedral. By the next month, £114,000 had already been subscribed.

July. The 1957 Franco-British Congress was held at the Training College. More than 60 French and 15 British delegates attended and were greeted by the Bishop at *Bishop Mount* and by the Mayor at the Town Hall.

The Bishop opened the Old People's Friendship Club's new headquarters in *Thorpe Prebend House*. This followed the decision of the Corporation to sanction its use for the club after the contents of the City Museum, formerly located in the house, had been dispersed. These included more than 100 cases of stuffed birds. The City Engineer reported some problems in the disposal of the cases and similar items.

Dr Philip Marshall, organist at Boston Parish Church in Lincolnshire, was appointed to Ripon to succeed Dr Lionel Dakers. Dr Marshall and the new precentor, the Revd Charles Buck, took up their appointments in November.

A national bus strike led to increased passenger traffic by rail, especially between Ripon and Harrogate. Villagers complained of not being able to shop in Ripon, but conversely some Ripon people shopped at home instead of in Harrogate. No absenteeism was reported by firms in the city.

The Royal Engineers presented wrought-iron 'Gates of Friendship' for the Spa Gardens. A large crowd watched the ceremony.

There was another fire at the Harper Barracks: the quarters of the single officers were destroyed and quantities of personal kit lost, including that of officers due to be demobilised within the next 24 hours.

St Wilfrid's Day was celebrated in beautiful weather. 'St Wilfrid' himself found difficulty in mounting 'Sally' and the 'monk' leading the horse lost a sandal in North Street.

September. For the first time in 20 years the Federation Festival of the National Federation of Old Choristers' Associations was held in Ripon.

A severe influenza epidemic affected many schoolchildren; nearly 600 were absent during the last week of the month. In the following week, 200 more cases were reported, with older pupils and adults on the list. Bus and postal services and church choirs had problems,but by mid-October the epidemic was on the wane.

October. The Ripon Horticultural Society was revived under the name of the Ripon and District Allotment Holders and Horticultural Society.

Despite a Council decision in September to delay any new scheme which would involve a bank loan until the current high interest rate fell, it was agreed to proceed with the new Grove Lane sewer. If this work was not undertaken, public health would be endangered.

The Hallé Orchestra made its first visit to Ripon Cathedral. Previous visits which had been mooted had always been shelved because objections had been made to charging the public for admission to the Cathedral.

Mr Harold Wilson, the Labour Party's 'Shadow' Chancellor of the Exchequer, addressed the Ripon and District branch of the National Union of Agricultural Workers at their annual dinner.

From 1 January 1958, the Post Office announced that many telephone calls would be reduced to 3d. The 'Ripon cheap call 3d area' would be extended to include Harrogate and Hawes.

December. Messrs Hepworth and Company Limited were shortly to close their brewery in Bondgate, established before 1822 by Richard Lumley, and now a subsidiary of Vaux Brewery. The premises were to be used as a bottle and barrel store to supply licensed houses in the area, and as many as possible of the employees would be retained.

The age-old custom of serving rum punch when the civic party returned to the Town Hall after the Christmas morning service in the Cathedral was revived.

A Ripon bellringer invented two new changes called 'St Wilfrid' and 'St Hilda'. He hoped to get recognition of these from the Bellringers' Federation.

The Mayor switched on the new radio for Ripon Hospital to provide individual 'pillow phones' for each bed. The appeal fund launched in the previous May had begun slowly, but finally reached £648.

During the year, the Ministry of Works made two grants for the conservation of Ripon's historic buildings. The first was given towards the cost of repairing the Wakeman's House and the second, in December, was for £1,000 towards an estimated £2,300 for repairs to the Town Hall. It was understood that the latter grant might have to be increased since the actual cost could not be known until the protective but disintegrating layers on the Town Hall facade had been removed. Even more extensive damage than expected was revealed when the facade was stripped, and the Ministry of Works was unwilling to accept the estimate given for the repair work. Meanwhile complaints were received by the Council because £10 a week for scaffolding had to be paid although no work was being carried out.

January. The City Prize Band and several hundred people greeted the New Year in the Market Place despite a fall of six inches of snow. Great indignation was expressed when the Christmas tree lights were switched off at 11.55 pm and Alderman King, chairman of the City Finance and General Purposes Committee, later apologised for the mistake.

Matins was televised from Ripon Cathedral, the first Cathedral service to be presented by Independent Television, and in June an ordination service was covered by the same network.

The slaughterhouse scales were found to be wildly inaccurate. A mouse's nest discovered in the control box had caused a variation in the readings of as much as 12 lbs according to how far the mouse ran in panic along the connecting rods.

February. The old-established firm of motor engineers, Croft and Blackburn, opened their new car showrooms and spare parts department in Kirkby Road. The firm was first established as the Victoria Carriage Works in 1742.

More heavy snow fell with drifts of up to six ft deep, even on main roads. Another blizzard at the end of the month cut off villages, totally disrupted bus services and made a mail van five hours late. Children who came into school in Ripon were unable to get home.

March. Mr Charles Harker announced that the publication of The Ripon Wakeman would cease at the end of the month because of increasing costs. The paper was a 1947 revival under the new name of the Ripon Advertiser, intended to encourage local writers and provide a digest of local news.

The Ministry of Housing and Local Government gave permission, previously refused, for the housing development in Allhallowgate to go ahead.

April. Major Bruce Eccles was re-elected for a fourth term as county councillor for the Ripon area.

The new Cathedral masons' workshops, in Dean's Yard on the north side of the Cathedral, were opened.

Improvements at Ripon racecourse included a new ladies' powder-room and a dining-room for owners and trainers. In July, a new handicap race for three-year-olds was run, named The Ripon Rowels, and the winning jockey received a silver replica of the spur said to have been presented to James I. The facilities were further improved in 1960 when a new Steward's box and windows to the totaliser were added, using a flat roof to the extension to give members a better view of the paddock. The extension included a canteen and 16 berths for stableboys and horse-box drivers.

1958-59. WILLIAM DAVIES TOULMAN, Garage Proprietor

Mayor 1957-58-59

May. Aldermen W. R. Dixon and W. N. Wells, both former mayors and long-standing members of the Council, announced they would not seek re-election when their term of office as aldermen expired in May. In October the City of Ripon conferred the Freedom of the City on Mr Dixon and on another former mayor, Mr Charles Harker, at a ceremony in the Lawrence Ballroom.

Five young Ripon string players each gained high distinction prizes at the Horsforth Musical Festival: Carol Corkish, Gillian Shufflebotham, Andrew and Stephen Orton and Susan Baines. In December Susan was chosen to play in the National Youth Orchestra. They were all members of the Ripon young people's orchestra, the Gilbert String Orchestra, conducted by Mr G. Shufflebotham, and were chosen to represent Yorkshire at a music festival in June 1959.

Ripon City Football Club became the winners of the Ripon League Senior Charity Cup by defeating the Boroughbridge team. A second football success was gained by the Ripon City Reserves who beat the Thirsk Falcons and so were awarded the Ripon League Junior Charity Cup. However, in the finals, Ripon City failed to win the Whitworth Cup and the Harrogate League Cup.

A Ripon couple, Mr and Mrs T. P. Pearson, were rescued by a ladder from their car when it was swept away by flood water as they were attempting to ford the river Skell at Firs Avenue; their car came to rest against a pier of the footbridge.

June. A Papal Bull of 1494 and Papal Indulgences of 1510 were discovered in the Cathedral Library. It was decided these should be sold but copies were to be made. The work of colouring the figures on the choir screen was begun.

Moorside Infants' School was brought into use. In

October, the formal opening ceremony was performed by Alderman W. R. Dixon; Alderman Hyman, Chairman of the West Riding Education Committee, was the speaker.

A tin-baling machine, purchased by the Council for about £1,500, proved its worth when the salvage department announced that during one month over 13 tons of crushed and baled tins had been sold for £111 7s 0d without incurring any extra labour costs.

The County Fire Service was concerned about the shortage of volunteers for Ripon Fire Brigade and appealed to the City Council to allow its employees to undertake part-time duty as firemen.

A Restoration Fund was launched for urgent work on the fabric of Holy Trinity Church and repairs, especially to the steeple, were to go ahead.

July. Mr W. M. Claye, former Town Clerk of Tenby in Pembrokeshire, succeeded Mr Rennison as Town Clerk of Ripon.

A Conservative rally on Ripon racecourse was addressed by the Minister of Pensions and National Insurance, Mr John Boyd Carpenter, whose grandfather had been Bishop of Ripon.

The town was invaded by swarms of small fawn-coloured moths, known as diamond-backs, part of a mass migration from the continent, to the great inconvenience of the population and of cyclists in particular.

The Mayor and Mayoress received a party of mayors from English and French towns and the mayors of Stalingrad, Leningrad and Belgrade, all of whom were attending a World Congress of United Towns at Harrogate.

The 119 Field Engineer Regiment (Territorial Army) presented silver plate to the City in appreciation of Ripon's hospitality.

August. Ripon City Cricket Club defeated Rowntrees' XI and, in September, received the trophy as winners in the York Senior League's First Division Championship

September. The Ripon and District Allotments and Horticultural Society held their first show, a successful revival of the society after nearly 20 years in abeyance.

The Cathedral succentor, the Revd J. E. B. Brunson, was found dead on the railway line at Littlethorpe. The verdict at the inquest was of suicide while the balance of his mind was temporarily disturbed.

October. Mrs Andsley was given a Royal Humane Society Award for her part in the rescue of a seven-year-old boy while on holiday at Barmouth. Her husband, Corporal Andsley, had won the same award for a rescue in Ripon during the previous year.

Seventy drawings by the local amateur artist, Jim Gott, were exhibited in the Cathedral. In December, the work of another local artist, George Jackson, was shown in the Christian Alliance Room in aid of the Holy Trinity Restoration Fund and this exhibition was opened by the Wensleydale authors, Marie Hartley and Joan Ingilby.

The 'hump-backed' Navigation Bridge over the canal in Boroughbridge Road was to be replaced by a road when the water from the canal would be taken through a culvert. Earlier in the year the Corporation had taken over the bridge from the British Transport Commission.

Ripon Golf Club held its Golden Jubilee dinner at the *Spa Hotel*.

November. According to a report by the City Engineer, damage during Bonfire Night was more extensive than usual, especially to play equipment and seats at the King Street playing field. Doubts were expressed about the advisability of continuing the custom of lighting a bonfire there.

December. The city was featured in Wilfred Pickles' radio programme *Have a Go*. Earlier in the year, Ripon children were recorded in the *This is My City* series on *Children's Hour*.

Mr F. W. Spence, managing director of T. and R. Williamson Limited, was elected as president of the National Paint Federation.

The Mayor and Mayoress enjoyed a 'blitz' lunch made in a dustbin cooker in the Corporation yard in Low St Agnesgate by the Ripon W.V.S., at the conclusion of a Civil Defence exercise. The menu was beef stew with creamed potatoes and greens, apple crumble with custard, and tea and rock buns.

Mrs E. L. England celebrated her 100th birthday in the Clova Nursing Home in Ripon. Although not a native of the city, she had lived most of her life at Sharow. She died in 1960 at the age of 101.

Lightning struck the home of Mr and Mrs Frank Smith in Lark Lane. Part of the roof was blown in and windows and a television set wrecked. Early the following morning a fire, probably caused by the storm, destroyed Mr L. Carling's garage in Trinity Lane; five coaches and a car were destroyed and the total damage was estimated at £7,000. Three fire brigades fought the blaze in a high wind for more than two hours before it was brought under control.

January. Ripon was chosen as one of the two West Riding areas for the experimental introduction of the 'Clegg Plan' for placing children in secondary schools. A feature of the plan was the replacement of selection tests by 'guided' parental choice.

The N.E.E.B. announced a change in voltage in Ripon and the surrounding area from 230 to 240 volts, to take place within the next six months.

February. There were reports of vandalism in the Spa Gardens where plants were wilfully damaged and in the *Palladium Cinema* where seats were slashed; 30 seats had been replaced since the previous August. In the graveyard of the Cathedral crosses had been pulled from their bases.

March. It was announced that Dr J. R. H. Moorman, Canon of Chichester Cathedral and a noted Church historian, would succeed Dr Chase on his retirement in April. Dr Moorman was consecrated Bishop of Ripon in York Minster on 11 June and enthroned in Ripon Cathedral on 29 June.

Dr C. H. Moody's book *Fountains Abbey and Fountains Hall* was published in the *Pride of Britain* series just before his 85th birthday.

April. It was announced that, on his retirement in July, Mr P. H. Molyneux would be succeeded as City Engineer by Mr L. M. Tebay.

Ripon's new fire engine arrived; costing £6,000, the vehicle was of the latest type and regarded as especially suitable for the narrow streets of the city.

Mr Christopher Ibbetson died at the age of 107 at Sharow View.

The Chief Guide, Lady Baden-Powell, visited a Ripon Guide Training Weekend held at the Training College.

A merger of the Ripon City and Rural Districts was suggested but the Ripon City Council was not in favour of the scheme.

1959-60. WALTER ROY BEAUMONT, Company Secretary

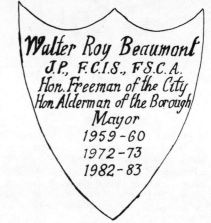

Walter Roy Beaumont
J.P., F.C.I.S., F.S.C.A.
Hon. Freeman of the City
Hon Alderman of the Borough
Mayor
1959 - 60
1972 - 73
1982 - 83

Born 1908 in Huddersfield; educated at Mirfield Grammar School and Halifax Technical College. Came to Ripon in 1944 as Accountant/Manager to one of the Allton Group of companies, became Group Secretary in 1945 and Director in 1947. Elected to Council in 1949, Mayor 1972-73, 1982-83. Member of Harrogate District Council 1974-80, Mayor of Borough of Harrogate 1976-77, Honorary Alderman of Harrogate. Member of North Yorkshire County Council 1974-82. Honorary Freeman of Ripon 1983. Awarded the Defence Medal 1939-45 and the Police Medal for long service as a special constable. A Magistrate, Commissioner of Inland Revenue, Governor of Ripon Schools, Grantley Hall Adult Education College and Harrogate Colleges of Further Education and Art, among many other official appointments. Organist of Holy Trinity Church for more than 20 years, Musical Director of the Ripon Amateur Operatic Society (and the Thirsk Society), served on the Executive Committees of the Yorkshire Arts Association and the Harrogate Festival; holder of the Long Service Medal of the National Operatic and Dramatic Association. Was Northern representative, Yorkshire Rugby Football Union; Honorary Life Member of the Ripon Rugby Union Club and of the Cricket Club of which he has been Secretary, Treasurer and Committee Chairman. A Freemason and a member and Past President of the Rotary Club.

June. The Ministry of Housing and Local Government approved the site of a new cemetery in Little Harries Lane off Kirkby Road.

The polio vaccination scheme made slow progress: only 40 per cent of young people between the ages of 15 and 25 in Ripon had come forward.

The Princess Royal presented the prizes at Ripon Girls' High School Jubilee Speech Day.

August. The work of laying a relief sewer in Clotherholme Road was completed and the road, closed from November 1958 to July 1959, was reopened to through traffic. The delay was caused by finding an unexpected stratum of sand.

New foundations were laid in preparation for the stone and concrete structure to replace the 97-year-old wooden Alma Bridge, which was in a dangerously decayed state.

The new police headquarters in North Road were completed at a cost of £32,500. Ten semi-detached and one detached houses were also built as police accommodation. The old police station in St Marygate (which had been the Ripon House of Correction) was sold to a private bidder for £1,540.

September. Low rainfall in July, August and September (only 0.11 ins. in September) led to appeals for cuts in water consumption, although the drought crisis was reduced by the greater quantities of water in the Harrogate reservoirs stored through the new Water Board's foresight. The corn harvest was good and came early because of the sun and dry weather, but root crops were said to be badly affected by the lack of rain. In the city a hosepipe ban was not imposed until the beginning of October, when it was questioned whether the Spa Gardens bowling green should be watered, when the flowers there were allowed to die. It was pointed out that the bowling green was given preferential treatment because a completely new green would have meant a considerable expense in the next season. A plague of caterpillars played havoc with Ripon allotments. It was the end of the year before the effects of the drought ceased to be of concern.

Two visitors to the city were the victims of road accidents. A pensioner from Mirfield was killed by a lorry which mounted the pavement outside the *Station Hotel* and a Greenock man was severely injured when his car crashed into the parapet of North Bridge.

The demolition of some of Ripon's oldest properties began on Bedern Bank.

October. The Ripon girls' dancing group the 'Tip-Taps' was disbanded because of a shortage of dancers, after seven successful years during which more than £800 had been raised for charity.

The Ripon Motor Club organised two TV Motor Cycle Scrambles at Hutton Conyers; an estimated 6,000 spectators watched national stars perform at both shows.

Sir Malcolm Stoddart-Scott (Conservative) retained his seat for the Ripon Parliamentary division with an increased majority. Dr Moody wrote to the *Gazette* to claim that the announcement of the polling results

31. Bedern Bank (Fossick)

in Otley was an affront to the city of Ripon. The Mayor and others supported Dr Moody, but Sir Bernard Kenyon, the returning officer for the West Riding, replied that the procedure was in accordance with the general rule of appointing his deputy in any area by seniority.

The last Methodist service at the 70-year-old Skellgate Mission Room was held. The following weekend, on 31 October, the opening ceremony and dedication of the new Methodist Church in Harrogate Road was performed in the presence of the Mayor and Mayoress. Mr Arthur Row, one of the trustees, opened the new building. The Revd F. Platt Green, chairman of York and Hull district, dedicated the church and the Revd A. Raymond George of Wesley College, Leeds, preached at the dedication service. The architect was Mr Francis Johnson of Bridlington. The congregation was so large that the service was relayed by loudspeaker to those standing outside.

Masons working on the restoration of Ripon Cathedral carved portraits of the Dean, the Archdeacon of Richmond and two of the canons.

Despite considerable objections, it was decided that traffic lights would be tried for a period at the junction of High Skellgate and Westgate.

The City Treasurer reported a growth of £4,182 in the rateable value of Ripon for 1958-59, reflecting a corresponding growth in the city. A similar increase for 1959-60 would make good the loss caused by the partial de-rating of commercial premises from April 1957.

December. Slum clearance plans proceeded. Orders were passed for the clearance of property in Blossomgate and Church Lane and were proposed for St Marygate.

On 23 December the death occurred of Lord Halifax, who, as the Hon. Edward Wood, had represented the Ripon Parliamentary Division from 1910-25, when he was appointed Viceroy of India.

January. Mr J. Garbutt's invention, the fibreglass boat, was now in full production at his workshop, Ripon Precision Services, in Stonebridgegate. The firm was turning out about four boats a week, only four years after the prototype had been built by Mr Garbutt.

March. A lorry crashed into a room used as a nursery at Pinfold Close in North Street: the driver was only slightly injured.

The Cathedral authorities announced the impending purchase of St Olave's Preparatory School. Choral scholarships would be given for boys to become Cathedral choristers. To enable the purchase to proceed, valuable books and manuscripts from the Cathedral library would be sold. Acute controversy was aroused at national as well as local level: some spoke of the reckless disposal of church treasures and their fear that the Caxtons would go to America: others considered the worship of the living church to be the greatest of its treasures. In May, two of the three Caxtons were auctioned, a first edition of a vocabulary and conversation book often referred to as *The Book for Travellers* sold to an American for £23,000 and now in Cambridge University Library; and the second, a copy of Laurentius Guillielmus's *Epitome Margaritae Eloquentiae* (the Pearl of Eloquence) being bought by the Brotherton Collection of the Library of the University of Leeds for £12,000. In all £40,270 was realised by these sales to help to refound the Cathedral Choir School.

April. A campaign to recruit men for a Territorial Army Troop of Royal Engineers in Ripon finished at the end of the month with 37 volunteers. The first river exercise took place on the Ure near Bishop Monkton.

Ripon's 'anthropoidal' sword, so-called because of the shape of its hilt, returned to the city after renovation by the Tolson Museum in Huddersfield, where its method of manufacture had also been examined.

The Bishop of Ripon dedicated the restored western end of the Cathedral undercroft for use as a Song School and Vestries.

Ian Eccles successfully defended his titles in the open events of the Harrogate Badminton League's tournament, and Miss E. Marshall won the Girls' Under-16 singles title at the Yorkshire Junior Badminton Championships and was later selected to play for the Yorkshire County Colts against Westmorland.

1960-61.   JAMES MILES COVERDALE, Solicitor

Born 1921 in Harrogate, son of Herbert William Coverdale, a Leeds solicitor. The family moved to West Lodge, Kirkby Road, Ripon in 1922. Educated Shrewsbury and Christ Church Oxford, read Law and rowed for his college. 1941-46, served with The Royal Artillery in France and Belgium, attained rank of major. Qualified as a solicitor in 1951 and practised in Ripon. Chairman of Young Conservatives. Elected to Council 1953, served on various committees and representative on the Association of Municipal Corporations. Laid the foundation stone of Claro Barracks. A Freemason. Played cricket with Ripon Nondescripts and had many hobbies: stamp collecting, model railways, photography, gardening. He left Ripon in 1978 and died in 1982.

May. The Cathedral Hall in High St Agnesgate was gutted by fire in the early hours of 15 May.

The Bishop of Ripon switched on the new floodlighting system at Fountains Abbey, an event arranged to coincide with the summer conference of the Illuminating Engineering Society being held in Harrogate. The abbey was floodlit only during the week of the conference, but in September the Studley Estate took over the system and switched it on again for several nights.

June. The Archdeacon of Richmond, the Ven. H. B. Graham, visited Ripon, Wisconsin, for the centenary of St Peter's School there, and received the honorary degree of Doctor of Sacred Theology from Ripon College. He took with him from Ripon, Yorkshire, gifts of a silver salver from the Corporation and of a silver spur from the Chamber of Trade.

The tenants of the new flats in Allhallowgate made a series of complaints about bursts in the internal water system, the failure to connect up the lights on the public stairways and the communal television area, and also stressed the need for better drying facilities.

The first tank moved along Ripon Road in Aden, a one-mile causeway across salt beds built by the 38 Corps Engineer Regiment in 23 days.

July. The former Methodist Mission Room in Water Skellgate was opened as the local headquarters of the

Assembly of God by Pastor J. Richardson of Sheffield, with Pastor Glyn Thomas, the local minister, officiating.

At the annual meeting of the Old People's Welfare Committee, the free chiropody service for old people provided by the W.R.C.C. was referred to with great appreciation. A report was received on improvements at *Thorpe Prebend House*, in use as their Friendship Club, including the provision of window shutters, a film projector and a screen for the upstairs room.

In his 80th year, Mr F. Smith sang on 31 July for the last time in the Cathedral choir which he had first joined in 1909 and in which he had sung, except for an interval of ten years, ever since.

The Cricket Club's gates to their Studley Road ground were hung, dedicated to the memory of Mr A. F. Newton who had bequeathed the money for these to the Club. Early in August the club, one of the oldest in the country, held a grand fête at the ground to celebrate what they believed to be their 150th anniversary, an event marred by grey skies and intermittent rain.

It was decided to paint the facade of the Town Hall, because a plain stone finish was not possible; oil from previous painting had penetrated the surface and the discolouration would be obvious.

The Northern section of the Veteran Car Club held its rally in Ripon. More than 40 cars registered between 1901 and 1916 were present. The special Mayor's prize was won by a 1902 Napier and the cars, which assembled in the Market Place, made a short run out to Masham.

Miss V. N. Hall, who had resigned from her post as Principal of Ripon Training College to become Principal of the Women's Training College at Cheltenham, outlined the changes due to affect the Ripon College. In September a three-year course would be introduced, numbers would be increased from 200 to 300, and the Girls' High School building would be taken over as a lecture block. Extensions to the existing buildings would include a new chapel, assembly hall and hall of residence. The old chapel would become an extension to the library.

August. A serious traffic jam occurred in High Skellgate, at that time a two-way street, when a bus tried to pass a parked car, which had to be jacked up before either vehicle could be freed. Traffic was diverted by way of Water Skellgate where a similar accident was only narrowly averted.

Mr D. Marston, a member of the Ripon Horticultural Society, who had already won prizes at the British Gladioli Society's International Exhibition in London, was again successful, carrying off six prizes, including one first. Mr Marston was well known as a leading exhibitor at local shows.

September. About 1,500 people watched a thrilling annual display by the Royal Engineers, including a re-enactment of the storming of the Kashmir Gate during the Indian Mutiny and the destruction of an enemy radar station by more modern methods. The scheme to fly in the Mayor by helicopter, however, had to be abandoned because of mechanical difficulties.

Mrs Barbara Allan of Ripon, dressed in an outfit made by her mother, won the title of the ABC Television Fashion Queen of Great Britain in the finals of the competition at Southport.

Mr L. H. Judge, the President of the Yorkshire Rugby Union, opened a new pavilion for the Ripon Rugby Club. It had been built at a cost of £900 and members had put in a great deal of the work themselves in their spare time.

The *Gazette* reported that a new line for the relief road had been accepted by the local authority, which would run farther to the west of the Cathedral and cut right through Kirkgate. The following week, the paper quoted public reaction as one of sheer disbelief coupled with a demand for a relief road to the east of the city. A Kirkgate shopkeeper's letter was published attacking the scheme as the 'Murder of Kirkgate', and detrimental to the whole city. Acrimony continued through October, when the Council denied its approval, affirmed it had never seen a plan like that produced by the *Gazette* and vented its suspicion of a leak by someone connected with the County Council. Only one Ripon Council voice was raised in favour of the new relief road and the majority expressed strong preference for a line east of the Cathedral.

Dr C. H. Moody bitterly attacked the Corporation plans to fell lime trees on Boroughbridge Road so that a formal garden could be made 'to improve the approach to the city' and he threatened to resign his 'Freedom' if the scheme were carried out. The Corporation refused to have a change of heart and in November Dr Moody withdrew his threat but asked not to be invited to any public functions.

October. Lady Masham and Miss Pauline Foulds of Littlethorpe won gold medals in the swimming events in the 9th International Olympic Paraplegic Games.

A Ripon taxi-driver, Mr Kenneth Simpson, was forced out of his vehicle at knife-point by his passengers at New Park, Harrogate. His taxi was later found abandoned near Harper Barracks and soldiers stationed at Ripon were charged with armed robbery.

The 100-foot chimney in the Ripon Corporation Yard was demolished brick by brick. Dr Moody had earlier condemned the Corporation for its refusal to remove this eyesore.

Mr Charles Harker presented the Cathedral with microfilm copies of the two Caxton volumes which had been sold.

November. The Mayor laid the foundation stone of the new Harper Barracks which were to be built at a cost of £640,000. He emphasised the importance of the city's links with the Royal Engineers.

The British National Ploughing Championships were held at Hutton Moor Farm, north of Ripon, with more than 150 ploughmen present. The *Gazette* stressed the contrast between the immaculate appearance of the manufacturers' machines on display and the shabby, battered array of ploughs brought by the ploughmen. At a special service in the Cathedral, the Dean blessed a plough.

After 4 November, 'Mischief Night', about £2,000 had to be spent by the Council to repair damage done to street nameplates and walls. However, when Bonfire Night was celebrated on 5 November, there was not a single fire-call in Ripon all weekend.

Tree felling in the grounds of *The Hall* by the Cathedral authorities brought forth yet another attack by Dr Moody.

A Public Inquiry considered an application to build a house in the angle of Studley Road and Bishopton Lane. The verdict was given against the proposal on the environmental grounds that the house would spoil the approach to Ripon from Pateley Bridge with the view of Bishopton Bridge and the 18th-century houses. In the event, however, the application was allowed.

Among the guests at the annual dinner of the Nidderdale Cricket League held in the *Spa Hotel*, Ripon, were Peter May, the England captain, Freddie Trueman and Brian Close.

A Compulsory Purchase Order for houses in St Marygate and Priest Lane, both clearance areas earlier approved by the Council, was confirmed after a Public Inquiry and another Clearance Order followed for houses in Blossomgate. Mr W. L. Ingham, the Public Health Inspector, reported to the Health Committee that the demolition of unsatisfactory houses was outpacing the provision of new accommodation and blamed lack of co-operation between the Health and Housing Committees for mismanagement.

December. A wooden panel representing St Willibrord, found in London by Mr G. Place and presented by him to the Cathedral, was fixed in position on the wall of the south choir aisle.

The rainfall in 1960 was 33.6 ins. Although this was six inches above the annual average, a heavier rainfall had been recorded in both 1946 and 1951.

January. The Ripon Highways Committee considered objections to Corporation workmen undertaking outside jobs in their spare time but decided to allow the practice to continue. Sanction was also given to the hiring of Corporation equipment at standard rates, a resolution later amended to permit the use of plant for Corporation contract work only.

A letter from Mr K. G. Dodds, Manager of Farrods Limited, affirmed that in his search for a site for a new work development in Ripon he had found the city 'a derelict slum behind a not very pleasing facade'. He suggested that as a 'face-lift' a new road should be built from Coltsgate Hill, passing west of the Market Place to bisect Westgate and Somerset Row to enter Harrogate Road at Borrage Bridge. There was no place for 'the old-world charm' in the lives of 'our younger generation'.

An editorial in the *Gazette* criticised the refusal of the Highways Committee to consider the suggestion to open up the bus access road from Queen Street to the Bus Station for private car traffic.

The Finance and General Purposes Committee turned down by one vote a proposed trial period of free car parking on Market Day in the Corporation's official car park, for which a charge of sixpence was normally made. Traffic congestion had occurred since the Bedern Bank site had been opened as a free park taking up to 100 cars. The income from car parking in the city was £320 per annum and the annual net profit £241.

The Ripon Accident Prevention Committee decided to write to the Corporation complaining that the junction of Whitcliffe Lane and Harrogate Road was too acute; it permitted only minimum visibility for vehicles driving out into the Harrogate Road and was therefore dangerous. A few days later, there was a collision at this junction between two cars, one of which landed in the front garden of the corner house, but no one was injured. As a result a petition was drawn up setting out the defects in the design of the junction which members of the public were asked to sign.

Dr Howard C. Strick, who for the previous eight years had been Director of the National Council for the Training of Journalists, was appointed Warden of Grantley Hall College of Adult Education.

February. The Finance and General Purposes Committee approved a report recommending the replacement of gas lighting in six streets in the centre of Ripon and 16 streets on the outskirts by electricity.

An editorial in the *Gazette* supported a letter written to the paper by Mr V. L. Winterburn, manager of the *Palladium Cinema*, detailing the growing number of complaints of alleged inefficiency in the Corporation in a number of areas and calling for the revival of the Ripon Ratepayers' Protection Association. Councillor Beaumont suggested these complaints were based on misrepresentation and that the public should exercise its right to attend Council Meetings: only a handful of citizens attended such meetings during the year. An inaugural public meeting was held in the Assembly Rooms with Mr T. H. Hudson in the chair, replacing Major E. Bruce Eccles who had withdrawn. Mr Hudson was formally elected chairman after a new draft constitution had been adopted, emphasising the non-political nature of the Association. Nevertheless, rumours spread concerning Mr Hudson's connections with the Ripon and Pateley Bridge Liberal Association, which forced his resignation. Mr C. E. Penty was elected vice-chairman and Mr Woodhead treasurer. Two hundred and fifty members attended a second meeting to ratify the constitution but decided not to put forward their own candidate for the Council; three members, Messrs C. E. Penty, K. G. Dodds and J. H. Ellis would be standing as Independents.

Aismunderby Close, a large detached house at the junction of the Quarry Moor and Knaresborough Roads, was purchased by the Pentecostal Eventide Housing Association Limited for conversion to a home for 30 old people. Admission would be completely irrespective of the applicant's income. The Association was closely connected with the Ripon Assembly of God, which had premises in Water Skellgate.

Plans for the Cathedral Choir School were now well advanced. The Dean and Chapter had realised £34,437 from the sale at Sotheby's of rare books from the

Cathedral Library and the money had been used to purchase St Olave's Preparatory School, founded in 1924. The cost of new buildings and extensions amounted to £10,546, which left the Chapter with a capital deficit of £6,109, but seven-year covenants by donors had reduced this to £2,072. During the past year £27,500 had been contributed for the endowment of 11 choral scholarships, each named after its founder. Canon W. E. Wilkinson was appointed Chairman of the Governors. The Revd Duncan Thomson, who had been Precentor of the Cathedral for five years before going to Aysgarth as chaplain and assistant master, returned to Ripon as headmaster of the new Cathedral Choir School. Dr Philip Marshall, organist and master of the choristers at the Cathedral, tested and accepted seven choral scholars to enter the school in September.

Canon D. M. M. Bartlett retired as Residentiary Canon of the Cathedral at the age of 87, but he announced his intention to stay in Ripon in Skellfield Terrace and retained his post as Cathedral Librarian. Canon Bartlett had worked in the diocese since 1902.

March. Ripon Magistrates fined two men for stealing a van containing 150 sticks of gelignite and 35 detonators from the car park of the *Spa Hotel* where the driver had stopped for a lunch break. The men had taken a raincoat and the van keys from the hotel and police had found the abandoned van astride the traffic island at the junction of Bondgate and Southgate. Smoke began to issue from the bonnet and fire broke out; when a constable pulled at the electrical wiring he found a two-ounce stick of gelignite on the floor near the smouldering wires. The rest of the explosives were found in an unlocked wooden box in the back of the van.

Mr Philip Hall, head of a Ripon store and President of the Chamber of Trade, initiated a five-day week for his employees, so that they could have one Monday and one Saturday free in each month. Mr Hall believed improved conditions led to a happier and therefore a more efficient staff. In July, the Ripon General Purposes Committee agreed to recommend a five-day week for Town Hall staff.

A sheep-dog, Bessie, was rescued from an ancient heating passage inside a wall in the garden of *Hollin Hall*, Ripon, by her owner Mr A. H. Boynton Wood after being trapped for two days. Bessie had travelled for some 75 yards along a maze of fire passages built in three tiers, each three feet high and 15 inches wide, which had once heated the wall for fruit-growing.

Mr M. W. Claye, Town Clerk of Ripon since 1958, announced his resignation on his appointment as Clerk to the Spalding Rural Council. He was replaced in May by Mr J. A. Berry who returned as Town Clerk for a second term of office after seven years in Kenya.

April. The Princess Royal visited Ripon to accept on behalf of the British Legion at Lister House a new coach provided by the Cheshire branches of the Legion.

1961-62.   James Miles Coverdale, Solicitor

Mayor 1960-61-62

May. A Leeds fisherman, Mr Stanley Kirkley, caught what he believed was a pike of record size in the River Ure at Bishop Monkton. An article appeared about the catch in an evening newspaper with a photograph of the fish. However, it subsequently appeared that Mr Kirkley had transgressed a number of by-laws, for which he was fined £3 with £1 1s costs: he had broken both the law and the record.

June. Both Hornblowers resigned, Mr J. H. Ellis in order to stand in municipal elections and Mr C. Hawley, his deputy, because of the pressure of other duties. Mr Hawley was the son of a previous Hornblower, and was interviewed for the B.B.C. programme *Radio Newsreel*. A few days later he received a letter from a well-wisher in Boston, U.S.A., to tell him that the radio reception of the broadcast had been excellent. In September the Council found it difficult to appoint a successor; Mr Hawley was persuaded to continue with an increase in salary from £52 to £200 a year and two weeks' annual holiday.

July. After prolonged discussion, the Ripon Housing Committee decided that the site of the now demolished Tomlinson Court in Blossomgate was too small to enable any building development to take place, and recommended it should become a car park. The Council referred back the resolution for consideration with the whole of the Blossomgate development scheme. In August the Minister of Housing and Local Government confirmed the Ripon City Council's clearance order for six houses at the entrance to Blossomgate from Westgate.

August. One of Ripon's oldest and largest stores, Maurice Ward and Company, Drapers of Queen Street, closed. The property was demolished in 1961 and Maypole Dairies, part of Lipton's Supermarkets, moved into a new building on the site. In September the old-established grocery business run by Mr Jack and Mr Kenneth Moss in the adjoining property, Moss's Arcade, built in 1906, was taken over by Moore's Stores Limited. There was speculation about the future of the arcade, which housed the photographic business of Mr D. T. Atkinson and a café at the Bus Station end. During World War I the arcade had been used for temporary housing and during the 1930s as a Labour Exchange; in 1963 it was demolished to improve the access to the Bus Station and car park.

September. A Ripon householder had his application for an improvement grant turned down by the City Council because the line of the proposed relief road had not been determined. Councillor Toulman suggested that if the people at 84 Allhallowgate were to wait until such a decision was reached they might well be waiting until the next millenary.

A demolition order was granted for the premises of the National Provincial Bank in the Market Square. The owners promised to make every effort to preserve the architectural character of the Square and to incorporate the figure of St Wilfrid, high up on the existing building, into the new facade.

November. The *Gazette* published an interview with Mr Philip Mortimer, the official winder of Ripon's public clocks. Every Wednesday morning he set out to wind the eight-day clocks in the Town Hall and the Clock Tower, calling at the Grammar School and the *Spa Hotel* where he also wound and maintained the clocks. Mr Mortimer, a jeweller and watchmaker, followed his father and grandfather, Mr John Mortimer, who had founded the family business in Kirkgate 50 years before.

Canon Turnbull, Vicar of All Saints, Gosforth, was appointed Archdeacon of Richmond and Canon Residentiary of Ripon Cathedral in succession to Dr H. B. Graham, who had resigned the previous September.

When the Council were informed that the land in Dallamires Lane scheduled for industrial development would be available early in 1962, it was decided to approach the British Transport Commission in order to transfer to them the ownership of the Ripon Canal from its basin to the Littlethorpe Road bridge, with a view to filling-in the canal and incorporating the extra land.

The Mayor launched an appeal for £1,000 to pay for new uniforms for the Ripon City Silver Band.

The Council referred for reconsideration a resolution which had been defeated at the Finance Committee Meeting to raise the wages of the Ripon Stave-bearers from 5s 0d to 10s 0d per duty.

December. An epidemic of 'teenage' influenza, lasting from four to seven days, swept the city and resulted in the absence of nearly half the secondary school population; in the Girls' High School, 110 out of 260 pupils; in the Grammar School, 80 out of 318; and in the County Secondary School, 350 out of 700.

A summer traffic census showed that of the 27,042 vehicles entering Ripon daily, 11,000 were local. Two-thirds of the total traffic used the A61 of which 61 per cent was through-traffic which could be accommodated by a bypass. The other three roads only required access to the city.

January. Major W. N. Wells, Mayor 1956-57, was awarded the C.B.E. in the New Year Honours List in recognition of his political and public services to Ripon.

A smallpox scare caused queues of people seeking vaccination to gather at Alma House Clinic and at the doctors' surgeries. The one known contact in Ripon and his family were among those vaccinated and the Medical Officer of Health declared there was no reason for panic.

February. The year had started with heavy snowfalls which did a considerable amount of damage. On 11 February an 80-mph gale swept the district leaving a trail of destruction. Trees were uprooted blocking roads in and around the city and causing severe damage to old-established parks such as Studley; vehicles were overturned, small buildings smashed, eight shop windows were blown in and goods scattered about the streets; the roof of Handley's butchers shop in North Street was blown off and a building at the *White Horse Hotel* collapsed. Train and bus services were disrupted. A second gale on 15 February blew in more shop windows and brought down more chimney stacks.

The Country Style Company which operated a chicken factory in the former Congregational Church in North Street negotiated with the Council to take over the whole of the land then available on the Dallamires Lane industrial estate.

March. The Council set a rate of 24s 6d in the pound, an increase of 2s 10d, which provoked much complaint, but most of the rise was due to the higher demands made by the W.R.C.C.

1962-63. CHARLES AUGUSTUS FEARN, **Bank Manager**

Mayor 1954-55-56, 1962-63

May. Thieves who carried out a 'smash and grab' raid at Kerridge's jewellery shop in North Street got away with diamond rings valued at £200.

June. Mr David G. Kendall, Fellow of Magdalen College, Oxford, was elected Professor of Mathematical Statistics and Fellow of Churchill College, Cambridge. He was the son of Mr and Mrs F. E. Kendall of Clotherholme Road and was educated at Ripon Grammar School and Queen's College, Oxford.

The Bishop of Ripon, Dr J. R. H. Moorman, was appointed as one of the Anglican observers at the

Vatican Council to be held in October, and in 1966 he published his impressions of the Council as *Vatican Observed*. In 1963, he had represented the Archbishop of Canterbury at the coronation of Pope Paul VI.

The first charity race meeting in the north of England was held at Ripon racecourse. It was attended by 15,000 people and £6,000 was raised for the National Playing Fields Association.

The Ripon Girls' High School was closed: its premises and the cottages on Coltsgate Hill which were used as a hostel were acquired by the College. The school had opened in 1909 with 12 pupils and three full-time teaching staff, plus visiting teachers for art, music and cookery. It was housed in a building designed for 80 girls and an evening institute. By 1962 it had 260 pupils and 14 full-time teaching staff, and a number of part-timers. At first its pupils were largely fee-paying with a sprinkling of 'exhibitioners', but the proportion of the latter increased and the school's maintained status meant that fee-paying came to an end after World War II. In its early years there were some citizens who expressed doubts about the need for such a school for girls and regarded it as an unnecessary charge on the rates, but during the head-ship of Miss M. W. Johnson (1916-1948), when most of the growth took place, this attitude disappeared and the school was accepted as playing an essential role in the life of the city. Miss Johnson was succeeded by Miss J. M. Cullingworth. The closure in 1962 came about primarily because the buildings and the site were not capable of providing for the expansion needed to bring the facilities up to modern standards, and because the school's numbers were not large enough to provide economically for a sufficiently wide variety of educational opportunities. These practical considerations combined with the educational theory of the time to suggest that a co-educational grammar school might best serve the interests of the young people of Ripon. Thus the school was amalgamated with the Grammar School where there was space for expansion. A new assembly hall and dining area, kitchens, laboratories and classrooms were built, the old assembly hall, 'Big School', was converted into a library and classrooms, and the swimming bath was improved and covered in.

The Cathedral Boys' School in Priest Lane also closed. It had opened in 1853 and the logbooks go back to 1862. Pupils were transferred either to the new Moorside School for 160 children, which opened under Miss D. E. Pratt in September, or to the Cathedral Girls' School in Agnesgate which became a Junior Mixed school. The Priest Lane buildings were later demolished and the *Ripon House* home for the elderly erected on the site.

August. A meeting of 20 local organisations was called by the Chamber of Trade early in the year to consider ways of enlivening and extending the Feast of St Wilfrid. As a result the City Band and the 'Saint' were followed by a cavalcade of 12 floats displaying tableaux of events in the history of the city. The Children's Day May Queen took part in the pro-cession which was followed by a pageant in the

Cathedral. A film of the procession was made which was purchased by the City Council and presented to the organisers.

After months of argument and petitions and polls from both sides, the City Council had decided in January that the St Wilfrid's Fair should be held in the parking ground because of the noise and disruption it caused in the Market Place. There were protests from the showmen and citizens and when the Council reconsidered the matter they were equally divided, and the Mayor refused to use his casting vote because four members were absent. At a special session in March it was eventually agreed to abide by the decision made in January. When the fair was held in the car park it provoked further complaints from the showmen, and from residents in the vicinity.

Gillian Shufflebotham, Susan Baines, Rita Eddowes, Carol Corkish and Andrew and Stephen Orton were among 12 young musicians from Yorkshire chosen to play in the National Youth Orchestra. Andrew and Stephen Orton both became distinguished musicians.

The Methodist Churches at Coltsgate Hill and Allhallowgate amalgamated and the last service was held at Coltsgate Hill on 26 August. The Allhallowgate Church, more conveniently sited and with room for expansion, would be a centre to strengthen Methodist work in the city.

The National Provincial Bank, originally the Claro Bank, and the shop next to the Town Hall were pulled down to make way for the present building. Demoli-tion revealed the timber-frame construction of the shop, and a bottle containing a worksheet with the names of those who were employed in building the bank in 1899 was found; today only the statue of St Wilfrid remains from that building.

September. The City Council's offer of £4,000 to purchase the hockey field in Mallorie Park Drive was rejected by the owner and the Council decided, by the casting vote of the Mayor, not to acquire it com-pulsorily. There had been much debate; the hockey field adjoined the football, rugby and cricket grounds and many people had looked forward to the possi-bility of a fine sports centre between Studley Road and Mallorie Park. Others thought that the sports fields were less used than formerly and spoke of Quarry Moor as a possible centre.

October. St Wilfrid's Roman Catholic Church celebrated its centenary. The Mayor and Mayoress at-tended the Centenary Mass.

The Local Government Boundary Commission con-sidered the revision of county boundaries. Harrogate Council wished to transfer to the North Riding, but Ripon City and the Rural Councils wanted to remain in the West Riding of Yorkshire. At a meeting of the Boundary Commission in York in February 1963, the Ripon representatives expressed Ripon's wish to remain in the West Riding, but if this were not possible the second choice would be for a united county of Yorkshire.

The Public Hall Committee which campaigned for an adequate hall for entertainments and functions in

Ripon had called a meeting in March, which urged the Council to seek powers to borrow money to erect such a hall at public expense. The Council finally accepted the opinion of the Finance and General Purposes Committee that the cost was too great and the matter was 'left on the table'.

November. On 1 November the curfew bell at the Cathedral was rung by hand for the last time. The installation of electrical mechanism was a boon to the vergers — no longer was it necessary to climb 70 steps to the tower every night. In June 1964, the Friends provided an electric winding motor for the clock which precluded the necessity for manual winding twice daily.

Bonfire Night passed without a call on the Fire Brigade, but 'Mischief Night' had left a trail of damage: telephone kiosks, lamps, seats and bridges were vandalised and a soldier fell through a hole in Coltsgate Hill where a grating had been removed from the pavement.

W. M. Abbott and Company announced that their factory in Kirkby Road would close at the end of the year but that the retail shop and workshop in North Street would continue. Abbotts started furniture-making in Allhallowgate in 1853 and the firm had long had a high reputation as makers of quality and reproduction furniture.

Forward planning by the Ministry of Health proposed the closure of the General (Firby Lane) and Princess Road (St Wilfrid's) Hospitals in Ripon on the completion of the new General Hospital in Harrogate in 1975. Firby Lane would be retained for geriatric and maternity cases only. The *Gazette* sponsored a petition against the proposed hospital re-organisation which would mean the end of Ripon Hospital as a general hospital. More than 7,000 people responded in the next two months and the scheme was abandoned.

The City Council agreed to go ahead with the building of 44 flats in Lead Lane despite the long-standing objections of some councillors who thought Ripon people would not want to live in flats. In June plans for old people's bungalows in North Road and Bondgate had been approved. A threat to increase Council house rents by 5s 0d per week, where gardens were neglected, had been fruitful and in 99 out of a hundred cases there had been an improvement.

December. The City Council approved and passed to the County Council a new plan for a relief road which had been first presented in April. The proposed road would pass to the east of the Cathedral and affect Camp Close and Paddy's Park, the Cathedral Schools and residential and business properties. The scheme was opposed by the Dean and Chapter and residents in the area.

January. A new access road from Littlethorpe Bridge to the racecourse was built, but other improvements to the course had to be deferred because an expected grant from the Betting Levy Board was not forthcoming.

A local boy, Brian Dunn, achieved success in the world of show business playing the Spanish guitar.

In less than a year he appeared in a show at the *London Palladium*, was on television 12 times and played in several recordings.

As a result of legislation which could make authorities liable to compensation for persons injured because of damaged pavements, the City Council decided to spend £20,000 on their improvement. The Health Committee authorised a pilot scheme for the use of refuse bags instead of dustbins.

The *Black Dog Hotel* in Skellbank was put up for auction. It was bought for £4,500 by Scottish Breweries and its name was changed to the *Highland Laddie*.

At a meeting called by the Mayor, representatives of local welfare societies agreed to set up a Ripon Council of Social Service (later the Council for Voluntary Service) to co-ordinate social and welfare activities in the city.

February. Mr George Cotson, the City Bellman since 1938, collapsed on a Ripon-Harrogate bus. The driver drove the bus straight to hospital but Mr Cotson was dead on arrival.

Severe weather had started in December and snow and frost continued for more than two months. The coldest day recorded was 25 February with 3°F; snow-clearing and road-gritting cost the Council £3,153 and there was much unemployment in the building and construction trades. Foxes were seen scavenging for food on the outskirts of the city, college students ran a pancake race through the snow on 20 February, and almost all football and rugby matches from mid-December to early March had to be called off.

New valuation lists had been made public at the beginning of the year; the rateable value of the city was increased from £121,129 to £302,833. It was at first thought that domestic ratepayers would see little change because of the reduced poundage, although business premises would suffer because of the abolition of 20 per cent and 50 per cent reliefs; but, when at the end of February the West Riding set a rate equivalent to an increase of 3s 3d on the old valuation, the City Council protested strongly to the County': 'The attitude of the W.R.C.C. makes one wonder whether the Council should reconsider its request to the Boundary Commission to remain in the West Riding'. In the end a rate of 11s 4d (28s 2d on the old valuation) was agreed.

April. Indignation at higher rates was increased by rises in Council house rents and a public meeting in the Co-operative Rooms resolved to form a Council Tenants' Association to protect their interests. The existing Ratepayers' Association was unable to find a candidate to contest the May elections.

1963-64. WILFRID HENRY PARNABY, Electricity Foreman

Born 1902 and educated in Harrogate. Joined the army at 16 and served in India and Ireland. Territorial Army until 1952; awarded the Territorial Medal with three bars, in charge of cadet training in Harrogate, Knaresborough and Ripon. Came to Ripon in 1929 as Instructor at the Drill Hall. Worked for Harrogate Electricity Department from 1936; B.E.M. for services

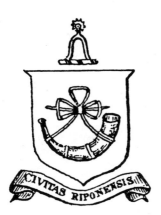

to electricity industry 1964. Elected to Council 1954, and to Harrogate District and North Yorkshire County Council 1973. Honorary Alderman of Harrogate, received the Honorary Freedom of Ripon 1982. During his mayoralty fought to save Ripon Hospital and Sharow View Old Peoples' Home from closure. Devoted to social work for which he received the Jubilee Medal in 1977. President, Citizens' Advice Bureau (which he established in Ripon), Royal British Legion, Age Concern, Council for Voluntary Service; Chairman Retired Men's Forum, etc. Organised lunches at which professional and voluntary social workers could meet. Said 'Ripon has the finest community of voluntary social workers in the county'. Mayor 1964-65.

May. Dr Martin Niemoller, the Lutheran pastor and former U-boat commander, famous for his courageous opposition to Nazi rule in Germany, visited Ripon. He was given a civic reception by the Mayor, and Allhallowgate Methodist Church was packed to capacity when he gave an address there.

At his installation the new Mayor, Councillor W. H. Parnaby, called for 'Hands off our hospital, our station and our boundaries'. Later in the month he presided over a public meeting in the Opera House to discuss hospital reorganisation. Local authorities and the constituency M.P. were urged to approach the Minister of Health on behalf of Ripon Hospital.

The Ripon, Wakefield and Bradford Diocesan Training College celebrated its centenary on 10 May. A considerable building programme had been completed and in the morning the Bishop of Ripon dedicated the new chapel in the presence of five other bishops. In the afternoon the Countess of Harewood officially opened a new assembly hall, music block, gymnasium and hostel accommodation. A Centenary Ball was held in a large marquee erected in the grounds, followed by a firework display. A history of the college, *The First Hundred Years* by Mrs A. M. Wilkinson, was published. More than 900 former students attended a centenary reunion in July.

There were many instances of vandalism throughout the year, and on the contractor's site on the Lead Lane housing estate the damage was so serious that a meeting was called to discuss preventive action. It was said that the equivalent of a day's work by two bricklayers was being destroyed every night. The co-operation of parents and the Tenants' Association was sought and the contractor was instructed to keep children clear of the area during the daytime.

June. The market-stall erectors worked to rule for two weeks because of a dispute with a dissatisfied stallholder. Traders who arrived early complained that this meant them being kept waiting instead of their stalls being put up immediately. The City Engineer mediated between the parties.

Sir Sydney Roberts, Master of Pembroke College, Cambridge; President of the Library Association and a friend of the Canon-Librarian the Revd D. M. M. Bartlett, reopened the Cathedral Library after a complete restoration had been carried out at a cost of £4,000 by the Friends of the Cathedral. The angelus bell-turret on the central tower of the Cathedral was replaced after repair; it had been taken down before the war because of its dilapidated state.

July. The Ripon members of the Women's Voluntary Service began preparations for a regular 'Meals on Wheels' service to elderly and disabled citizens. The Mayor inaugurated the service on 3 September by serving the first of 36 meals which had been prepared for delivery at the *Café Victoria*.

August. Twenty-five floats took part in the St Wilfrid's procession; the theme was 'Aspects of Life in Ripon from A.D. 700 to the present day'. The residents of Southgate revived the custom of providing refreshments, including 'Wilfrid tarts', to the participants.

September. The police refused to allow members of the Ripon branch of C.N.D. to hand a letter to the Prime Minister who was on a visit to Swinton Castle. The M.P. for Ripon subsequently wrote to Mr Macmillan regretting the intrusion on his holiday and assuring him that the C.N.D. branch, with a membership of 20, was not typical of Ripon.

New buildings at Claro Barracks costing £700,000 were opened by Mr James Ramsden, M.P. for Harrogate and Under-Secretary of State for War. Mr Ramsden confirmed that Ripon would continue to be home for a major unit of the Royal Engineers and an important centre for the Territorial Army.

The Minister of Health, the Rt. Hon. Enoch Powell, visited Ripon Hospital. The Mayor was not originally invited but he asked if he might be present and was thus able to speak to the Minister about the future of the hospital.

October. Mr C. Dalton, the last of Ripon's horse-cab drivers, died aged 84, and in the same week one of the first motor-bus drivers, Mr E. Sykes, retired after 41 years' service.

November. The President of Iceland, who was on a tour of Great Britain, was the guest of Sir Richard and Lady Graham at *Norton Conyers*.

December. A Compulsory Purchase Order (prior to demolition) for cottages and property in Somerset

Row was confirmed by the Ministry of Housing and Local Government.

A large hole appeared in the road outside the Police Station in North Street; it was found that a brick culvert had collapsed and this was replaced by an iron sewer pipe. Further inspection by closed-circuit television revealed that the main sewer from North Street to the Clock Tower had virtually collapsed, causing continual flooding in Princess Road. A scheme for renewal of sewers in this part of the city was given high priority. Sewerage problems also hindered development on the Dallamires Lane Industrial Estate, so much so that Country-Style Chicken Packers threatened to withdraw from the site. The problems were finally resolved and the firm moved to the new factory in August 1967, where they hoped to have nearly 200 employees.

Despite warnings by the City Council, the railway unions and the stationmaster, citizens remained apathetic about the possible closure of the station. An attempt to set up a Railway Defence Committee attracted little support and a press campaign met with a poor response. At the end of the year Alderman M. Coverdale declared 'Ripon is quite capable of burying its head in its ancient charms and losing its railway station'.

January. The Cathedral organ was rededicated by the Bishop after a thorough cleaning and rebuilding. Work on renewing the masonry of the central tower, one of the major items in the restoration programme, neared completion.

February. On 2 February, the Feast of the Purification of the Blessed Virgin Mary, the Candlemas ceremony, was revived at the Cathedral. After Evensong, a congregation of 200 processed around the building carrying candles. The ceremony was to prove increasingly popular in later years. The ancient custom had long survived the Reformation in Ripon and a visitor recorded seeing the Minster ablaze with candles in 1790.

Wrestling matches staged at the Opera House drew a very large audience and the management hoped to make such promotions a regular feature of entertainment.

A decision by the Council to mark out parking spaces in the Market Square aroused continuing controversy. It was alleged that difficulties were caused for motorists, that there were more cars on the Square than previously and that insufficient space had been left for the Hornblower. Complaints continued after a modification of the scheme in July left more space around the obelisk, but the Council refused to enclose it within a post-and-chain fence because of the expense.

Notice was given of Compulsory Purchase Orders for the clearance of sub-standard housing in Stonebridgegate, Low St Agnesgate, Bondgate and Bedern Bank.

March. A suggestion by its M.P., Sir Malcolm Stoddart-Scott, that Ripon should seek to persuade the government to establish one of the new universities in Ripon caused much comment. Possible sites, the suitability of the town, and the possible impact on the community were debated; the abortive schemes in the reign of Elizabeth I were recalled. In November a committee with the M.P. as chairman was set up to stake Ripon's claim without success.

April. Progress was made on the development of the Dallamires Lane Industrial Estate. Two sites were let and a further six acres of land purchased by the Corporation. Sanction was at last given to proceed with the sewerage scheme there, which had been the cause of much delay and uncertainty.

Three red-ash hard tennis courts were laid down by the Ripon Tennis Club in Mallorie Park where previously only grass courts had been available. The Ripon City A.F. Club won the Senior Charity Cup for the seventh successive year.

Mr J. H. Gough, Town Clerk of Ripon from 1920 to 1942, died aged 86 in Llandudno.

Ted Moult, the television personality, opened *Harvester House*, the new premises in Kirkby Road of Croft and Blackburn. Their garage in the Market Square continued; the new premises, formerly Abbott's Furniture Factory, were to house the farm equipment and used car divisions of the business.

1964-65. WILFRID HENRY PARNABY, Electricity Foreman

Mayor 1963-64-65

May. General Sir Colin Barber of *Quarry Moor* died while on holiday. Sir Colin, who had retired in 1955 as G.O.C. Scottish Command and had been Governor of Edinburgh Castle, was an unmistakeable figure in Ripon and was reputed to have been the tallest general in the British Army.

Additional married quarters were needed at the barracks, and a start was made on the erection of 159 new houses on Clotherholme Road.

June. The residents of Lead Lane protested about the nuisance arising from the children's playground on the estate. The Council first suggested distributing the equipment around several sites, but this led to further protests and it was eventually decided to re-site all the equipment on Greystone Meadow where it would also be convenient for children living in the Gallows Hill area.

The Mayor, Alderman W. H. Parnaby, was awarded the B.E.M. in the Queen's Birthday Honours List.

A nursery unit costing £19,000 at Dr Barnardo's School at Springhill for mentally handicapped children was opened by Lady Graham.

July. A town map and a report on Ripon's traffic problems were published by the W.R.C.C. and sent to the Ministry of Transport for approval. The report recommended a relief road to the east of the Cathedral, on the grounds that a complete bypass was unsuitable because Ripon was an important market and tourist centre and there was a high proportion of local traffic. However, it was essential that the centre of the town be relieved of congestion. The M.P. approached the Minister of Transport and was told that the relief road had a very low priority and Ripon would have to wait.

An application to install 'one-armed bandit' machines by the Racecourse Company and three public houses led to eight months of argument between the City Council and its Finance and General Purposes Committee. The Committee wished to reject the application outright, but the Council insisted on further consideration being given; eventually the Committee gave way and the gaming machines were approved.

August. Naomi Jacob, the well-known writer, who died on 27 August, was born in Ripon and spent her early years there. She was the daughter of Dr Jacob the headmaster of a school in St Agnesgate, where they lived. A major influence in her life was her grandfather Robert Collinson, proprietor of the *Unicorn*, and four times Mayor of Ripon. She became a pupil teacher at Middlesbrough and hated it; involvement in the theatre followed, but due to recurring tuberculosis she left England and went to live in Italy until World War II when she returned to England and joined E.N.S.A. Among her numerous novels, many with a north-country background and some based on Ripon, her finest writings were the 'Gollantz Saga', the story of a Jewish family which brought her outstanding success. Her autobiographical works covered all periods of her life, but we of Ripon owe her a debt for the family chronicle *Robert, Nana and Me*, published in 1952, which gave a vivid picture of Ripon in the time of Robert Collinson.

September. The Council Tenants' Association was wound up after only 16 months because of lack of support. A mere 10 members attended the final meeting.

The British Railway Board gave notice that the Harrogate-Ripon-Northallerton line would be closed for passengers on 30 November if no objections were lodged. By mid-November 96 local objections had been received, and these were referred to the Transport Users' Consultative Committee.

Two rare books, *De Consolatione Philosophiae* by Boethius, printed by Caxton, and a 14-century illuminated *Hours of the Virgin Mary* were found to be missing from the Cathedral Library. Suspicion fell on two men who had recently visited the library by appointment. The books, thought to be worth £29,000, were later returned by post in a brown paper parcel with an Irish post-mark.

October. The Y.M.C.A. celebrated the Golden Jubilee of its work in Ripon with a fête in July and a reunion in October.

On 20 October no Hornblower arrived to sound the Horn at 9 pm at the Market Cross. The acting Hornblower, busy with other things, had forgotten he was on duty that night; reminded by his wife on his return home, he hastened to perform the ceremony at 10.30 pm.

Sir Malcolm Stoddart-Scott (Conservative) was re-elected as M.P. for Ripon with 18,503 votes: R. H. H. Duncan (Liberal) won 7,814 votes, and P. O'Grady (Labour) 7,314 votes.

Many instances of vandalism were reported. The former church hall in Coltsgate Hill was wrecked, and the damage to public conveniences was such that the Council decided to close the Minster Road toilets at night. At the *Palladium Cinema*, where 80 seats had been damaged, the manager placed a notice in the foyer requesting the public to concentrate their efforts on those already damaged if they *must* slash seats. There was a serious affray in the Market Square, where a mob of 150 teenagers attacked police officers who tried to question some of them. An inspector was dragged along the ground and only one person among many onlookers, a taxi-driver, tried to help. The situation was brought under control after the arrival of an army vehicle. Subsequently eight youths received prison sentences.

November. Miss Pauline Foulds of Littlethorpe, and Lady Masham, both of whom had suffered spinal injuries in riding accidents, did well in the Paralympics (paraplegic games) in Tokyo. Miss Foulds won three gold and Lady Masham a gold and four silver medals. On their return there was a celebration in the village hall at Littlethorpe and they were given a civic reception at the Town Hall.

January. 'Not too old at 60': the Rotary Club appealed to local businessmen to consider the employment of older people in a part-time capacity. Several such jobs had already been provided to the mutual satisfaction of the pensioners and their employers.

The Grammar School acquired the organ from the former Methodist Church in Coltsgate Hill. The organ was to be rebuilt and installed in the assembly hall of the school under the direction of the Cathedral organist, Dr Philip Marshall, and Mr P. H. Miles of the Grammar School. The estimated cost was £2,500 and fund-raising events followed later in the year. The work was completed by July 1967 when the organ was put into use.

February. The Cathedral was crowded for a memorial service to Sir Winston Churchill. Civic and Service dignitaries attended and the sermon was preached by the Dean.

Following a public meeting in January to discuss the future of Quarry Moor, a plan to develop the area as a children's playground was put before the Council.

Mr Charles Harker, Freeman of the City and Mayor of Ripon 1926-28, died on 22 February at the age of 90.

March. The Chamber of Trade launched its plan to promote Ripon as a provincial shopping centre. It was urged that parking in the city should be completely free, and the slogan 'Park in Comfort — Shop in Comfort — Shop in Ripon' was the message of a widespread advertising campaign which aimed to attract shoppers from larger centres where parking was said to be difficult. In July an anonymous objection to advertisements on Leeds Corporation buses was thought to have been officially placed, but Leeds Corporation and Chamber of Commerce denied responsibility. At the end of the year the campaign was judged to have been successful and it was extended into the following year. The Chamber also discussed full-day closing in Ripon — on Mondays or Wednesdays — but opinions were divided and the matter was deferred.

1965-66. NEVILLE STEPHENSON, Postmaster

Born 1920, the son of Walter Stephenson of Ripon. Educated at Ripon Cathedral School and the Grammar School. Assistant Head Postmaster at Ripon. Elected to Council 1958. Alderman 1967. Resigned from the Council on his appointment as Postmaster at Northallerton in 1971. He was Vice-Chairman of the Governors of the Grammar School and fought for its retention; also a governor of Moorside Junior and the County Secondary Schools. Served on the District Education Sub-Committee and represented the Council on the Education Committee of the Association of Municipal Corporations. Past secretary of the Ripon City Club. Many sporting interests — cricket, rugby, walking, billiards and snooker.

May. For the first time a Communist was among the candidates standing for Council at the municipal elections; in the event, however, all five seats went to Conservatives.

Dr Charles Henry Moody, organist and Master of the Choristers of Ripon Cathedral from 1902-54, died at the age of ninety-one. Born at Stourbridge, Dr Moody was trained at Bangor Cathedral and held appointments at Wells Cathedral, Wigan and St Michael's Coventry before coming to Ripon. He gained an early reputation as a choir trainer and throughout his career strove to maintain the highest traditions of cathedral music, particularly during the difficult years of the two World Wars. He had many engagements as an organist and conductor, but in Ripon was perhaps best known for the performances of his Amateur Operatic Society. He received the C.B.E. in 1920 and the degree of Mus.D. Cantuar in 1922. Second to music his interest was architecture, expressed in his love and knowledge of the Cathedral and Fountains Abbey. On the Golden Jubilee of his appointment he was made a Freeman of the City, an honour he valued above all others, but typically threatened to resign when the Council proposed to cut down some lime trees which gave him great pleasure. In character to the last, his death was occasioned by falling in an attempt to shave himself — 'I did not want to meet my Maker unshaven'.

Mr Raymond Webster, who had had a stone Madonna and Child accepted in 1964, was again successful at the Royal Academy. The exhibit on this occasion was a bronze and polyester head of Margaret Sweeney, a pupil at Aldfield School where Mr Webster's wife was the head teacher. There is a head of Dr Moody by Mr Webster in the Council Chamber at the Town Hall.

The committee preparing the case for Ripon as the venue for a new university resolved to continue its work, despite disappointment at a Ministry statement that no more universities would be needed for 10 years at least.

June. Miss Joan Cullingworth, who succeeded Mrs F. Smith as District Commissioner for Girl Guides, had been connected with the Movement since 1928. From 1950 to its closure in 1962 she had been headmistress of the Ripon High School for Girls and returned to Ripon again after teaching for some years in Nigeria.

The Council abandoned its plans for a roofed sun shelter in the Market Square in favour of making a garden above the public conveniences.

August. The change to a late August Bank Holiday was not welcomed in Ripon where the day had locally been associated with the Feast of St Wilfrid. The celebrations took place on the traditional date with a procession of floats on the theme *The Craftsmen of Yesterday* and a pageant in the Cathedral. When the Bank Holiday came the weather was poor and there was little interest, although a crowd of 20,000 attended the race-meeting.

The Appleyard Group of Leeds acquired Glovers, Motor Dealers and Agricultural Engineers, for £325,000. Mr Sidney Glover started a motor cycle business in 1914, later selling motor cars, and in the 1930s built the well-known showrooms and workshops near Borrage Bridge called Glovers' Garage. He later extended his business to Harrogate.

September. Fragments of pottery turned up by
cattle at Winksley led to the discovery of medieval
kilns. An excavation was carried out by Mr C. V.
Bellamy of Leeds University and a local archaeology
class, which dated the finds to the 11th and 12th
centuries, contemporary with Nicholas and William
the potters of Winksley, who are mentioned in the
Fountains Charters and *The Memorials of Ripon*.

Great apprehension about the future of Fountains
Abbey and grounds followed the sale of the Studley
Royal Estate (19,000 acres) by Mr Henry Vyner in
August. The purchasers, Broadland Properties,
(Scarborough Limited), indicated their willingness to
re-sell the Abbey and Studley Park, and many
approaches were made to the Government and other
bodies.

October. The window frontage of Mr Jack Thompson's cycle shop in North Street was dismantled and
taken to York to be re-erected in the 19th-century
shopping street being constructed in the Castle
Museum. Small portions of other Ripon buildings had
already been incorporated there.

'The Ripon Doctors' wrote to the press, 'There are
hundreds of new houses and bungalows going up
all over the town and few of them have a number
. . . tramping about in the mud in the middle of the
night trying to find a patient can be very frustrating.'

November. The Ministry of Defence announced the
closure of the ex-Bomber Command Station at
Dishforth, although the airfield would be retained as
a relief landing ground. There were fears for the loss
of many civilian jobs; shortly after, it was stated that
some of the buildings would be used as a Police
Training School.

On the grounds that it would be detrimental to the
amenities of the Cathedral, the Dean and Chapter
vetoed a proposal by the Council to construct an
access road from the top of Bedern Bank to the
parking ground. Earlier in the year the Council had
decided not to ask the United Bus Company to allow
other traffic through the access to the bus station from
Queen Street which was restricted to buses only.

December. Exceptionally heavy snowfalls caused
chaos; cars, buses and an ambulance were marooned
in drifts, the villages were cut off and many children
were unable to get to school. The Claro Water Board
announced that all its reservoirs were full for the first
time in its history.

The Hall, formerly the residence of the Oxley family,
had been purchased by the Dean and Chapter some
years previously. They now announced that, with the
help of grants from the Ministry of Public Buildings
and Works and the Church Commissioners, it would
be restored as nearly as possible to its original state
to become the new Deanery, *Minster House*.

January. To ring in the New Year, most subscribers
on the Ripon telephone exchange were given new
four-digit telephone numbers.

February. The City Council approved 'No Waiting'
orders in five main city streets — High Skellgate,
Market Place West, Fishergate, Coltsgate Hill, Old
Market Place and Queen Street — despite strong

protests from the Chamber of Trade.

Dr Philip Marshall, Cathedral Organist and
Choirmaster, left Ripon for a similar appointment at
Lincoln. He was succeeded by Mr Ronald Edward
Perrin, formerly sub-organist at York Minster.

Mrs Mary Moorman, the wife of the Bishop of
Ripon, won the James Tait Black Memorial Prize for
the best biography of the year with her book *William
Wordsworth: a biography of the later years, 1803-1850*,
published by the Oxford University Press.

Comprehensive education became a major issue in
Ripon and district. The majority of grammar school
parents voted against it, but most primary and county
secondary parents were in favour of some form of
comprehensive education, with a leaning towards a
two-tier system in Ripon. In October, when the
W.R.C.C. sent a scheme for the introduction of comprehensive education in the city, it did include a
proposal for two tiers, ages 10-13 and 13-18, within
the overall pattern.

March. After protracted discussion the Claro Water
Board finally refused to introduce fluoridisation.

Exhibitions were held in Ripon during the year:
'Yorkshire Maps' in March, 'Yorkshire Natural History'
in August, and 'Rockingham Ware' in November and
December, all in the Town Hall; one on 'Home Safety,
Accident and Crime Prevention' was shown in the
Victoria Ballroom in March and there was a Royal
Engineers' display of equipment in the Market Place
in July.

In the General Election, Sir Malcolm Stoddart-Scott
won a Conservative victory for Ripon, retaining his
seat by a very comfortable majority, when throughout
the country his party were losing at the polls.

April. Michael Nutter, a Ripon boy, was the runner-
up in the Portuguese Amateur Golfing
Championship.

Extensions to Allhallowgate Methodist Church,
including a concert room and a Sunday-school room,
were opened by Mrs W. Pickering, wife of a former
superintendent minister of the circuit.

The inadequacy of the city sewerage system led to
plans for relieving the city sewers of storm water. The
first plan, affecting the Clock Tower and Skittergate
Gutter, had been approved by the Ministry and was
ready for tender; the second, for the Camp Close
district, was then about to be submitted to the
Ministry and would later be extended to the Lead
Lane area, which had been subject to recent flooding.
As a short-term solution to the latter hazard, these
sewers were linked to Grove Lane later in the summer,
a measure some felt would merely transfer the
problem. After more flooding in December when the
sewage again overflowed into Ripon streets, the
Council rushed through a £300,000 scheme.

1966-67. NEVILLE STEPHENSON, Postmaster

June. A team of young archers from the County
Secondary School was awarded the Champion Team
Trophy in the Yorkshire Association Junior Championships for the third time in four years, and for the
second year running Gordon Shipley won the

NEVILLE STEPHENSON
MAYOR
1965-1967

Mayor 1965-66-67

individual Junior Archery Championship.

The open tennis tournament at Ripon had to be cancelled because of lack of support.

July. The Co-operative Bakery was closed for seven weeks, as more than half the staff contracted food poisoning on an outing to Scarborough.

The Fountains Abbey estates figured in the news. First came the announcement of the purchase of the Abbey, Studley Park and Studley Royal House from the owner, Mr Henry Vyner, by the W.R.C.C. for £250,000. In October the Ministry of Public Buildings and Works took over the guardianship of Fountains Abbey, assuming responsibility for repairs and upkeep there. Later that month Commander Clare Vyner bought back Fountains Hall, which had been sold by his son. In December, the W.R.C.C. bought seven of the eight statues in the landscape gardens of Studley Park, sold by auction in the grounds.

The Station Commander of R.A.F. Topcliffe presented a plaque to the Mayor to mark the 'happy relationship' between the city and the R.A.F. base.

August. Great pleasure was expressed in Ripon when the Minister of Housing and Local Government rejected the proposal of the Local Government Boundaries Commission to transfer Harrogate, Ripon and district to the North Riding.

September. The Minister of Transport agreed to the closure of the Harrogate-Northallerton railway line to passenger traffic subject to the provision of certain additional bus services. She refused to see a Yorkshire deputation protesting against the closure, as her decision could not be reversed and in December it was announced that the last passenger train would run on 6 March 1967.

October. Mr Percival Smith, a keen local historian, published his book *The Jepson Story*, a history of the Ripon Bluecoat School.

November. Ripon City Prize Band started a Band Supporters' Club to help to raise funds and converted a disused shop on the ground floor of their headquarters into a clubroom.

The Mayoress opened the temporary Solid Fuel Advisory Centre, the first in Yorkshire.

The W.R.C.C. gave its approval for an expenditure of £40,000 to buy land at the rear of Church Lane and Kirkby Road, for a proposed Roman Catholic Primary School, and for additional land for the County Secondary School.

December. Ripon's first communal development for elderly people, Russell Dixon Square, was officially opened by County Alderman Mrs J. Smith.

The Ripon *Gazette* changed its day of publication from Thursday to Friday.

Two Ripon stores, Gallon's and Moss's, engaged for three days in a cut-price war to reduce the price of cigarettes by 3d to 5d as part of a struggle over resale price maintenance. Both stores belonged to Moore's Group and one manager reported a fivefold increase in the sale of cigarettes. The Chamber of Trade condemned price-cutting.

A new animal-feed manufacturing and distribution plant was established by Feed Services (Liverpool) Limited on the Dallamires Lane Trading Estate, the first of several proposed developments there.

A summer of road chaos in Ripon was forecast. Police and highways officials were already discussing traffic problems likely to be caused during the summer by three major roadwork schemes: a new sewer network in North Road and Magdalen Road; the North-Eastern Gas Board's new trunk main scheduled to run from Harrogate along the railway embankment via Magdalen Road and so on to Thirsk; the North-Eastern Electricity Board's new trunk cable to be laid from Bondgate, past the Town Hall and down Westgate. In all, 13 roads and streets would be taken up. Parts of the A61 might be reduced to one-way traffic and the alternative route to the A61 down Magdalen Road might also be affected.

March. The Ripon Rotary Club published a free *Pensioners' Guide*, with useful information and advice for the elderly.

The public convenience extension and garden in the Market Place were completed at a cost of £6,000. These were the subject of contention because of their cost and appearance, and the object of serious vandalism during the summer.

April. Whippet racing began in Ripon on a track made on a corner of the racecourse between Boroughbridge and Littlethorpe as a temporary arrangement, and in August a permanent track was made near the Red Arrows' football pitch in the Boroughbridge Road. Later a Ripon and District Whippet Club was formed.

The City Council planned to buy the Drill Hall (now Hugh Ripley Hall), relinquished by the Territorial Army, for £10,000. In August the Public Hall Executive Committee voted to hand over their fund of £410 to help the purchase, on condition that the building remained a public hall for at least five years.

Mr C. Hawthornthwaite, District Commissioner Ripon and District Boy Scouts, was awarded the Scout Movement's highest award, the *Silver Wolf*, in recognition of his 50 years' work for the movement.

1967-68. FREDERICK WALTER SPENCE, Varnish Manufacturer

Born 1908, son of Thomas Fowler Spence, mayor 1927-28-29. Educated Ripon Grammar School and Loughborough College. Chairman and Managing Director of T. and R. Williamson Limited. 1939-45, Flight Lieutenant R.A.F. Elected to Council 1960, to Harrogate District Council 1973, and to North Yorkshire County Council 1982. President National Paint Federation. Member of the National Liberal Club, the Yorkshire Agricultural Society, the Yorkshire County Cricket Club, the Ripon Golf Club and the City Club. Chairman of the Governors of the Grammar School and governor of the County Secondary School. His mayoral effort was in support of the appeal for the Ripon Y.M.C.A., of which he was President. Served for many years on the District Highways Committee and was a leader of the opposition to the Inner Relief Road. Also mayor in 1968-69 and 1978-79.

May. A public inquiry was held into the W.R.C.C.'s proposed scheme to close the public footpath leading from Whitcliffe Lane and Studley Roger to Fountains Abbey. In 1968 the W.R.C.C. decided to keep the footpaths open.

Starting stalls were used for the first time in Yorkshire on the Ripon racecourse at the Variety Club Charity Meeting.

The Very Revd Frederick Llewellyn Hughes, Dean of Ripon, died suddenly at the age of 73, on 4 June. Dean of Ripon since 1951, educated at Christ's Hospital and Jesus College, Oxford, he was in King's (Liverpool) Regiment and on the General Staff in World War I. He was ordained in 1922. In World War II he was Chaplain-General to the Forces from 1944-51 and chaplain to King George VI between 1946-52.

A new music and recreation block was built at Ripon Cathedral Choir School as a memorial to the late Dr C. H. Moody.

July. A newly-formed local group, *The Wakeman Singers*, gave a recital in the Cathedral Library.

A severe storm caused cellars and roads in the city to flood and the Fire Brigade answered many calls to pump out water. Even road surfaces were torn up by the force of the water.

The district of Clotherholme was given its own parish council.

August. To follow the successful production of Benjamin Britten's opera *Curlew River* in the Cathedral in 1966 during the Harrogate Festival of Arts and Sciences, his opera *The Burning Fiery Furnace* was given its first production in Yorkshire in the Cathedral at the 1967 Festival.

The British Waterways Board drained Ripon Canal in order to repair the lock near Littlethorpe. They omitted to notify the Piscatorial Association in time, and the Association blamed the Board for the loss of an estimated 65,000 fish.

On 26 August the *Opera House*, which had shown films for more than 50 years, was used as a cinema for the last time. It would become a hall for bingo, meetings and functions.

A firm of developers wished to purchase and demolish the *Café Victoria* and replace the buildings with two shops. The local authorities did not disapprove of the change of use, but objected to the developers' plans for access from Westgate.

September. The Vaux group of breweries planned to sell the *Unicorn Hotel*, and a Bradford-based property group applied for outline planning permission for a supermarket and office block development. Public outcry against both these plans, for the *Café Victoria* and the *Unicorn Hotel*, resulted in the formation of a pressure group to save them. The Society for the Protection of Ancient Buildings gave its support and a petition was sent to Ripon's M.P. A meeting was called to form a Ripon Civic Trust or Preservation Society in November and by the next month the application to turn the *Unicorn* into a supermarket and offices had been withdrawn.

On 25 September the Ripon Citizens' Advice Bureau opened at 10 Westgate in premises supplied by the Ripon and Pateley Bridge Rural District Council.

The death occurred of Canon W. E. Wilkinson, Residentiary Canon of Ripon 1948-65. Canon Wilkinson was ordained in Ripon Cathedral in 1923 and became an authority on the history of the building. He served as Cathedral treasurer and had latterly been librarian. His devotion to the missionary work of the Church both overseas and at home found expression in the Diocese, especially in his connection with Ripon Training College.

October. On 20 October, the first issue of the *Gazette* to be run from the newly-installed Crabtree Rotary Press, which could print up to 20,000 copies an hour, was published. The former rotary press had been in use for more than 40 years.

The obelisk in the Market Place was enclosed in scaffolding for repair.

About five hundred officers and men were due to return from Germany to Ripon and about 200 of these would require family accommodation. The army had bought some houses and planned a meeting with Ripon landlords to persuade them to let flats and houses to soldiers. The army offered to rent the premises and then allocate them to families. It was realised that the influx of so many army personnel would also place an additional strain on the city's educational resources.

November. A 15-year-old Ripon swimmer, Yvonne Farrer, had a very successful year, including the award of two bronze medals and one silver medal in the national championships.

The Ripon Rowel Players presented *Love in a Mist* at the Claro theatre at the R.E. Barracks, deprived as they were of their usual venue of the *Opera House*. Special buses took playgoers to and from the theatre to the bus station during the five-day run of the play.

December. Mr Cyril Hawley, the Hornblower, resigned in protest against the Council's decision to deny him space in the Market Place. He claimed that parked and moving vehicles had made his work un-dignified and even dangerous.

On the initiative of the Rotary Club, the Ripon Men's Forum for retired men was formed.

The W.R.C.C. Education Committee approved the building of extensions to Ripon Grammar School at a cost of £122,604 to turn it into a seven-form entry comprehensive school for 13- to 18-year-olds.

In an interview the Ripon artists Mr and Mrs H. A. Clarke said that in recent years they had had many paintings accepted for exhibition by galleries in Yorkshire and in London by the Royal Society of British Artists, the Royal Society of Painters in Oils, and the Guildhall.

The automatic telephone service was inaugurated by the Mayor from the new exchange in Allhallowgate.

Ripon boy, Philip Curry, won a place in the National Youth Orchestra, upholding the city's growing reputation for music in schools.

It was announced that the new Dean of Ripon would be Canon Frederick Edwin le Grice, the sub-dean of St. Alban's Cathedral.

January. The administration of Ripon's Post Office became the responsibility of the Harrogate Post Office, where new mechanical sorting equipment had been installed.

Concern was caused by the lack of applicants for the post of Hornblower but eventually Mr Brian Waines was appointed.

February. The former Congregational Church in North Street, once used as a chicken factory, was demolished.

The 'People Next Door' campaign launched a street-warden scheme to involve about 150 people acting as liaison between residents and welfare organisations.

March. A team of scientists working for the Marine Division of the Pinchin Johnson Association's Ripon factory invented a method of combating vegetable growth on ships' hulls.

The worst floods for over 100 years swept through the city. The high water mark at North Bridge was only a few inches below that recorded in 1883. Roads were impassable, cellars and ground floor rooms were flooded, and the racecourse was under water. Much damage was caused to farmland and livestock was endangered. On 2 July, a violent storm of rain and

hail with gusts of wind up to 66 knots caused greater havoc. Every street in the city centre was flooded; shops, offices, banks and the college were seriously affected and even houses on the outskirts did not escape. The wall of the Spa Gardens collapsed on to Skellbank. The damage done to farms in the Ripon area was estimated at over £250,000.

The City Council made a preservation order, giving the Council power and control over any proposals to change the appearance of the *Unicorn Hotel*, par-ticularly the front elevation; but the Council felt obliged to approve the change of use subject to con-ditions laid down.

April. The W.R.C.C. cut its grant to the Ripon Y.M.C.A. Youth Club by 50 per cent and it proved therefore impossible to retain the services of a full-time leader. An appeal for local support was endorsed by the Mayor in May who asked for £1,500 to support the Club.

The Ripon *Gazette* moved from its premises off the east side of the Market Place to 5 Kirkgate.

1968-69. FREDERICK WALTER SPENCE, Varnish Manufacturer

Mayor 1967-68-69, 1977-78

May. Hooligans smashed panes of stained glass in windows on the north side of the Cathedral.

At a meeting in the *Wakeman's House* a 'Ripon Soc-iety' was formed with a committee of 11 to continue and extend the activities of the group originally formed to safeguard the *Unicorn Hotel* and the *Café Victoria*. On 27 June, the Ripon Civic Society was founded with Sir Richard Graham of *Norton Conyers* as President and Dr R. M. H. Anning as Chairman. Initial plans included clearance of the river and canal areas, bulb-planting and restoration work at St Anne's Chapel.

On 18 May, the Very Revd F. E. le Grice was installed as Dean of Ripon.

Ripon's first woman Special Constable, Miss Susan Knowles, began her duties outside the Cathedral dur-ing the Mayor's Sunday procession.

June. The Christian Alliance clubhouse in Trinity Lane, which had been destroyed by fire, was re-opened. Serious damage to the work of reconstruction during the January gale caused only minor delay.

HRH Princess Margaret, President of Dr Barnardo's, visited the two homes of the organisation in Ripon, Red House Nursery Home and Springhill School.

Mrs Eleanor Dunning was awarded the B.E.M. in the Birthday Honours List for her service to the National Savings Movement.

It was announced that Ripon would have its own 'Pride of Lions', when the city's branch of the Lions' Club for men over 40 was formed. Its first task would be to help with a free taxi-service for the elderly.

Mrs Mary Moorman received the honorary degree of Doctor of Letters of the University of Durham.

Dr J. R. H. Moorman's book *A History of the Franciscan Order* was published by the Clarendon Press; it was a fuller study than his previous works on the subject.

August. Vaux breweries proposed to close their Ripon depot in September with the threat of redundancies.

September. 4 September marked the introduction of disc parking, a measure confined to the Market Square. To begin with, many cars omitted to display discs.

At the request of the Institute of Geological Sciences, the Ripon Health Committee agreed to leave open a section of the Quarry Moor rubbish tip so that geologists could inspect a rare outcrop of rock, a fossil beach deposit similar to the coast of the Persian Gulf today. The provision emphasised the outstanding scientific value of Quarry Moor which offers not only an exposed face of magnesian limestone laid down over 200 million years ago, but a habitat where plant species of great interest flourish on the floor of this ancient quarry. This important geological and botanical site belongs specifically to Ripon City as the owners under the will of the donor of the land.

October. After one hundred years of service to Riponians, Winsors fish and game shop at 15 North Street closed on the retirement of the proprietor.

November. The supporters of Blackburn Rovers football club rioted in the city centre when their coaches stopped on their way home from Middlesbrough. The damage was mostly to shop windows, but there was one alleged assault on a Ripon boy.

December. Crompton Parkinson's electrical workshops opened in the *Black Swan* Yard in the former laundry premises.

The Royal Engineers based in Ripon gave assistance to the civilian population by installing central heating in the Y.M.C.A. hall, and by raising a lead statue from a pond in Studley Park.

The Mayor held a transatlantic telephone conversation with his counterpart in Ripon, Wisconsin, on Christmas Eve; the exchange was to be broadcast in Wisconsin by the local commercial radio station.

The Cathedral was floodlit at Christmas-time as an experiment: nine floodlights were rigged up by arrangement with R.A.F. Topcliffe.

1969-70. GEORGE FEATHER, Estate Agent
Born 1914 in London. Son of Handel Feather, a violinist. Educated in Croydon and worked in

jewellery trade. 1940-46, served with Royal Artillery. Spent holidays with relatives in Ripon as a boy and his first wife was the daughter of Joseph Hurst, a City Councillor. Came to Ripon in 1953 and held positions with Hepworth's Brewery and Renton and Renton, Estate Agents. Elected to Council 1963 principally interested in housing and estates. Presented the Freedom of the City to Sir Malcolm Stoddard-Scott. Hobbies, gardening and reading.

May. The Freedom of the City of Ripon was presented to R.A.F. Topcliffe with traditional pomp and ceremony. Rain, which threatened just before the ceremony, held off while the four flights, 120 men altogether, lined up in ranks on the Market Square. The Dean of Ripon led the prayers and the Mayor presented the illuminated Freedom Scroll. The timing of the fly-past of Varsity and Jet Provost aircraft from Topcliffe and R.A.F. Linton-on-Ouse was perfect. The two formations zoomed over the city centre as the newly-presented scroll and the Queen's Colour were paraded round the Square. After the parade, the Queen's Colour Squadron detachment marched through the city centre, with bayonets fixed, drums beating and the R.A.F. Regiment band playing. Group Captain N. Poole, Officer Commanding R.A.F. Topcliffe, presented an inscribed silver tray to the city to mark the occasion.

June. Alderman F. W. Spence called for the Council to produce a development policy for Ripon and decide whether emphasis in the future should be placed on attracting tourists or factories to the city; this was the start of what was to be a continuing debate for months to come. In August Councillor Barrie Price brought forward a three-phase plan to attract new factories to the Dallamires Lane industrial estate. There was some opposition to the scheme and a proposal to allocate £500 for an advertising fund was rejected.

September. Ripon's first festival of the arts was opened at the Hugh Ripley Hall by Sir Richard Graham, the Chairman of Yorkshire Television. It was hoped that the two-week event would become important among northern artists who put on show 108 works, both paintings and sculpture. Among the artists from the Ripon district who exhibited works were Raymond Webster, Peter Sarginson and Philip Jones. In addition to the art exhibition, the three main events were a public lecture on the works of Wordsworth by Mary Moorman, a concert by the Wakeman Singers conducted by their founder Alan Dance, and a poetry reading by the Leeds playwright Brian Thompson.

October. At the first annual meeting of the Ripon Civic Society the Chairman, Dr R. M. H. Anning, said the city would have had a bypass road a long time ago if there had not been such tremendous opposition to the idea. He said that members must back proposals for a relief road with all the strength they had. He welcomed the improved relationship between the Society and the City Council.

Work started on a new bridge over the River Nidd at Killinghall on the A61 Harrogate to Ripon road. The project would cost £240,000 and take 18 months to complete. The old bridge was set askew to the line of the approaching roadways, which were themselves on bends, thus causing frequent damage to the wide walls of the bridge by both cars and heavy vehicles. Lady Ingilby cut the ceremonial tape across the completed roadway in May 1971.

The last goods train to run from Ripon goods station departed for York at 8.30 am on 3 October. A group of railway enthusiasts took photographs of the end of an era of transport in Ripon.

Representatives of Ripon Education Committee, school managers and other guests attended the opening of the new Ripon Holy Trinity (Controlled) Junior School in Church Lane. Alderman Mrs L. I. Fitzpatrick, Chairman of the West Riding Education Committee, opened the school and the Bishop of Ripon dedicated the building.

Memorial services were held in the Cathedral and at St Wilfrid's Church, Harrogate, for Canon Donald M. M. Bartlett. He had been vicar of St Wilfrid's for 21 years and successively Archdeacon of Leeds and Richmond. Canon Bartlett had worked in the Diocese since 1902. He was a greatly-loved personality in the Church in the North and was renowned for his ability to inspire affection among all sorts of people, and not least for his championship of the gypsies' cause. On his retirement in 1961 as Residentiary Canon of Ripon Cathedral, he retained his post as Cathedral librarian. Only a few weeks before his death, a booklet of reminiscences of his life was compiled and published by Mrs A. M. Wilkinson.

A public enquiry conducted by the Ministry of Housing and Local Government was held at the Town Hall on an application by Mr Charles Doubtfire to convert an 18th-century property in Kirkgate into an amusement arcade, a proposal which caused heated controversy for some time. Mr Ted Pearson, a member of the Ripon Civic Society, said that Ripon could not continue as a decaying town; it should generate more opportunities for local employment and enhance its reputation as a tourist centre, but to allow amusement arcades into the city was a retrograde step, and not one that would help its image. The Dean of Ripon objected to the application on both moral and planning grounds. He described Kirkgate as having something of the character of a 'Pilgrims's Way', and said it was unthinkable that an amusement arcade should be allowed within 100 yards of the west door of the Cathedral. Mr R. C. Hague, Chief Planning Assistant for W.R.C.C., maintained that Kirkgate was predominantly a commercial street and use as an amusement arcade was no different from any other commercial use. The final stroke against the plan came when Councillor Barrie Price presented a successful petition signed by 1,339 residents against the proposals.

November. The Mayor of Ripon gave his full support to a scheme by Ripon Rotary Club to provide holiday chalets for old people at the Municipal caravan site at Ure Bank. The scheme was run in conjunction with the National Association for the Welfare of the Elderly and 25 local organisations pledged their support.

December. West Riding Education Committee approved the reorganisation of education in the city based on the Middle School System, whereby children would attend primary schools until they were ten; they would then go to one of two middle schools, one of which would be housed in the secondary modern school and the other in a new building. At 13 all would transfer without selection to the Grammar School buildings, suitably extended. This decision was made despite the opposition expressed by the Chairman of the Board of Governors and the Headmaster of the Grammar School, who in a letter to the Gazette had said 'We reject the comprehensive idea and we intend to preserve Ripon Grammar School as an academically selective School'. In April 1970 parents at the Grammar School set up an action committee which organised a petition with 4,000 signatures against the W.R.C.C. scheme. Discussions continued until November 1970, when the County Education Committee arranged a public meeting in the Claro Theatre which was attended by 1,000 people, and at which the Chairman of the Committee asked whether the existing system should remain unchanged in Ripon or whether selection at 11 should be discontinued. In January 1971 the County Education Committee decided not to introduce comprehensive education in Ripon, and also that the secondary modern school should be enlarged to cope with the extension of the school-leaving age to 16 in 1972.

January. The Redcliffe-Maud Report recommended the adoption of new boundaries for the counties of England and Wales and a three-tier system for local government: a top tier of modified county councils and new metropolitan councils for the heavily populated and industrial areas; a new second tier of district councils responsible for amalgamated combinations of existing boroughs and rural districts; and a third tier of parish councils, which would include the existing ones and most of the existing small municipalities which would adopt parish status. Under the Maud proposals the areas north of Leeds in the West Riding would be absorbed into a vast metropolitan area based on Leeds. In order to avoid this, representatives from Harrogate, Ripon, Knaresborough, Nidderdale, Ripon and Pateley Bridge and Wath areas unanimously agreed to recommend to their respective councils a voluntary amalgamation into a single unit, with a district council of 40 members, serving a population of more than 120,000. At the Ripon Council meeting in January 1970, called to ratify the recommendation, the Mayor twice used his casting vote to avoid the proposal being turned down. Councillor Mrs Boddy, attacking the proposal, said that the most appropriate description of the amalgamation was 'the pedigree sow with her litter of five; Harrogate being the sow and Ripon one of the piglets'.

In the White Paper, the Government expressed agreement with the incorporation of the northern West Riding areas into the proposed West Yorkshire Metropolitan area. This prompted the existing authorities ranging from Wetherby and Tadcaster in the east to Skipton in the west and Harrogate, Knaresborough and Nidderdale to the north to argue with the Ministry, both individually and jointly, the case for transfer to the proposed Area 5, part of North Yorkshire. On the assumption that the Government would not change its mind about the inclusion of Harrogate and adjoining areas in the Metropolitan unit, representatives from Ripon City Council, Wath and Ripon-Pateley Rural District Councils met to discuss an amalgamation of their own areas and other adjacent areas to form a Dales District, excluding Harrogate, Knaresborough and Nidderdale. By the end of October, Ripon was suggesting a combination of existing small authorities, ranging from Boroughbridge to Skipton and serving a total of 90,000 population. However, in October 1971 the boundary changes included in the Local Government Bill were announced and Harrogate, Knaresborough and the whole of Nidderdale were not included in the Metropolitan area. Thus the original suggestion of a new district consisting of Harrogate, Knaresborough Urban, Nidderdale, Ripon-Pateley Bridge, Masham and Wath Rural Council areas, already in the hands of the Ministry, became a practical possibility and was ultimately accepted by all concerned. Before this, Ripon City Council, still adamant about its aversion to joining Harrogate and its neighbours, decided in December by nine votes to three to tell the Minister that Ripon continued to favour a Dales District authority with a total population of 77,189. The Council also emphasised to the Minister that, whatever the outcome of local government reform should be, it felt it was essential that Ripon should retain its status as a historic city.

Lady Masham, the wife of Lord Masham (heir to the Earl of Swinton), received a Life Peerage in the New Year Honours List for social services and services to the handicapped. She chose the title of Baroness Masham of Ilton and at the age of 34 became the youngest life peer.

March. The Ripon Sergeant-at-Mace collapsed and died in Allhallowgate Methodist Church, where a civic party was attending the funeral service of a former Mayor and Freeman, Mr W. Russell Dixon. Mr Edward Bourke, who was 62, had led a procession of robed Aldermen, Councillors and other civic heads from the Town Hall in freezing weather. He had just taken his seat when he collapsed and a few minutes later it was announced that he had died. Mr Bourke, an Irishman, joined the Royal Marines in 1928 and served for 23 years. Soon after joining, he became personal orderly to the Commander-in-Chief of the Mediterranean fleet. He served in the Far East during World War II and after returning to England he was selected along with a C.P.O. to accompany the First Sea Lord, Admiral Sir John Cunningham, for the presentation to Princess Elizabeth of a cheque from all ranks of the Royal Navy as part of its wedding present. He joined the Cunard Liner *Queen Mary* as Master-of-Arms in 1951 and in 1956 was appointed Sergeant-at-Mace in Ripon and became a member of the Guild of Mace Bearers. He was responsible for training cadets at Ripon Grammar School and was appointed cadet officer for the R.N. Reserve for the Harrogate area.

The City Council approved in principle phases one and two of the W.R.C.C. four-phase scheme to provide a western relief road. The two phases involved the building of a link road from Borrage Bridge through a new roundabout at Somerset Row and on to join Park Street at the Westgate/Blossomgate junction. A61 traffic, having travelled north on this new road, would then continue up Blossomgate into Trinity Lane and down Coltsgate Hill to join two-way traffic near the junction with North Street. This one-way system was planned to be replaced in phase three by a new road crossing from Westgate over the area west of Fishergate to rejoin the A61 at Coltsgate Hill. In September 1971 the W.R.C.C. decided to drop the one-way scheme and hoped to proceed with the complete new link road (i.e. phases two and three, carried out at the same time). Phases two and three were adopted by the North Yorkshire County Council after reorganisation in 1974 as the basis of the Ripon Inner Relief Road which was to cause controversy over the following decade.

April. A letter appeared in the *Gazette* announcing the Dean Hughes Memorial Fund. 'The Dean and Chapter has decided that the memorial should take the form of the reconstruction of the forecourt of the Cathedral. This was an improvement much desired by the late Dean and will enhance the beauty of the Cathedral which he so deeply loved and indeed the city of Ripon for which he so greatly cared'. The completed forecourt was dedicated by Dean Edwin le Grice in the presence of Mrs Dorothy Hughes. The inscription on the plaque at the extreme right of the cobbled forecourt reads: 'This forecourt was restored in 1970 in memory of Frederick Llewellyn Hughes, Dean of Ripon 1951-67. A servant of God and a friend of the people'.

Ripon Estates and Baths Committee recommended that a stained glass window, depicting the presentation of a pair of Ripon's famous spurs to King James I, which had been removed from the Spa Baths where it had been damaged by fire and vandals, should be preserved and displayed in the *Wakeman's House*.

1970-71. GEORGE FEATHER, Estate Agent

Mayor 1969-70-71

July. Econ Engineering Limited, manufacturers of industrial heaters and grit-spreading machines, who had moved into the former Hepworth Brewery premises in Bondgate at the beginning of the year, wished to close Brewery Lane and a short footpath (a right of way) which divided the company's buildings. The firm wished to erect a building across the footpath and said that additionally they were concerned for the public safety as 60 lorries per day passed down from one side of the footpath to the other.

After 20 years as producer for the Ripon Amateur Operatic Society, Mr Frank Lowley announced his retirement. He joined the Society in 1930 and for a long time was one of the principal players, taking part in many productions. Mrs Veronica Robson of Harrogate, the Society's dance mistress for 15 years, accepted an invitation to produce the next show, *Hello Dolly*.

September. New floodlighting at Fountains Abbey was switched on by the Minister of Public Buildings and Works, Mr Julian Amery. The system was installed in such a way as to avoid damage to the fabric of the Abbey. The floodlighting was on from 8 pm to 10 pm each evening for four weeks, and attracted 8,000 visitors.

October. Ripon Fire Brigade left its old headquarters in Blossomgate, after more than 50 years in the premises which had been the Ripon Stallhouse, and moved into a new building in Stonebridgegate. The new fire station had a garage for two appliances and a radio van. The reception and control room was equipped with the latest call-out and communications system which did away with the old bell alarms. There was also a five-storey drill-cum-hose drying tower.

December. The City Council decided to consider purchasing the *Opera House* for conversion to a community centre if at any time its site value seemed reasonable. In June 1971 a sub-committee was formed to consider the matter further.

Consideration was given to changing the method of selecting the Mayor. Councillor Barrie Price asked the committee to reconsider the practice of inviting a Mayor to serve a second year. Alderman W. R. Beaumont explained that on many occasions it had been in the interests of the Council for the Mayor to serve a further year, as, if he did not do so, since there were only 16 councillors and aldermen, it might be necessary to consider a councillor who had served only one term. He said the present system saved embarrassment.

January. Both the Sergeant-at-Mace, Mr Frederick Jobling, and the Hornblower, Mr Brian Waines, announced their retirement.

Stone masons working in the Old Courthouse, Minster Road, uncovered inscriptions dating back to 1613 on one of the outside walls when stripping off damaged plaster. Quite high up and etched into the surface was the date 1613 and the symbol of two crossed keys. Immediately below this was a plaque inscribed with the date 1846 and the crossed keys again; some writing in pencil recorded a marriage and the names of workmen: 'Ripon Feby 24th 1846 Pancake Tuesday Married by the Lord Bishop of Ripon at . . . Church — E. H. Reynard Esq. of Sutherland Wick to Miss Mason of Copt Hewick'. 'Thos Harrison — gaoler, James Harrison — painter, Edward Orton — bricklayer master, Joseph Renton — journeyman, William Leeming — labourer.' The theory of one of the stonemasons, Mr Ken Batty of Pateley Bridge, was that the original structure had been repaired in 1613, when the workmen made the first inscription; that in 1846 the wall was covered with plaster, the plaque fixed and the pencilled record made before the Victorian workmen sealed the wall.

After two years of discussion about the possibility of preserving four 18th-century cottages in Bondgate, the City Council decided the buildings were not worth retaining and should be demolished to make way for a modern development. In July the Council decided that the site would be used to build 40 units: 28 bed-sitters and 12 one-bedroomed flats for protected accommodation for the elderly.

February. Decimal day, when the new coinage came into use, produced few difficulties in Ripon except at the Post Office where because of a strike there had been no staff to make the necessary preparations. The Head Postmaster, Mr E. G. H. Potter, said that even when the staff returned to work the Post Office would not open until everything was ready for decimalisation.

Miss Florence Bone, the Ripon novelist, died in a Ripon nursing home aged 96. Her novels dealt with Yorkshire history: one of her earliest books published in 1907, *The Morning of Today*, told of the actions of Jacobites and Methodists in the North Riding: in 1910 she wrote *A Rose of York* about General Fairfax's siege of York during the Civil War and later used a similar subject in *The Sapphire Button* (1920). Her best known book was *Clacking Shuttles* (1933) in which she described life in Northallerton in the 1840s. In 1952, when 77, Miss Bone wrote *Midsummer Candles* about the detention of Mary, Queen of Scots, at Bolton Castle in Wensleydale. She served as president of the Ripon Women's Luncheon Club, was associated with the Business and Professional Women's Club and lived for many years at 4 Spring Bank, Ripon.

March. A shortage of bed space at Firby Lane Hospital was caused by the restriction of admissions to Sharow View Old People's Home because of its forthcoming closure in 1972. Normally, after treatment at Firby Lane, elderly patients were transferred to St Wilfrid's Hospital for rehabilitation before being discharged to Sharow View or back to their homes. The running-down of Sharow View had meant placing beds in the middle of wards at Firby Lane because of overcrowding at St Wilfrid's, which had only 32 beds and was insufficient to serve the needs of the community. Later in the month, the County Council Health Committee decided to purchase land in Residence Lane for the erection of a new old folk's home (*Ripon House*) and to delay the closure of Sharow View until this building was completed.

April. Up to 45 jobs were provided in Ripon by the end of the year as a result of the purchase by Yorkshire Heating Supplies Limited of four acres of the former Pinchin Johnson paintworks site, which had stood empty for 18 months. The Company's headquarters was transferred to Ripon from Leeds in June; it had branches covering the area between Edinburgh and Leicester and already had a warehouse in Ripon in Magdalen Road.

The Studley Royal and Aldfield Estate of about 3,000 acres was put up for sale by the executors of Mr Arthur Holmes and was expected to realise over £500,000. The estate comprised *Wheatbriggs House*, a period property overlooking Studley Park; cottages, woodlands, fishing in the River Skell and a 23-acre lake; shooting rights on Spa Gill and Mackershaw moors, together with Fountains Abbey Park, the famous home shoot of the second Marquess of Ripon.

Earl Mountbatten of Burma, wearing driver's cap and goggles, drove the 10¼-inch gauge *Royal Scot* and a trainload of excited children for the first time on *Newby Hall's* miniature steam railway line. The *Hall's* launch on the Ure, navigated by Mrs Robin Compton and carrying other adult guests, kept pace with the train. Earlier the guests, who included the Earl and Countess of Harewood and Sir Malcolm Stoddart-Scott, had been welcomed by Mr Robin Compton. Another new feature for the tourist season was the display of the late Robert de Grey Vyner's collection of old chamber pots, collected from all over England and the Far East, ranging from unique 16th-century peasant ware to the finest examples of 18th- and 19th-century china.

At a ceremony at Ripon Grammar School, Colonel Sir Malcolm Stoddart-Scott, M.P., was admitted as an honorary Freeman of the City. The Town Clerk, Mr J. A. Berry, read the resolution passed by the Council at its special meeting in March: 'That the honorary Freedom of the City be conferred upon Col Sir Malcolm Stoddart-Scott, Knight, officer of the most Excellent Order of the British Empire, upon

whom has been conferred the Territorial Decoration, Doctor of Medicine, Colonel late Royal Army Medical Corps, Deputy Lieutenant of the West Riding of Yorkshire, Member of Parliament, thus acknowledging his distinguished representation of the Ripon Division in Parliament during a continuous period of twenty-one years, recognising his eminent services in the public interest, particularly in the spheres of medicine, medical research and social welfare and expressing the high esteem in which he is held by the citizens of Ripon'.

A grant of £1,200 was made by the City Council to the Ripon City Development Association, set up to encourage firms to site new factories in Ripon. The Chamber of Trade asked its 115 members to contribute £1 each to the Association.

1971-72. Norman Wilfrid Pollard, Works Foreman

Born in 1910 in Stonebridgegate and attended St Wilfrid's Roman Catholic School. His first job was as an errand boy with Moss's Grocers; later worked at Crombie's Quarry and the Camp. Called up to the Royal Artillery 1940, captured in North Africa and taken to Italy where he escaped, but was recaptured and sent to Germany. Learnt the art of embroidery in captivity. Repatriated 1945 and began work at Allton's Steel Works. An active member and official of the Amalgamated Engineering Union and the Labour Party; organised many social events. Elected to Council 1960. He died in 1974.

May. A telegram of congratulations was received from the leader of the Opposition, the Rt Hon Harold Wilson M.P., by Councillor Norman Pollard shortly before he was installed as Ripon's first Labour Mayor.

June. Mr E. Woodhead and Mrs P. Wright started work as attendants at the new Tourist Information Kiosk set up in the Market Square ready for the 1971 tourist season. A visitors' book was available for tourists to sign and make comments. After considerable discussion, the City Council agreed to share the costs of installing a telephone in the kiosk.

July. The City Engineer received a letter from British Rail asking whether the Council had any objection to the removal of the steel viaduct which had carried the Harrogate-Northallerton railway over the River Ure at Ripon. The Board intended to start work in December.

August. The National Westminster Bank decided to close the branch at the corner of the Market Square and Kirkgate, which before the amalgamation of the two Banks had been the Ripon branch of the former Westminster Bank, and to continue business at the St Wilfrid branch of the former National Provincial Bank in the premises next to the Town Hall.

September. The Mayor presented a National Certificate in recognition of the high standard of service to the public reached by the Ripon Citizens' Advice Bureau. The award was received by the Bureau's Joint Organisers, Miss N. Wilkinson and Mr Ben Smith. Councillor W. H. Parnaby, Chairman of the Standing Committee, speaking at a social held in the Town Hall, recalled that the Bureau had been set up in 1968. He thanked the legal and professional representatives who had helped with training and the local authorities for their help and encouragement.

October. Extensions to the Fishergreen sewage disposal works, which had cost £322,000, were officially opened by Alderman F. W. Spence, Chairman of the Highways Committee. The new facilities would be adequate for the city's needs well into the 21st century.

A bomb disposal expert was called to examine a package believed to be an unexploded bomb in a litter basket at Ripon Bus Station, found by a Corporation workman. It proved to be two tobacco tins full of 0.22 ammunition. The expert said the package was similar in appearance to real bombs he had dealt with in Northern Ireland.

December. The Royal British Legion Home, *Lister House* at Sharow, received two gifts at an interval of six weeks sent anonymously through the post. Each gift was made up of £100 in £5 notes in a heavily taped envelope accompanied by an unsigned message. The messages read 'Please use the enclosed cash to give all your inmates a little bit better Christmas. Probably better television or food, drink, books, etc., anything which will make a good time. From a well wisher, Happy Christmas to all'.

The Finance Committee recommended the Council to guarantee the costs of the 1300th anniversary celebrations of the foundation of Ripon Cathedral up to a loss of £2,000. In addition, the Committee recommended the contribution of £100 towards a newspaper supplement of details of the programme and £370 to meet electricity charges and maintenance costs of floodlighting the Cathedral.

Work was completed on the reconstruction of two flying buttresses on the north choir aisle of the Cathedral. Mr Frank Marshall, one of the masons, had carved stone heads of the Dean, Canon R. Emmerson, Canon J. G. B. Ashworth and the late Venerable H. Graham.

January. Alderman W. R. Beaumont, Chairman of the Finance Committee, reported that he had authorised the Parks Superintendent not to purchase flowers to be worn during the civic visit to the hospitals on Christmas Day. He had done this after being told that the cost of the buttonholes would be 30p each. He asked members to consider whether the Council was justified in spending £20 per year in this way. The Committee was divided when it came to the vote, but buttonholes won the day.

February. As Ripon moved into its second week of blackouts as a result of the miners' strike, almost all industry in the area had been affected although no workers had been laid off. At T. and R. Williamson Limited's Varnish Works, paint had had to be made as in the old days — by hand in small quantities. With advance warnings of cuts from the C.E.G.B. and the co-operation of their own workers, Country Style managed to keep up its production. The Employment Exchange made special arrangements for workers who had been laid off to receive benefits. Supermarkets were finding it difficult to keep open during cuts and reported that some people were stocking up with foodstuffs, fearing a shortage.

March. The last mail to bear the 'Ripon' postmark was collected on 5 March. The replacement of the postmarks of Ripon, Knaresborough and Pateley Bridge by the 'Harrogate' mark was part of an economy drive in the Post Office. Local authorities and the Post Office Advisory Committee had failed to come up with a mutually acceptable name other than 'Harrogate', although a spokesman said that this was not necessarily permanent.

Canon Ralph Emmerson, a Residentiary Canon of Ripon Cathedral since 1966, was consecrated Bishop of Knaresborough in York Minster, in succession to the Rt Revd Howard Cruse, who had given up the suffragan bishopric because of failing sight.

April. Although the Ripon representatives indicated that the Ripon City Council preferred the generic title 'Claro' for the second tier authority, the Joint Committee organising the administration decided on the name 'Harrogate District Council'. As a result of consultation, the Joint Committee agreed to support Ripon's application to retain its Mayor and civic ceremonial. The Clerk, Mr Neville Knox, reported that the new Local Government Bill would go to the House of Lords on 10 May and it was expected to receive the Royal Assent later in that month.

At a meeting between representatives of the City Council, the Dean and Chapter, the Cathedral architects and the W.R.C.C., various methods of diverting traffic away from the Cathedral were discussed. It was finally agreed that a temporary solution would be to divert heavy traffic from Stonebridgegate along Priest Lane over a Bailey bridge at Low Mill and on to the Boroughbridge Road via Firs Avenue. The suggestion attracted violent opposition and was dropped.

The grand three-month Festival to commemorate the 1,300th anniversary of the building of the first church by St Wilfrid on the Cathedral site started at the beginning of May. Almost every aspect of church life in the Diocese had its place and many organisations and individuals worked hard in its preparation and in its celebration. Major-General Sir Charles Dalton of Grewelthorpe organised the Festival appeal, which not only financed events in the Festival itself but also provided a permanent system of floodlighting to the exterior of the Cathedral and portable staging for productions of all kinds. A limited edition of 1,300 commemorative plates was made by Spode. The Diocesan Youth Committee organised a multi-media service when the pews were removed from the nave and the altar placed on a central dais so that the congregation stood or sat round it. During the Eucharist, the Communion Elements were brought to the altar in dance; music was provided by live guitars and selections were played from both *Godspell* and *Jesus Christ Superstar*.

The main children's contribution to the Festival was the splendid performances of Benjamin Britten's *Noye's Fludde* on three successive evenings. More than 200 Ripon school children took part, the highlight being the Procession of Animals with children wearing beautifully-fashioned masks.

June began with the combined Ripon, York and Scarborough Choral Societies singing Bach's *Mass in B Minor*. Crowds were expected to reach 40,000 at a two-day Edwardian and modern Steam Fair on Ripon racecourse, but in fact scarcely totalled 9,000 as a result of wet weather. The joint organisers, Mr Charles Doubtfire and Ripon Rugby Club, only just managed to recover expenses. Despite the rain and mud under foot the majority of the attractions went ahead, ending with a gigantic firework display on Saturday night. The next day the Dean conducted an open-air service, when a fairground organ provided music for the hymns. The three Northern Cathedral choirs from Ripon, York and Durham sang Evensong in the Cathedral and for the first time gave a concert in the assembly hall of the Secondary Modern School. Local children participated with students of Ripon College in a production of a children's play *Rippondell* staged in the garden of *Minster House*. Ripon College students and staff also performed William Walton's oratorio *Belshazzar's Feast* in the Cathedral. July saw recitals by Mr Alan Cuckson on the harpsichord, by brass bands conducted by Mr Harry Mortimer and a 100-strong male voice choir.

The principal event of the Festival was the visit of Her Majesty the Queen Mother to attend the Mothers' Union Festival Service in the Cathedral. Her Majesty was presented with No. 1 of the Spode plates, and she took tea with 2,000 of her fellow Union members in the garden of the *Spa Hotel*.

In August, 'St Wilfrid' was again played by Mr Geoffrey Tanner, leading the procession of 20 floats decorated on the theme *Thirteen Hundred Years*. The Mayor of Ripon, Wisconsin, U.S.A. and his party who were visiting the city joined in with the festivities and attended in the evening a morality play, *Rex Vivus*, presented by the 'Elizabethans'. The American guests accompanied the civic procession to the Cathedral for the final event of the Festival, an ecumenical service at which His Eminence the Cardinal Archbishop of Utrecht preached the sermon.

1972-73. WALTER ROY BEAUMONT, Company Secretary

Mayor 1959-60, 1982-83

May. The Dean revived an ancient custom when he led members of the Cathedral congregation in a perambulation round the city. Boys from the Choir School, carrying branches of palm as the Blue Coat boys did in 1795, were at the front of the procession and followed the same route singing at traditional places where prayers were said for city and home. The Ripon Perambulation probably originated as a Rogationtide procession when a blessing was asked for the crops and work on the farm.

Mr George Simpkin became the Ripon Hornblower on the retirement of Mr Brian Waines.

Councillor J. B. Briscombe resigned from the City Council because he felt he could not work with the newly-elected Labour candidates on the East Ward, Councillors J. McGarr and N. Fortune. Mr Briscombe said he would probably contest the 1973 first election for the new Harrogate District Council.

June. An exhibition was mounted of Canon J. B. Ashworth's drawings, which traced the history of the Cathedral's architecture, starting with imaginative pictures of St Wilfrid's original church which was described by the Saint's biographer as being made of polished stone with pillars and porches. The drawings were later published under the title *Prospects of Ripon*.

Mr J. Crossley Eccles, Sales Director of T. and R. Williamson Limited since 1944, retired after almost 50 years' service. He was well known for his skill as an artist; examples of his work are the Freedom Scrolls presented by the city to R.A.F. Topcliffe in 1969 and to Councillors Beaumont and Parnaby in 1980.

July. The Ripon Civic Society published *Ripon — Some Aspects of its History*, compiled by six members of the society who had each specialised in a particular aspect of the city's history: 'Administration of Local Affairs' by J. M. Hagerty, 'Medieval Society' by Mary Mauchline, 'The Ancient Hospitals' by E. Pearson, 'The Georgian Town' by Kathleen Bumstead, 'Victorian and Edwardian Times' by J. M. Younge, and 'Country Gentry and Estates' by W. J. Petchey.

September. The newly-formed Ripon and District Abbeyfield Society launched an appeal to raise £2,000 towards the purchase and conversion of a suitable house for use as an Abbeyfield Home to accommodate six or eight elderly people. This paved the way for the establishment of a home in Church Lane.

October. Queues formed at the west door of Ripon Cathedral when nearly 8,000 people attended the Festival of Flowers designed by Mrs Feodora Humphreys. It was hoped that any profits would help to pay off the outstanding costs of the Cathedral floodlighting.

Mr Harry Pearson retired after 38 years as verger at the Cathedral. The Dean presented him with a cheque for £132 from parishioners at a Harvest Supper. Mr Pearson had received letters of appreciation and goodwill from many people, one contribution coming from a doctor in California who had visited the Cathedral on a number of occasions.

November. Mr Charles Doubtfire, the well-known showman who had based his amusement empire in Ripon since 1939, died aged fifty-five. He had started as a hoop-la stall boy and gradually built up his own amusement empire. His fun fairs in the Market Place and the Bus Station car park (whichever site was in favour with the City Council at the time) had become a part of the city's traditions. Mr Doubtfire's only son declared his intention of continuing the business.

December. The question of providing sports facilities at Quarry Moor was again considered, this time by the Estates and Baths Committee, who decided that the Ripon Amateur Athletics Club should be asked to reduce its minimum requirements. Mr Alan Williamson, the City Engineer, had said that the standard of facilities which had been suggested would cost £50,000.

Mr T. G. Smallwood, the executive manager of the Ripon City Development Association, said that during its first 12 months new factories had been attracted to provide 100 extra jobs. This was halfway towards the initial aim which was to replace the 250 jobs lost when the paintworks closed in 1969.

January. Peter Alliss, the Ryder Cup golfer, opened an extension to the clubhouse built by voluntary labour at the Ripon Golf Club.

The Revd Walter Dillam, vicar of St Wilfrid's Church, Harrogate, was installed as a Residentiary Canon of the Cathedral, in place of Archdeacon Turnbull who had resigned his administrative membership of the Chapter. Canon Dillam was to be treasurer and to have the oversight of the maintenance of the Chapter's property.

A Ripon Canal Restoration Association was formed at a public meeting held in the *Unicorn Hotel* to support a £213,000 scheme for the reopening of the canal and the construction of a boating marina near the canal basin in Dallamires Lane. An action committee was set up to prevent the land proposed for the marina from being developed as a light industrial site. The Ripon City Council reacted strongly and wrote to the W.R.C.C. asking it not to give planning permission for a marina on the site but to allow Nor-Farm Services Limited to build a factory. The marina application was refused and the Canal Association lodged an appeal which was rejected by the Department of the Environment in May 1974. Strong opinions were expressed on both sides and the controversy flared up at a Ripon Planning Committee meeting in March, when Councillor David Fisher was ousted as the Committee's chairman because of his support for the marina.

February. Alderman F. W. Spence was chosen to be the Chairman of the governing body of Ripon Grammar School, following Major Norman Wells who had been Chairman for the previous five years.

The Bishop Monkton Village Society called a meeting to promote opposition to the 'Blue Route', the preferred route for the planned Dishforth-Pudsey motorway. The Ripon Civic Society and the City Council both wrote to the Department of the Environment giving support for the motorway.

Documents from 1108 onwards relating to the administration of Fountains Abbey, in the collection of the late H. L. Bradfer-Lawrence of Sharow End, Ripon, were given to the Yorkshire Archaeological Society by his family. Subsequent research proved these records to be of inestimable value in constructing the economic history of the Abbey.

March. The W.R.C.C. Forward Planning Department considered various schemes for the development of the Deanery Fields between the Bus Station and the Cathedral. Four draft schemes were considered for the site: a group of maisonettes, a supermarket of 14,000 square feet, eight shops, or car parking.

The G.P.O. announced that it hoped to acquire the Dissenters' Graveyard, adjoining the telephone exchange in Allhallowgate, as a site for future extension. The Civic Society, who hoped to improve the amenities of this quiet 'oasis' in the town centre, wrote to the City Council opposing the application. The graveyard had been disused since 1871 when a new Congregational Church had been built in North Street to replace the now demolished Temple at the rear of the burial ground.

While the stonework above the crossing in the Cathedral was being repaired the altar was moved closer to the congregation in the nave. The Dean reported in the Cathedral *Newsletter* that there had been enthusiastic approval of the general idea of clearing the crossing and bringing the altar further west.

An outline planning application was made by the Harewood Housing Society to build 40 flats at *The Knoll* in Palace Road.

April. Mr John Spencer's devotion and service during his 20 years as headmaster and superintendent of Dr Barnardo's Springhill Boarding School were praised by Mr Leon Smallwood at a meeting of teachers, children and friends of the school to mark Mr Spencer's retirement.

The Mayor, Alderman W. R. Beaumont, and Councillor W. H. Parnaby were elected as the City's representatives on the new first-tier authority until April 1974 when the North Yorkshire County Council would take over.

1973-74. WALTER JACK BAILY, Works Superintendent

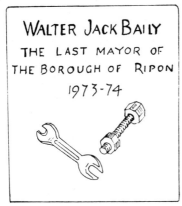

WALTER JACK BAILY

THE LAST MAYOR OF

THE BOROUGH OF RIPON

1973-74

Born 1921 in Camberwell and educated Peckham Central School and Beaufoy Technical College. Served seven years with the Royal Engineers. A trained fitter and turner, he was employed by the Allton Group on coming to Ripon. Elected to Council in 1955 and has sat continuously ever since. The last mayor of the municipal borough and the first of the City Council. Justice of the Peace 1962-79. Chairman of the Ripon branches of the Royal Engineer Association and Age Concern, Secretary A.U.E.W., and associated with the Amateur Operatic Society for 25 years. Treasurer of Ripon Children's Sports Day for 20 years; in the *Year of the Child* his appeal refurbished the Children's Corner in the County Library Branch and provided additional books for junior and infant schools. Also Mayor 1979-80.

May. Exploratory excavations on the outside of the north transept showed the Cathedral to have been built on cobbles and red sand. Mr C. Ward, the Cathedral architect, said that sand was a sub-soil in many areas of this country and the fact that there had been a building on the Cathedral site for 1,300 years was reassuring. However, he was concerned that the heavy traffic on Minster Road should be re-routed.

Parents of 320 children who would attend the new Greystones School threatened to keep them at home if the City Council did not provide a footpath and safety barriers alongside Quarry Moor Lane. The completion of the buildings was delayed due to a shortage of labour and materials, and the children received part-time education at Moorside School until 19 November when the new school opened.

June. The elections took place to choose the six Ripon members of the second-tier authority which would form the new Harrogate District Council. Councillor Graham Scott was voted Chairman of the new Council. The Home Office informed the Town Clerk that it would not be necessary for the City Council to make a formal application for the continuation of city status; at the appropriate time, the Home Secretary would advise the Queen on the continued use of all prerogative titles of Ripon. The successor council received the approval of the Queen in December.

The death occurred of Colonel Sir Malcolm Stoddart-Scott, who had been M.P. for Ripon for more than 25 years. A memorial service was held in Ripon Cathedral on 29 June.

July. The Yorkshire and Humberside Sports Council included a scheme for a sports complex in their 1975-76 list, and the City Engineer said that levelling of the former refuse tip at Quarry Moor would start later in the year.

The three major appointments to the staff of the new Harrogate District Council were announced: Chief Executive and Director of Administration, Mr J. Neville Knox (former Town Clerk of Harrogate); Director of Financial Services, Mr Ronald Wooley (former Borough Treasurer of Harrogate); Director of Technical Services, Mr Robert Mayo.

The Ripon Civic Society asked the Minister for the Environment to intervene and stop the demolition of two shops, Boots Limited and the Army and Navy Stores, the last remaining examples of 18th-century architecture on the east side of the Market Place. The owners wished to replace the buildings, which needed major structural repairs.

Mr David Austick (Liberal) was elected M.P. for Ripon in the by-election caused by the death of Sir Malcolm Stoddart-Scott. He won the seat with a majority of 946 over the Conservative candidate, Dr Keith Hampson.

August. Police Sergeant Edley Grindle was awarded the R.S.P.C.A. bronze medal, and a commendation for bravery, for his part in rescuing 16 bullocks from a submerged cattle wagon which had toppled into the Ripon Canal near Ox Close.

September. The Department of the Environment decided not to intervene in a dispute between residents of Redshaw Close and Econ Engineering who had erected a factory building only 22 feet from three bungalows in the Close. The firm offered to 'camouflage' the 28-foot high wall by the use of creeper vegetation.

Mr Joseph Cooper, who had taken over as headmaster at Ripon Secondary School, said that he was determined to play his part in dispelling the 'second-best' image which he claimed secondary modern schools had in comparison with grammar schools.

The Dean announced that the Chapter was seeking permission to move the fine 18th-century memorial to Sir Edward Blackett of *Newby Hall* in the north transept to a place under the south-west tower of the Cathedral. The four-ton memorial, which stood over the family burial vault, was in danger of collapsing because of cracks which had appeared in the transept wall. The 15 lead coffins from the vault would be buried in the churchyard.

Throughout the year references and statements were made concerning the possible start of the W.R.C.C.'s planned relief road, ending with an announcement in December by Lieutenant-Colonel G. A. Leech, Highways Engineer for the North Yorkshire County Council, that it was unlikely to begin before 1975.

November. Alderman F. W. Spence suggested that after local government reform in April 1974 the Mayor should become known as the Wakeman. He said that as the new Harrogate District would have a Borough Mayor, Ripon's Mayor should be called by the ancient title given to its medieval law officer.

William Morrison Supermarkets Limited sought outline planning permission for a five-acre shopping and community centre complex, which would incorporate the Croft and Blackburn garage with its frontage on the Market Square. The plans included parking space for 430 cars and provided for an arcade of shops running from the garage to link with the new supermarket and community centre, an alteration to the bus station with new queuing stands and further parking on Deanery Fields. A model of the proposed development was put on display to the public in December. The development caused widespread controversy over the next 18 months. Ripon traders formed the Ripon Independent Shopkeepers' Association and wrote to the W.R.C.C. objecting to the proposals, pointing out that there were already eight small self-service stores in the city.

The Civic Society issued a statement pointing out that this was the first time that a coherent scheme had been produced for the development of the deteriorating area on the east side of the Market Place. However, they warned that the development of a supermarket of the proposed size, a shopping arcade, the retention of the bus station on the east side and the extra car parking would move the centre of gravity of the city eastwards, at the expense of businesses on the west side of the Square. The Society was opposed to the sale of public land for use as a public car park which would fall under the control of a private firm. At a public meeting held at the Hugh Ripley Hall in March 1974, an action group was formed to lobby the Harrogate District Council which would take control in April. Again, the major objection was the sale of civic-owned land for the project. Councillor John McGarr was the main supporter of the scheme, and he campaigned for it throughout.

At the end of March, Morrisons offered an additional £35,000 to help pay for a community centre or public hall as part of the scheme, in a letter to the City Council. The Council's debate ended with acceptance in principle, and the passing-on of the proposals to the Harrogate District Council for the resolution of the financial details. The main topic of the election in April for two representatives for Ripon on the District Council was the supermarket proposal: only the two Liberal candidates were opposed to the scheme. In June 1974, the Ripon Successor Council reaffirmed its support for the proposals by 10 votes

to three. A week later the Harrogate Council turned down the application.

The *City Café* in Ripon Market Place North was sold to an unnamed buyer for £94,000. The Wakefield firm of bakers, Charles Hagenbach and Sons Limited, later opened a retail bread and confectionary shop and self-service restaurant.

December. Mr Brian Waines, who had resigned the job of Ripon Hornblower in 1972, returned to the post.

February. Mr Gavin Macpherson, Lecturer in Transport Engineering, of Magdalen Road, published a report on *Ripon and Traffic* in which he suggested a bypass between Harrogate Road and North Bridge taking a route along the old railway line.

It was reported that most factories were managing to cope despite threats of short-time working because of the national power restrictions. Ripon firms were using generators and rearranging schedules. The W.R.C.C. prepared plans to open 28 emergency centres of fuel and power if the situation became worse.

The Mayor opened a new Youth Centre at Ripon Secondary Modern School. The centre was fully equipped for football, badminton and volleyball, and in addition had a modern coffee bar, disc-jockey booth and dance floor. The centre would be under the leadership of Mr David Uffindall, youth tutor to the school.

March. A civic funeral was held at Ripon Cathedral for Mrs Elizabeth M. Boddy, a member of Ripon City Council and the new Harrogate District Council. Her greatest interest had been her work as Chairman of the Ripon Housing Committee, and she had been instrumental in getting the Bondgate old persons' flats project under way.

Dr Keith Hampson, Conservative candidate, was elected as M.P. for Ripon with a 4,000 majority over the sitting Liberal member, Mr David Austick. The Ripon Successor Council decided to consider planning applications forwarded by the Harrogate District Council for observations in full council.

Mrs Joan Connor was appointed Clerk to the Ripon Successor Council.

The Ripon Group of the Ramblers' Association called for an inquiry on proposals by Cawood Wharton Limited to excavate gravel from 150 acres of farm and parkland between *Studley Royal* and Ripon.

Ripon's first streaker, a 20-year-old soldier from Claro Barracks, was fined £50 by the city magistrates. The defendant was first seen jogging down North Street from the direction of the Market Square completely naked on a Saturday morning. He then disappeared through the archway of the *Saracen's Head* and two police officers found the defendant getting dressed in the public house. The Chairman of the Bench, Mr F. T. Collinson, commented 'I don't know from where this name streaker originates; it should be more like freaker'.

A number of people were injured and damage estimated at £60,000 was caused by terrorist bombs exploding at Claro Barracks. The main damage was to the N.A.A.F.I. building where one wall was ripped away. It was thought three of four persons were involved, one of them probably female.

April. Ripon Court House sat as a court for the North Yorkshire Police area for the first time on 3 April.

At midnight on Sunday 7 April, local government old-style ended and a new District Council which by Charter is known as the 'Council of the Borough of Harrogate', responsible for the administration of 515 square miles, came into full operation. The new authority lost responsibility for libraries, consumer protection and most of the County's highways, but acquired more responsibility for housing and planning matters.

Workmen discovered a door which had been invisibly encased in an outer wall of the Old Deanery for an estimated 150 years. The original wooden door was still on its hinges and it was decided to use it as the main entrance to the restaurant.

Mr Moe Sawyer, who started his apprenticeship with R. Ackrill Limited at the age of 14 in 1923, retired. His first experience of printing newspapers was in 1926 during the General Strike, when the only way of getting newspapers on the street was by using the services of apprentices and management.

1974-75. EDWARD IVOR JONES, Store Manager

CIVITAS RIPONENSIS

Born 1905 in Liverpool and educated at St Margaret's Higher Grade School and Liverpool Institute. First worked for G. H. Ireland and Sons, Importers of Maize, but from 1930 was employed by F. W. Woolworth and Company at various locations in Lancashire and Yorkshire. Appointed manager at Ripon in 1950. Retired 1965. During the war a W.O. II with the R.A.O.C. and served in the U.K. and in Palestine. Elected to Council in 1965; Mayor in the year following local government reorganisation; the Council had resolved that the title of Mayor should be retained and a Royal Charter was obtained to preserve Ripon's style as a City. Helped by the Clerk, Mrs Joan Connor, and fellow councillors, the main task of his year was to adjust the work of the City Council to the changed circumstances. At the close of his year attended the annual Festival of St John of Beverley in Beverley Minster.

May. Theakston's of Masham, an independent family brewery since 1827, signed a contract to take over the state-owned Carlisle Brewery.

The B.B.C. *It's a Knockout* contest was held on Ripon racecourse with teams from Ripon and Rotherham. The latter won by 13 points to nine.

Mr Philip Harrison, 21-year-old history student at Ripon College, undertook to carry out the Hornblower's duties during term time and Mr Cyril Hawley, the Mayor's Sergeant-at-Mace and previously the Hornblower, agreed to blow the Horn during the College vacations.

June. Harrogate Borough Council were unwilling to pay the cost of the current maintenance of Ripon Cathedral's floodlighting for 1974 as there had been no provision made in the estimates.

A farewell party was held for Ripon's only Church Army Sister, Sister Mary Crathorne, on her retirement. She was presented with two cheques, one from friends and the other from the Dean and Chapter.

July. As under the 1972 Local Government Reform Act no elections could be held until after December 1975, two vacancies on the City Council were filled by co-option. Mr Archie Keighley, Labour, and Councillor Jack Briscombe, Independent, were appointed.

A 'clean-up' of the River Skell was carried out by pupils of Ripon Secondary School. Ten tons of rubbish were removed from a one-mile stretch of the river and part of the Laver. They were supervised by Mr David Uffindall.

William Morrison Supermarkets Limited produced a new scheme for the conversion of the former Croft and Blackburn garage premises into an arcade with four shop units and two kiosks leading to a new supermarket at the rear. The upper floors of the Market Square building would house administration and staff facilities and the facade facing the Square would be left substantially untouched. Plans included a service yard and a staff car park. The site area would be 3,704 square metres. Office staff would number 10 and other staff about a hundred. There were no proposals for additional car parking space to cater for the customers of the proposed store and it was largely because of the omission of this provision, a requirement of the original consent, that Harrogate District Council refused the application. The Company took the refusal to Appeal in January 1976 and the Department of the Environment announced their decision to allow the appeal in July 1976.

August. A petition signed by almost 300 people was handed to Ripon City Council for a clean-up of the Alma Weir and the basin, which had become eyesores.

Harrogate Council operated a summer play scheme at Moorside Junior School during the holidays, in which over 100 children enjoyed football, cricket, rounders and tennis. There was also painting, knitting and a dolls' house for the younger ones. Both the Fire Service and Police Force put on displays.

Ripon's 1690 Horn was missing when the City's *It's a Knockout* team arrived from Bayreuth at Manchester Airport. Mr Cyril Hawley, the Sergeant-at-Mace, had discovered that his suitcase which contained the Horn was not on the plane. A thorough search by the airport authorities recovered the property and the Horn was returned to Ripon the next day. The Mayor, Councillor Ivor Jones, who accompanied the party, had presented two pieces of the municipal Spode china, dated about 1787, to the Burgomaster of Bayreuth and his wife. There was considerable criticism of this action by the Council, who asked the Clerk and Councillors Spence and Parnaby to carry out a complete inventory of the City's treasures. Mr Robert Copeland, a director of Spode Limited, visited Ripon in 1975 to examine the dinner service and said that it was historically important as he thought it was the earliest known municipal-crested service to be supplied by his firm. One of the hand-painted dishes was presented on permanent loan for display in the famous Spode museum at Stoke-on-Trent.

September. Army bomb disposal experts from Catterick were called to Claro Barracks to examine a cellophane package which was found in one of the accommodation blocks. The police and fire brigade were called and the camp was evacuated. In the end, the parcel proved to be completely harmless.

October. Ripon was one of the four towns, with York, Selby and Skipton, in the new county where comprehensive secondary education had not yet been introduced, and there was speculation about the intentions of the Council. Mr Brian Stanley, the new headmaster of Ripon Grammar School, said to parents at Speech Day that he would support any campaign which would prevent the school becoming part of a comprehensive education system. In November, a group of teachers and parents called the Ripon Action for Comprehensive Education, was set up under the chairmanship of Mr J. H. Cooper, headmaster of the City Secondary School. Later in the month, Dr Keith Hampson, M.P. for Ripon, affirmed his support in principle of comprehensive education. These differences in opinion were to sharpen over the next 18 months while the County Council decided its policy in the matter.

In January 1975, a working party was appointed by the North Yorkshire Education Committee to consider the reorganisation of secondary education in Ripon in accordance with the government's requirement for local authorities to report progress in the introduction of comprehensive education in their areas. As a result of the party's work, the Education Department issued in October 1,500 copies of a consultative paper, showing how Ripon's schools might be absorbed into the County's comprehensive system. The working party's report stated that it was important to retain the 110 places for boarders at the Grammar School and that provision should be made for future growth in numbers. Schemes which involved a separate sixth-form college were rejected because of lack of numbers, and the three-tier school system was thought to be impracticable. The document put forward alternative schemes: an amalgamation of the two present schools to form one ten-form entry comprehensive, or for each of the two present schools to be converted to five-form entry schools. It was hoped that consultation could be

completed for the working party to report to the March 1976 meeting of the Education Committee. The discussions revealed deep divisions between the supporters of comprehensive education and those who wished to retain selection and separate grammar secondary schools. Dr Hampson suggested there should be a referendum of parents in the city.

The Harrogate General Purposes Committee voted 32 to 15 in favour of a single school and parents and staff at a meeting of the County Secondary School voted overwhelmingly the same way. Parents and staff at the Grammar School, however, were equally determined to retain the existing system and set up an action group. The Thameside Council's victory in the Appeal Court over the Education Secretary, Mr Fred Mulley, heralded a stay of execution for authorities opposed to comprehensive education and gave encouragement to the Grammar School Action Group. The teachers of the County Secondary School approached Mr Mulley by letter calling for an end to the delays in implementation. In October, the action groups of Ripon and Skipton Grammar Schools and the Skipton Girls' High School joined forces to fight the N.Y.C.C.

The North Yorkshire Secondary Schools Sub-Committee in December 1976 at last approved the single split-site school for 11- to 18-year-olds for Ripon. It was expected the school would take 1,730 pupils including a sixth-form of two hundred and thirty. The Education Committee endorsed the decision, and pressed on with public meetings at which officials and Chairmen of both the Education and Finance Committees attended to explain the plan. However, in July 1977 the full County Council backed the alternative two-school scheme and instructed the officials to send this plan to the Minister for approval. In September the Secretary of State, Mrs Shirley Williams, directed the Council to prepare for a single comprehensive school in Ripon and required a reply by the end of the month. The Council decided to take legal advice, which ruled that Mrs Williams had exceeded her powers. However, the High Court decided that she was legally within her rights to act in the matter. In January 1979, the Council decided to appeal but before the case was heard the new Conservative Government announced that local authorities would no longer be compelled to introduce or to extend systems of comprehensive education.

November. A third bomb scare at Ripon's Claro Barracks resulted in the evacuation of 150 soldiers, wives and children. An aluminium keg similar to some bombs used in Northern Ireland had been found.

December. The County Highways Sub-Committee turned down a request for the imposition of a weight restriction on heavy traffic using Minster Road to protect the Cathedral.

The Ripon Choral Society, with the Harrogate Chamber Orchestra conducted by Ronald Perrin, gave a performance of *The Christmas Story*, set to music by Heinrich Schutz. Two hundred people attended, bringing rugs and hot-water bottles to withstand the cold in the Cathedral.

January. The Countess of Dartmouth, Chairman of the Historic Buildings Commission, visited Ripon in connection with European Architectural Year. She was received by the Mayor at the Town Hall and later viewed various buildings in the city including the Gazebo behind Park Street where Sir Richard Graham, President of the Civic Society, explained the plans which the Society had prepared for its restoration. The Gazebo takes the form of two small towers with pantiled roofs, joined by an elevated terrace walk, and was probably built about 1702, the same time as the Obelisk. The building had deteriorated over the previous two decades and was in urgent need of restoration. The Department of the Environment agreed to fund half the cost of £16,000, and negotiations were carried out over the following two years in order to get the work under way. However, early in 1977, the Society decided to shelve the scheme because of the national economic situation.

February. The Dean discussed in his *Newsletter* the question of floodlighting the Cathedral during a time of crisis and energy conservation. The Chapter had taken a compromise course of maintaining full floodlighting at weekends and illuminating the central tower alone on other evenings.

The first statement of the year on the Ripon Relief Road was made by Colonel Leech. He reported that the current estimated cost of the scheme was £919,000, including the purchase price of property and construction work. The relief road would be included in the County Transport Policy and Programme of Works to begin in the year 1976-77. A sketch map was released to show the line planned for the new road: it led from Borrage Bridge crossing Somerset Row to the east of Firby Lane through the present junction of Park Street and Blossomgate, then bearing across St Wilfrid's Place to rejoin the A61 in North Street to the north of Coltsgate Hill. A roundabout would be formed at the Somerset Row junction and the new carriageway would be 10 metres in width with a three metre wide footpath on either side. To ensure a free flow of traffic in the east-west direction, it was proposed to improve Water Skellgate and Skellgarths. The city's representatives on the County Highways Sub-Committee welcomed the scheme; however, Mr Ian Collinson, the President of the Chamber of Trade, and Mr E. Pearson, Chairman of the Civic Society, warned that the route would do nothing to remove heavy through-traffic from the city and that a bypass or the 'Blue Route' of the Pudsey-Dishforth motorway was required as well.

March. Harrogate Planning Committee refused permission for Redlands Quarries Limited to build 500 houses in Doublegates Quarry, Clotherholme, which would have increased the Ripon population by 10 per cent.

Ripon's oldest man, Mr John Henry Wray, died two days before his 100th birthday. He had lived in Ripon all his life, had attended the Grammar School and had continued the shoemaking business in Queen Street which had been founded by his grandfather in 1863. He had retired only four years before his death.

April. There was considerable opposition to the N.Y.C.C. plan for double yellow lines along the sections of the A61 within the city centre, particularly amongst traders in the area. The objectors maintained that the restrictions would enable heavy lorries to travel much faster through the centre. A similar worry was expressed by the Dean with respect to vehicles passing the Cathedral after the improvements were completed in St Marygate.

1975-76. JOHN HENRY RICHMOND, Hotelier

Born 1936 at Kirkby Malzeard, of a well-known 'Highside' family and a descendant of the Richmonds of Laverton Hall. Proprietor of the *Nordale Hotel* in North Road. Educated at Ripon Grammar School. Elected to the City Council in 1967 and, after the local government reorganisation, to the Harrogate District and North Yorkshire County Councils. He was the youngest mayor for many years. In the American Bicentenial Year (1976) went to Ripon, California, for the first meeting of the Mayors of the three Ripons: in Yorkshire, Wisconsin and California. Chillingham Horns were presented to the American cities. This visit promoted further contacts and exchange visits of golfers. Held office in the Chamber of Trade and Tourist Association and active in the promotion of light industry and tourism. Strongly advocated the retention of selective secondary education in Ripon and a leading advocate of the inner relief road. A member of the Rotary Club and a Methodist lay preacher.

May. The Harrogate Planning Committee approved planning permission to convert the *Café Victoria* in the Market Place to a store for Boots the Chemist. The new store would have a sales area of 6,000 sq. ft. and a stock area of 3,000 sq. ft. The adjoining pedestrian way would provide a link to Blossomgate and a rear service access would also be made. The permission required the retention of the 15th-century timber-framed building fronting the market place. Originally a burgage property, Roger Wright, a mercer and Mayor of Ripon in 1677, 1695 and 1707 lived here; later owners followed various trades and in the 18th century the building became the *York Minster Inn*. Much later it became the *Café Victoria*, coming into the Oliver family

in the early 1920s and passing through four generations up to the time of the sale. During the erection
of the new store behind the old Market Place building,
the latter was propped up awaiting the final stage of
joining the old with the new. At the end of March
1977, the architects in charge of the development
declared that the frontage was unsafe, gave the Harrogate Council notice of demolition and two days later,
on a Sunday morning, the demolition gang moved
in. The Council insisted on the erection of a near-
exact replica. Some of the ancient roof timbers were
preserved and put on permanent display on the
archway wall.

T. and R. Williamson Limited celebrated the
bicentenary of the foundation of the company with
a dinner at the *Ripon Spa Hotel*. The company was
founded by Daniel Williamson, a banker, who settled
in Ripon in 1745. He was also an artist and heraldic
painter who had learned the secrets of varnish making from the French. In 1975, the firm employed over
100 people.

The Department of the Environment published a
public consultation paper and held an exhibition in
Ripon of plans and other relevant material on the
Dishforth motorway spur. In addition, mobile exhibitions were held in all the villages and towns near the
routes. The public were asked to express their views
on the four alternative schemes. The City Council,
the Civic Society, and the Chamber of Trade were all
in favour of the 'Blue Route', but Dr Hampson, M.P.
for Ripon, expressed his opposition to this scheme
and thus attracted much local criticism. West Yorkshire
Council and Harrogate District Council also strongly
backed the 'Blue Route'.

The Harrogate Council announced an improvement
scheme, at a cost of £80,885 including landscaping,
of derelict sites in the Lickley Street area.

July. The Yorkshire and Humberside Regional
Office of the Department of the Environment published an important survey of Ripon. The main aim
of the study was to investigate ways in which the city's
environment could be improved in the short term
while retaining longer perspectives. Schemes were
put forward to improve the River Skell area from the
Rustic Bridge to its confluence with the Ure by providing foot underpasses to the road bridges, restoring
and landscaping the Alma Weir basin and providing
seats. It was recommended that the Market Square
should be partially pedestrianised and that the
derelict areas on both sides be improved. The report
suggested there should be a traffic management
scheme and that, when tipping was completed on
the Deanery Fields, the area should be landscaped
as a park and picnic area, and that any proposals to
use the site for car parking should be resisted. One
of the main recommendations was the formation of
a conservation committee for Ripon to prepare a
policy and plan for the conservation area and to
advise on the implementation of the proposals.

August. Two thousand people, representing Royal
British Legion branches from all over the north of
England, attended the 25th anniversary of the

opening of *Lister House*, Sharow. To mark the occasion
the Legion's National Chairman, Mr T. S. C. Busby,
officially opened the residents' new recreation room.

September. The Saxon crypt in the Cathedral was
converted into a treasury with a grant from the
National Trust to house an extensive range of priceless
communion plate gathered from all parts of the
diocese.

A Quarry Moor action group of interested bodies
was set up to study the possible use of the land as a
sports complex. Eoin Development Limited, Leeds,
wanted to lease the land and build a complex costing
about £130,000. The City Council, however, was
opposed to development by private enterprise.

October. A layout for an extension of the Dallamires
Lane Industrial Estate was agreed at a meeting of the
Ripon Development Association, and it was expected
that the first new factories might be ready by the end
of 1976 with the ultimate provision of 200-500 new jobs.

All Roads by William Mayne, a play telling the story
of St Wilfrid, his work and travels, was successfully
staged in the nave of the Cathedral. Sixty people from
all parts of the area had been preparing for this
production for eight weeks. The play was directed by
Mr Derek Stevens, head of creative arts at the City
School.

A table made about 1850 by William Moss at his
works in the Market Place was purchased by the
Harrogate and Ripon Councils at an auction sale in
London. The piece is now housed in the Council
Chamber at the Town Hall.

November. The death was announced of Councillor
David Fisher. He had been educated at Ripon
Grammar School and his home was at *Field House*,
Canal Road. Councillor Fisher had taken particular
interest in education and planning matters in the city
and had been chairman of the City Planning
Committee.

December. The Rt Revd Hetley Price, Suffragan
Bishop of Doncaster, was appointed Bishop of Ripon
to succeed Dr John Moorman. The new Bishop was
enthroned before a congregation of 1,500 in Ripon
Cathedral on 10 April. The Bishop suffered a stroke
in September 1976 and after a second one supervened
in March 1977 he announced his resignation. This
news, coming only 11 months after his enthronement,
brought great sadness to the people of the diocese.
Bishop Hetley Price died only a fortnight later. A
funeral service was held in the Cathedral which the
Archbishop of York, the Bishops of Knaresborough
and Manchester, and civic dignitaries from throughout
the diocese attended.

Miss M. D. Gage retired as Principal of the College
of Education. The Revd Herbert Batey succeeded her
as Vice Principal of the new united College of Ripon
and York St John.

January. Mr Chris Martins, a former director of
tourism for York, published a report on a survey of
Ripon in terms of tourist promotion which had been
commissioned by the City Council. He maintained that
Ripon had a mass of attractions to offer the tourist and
strongly recommended the setting up of a Ripon

Tourist Promotion Association. The City Council agreed to put up £1,000 to start an association and in March the Chamber of Trade called a special meeting at the Town Hall and agreed to support the idea. At a public meeting in May, Mr Harry Whitaker, Director of Yorkshire and Humberside Tourist Board, offered full backing. Councillor John Richmond was elected Chairman and Dr John Whitehead was appointed part-time secretary at the first meeting of the Association in December.

February. The Dean announced that the Chapter was facing a financial crisis over the costs of repair and maintenance work on the Cathedral fabric, and said that the workforce would have to be reduced from three stonemasons to one, who in the immediate future would carry out routine maintenance only.

District Councillors made a tour of the city to assess the changes suggested in the Department of the Environment Survey. This resulted in the Planning Committee setting up a Special Conservation and Environment Committee to advise on some of the Report's recommendations and to initiate individual projects. The new Committee (of 12 members) included representatives from the three local authorities, local organisations such as the Civic Society, the Chapter, the College, the Chamber of Trade and the Women's Institute, and also specialist groups (Harrogate and Yorkshire Dales Society of Architects, York Georgian Society, and North Yorkshire Vernacular Architecture Group). The Special Committee held its first meeting in May under the chairmanship of Dr John Whitehead, the Secretary of the Ripon Civic Society.

The 18 almshouses of the Hospitals of St John and Mary Magdalen were reopened after extensive renovation to provide indoor toilets and bathrooms and modern kitchens. The work had cost more than £35,000, raised by the Trustees who sold some capital assets, with help from the Harrogate Council who gave an improvement grant and a mortgage loan.

March. The Mayor, Councillor John Richmond, and the Sergeant-at-Mace made a goodwill visit to Ripon, California. At a special reception the Sergeant-at-Mace blew the 1690 Horn at 9 pm and the Mayor presented a piece of Westmorland steel plate bearing the city crest and the motto 'As true steel as Ripon rowels' to Mayor Feichtmeir.

April. Ripon's Conservation Area was extended by the Department of the Environment to include: land west of the Market Place from Blossomgate to Coltsgate Hill (to control the area affected by the proposed relief road); the Clock Tower, North Parade and Crescent Parade; the Alma Weir and the canal basin.

1976-77. Michael F. Falkingham, **Manager**
Born 1935 in Allhallowgate, Ripon. Educated Ripon Cathedral School and the County Secondary School; a chorister at the Cathedral. Joined the Royal Air Force at 17 and served for five years. Employed for 15 years at Jacksons, Outfitters, Westgate and at the time of his death by Austin Reed, Thirsk. Elected to Council 1970 and to Harrogate District Council 1977. Chairman of the Planning Committee, promoted bulb-planting on

the approach roads to the city. Responsible for the B.B.C. *It's a Knockout* on the racecourse and later took a team to Germany. A very keen sportsman, he had been a member of the R.A.F. Athletics Team, winning many trophies; was Secretary of the Ripon Nondescripts Cricket Team, President of the Sub-Aqua Club, and a member of the Rugby and Golf Clubs. A Governor of the Grammar School and a member of the Chamber of Trade. He died in 1982.

May. There was controversy over protocol involving the city's new Mayor and the newly-elected Mayor of Harrogate. The dispute began after the Ripon Mayor-making ceremony. The Mayor of Harrogate, Councillor Roy Beaumont, attended in a dual capacity: as the longest serving city councillor at the ceremony in the Town Hall, and later as Mayor of Harrogate at the civic lunch in the *Spa Hotel*. It was originally planned that Councillor Beaumont would act as host at one of the tables for the lunch, but at the last moment the Chief Executive of the District, Mr Neville Knox, intervened and Councillor Beaumont was seated at the high table to the right of the new Mayor. Mr Knox pointed out later that the 1972 Local Government Act made it clear that 'The Chairman of a district shall have precedence in the district but not so prejudicially to affect Her Majesty's Prerogative. That means unless the Lord Lieutenant is present, who is the Queen's personal representative, the Mayor of the District is entitled to precedence'. Both the Department of the Environment in London and the Home Office later confirmed that Mr Knox's interpretation of the law was correct. The City Council's disappointment with this ruling has continued through the years.

June. Concern was expressed that of 120 teenagers who had left school at the end of the summer term nearly 50 per cent had been unable to find jobs.

Teenage vandals hit the first voluntary clean-up project being carried out by members of Rotaract under the auspices of the new Environment Committee. During the lunchbreak teenagers stole a saw, cut up the timber being used to repair a riverside bench, and later drove motor scooters over a newly-dug drainage trench. A week later the teenagers responsible approached the Rotaract club president, Mr Dennis Broadland, and apologised for their action.

July. Three previously unemployed men and a school leaver were employed under the Job Creation Scheme to construct a riverside footpath between the Alma Weir and Bondgate Green Bridge.

August. Ripon had steered clear of problems posed by the long summer drought, but industrial undertakings in the city were now beginning to feel the effects. Ross Poultry's Dallamires Lane factory had managed by using two boreholes on the site, but this water was too hard to be used in refrigeration equipment. If the Drought Act had been enforced in the area the firm would have faced considerable difficulties.

Mr Geoffrey Tanner as 'St Wilfrid' headed the largest procession for many years consisting of nearly 40 floats. St Wilfrid wore a completely new outfit of mitre and robes, and the Lofthouse Colliery Band led the parade. The Committee was able to pass on £100 to the city's Round Table to be distributed among Ripon charities.

October. Canon J. Paul Burbridge, a former Residentiary of York Minster, was installed as Archdeacon of Richmond and Residentiary Canon of Ripon Cathedral before a large congregation.

November. Plans were announced for the amalgamation of two supermarkets in the Market Square: Liptons and the adjoining store, Moores, then operating as separate businesses.

The County Planning Development Control Sub-Committee turned down by six votes to three the inner relief road scheme. The decision came as a major shock to the City Council, as it had expected that approval would be a mere formality following the observations from the Harrogate Council approving the scheme in principle. The Mayor, Councillor W. R. Beaumont, Ripon's County Councillor and Chairman of the Area Highways Sub-Committee, and the Dean all expressed astonishment and declared that they would fight to get the scheme reinstated. In January, the Planning Sub-Committee reversed its decision. In April 1977, the Secretary of the Environment, Mr Peter Shore, called in the plans for the road to decide himself whether the scheme should go through after a public inquiry. The Assistant County Surveyor said in June 1977 that the Council would ask that the inquiry on the inner relief road should be delayed, until after a decision had been made on the route of the Pudsey-Dishforth motorway spur. A fortnight later the Minister of Transport, Mr William Rogers, announced that he favoured a new extension from the A1 at Wetherby and that the 'Blue Route' was environmentally unacceptable.

December. Mr Fred Collinson, having reached the statutory retiring age of 70, stood down from the Ripon Bench after serving 27 years. He had been appointed Chairman in 1960. After his last appearance in court, tributes were paid by the succeeding Chairman, Mr John Bostock, by Mr Ken Harding on behalf of the Clerks, and by Chief Superintendent George Templeton on behalf of the police.

The Council asked for an estimate for a complete renovation of the Mayor's chain of office, probably the first since it was specially made in 1859 by the firm of Hunt and Raskell and supplied by Blakeborough and Hunt, Jewellers, Ripon. The chain is among Ripon's most valuable city treasures, being made of gold and weighing 1 lb 11 ozs. It was bought by public subscription. The main portion displays the city coat of arms surrounded by the Ripon motto, and the many minor badges are those of the old Ripon trade guilds, now defunct.

January. There was disappointment that the work of clearing the site for the Morrison supermarket had gone too far for an archaeological investigation to be carried out. The firm claimed it had never received the letter from the Department of the Environment requesting the search. The supermarket was formally opened by the Mayor, Councillor John McGarr, in September.

February. Seventy-three children were sent home from the County Secondary School by the Headmaster for being 'incorrectly dressed'. Mr Cooper said he would continue to ban any child who did not come up to the approved standard of dress. Two mothers of children who had been sent home obtained 200 signatures to a petition asking that the rules for fifth formers who were taking C.S.E. examinations be relaxed, because the ban was causing them to lose vital tuition.

Ripon City Golf Club had hoped to extend the course from nine to 18 holes by acquiring a share in the 52 acres of land adjoining High Common Farm. However, at the auction sale in Boroughbridge, a local industrialist purchased the farm.

The Special Committee for the Environment successfully approached the probation service to use the Community Service scheme, under which the courts can order offenders to do useful community work in place of conventional punishments. This help boosted the volunteer force which was already carrying out projects on derelict sites in the city. The main work was on the land adjoining the footpath connecting the car park and the Cathedral. This site was cleared of tons of debris, levelled and the land prepared for seeding, all by voluntary labour. The Civic Society provided trees as part of its Silver Jubilee planting and the Ripon Business and Professional Women's Organisation provided two seats.

The City Council decided not to support a scheme put forward by the Mayor to purchase the *Opera House* site for conversion into a community centre. The building had been gutted by fire in 1976 in the biggest fire in Ripon for 20 years.

Paul Richmond, the 17-year-old son of ex-Mayor John Richmond and a sixth-former at Ripon Grammar School, became the Ripon Hornblower in place of Philip Harrison, who had to relinquish the office when his Ripon College course finished in June.

March. The N.Y.C.C. gave planning permission for the development of an educational farm and country leisure park at Lightwater Valley, North Stanley to Mr Robert Staveley; and for the building of a marina to accommodate 177 pleasure craft by the side of the Ripon Canal to the Ripon Racecourse Company.

April. The Ripon Bypass Group, founded earlier in the year by Mr R. W. Ellis to lobby the authorities to provide a bypass for Ripon as an alternative to the inner relief road, collected 2,852 questionnaires out of 4,000 delivered to Ripon households in a referendum. Ninety per cent of the returned forms were opposed to the inner relief road scheme.

Mr J. E. R. Seeger, who had successfully converted the House of Correction, built in 1686, into a private residence, applied to the Harrogate Council for permission to convert the adjoining disused Ripon Liberty Prison, built in 1816, into two houses. The application was supported by the Ancient Monument Society and the York Georgian Society, as both bodies were anxious to bring the building into use. The Civic Society strongly opposed the plan as they believed conversion could not be achieved without completely destroying the character of the building, which retained the original heavily-barred prison features including the cell doors and Victorian ventilation system. The Society suggested that the building should be taken over by the Council as a law and order museum. This ambition was fulfilled when the Ripon Museum Trust, set up in 1981, opened the present Ripon Prison and Police Museum in 1984.

The Department of the Environment designated the Ripon City centre as a Conservation Area of Special Merit, which meant that some conservation projects became eligible for special Government grants.

1977-78. JOHN McGARR, Civil Servant

Born 1921 in Carlisle. Educated Caldergate School, Carlisle, and in the Royal Air Force in which he served from 1938 to 1950. Civil servant with the Ministry of Defence. Elected to Council 1972, to Harrogate District Council 1974, and North Yorkshire County Council 1981. As Mayor in the Silver Jubilee Year of Queen Elizabeth II, he was responsible for the commemorative fountain erected in Minster Road. In his second mayoralty his appeal was for the benefit of the mentally handicapped. Mayor in 1985 when the Queen attended a civic lunch at the Town Hall following the distribution of the Royal Maundy at the Cathedral. A defender of Ripon civic tradition, particularly the dignity of mayoral office, and a supporter of many local organisations. Prominent in efforts to save Hellwath from quarrying and in opposition to the inner relief road.

May/June. The Mayor, Councillor John McGarr, launched an appeal for funds to erect a fountain on the Market Place as a tribute to the Queen during her Jubilee Year. The original idea had been made by Mr R. K. Wilson, then President of Ripon Men's Forum, and the appeal reached a total of £1,337. Mr Frank Marshall, the Ripon stonemason, produced the final designs in December 1978 and these were submitted to the Harrogate Planning Committee. A decision was deferred because they were not satisfied that the proposed site between the Town Hall and the Obelisk was the most suitable one. Councillor McGarr, however, was adamant that the fountain should be on the Market Place. He carried out a referendum which revealed that 500 people agreed with the market place site and 113 would prefer the fountain to be placed elsewhere; the City Council supported Councillor McGarr.

The Dean announced a scheme for colouring the angel corbels on the north and south aisle walls of the Cathedral; the estimated cost of colouring one corbel would be £120. He suggested that individuals, families or groups might like to sponsor particular corbels.

Ripon celebrated the Silver Jubilee on the three days 5, 6 and 7 June, starting with a civic service on Sunday at the Cathedral which was taken by the Dean and attended by the Mayors and Councillors of Harrogate and Ripon. A spectacular gala was organised in the afternoon by the Ripon Rugby Club; 50 primary school children took part in a parade beginning at the Market Place and, led by the Kerry Pipers' Band, they processed to the ground where a crowd of 4,000 witnessed the decorated bicycle competition and took part in a number of other attractions. On Monday, there was an *It's a Knockout* competition on the Market Square followed by the crowning of Ripon Children's Day Queen, 12-year-old Susan Crockett. The Mayor and Councillors braved the showers and toured all the decorated streets to decide the winner of the Silver Jubilee Street Plaque; the honour went to Ambrose Road. On Tuesday, the Ripon Rotaract Club organised a colourful human chess game on the Market Square.

September. A report by the County Archaeologist's Department identified six areas of the city which were of special importance. It warned that future developments were likely to damage archaeological remains and that there was a need for more excavation. Top priority was given to the Cathedral area as it was probably near the site of the earliest settlement with remains of ecclesiastical buildings and Anglo-Saxon structures; to the Market Place as the heart of the medieval town; to Skellgate as the centre of the medieval woollen cloth industry; to Bondgate as a settlement of the Archbishop's agricultural tenants; and to St Marygate.

In an archaeological dig on the site designated for building beside the old Deanery, the major find was an Anglo-Saxon circular brooch about one-and-a-half inches in diameter made of gold and inlaid with garnets and amber in the form of a cross. The brooch is now on display in the Treasury at the Cathedral.

October. The Venerable David Nigel de Lorentz Young, formerly Archdeacon of Huntingdon, and Honorary Canon of Ely, was enthroned as 11th Bishop of Ripon in the Cathedral by the Dean of Ripon before a crowded congregation. The new bishop then walked in procession with church and civic dignitaries to the Town Hall for a reception given in his honour. Bishop Young became the youngest bishop in the Church of England.

November. The Chamber of Trade pressed the City Council to change its mind over the future use of the *Wakeman's House.* By the casting vote of the Mayor, the Council had voted that the building should remain as a café, a role it had filled since 1968. The Chamber of Trade, the Civic Society and the Tourist Association all supported its use as a tourist information centre and the Harrogate Housing and Property Committee agreed.

December. A stained glass window depicting the life of St Wilfrid was placed in the north transept of the Cathedral in memory of Charles Sykes by his widow. The artist was Harry Harvey of York.

January. The Harrogate Council proposed to extend charges at the Victoria Grove and main car parks to include Saturday parking as well as the existing charge on Thursday. Income for the previous year was expected to show a surplus over expenditure of £2,470. The estimated surpluses for 1978 were £5,690 for Thursday charging and about £7,000 if Saturday charging were to be introduced. The proposals brought protests from all sections of Ripon residents.

February. The Revd George Parr announced his retirement after 19 years as Vicar of Holy Trinity Church. He had also been Chairman of the Governors of the County Secondary School and of the Managers of Holy Trinity School, as well as being involved with the Army Cadet Force and Ripon Rugby and Golf Clubs.

Massive opposition was launched against proposals by Cawood Aggregates Limited, who proposed to implement planning permissions granted between 1949 and 1963 to extract sand and gravel from a site extending from Hellwath to the River Skell behind the Cathedral Choir School and Whitcliffe Lane. It was estimated that the site contained a million tonnes of material which the company would extract over a seven-year period. The opposition was led by the ex-Mayor and County Councillor John Richmond, supported by the Civic Society and the Ripon Group of the Ramblers' Association. Of particular concern was the loss of playing fields and beauty spots reaching right into the city. A petition organised by the Civic Society collected 3,300 signatures and the County Planning Officer received 127 letters of objection from individual residents and 14 from organisations. The Harrogate Planning Committee

called for revocation of the plans, but were asked by the County to consider an exchange of land owned by the District on Ripon Parks for the Cawood land at Hellwath. They refused the exchange. In October 1978, the County Council allowed the permissions to go through, a decision which produced a massive reaction and an approach was made to the Department of the Environment. The Harrogate Planning Committee again called for revocation and offered up to £120,000 towards compensation without success. In the event Cawood carried out only minor works and allowed the children's play area to continue. Finally, in 1984 Redlands Quarry Limited, who had acquired the land, were granted outline permission to develop some of it for housing purposes.

A team of 10 golfers from Ripon Golf Club, led by ex-Mayor John Richmond, left on a goodwill trip to Ripon, California. They carried with them an oak plaque commemorating the visit and a pencil portrait by Lynda Birkinshaw of Mr Talbot Kendall, President of the Ripon California Chamber of Commerce, who had made the trip possible.

Mr Terry Harding was appointed Sergeant-at-Mace to succeed Mr Cyril Hawley who had been the Ripon Hornblower before becoming the Sergeant-at-Mace, and was now retiring.

March. The Ripon Amateur Operatic Society put on an ambitious production of the musical *Oliver* at the Claro Theatre, with nine-year-old Gerard Price in the title role and 13-year-old Richard Wray as the Artful Dodger.

April. The Mayor and the Sergeant-at-Mace were two of the passengers to travel from Ripon to London by stage-coach on a trial run before Farnell Touring started its five tours scheduled for the end of the year. The cost of a nine-day holiday would be £790 per person and would include five days on the road and two days each in Ripon and London. The stage-coach being used was the *Gay Gordon,* built in 1832 for the Edinburgh-London run. The Mayor carried with him a silver salver for presentation to the Lord Mayor of London.

The proposals to develop the Deanery Fields went a stage further with an offer to build a free car park at a cost of £65,000 by William Morrison Supermarkets Limited.

1978-79. FREDERICK WALTER SPENCE, Varnish Manufacturer

May. There was a three-week Cathedral Spring Festival when a varied programme of concerts, exhibitions, displays and lectures was presented. This second triennial event centred on a vast floral display in the Cathedral during the Spring Bank Holiday, organised by the Ladies' Flower Guild. Arts and crafts displays included work from the Grammar and County Secondary Schools and the Grewelthorpe Handweavers. An exhibition of church vestments was mounted in the north transept. The musical programme included concerts by the B.B.C. Northern Symphony Orchestra, the Harrogate Choral Society,

Mayor 1967-68-69, 1977-78

Atorah's Band, and organ recitals by the Leeds organist Simon Lindley and the American concert organist Carlo Curley. A display of early books and paintings entitled *The World of Sir Thomas More* organised by Mary Mauchline was shown in the library.

June. The Mayor received the first copy of a history of the city entitled *The Book of Ripon* which was written by Celia Thomson and published by Barracuda Books Limited.

The County Council published its draft Structure Plan. It proposed that Ripon should continue as the main shopping and service centre for the northern part of the Harrogate District. The level of new housing should cater for local needs and could be satisfied by existing planning permissions. Provision would be made for additional light industrial development with preference being given to small firms providing local employment needs, and Ripon should be encouraged to develop increased accommodation and other tourist facilities.

Mr Charles Barstow Hutchinson died aged 74 at his Markington home. He was a member of the Hutchinson family, which had first come to the area 200 years before to mine lead at Pateley Bridge. About one hundred years ago Mr Hutchinson's father became a solicitor, moving to Ripon in 1880 and later joining with Mr R. W. Buchanan to form the firm of Hutchinson and Buchanan. Mr Charles Hutchinson followed his father in the firm after qualifying in 1927. He inherited his father's interests in the racecourse and the *Spa Hotel* and 50 years ago became Company Secretary and Managing Director of both. He was also Chairman of the Car and Agricultural Machinery Company of Croft and Blackburn. In the 1930s Mr Hutchinson formed the Meads Trust Limited, a holding company for the various companies based on Ure Bank, which included Allton Engineering Limited, Ebor Concretes Limited, Allton and Company (Contractors) Limited, and W. E. Dixon (Ripon) Limited. The Meads Trust was named after his birthplace, *The Meads*, South Crescent. These many interests earned him the name of 'Mr Ripon'. He had been President of the Ripon Conservative Association, the Boroughbridge Agricultural Society

and Ripon Chamber of Trade. He worked for his local church at Markington, was solicitor for the Dean and Chapter, and a member of the Diocesan Board of Finance.

July. North Yorkshire Magistrates Committee's application for planning permission to add a temporary structure linked by a corridor to the northern side of the court-house, a listed building, was severely criticised by the City Council and the Civic Society. The Council was warned that, without the proposed extension, the Ripon Magistrates' Court might have to close.

August/September. The Ripon Town Scheme was started, whereby owners of listed buildings in the city centre could obtain grants of up to 50 per cent for repairs and restoration. The Department of the Environment provided a quarter of the cost and the N.Y.C.C. and the Harrogate Borough Council jointly the other quarter. The latter bodies also administered the scheme.

A successful drive was made to form a Ripon Conservation Volunteer Group to carry out cleaning-up projects on some of the derelict areas in the city centre. The first task for these volunteers was to deal with the area behind the Bus Station. Over the next months the volunteer force (with help from the Community service Unit) cleared and levelled the site, laid down limestone paths and planted trees provided by the Civic Society. One chestnut tree was given by the Wath Women's Institute to celebrate its Silver Jubilee. The Harrogate Council later provided extra topsoil, seeded the area and provided two wooden benches.

October. Hinton's Supermarket in Fishergate closed, with the loss of 15 jobs. The Managing Director, Mr Patrick Hinton, said the closure was due to declining business.

Mr Joel Bastow, an American living in Ripon, became the Deputy Hornblower.

November. Mr Ted Pearson, Chairman of the Hellwath Action Committee, resigned his chairmanship of Ripon Civic Society. He had been in the forefront of the conservation challenges in Ripon over the previous six years and was made a Vice-President in recognition of the work he had done for the Society.

The Mayor launched the Ripon Lottery. There was to be a monthly draw with tickets selling at 10p each. It would be run in direct competition with the Harrogate District Council's civic lottery, although that had not been the City Council's specific intention. Its aim was to launch an exclusively Ripon scheme, to give Ripon people the prizes and Ripon the benefit of the profits.

December. At the Ripon County Secondary School's first speech day the Headmaster, Mr J. Cooper, outlined its links with local industry. In this he included the annual industry and education symposium, when employers and staff met to discuss opportunities for school leavers and the requirements of local firms. Fourth and fifth year students were attending part-time courses at Harrogate College of Further Education in typing, office practice, auto-engineering, health, welfare and engineering craft.

The Bishop of Ripon instituted the Revd Roger Wilde to the parish of Holy Trinity, Ripon. Mr Wilde was presented to the Bishop by the Revd John Cockerton, a former principal of St John's College, Durham, on behalf of the Simeon Trust who are patrons of the living.

Now that there were doubts concerning the construction of the Pudsey-Dishforth spur, the County Planning Officer, Mr Cooper Kenyon, examined the environmental factors which would affect both inner and outer relief routes for Ripon. A direct comparison was not possible as only a general line had been put forward for the outer relief road. The principal advantage of the inner relief road (IRR) was that it would take through traffic and a large proportion of local traffic away from the Market Place, Kirkgate and the adjoining streets, which form the most important and sensitive part of the conservation area. The main disadvantages of the IRR were: it would involve the demolition of a number of buildings in the conservation area, some of which were grant-aided under the Town Scheme, and would have an adverse impact on historic areas; there would be an increase of noise and intrusion through the western fringe of the city centre; there would be disruption and closure of a number of commerical enterprises and the loss of a number of homes; and the road would open up to view semi-derelict areas and unattractive backs of buildings. The principal advantage of an outer relief road (ORR) would be the reduction in the level of heavy and through traffic in the urban area as a whole, not only in the city centre but also in Harrogate Road and North Road. Coupled with traffic management in the central area, the environmental benefit to the historic core could be similar to that of the IRR, but at the possible greater inconvenience of local traffic. A secondary benefit would be a positive use of the derelict disused railway line. The main disadvantages of the ORR were: if elevated, the road would be noisy and intrusive for the residential areas on the east side of the city; there would be a detrimental effect on attractive areas, particularly at North Bridge and between Littlethorpe and Ripon; there would be severance of some agricultural holdings and the loss of some good quality (including grade II) agricultural land. Mr Cooper Kenyon commented that it was difficult to assess accurately the environmental factors relating to the ORR, as a detailed plan had not been made. There were no details of the level or final line of the road and no indication of whether the embankment should be kept or removed. He concluded that there could be a greater justification of the IRR than the ORR purely on economic grounds, but on environmental grounds the ORR might be the more acceptable.

January. Peter Squires of the Harrogate Rugby Club and Ripon became the most capped winger in the history of English rugby, with 26 caps.

February. Members of the National Union of Public Employees threatened to close Ripon Grammar School indefinitely because the Headmaster, Mr Bryan Stanley, refused to close the school on the national 'day of action' strike by N.U.P.E. The union area organiser, Mr Malcolm Reid, instructed the school caretaker and his assistant to strike indefinitely and later called out the catering staff. The following week the union stepped up its action, calling out all N.U.P.E. members in the city's eight other schools with the effect of closing some of them.

P.C. Roger Smith of North Yorkshire Police was presented by the Mayor of Ripon with a Royal Humane Society certificate for bravery. P.C. Smith had jumped into the River Ure at Bellflask, North Stainley, and swam through the swollen river to free Mr Rupert Cawthra of Ripon who had been fishing and found himself trapped by a sudden rise in the river.

The Civic Society, which had always insisted that the first priority in solving Ripon's traffic problems should be the removal of through traffic from the city, declared its intention to campaign for a bypass now that the 'Blue Route' had been abandoned. The City Council also declared for the bypass, and in March the Harrogate Borough Council followed suit.

March, Econ Engineering, which was occupying the premises of the old Hepworth Brewery, applied for permission to expand the Bondgate factory into Redshaw House Fields opposite housing in Heckler Lane. The application brought considerable opposition as the area had been designated for housing and, in order to determine the degree of public support, the firm inserted a referendum form in the *Gazette*. The Managing Director warned that if the development was turned down, the firm would leave Ripon, with the loss of 50 jobs. The application was refused, but a suitable site was found to accommodate the firm's expansion on land between the Boroughbridge Road and the River Skell adjacent to the city's sewage works. Econ retained the Bondgate premises.

The police issued a warning for people in Ripon to be on their guard against an arsonist who had started fires at the County Secondary School, under a caravan on the caravan site, and under a car, all within a week.

1979-80. WALTER JACK BAILY, Works Superintendent

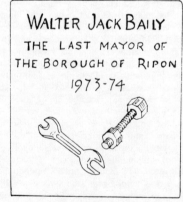

WALTER JACK BAILY
THE LAST MAYOR OF
THE BOROUGH OF RIPON
1973-74

Mayor 1973-74, 1979-80

May. Dr Keith Hampson, M.P., returned at the recent parliamentary election, was appointed Parliamentary Private Secretary to Mr Tom King, Minister of State for the Environment.

July. Although *Fountains Hall* was the property of the N.Y.C.C., the contents still belonged to its last private owners, the Vyner family. The family decided to remove the collection of fine furniture, pewter and pictures as the Council was not willing to install an adequate security system. Negotiations were also being conducted between the Council and Mr Neil Balfour, Euro-M.P. for North Yorkshire, for the purchase of *Studley Hall*, the former home of the Vyners, made by converting the stable block after the *Studley Royal* mansion was destroyed by fire.

September. Women students at the College of Ripon and York St John were warned not to go out alone at night while the Yorkshire Ripper, a murderer who had already raped and murdered a number of young women in West Yorkshire, was still at large. The Principal, Mr John Barnett, reminded the students that Ripon was only 30 miles from Bradford and 25 miles from Leeds.

October/November. The Dean condemned the Harrogate Council's decision to axe a £650 grant for Cathedral floodlighting. The Cathedral tower had been lit every night of the year and the whole building was illuminated at weekends and in holiday seasons. After the Council grant for electricity and repairs had ceased at the end of the year, the floodlights would be used only on special occasions such as Easter and Christmas. The Ripon Chamber of Trade agreed to support the lighting with a grant of £150 which enabled the Cathedral to be floodlit at weekends. In January 1980 the Dean announced that local people had raised £690, enough to keep the lights on until well into 1981.

Mr Ted Hudson, aged 70, Ripon Cathedral's longest serving bellringer, collapsed and died during the All Saints' Sung Eucharist in the Cathedral. He was a former captain of the Cathedral ringers, Secretary of the Yorkshire Association of Change Bellringers, and had recently been made an honorary vice-president of the Association. Mr Hudson had been employed by T. and R. Williamson Limited for 54 years before his retirement in 1974.

The Ripon Civic Lottery was suspended indefinitely because of declining public support: there had been only £20 profit from the previous month's draw. In March the Council decided to wind up the project; awarded £1,000 to Quarry Moor Development Association and divided £900 between five other groups. A sum of £500 was set aside to provide seats to be placed on the banks of the River Skell.

December. The Harrogate Borough Council put forward a package of four schemes to reduce congestion in the Harrogate, Knaresborough and Ripon areas in its submission to the A1 improvement public inquiry. The new roads suggested were: a Ripon bypass; a south of Knaresborough and Harrogate bypass; a Killinghall bypass; or a Killinghall bypass and an upgrading of the A61 between the proposed

Ripon bypass and the Ripley roundabout. In January the Minister of Transport, Mr Kenneth Clarke, rejected a western route for the Kirkhamgate-Dishforth motorway link, stopped the three-month-old inquiry and said less costly Government proposals would be introduced for minor improvements to the A1 north of Wetherby and a scaled-down Ripon Route. Following this decision, the Chairman of the N.Y.C.C. Highways Committee called for a public inquiry into the Ripon inner relief road to be held as soon as possible.

January. William Morrison Supermarkets Limited offered £85,000 to take up a 35-year lease on the Council-owned main car park under the same conditions as those previously offered and turned down by the Borough Council, that £40,000 should be spent in developing the Deanery Fields for parking and a picnic area. The Borough Council decided to keep control of all public parking in the city and to fund the Deanery Fields scheme itself.

The Ripon City Council decided to fight the threat to close the Registrar's Office in the Town Hall, which was open on Tuesday and Thursday mornings for the recording of births, deaths and marriages. The proposed closure was part of the County Council's economy plans.

After many years of fruitless attempts, Mr Arthur Yates of Littlethorpe established radio contact with Ripon, California, U.S.A., when he spoke to Mrs Marylin Van Dyk, a Ripon U.S. housewife. Mrs Van Dyk explained that she had taken up the pastime to keep her busy when her husband, a truck driver, was away from home.

February. The Dean invited representatives of various groups to attend a public meeting at the Town Hall to discuss ways and means of increasing the contributions of visitors towards the maintenance costs of Ripon Cathedral. On average the 150,000 visitors who passed through in 1979 gave 3p each. He explained that the Cathedral was run on an annual budget of £60,000, costing 30p per minute to keep the building open. The Dean and most of the people at the meeting were opposed to the imposition of a compulsory charge as had been introduced at Salisbury and Chichester. Instead, it was proposed to introduce a Ministry of Welcome, which would involve a rota of volunteers to welcome visitors to the Cathedral. There would be a notice which welcomed visitors and pointed out that to maintain the Cathedral and extend its work a gift of at least 30p was needed from every adult. The scheme was successful during its first year when visitors' donations amounted to £22,000.

Seventy-nine-year-old Mr Charlie Skirrow retired from his office of official Stavebearer to the Mayor, a throwback to the days when Ripon had its own constables who carried staves to preserve law and order. The Mayor presented Mr Skirrow with an inscribed tankard at a special ceremony in the Town Hall.

The Ripon Tourist Association introduced two new tourist brochures, the first being *Historic Buildings in and around Ripon*, containing histories of buildings in the area, prepared by members of the Civic Society, and the second was *Motor Trips around Ripon*.

March. Redlands Aggregates Limited, owner of the 50-acre site at Doublegates Quarry, applied for outline planning permission for a multi-million-pound project for 338 houses which would satisfy three-quarters of Ripon's needs for new housing over the next decade. In September, the Harrogate Borough Council released a survey of housing needs in Ripon and suggested that during the next ten years new development should be concentrated on four sites: at Red House in Palace Road, Doublegate Quarry, Kirkby Road and Clotherholme Road. It was estimated that a total of 350 new homes should be built and the report included a proposed rate of building in each year.

The Ripon Scout Troop committed itself to removing all the rubbish which had been dumped in Deep Ghyll instead of into the rubbish skips sited on the adjacent Gallows Hill. For some time there had been growing anger at the accumulation of rubbish on the Council-owned land and the lack of action by the local authorities. It was felt that Ripon should be provided with an amenity tip on an alternative site, and there was prolonged agitation until the County Council opened a tip for domestic refuse in Dallamires Lane.

April. Ten people were injured after a gas explosion blew out the front of Kings Bakery in Queen Street. Gas Board workmen had been called to the shop just before the blast after the assistants had complained of the smell of gas. The explosion highlighted the problem of heavy traffic causing fractures in the gas main on the east side of the Market Square and plans went ahead to replace it.

Ripon came to a standstill on Easter Monday as traffic queued bumper-to-bumper through the city on its way to the newest attraction in the area, the Lightwater Valley Leisure Park, North Stainley. Cars stretched back to Quarry Moor on the Harrogate Road and to Sharow Village on the Dishforth Road. The leisure park had 10,000 visitors on each day of the holiday.

1980-81. Barrie Price, Accountant

Born 1937 in Bradford and educated at St Bede's Grammar School there. Qualified as a chartered accountant at 21. Came to Ripon in 1962 after two years' National Service and joined the partnership which became Lishman, Sidwell, Campbell and Price, with offices in surrounding towns, and business consultancy and financial services. Elected to the Council in 1968 and to Harrogate District Council in 1974. His mayoral appeal was in support of the children's ward at the Hospital, to which he devoted the savings made by substituting afternoon tea for the customary mayoral lunch — he later invited the Council to a pre-Christmas dinner at the *Unicorn Hotel*. A Roman Catholic and office-holder at St Wilfrid's Church; the Council attended Mass there on St Wilfrid's Feast in October. Instrumental with Dr Keith Hampson, M.P., in recovering the City's right to grant the Honorary Freedom and the mayor's inclusion on the invitation list to Royal Garden Parties. Negotiated with the N.Y.C.C. for the transfer of the City's archives to their care. Has devoted great efforts as Chairman of the 1986 Committee to organising and co-ordinating the preparations for *Ripon 1100*.

May. Mr Terry Harding, the Sergeant-at-Mace, resigned in order to take up a new post as Beadle to Peterborough City Council. When considering a new appointment, the Harrogate Council recommended that the historic post should become a part-time job. In the past the Sergeant was both the Mayor's attendant and the Town Hall keeper. He was also responsible for giving talks to visitors on the civic regalia; he thus had to serve three masters: Harrogate Council, the Mayor of Ripon and the Clerk to the City Council. The City Council preferred to retain the combined appointments and asked the Harrogate Council to revise its decision. Mr David Marshall, who had recently left the Royal Engineers, accepted the joint post in September.

The new Mayor of Ripon, Councillor Barrie Price, decided to replace the traditional civic lunch following the Mayor-making ceremony with a less costly afternoon tea and to donate the money saved to charity. The decision brought protest from other members of the Council.

June. Dr Keith Hampson, M.P., tabled a motion asking that a Government Bill then going through Parliament be altered to restore the power of granting city freedom to Ripon, Chichester, Bangor, Caernarvon, Truro, Ely and Wells. Ripon lost this privilege after the Local Government Act of 1972. The origin of the tradition lies in the former power of trade guilds to restrict trade and manufacture to those whom they admitted to membership. The Freedom gradually lost its links with trade and, with the passing of the Honorary Freedom of Boroughs Act in 1885, it came to be seen as the highest civic honour a council could bestow.

July. The annual dispute in the eternal saga of whether St Wilfrid's Fair should be held on the Market Place took on a new aspect. The row was not over the actual site, but over the charge for letting the site for the four days of the fair. The Borough Council recommended a figure between £650 and £850, whereas the City Council thought £650 was too high.

August. Unemployment in the city reached 5.6 per cent, an increase of 2 per cent over the past year. Ripon's biggest event of the year, the St Wilfrid's Procession, showed the effects of rising prices and general economic depression; there were only 20 floats, half the number entered two years before.

October. The City Council was divided over a call by Councillor John McGarr for the disbanding of the Special Committee for the Environment which had been set up in 1976 following the survey of Ripon by the Department of the Environment. The Report had suggested many ways in which local people could improve the environment of the city at all levels. A major recommendation had been the establishment of this Special Committee to carry out small works and to advise on larger projects: but dissenting City Councillors considered that these matters should only be discussed by elected members, and were opposed to work which was deemed to be the responsibility of the Borough Council being carried out by voluntary labour. They also objected to the attendance at the Environment Committee meetings of a Planning Officer responsible for conservation in the areas and to secretarial help given by the Harrogate Council. The District Planning Committee considered the complaints and decided to continue their support of the committee. The Environment Committee undertook to send its minutes to the City Council, offered it larger representation and made the Mayor an ex-officio member.

November. Councillor Jack Baily opened a new children's section at the County Library in Ripon, funded from his Mayoral Appeal Fund which had been devoted to the International Year of the Child and had raised £2,500. Five hundred pounds had been given to the Child Assessment Centre in Harrogate, and the rest of the money had been used for the new shelves, bookcases and decoration of the Children's Library section.

The Mayor and Mayoress officially opened the renovated children's ward at the Ripon and District Hospital. The League of Friends of Ripon Hospitals had raised £6,000 to pay for the project.

December. An ancient custom was revived when the Mayor hosted a special Christmas dinner at the *Unicorn Hotel* following the December Council meeting. A similar event was recorded in 1691 when the Mayor, William Waterhall, conducted council business over dinner at Christmas.

January. Mr Stanley Josephs, Headmaster of Cordeaux High School, Lough, became Principal of Grantley Hall Adult College.

February. Concern was expressed that the N.Y.C.C. might take over the upkeep of Fountains Abbey. Mr Henry Vyner, a former owner of the estate, in a letter to *The Times* pointed out that since he sold the estate the Department of the Environment had held guardianship of the abbey and had undertaken a massive and continuing programme of works. On the other hand he alleged that *Studley House* had been nearly lost through neglect by the County Council, while work on the other buildings had been treated with little enthusiasm and replanting schemes for the park had been abandoned. In September, the Ancient Monuments Commission condemned the suggestion that the N.Y.C.C. should take control and the Secretary of State promised to take further advice before allowing any change. In May 1982, the N.Y.C.C. agreed to sell the Fountains Abbey and Studley Royal estates to the National Trust for £191,000, the loan debt on the land. In January 1983, Mr Heseltine, the Minister for the Environment, allowed the sale.

March. A detailed map of the Ripon IRR went on display at the Town Hall. The route, changed slightly from the 1976 plan, swung eastward and away from St Wilfrid's Place, where six houses previously planned for demolition would be saved. A public protest meeting was called in the Town Hall when more than 200 people packed the Council Chamber and overflowed onto the landing and staircase.

The IRR was the major if not the only issue of the County Council elections and overwhelmingly decided the fate of the Ripon candidates. City Councillors John McGarr and F. W. Spence, both declared opponents of the IRR, replaced the sitting members, Councillors Roy Beaumont and John Richmond. Councillor Beaumont had been the Chairman of the County Highways Committee which was responsible for the road proposals, and Councillor Richmond was a strong supporter of the road. Councillor Richmond announced his retirement from the City Council after he had heard the result of the County Council election.

In the summer, a mobile exhibition of the plans for the IRR was mounted in the Market Place and the Deputy Surveyor promised that a public inquiry would be held, after which the Minister would make his decision. In November, Councillor John McGarr organised a referendum in which 5,881 completed questionnaire forms out of the 8,850 issued were returned: 5,315 people were in favour of an outer bypass and only 566 voted for the IRR. In December, the Highways Committee voted for the IRR by 13 votes to four and in February 1982 the full Council confirmed the decision by a narrow majority of four votes.

April. An appeal for £100,000 was launched to provide a new building to cater for indoor sports and concerts at the Ripon Cathedral Choir School. The new facilities would include a boarders' common room, changing rooms, a music practice room and an art and craft centre. The growth of the school and the recent admission of girls made the need for the extra facilities urgent. A second aim was to raise money for endowments for choral scholarships to ensure that musically-gifted children, especially choristers, should not be excluded from the school on financial grounds.

Mr Ronald Perrin gave a recital on the £20,000 Makin electronic organ given to Ripon Cathedral by an anonymous donor. The organ, installed in the nave, has a tone similar to a pipe organ. It was not intended to replace the famous 100-year-old Harrison Organ, one of the finest in the country.

1981-82.   Robert Winster Bracken, Wing Commander (Retired)

WG.CDR. R.W. BRACKEN
C. ST. J., M.B.E.
MAYOR 1981-82

Born 1914 at Howgill, near Sedbergh, a farmer's son. Educated Sedbergh and Durham University. Metropolitan Police 1935-38, and Cumberland and Westmorland Constabulary 1938-49. A German linguist, he was seconded to the Military Government (Special Branch) in the British Zone of Germany, 1946-49, dealing with war criminals, traitors and denazification. He resigned from the Police Force to take a permanent commission in the Royal Air Force, in which he had served in 1944-45, followed by home and overseas postings. Following retirement from the forces, became a Regional Administrative Officer with the Agricultural Training Board. Elected to City Council 1979. In the International Year for the Disabled he completed the previous mayor's appeal for a specially adapted vehicle for use in Ripon. His Mayoress was his daughter, Mrs Evelyn Burr. County Director of the St John Ambulance Association, he is a Commander of the Order of St John of Jerusalem. An M.B.E. and holder of the Coronation Medal (1953). President of the Ripon R.A.F. Association, member of the C.A.B. and other community bodies. Home Defence Community Adviser in Ripon. A sportsman, and has represented the British Police in athletics and rugby, also played for the Yorkshire Wanderers.

May. Mrs Jennifer Jenkins, wife of Mr Roy Jenkins and Chairman of the Historic Buildings Council, officially opened four 18th-century cottages in Bondgate Green which had been restored by the Yorkshire Buildings Preservation Trust, set up in 1979. The Ripon restoration was the Trust's first project and the Ripon Civic Society had made an interest-free loan of £1,500, which on repayment would be used to renovate other old property in Ripon.

The Revd A. E. Hosband, a former Rector of Wath, of *Greenroyd*, Studley Road, presented the city with an oil painting by Mary Ethel Hunter, a Ripon artist who had died 45 years before. The painting of flowers, which remained on exhibition for a year in the Royal Academy, was left by Miss Hunter to Mr Hosband on condition that he should give it to the city at 'the end of his days'. The painting was hung in the Town Hall where another painting by Miss Hunter, of children in a paddling pool, was already on show. Mr Hosband said he had had great pleasure from the painting and had always intended to make the presentation when he reached the age of eighty-five.

An extension to the early 19th-century court-house was officially opened by the Lord Lieutenant of North Yorkshire, the Marquess of Normanby. The facilities included a second court room, two waiting rooms and a magistrates' retiring room, housed in a handsome building made of stone to match the court-house.

June. Mr Fred Collinson died at the age of 74. Originally from Spennymoor, he settled in Ripon in 1939 and moved to the Sports, Toys and Luggage business in North Street in 1953. Mr Collinson was a city magistrate for 27 years and chairman of the bench for 17 years before retiring in 1977.

July. Mr Joe Cooper, Headmaster of the Ripon County Secondary School, expressed concern at the drop in numbers entering the school. His school was 150 pupils below capacity and he estimated that some 200 children were travelling to neighbouring comprehensive schools.

The Mayor and Mayoress attended a garden party at Buckingham Palace; this was the first time that Ripon had been represented at a Royal Garden Party since the local government reorganisation in 1974.

Ripon celebrated the wedding of the Prince of Wales to Lady Diana Spencer, bedecking the city with red, white and blue bunting. The Mayor and Mayoress, Councillor R. W. Bracken and his daughter Mrs Evelyn Burr, with the Deputy Mayor and Mayoress, toured the city, dropping in on many of the street parties, and attending a special thanksgiving service in the Cathedral in the evening.

August. There was a break in tradition when 'St Wilfrid' had to abandon his place at the head of the Festival procession and join the Mayor and Mayoress in their carriage. *Morning Coffee*, the white horse trusted to carry the Saint, reared and bucked away from the band, dragging one of his handlers along the ground. The horse was calmed down and led to the front of the procession but his frolics continued and he was withdrawn. Mr Jack Longley of Healey near Masham said later that the horse had been stung just behind the saddle and must have been in considerable pain.

A 30-strong group of young people spent a week working at Ripon Cathedral carrying out some of the small labour-intensive jobs which the Dean and Chapter could not afford to have done. The group, working under three leaders, painted the undercroft, varnished the west doors, repointed walls and repaired gravestones.

September. The well-known haunt of booklovers, St Margaret's Bookshop in Kirkgate, built up by Jack and Edna Ellis over the previous 30 years, changed hands. The late Mrs Ellis, who had been Hornblower in the 1950s, was a skilled bookbinder and there are examples of his work in the Town Hall and the Cathedral. Mrs Ellis continued in business as an antiquarian bookseller.

October. The Ripon Museum Trust was set up to improve museum facilities in the city which had been sadly lacking since the City Museum at *Thorpe Prebend House* had been closed in the early 1950s and most of its exhibits dispersed. Apart from the tiny museum in the *Wakeman's House*, no municipal provision had since been made. The Ripon Civic Society had made a small collection of Ripon memorabilia and had mounted summer exhibitions organised by Mrs Edna Ellis during the previous few years, illustrating life in the city in past times. Earlier in the year, the Society had been offered a lease of part of the old Liberty Gaol in St Marygate and it was decided that a separate trust should be established to set up and administer a Prison and Police Museum in the building.

November/December. The Mayor swam the first two lengths to start a 24-hour sponsored swim at the Spa Baths. The event was organised by P.C. Tony Lockwood and the cadets of Ripon A.T.C. and attracted more than 20 volunteers who swam for 15 minutes each to raise more than £1,370 for Dr Barnardo's. The Mayoress, Mrs Evelyn Burr, also swam 20 lengths to help the cause. The Mayor's own appeal fund during the International Year for the Disabled was to provide a specially adapted vehicle for handicapped people and reached £6,500. One thousand pounds had already been spent on providing holidays.

February. Council tenants, temporarily moved into mobile homes at Camp Close while their houses in Wakeman Road were being modernised, sought compensation for the appalling conditions they had endured over the winter. During the severe spells of weather before Christmas they were without water, they had to bring their own heating appliances and their clothes and bedding were ruined by condensation.

The Dean held the annual Shrove Tuesday Supper in honour of Charles Dodgson, better known as Lewis Carroll, author of *Alice in Wonderland*, who was born 150 years before. Charles Dodgson had a close association with Ripon from his boyhood. His father was chaplain to Dr Longley, first Bishop of Ripon, and in 1852 was installed as Residentiary Canon. Although the real-life Alice was Alice Liddell from Oxford, the famous illustrations by Sir John Tenniel were not of her but of Mary Hilton Babcock, daughter of the Principal of Ripon Training College; Dodgson had taken a photograph of Mary which he had sent to Tenniel. His interest in photography may have started during a Christmas vacation with his family in Ripon when he visited the studios of Mr Booth, a commercial photographer in North Street. Charles Dodgson recorded in his diary on 10 January 1855 'After three failures he produced a tolerably good likeness [of me], which half the family pronounce the best possible and the other half the worst possible'.

A memorial service was held in the Cathedral for Sir Richard Graham of *Norton Conyers* who had died at the age of sixty-nine. He was the tenth baronet and his Jacobean house near Wath, to which he was devoted, had been in the family since 1624. Sir Richard loved the Yorkshire countryside and was a member of the Bedale Hunt. During World War II he was abroad on active service and became Chief Intelligence Officer to the Desert Air Force and was awarded the O.B.E. (Military Division); after the Sicilian and Italian campaigns he was finally brought back to Normandy. Sir Richard had been chairman of Yorkshire Television from the birth of the company in 1967 until he retired at his own request at the end of January and had agreed to continue as a member of the Y.T.V. board until May when he would have been 70. A High Sheriff of Yorkshire in 1961, he was also a former president of the Yorkshire Agricultural Society and a former chairman of the Yorkshire Insurance Company Limited and the Tees and Hartlepool Port Authority. He had only recently given up the Pro-Chancellorship of the University of Leeds. A regular attender at St Mary's Church at Wath, where he was church warden for 22 years, he was deeply involved in the life of the village and a supporter of its cricket club. Music was a life-long joy and he sang in the Ripon Choral Society for several years. He had indeed a particular regard for the city of Ripon, especially the preservation of its heritage, and was influential in the foundation of the Ripon Civic Society in 1968 of which he was the first President.

April. Associated Tower Cinemas submitted an outline planning application for the demolition of the *Palladium Cinema* in Kirkgate and the redevelopment of the site. The picture house, originally built in the mid-19th century as a workshop for the coach-building firm of Croft and Blackburn, had lost money over the previous year; its closure would cause 12 redundancies.

Councillor W. R. Beaumont, J.P., and Honorary Alderman W. H. Parnaby received the Freedom of the City from the Mayor at a ceremony held at the Ripon College.

Easter Monday again saw chaos on Ripon's roads with cars queuing through the city and for several miles back from the city centre. The problems started when Lightwater Valley Leisure Park reached its capacity of 10,000 visitors by lunchtime and vehicles were turned away. Many returned to Ripon and the Cathedral had 1,000 visitors during the day. The police flashed messages to national and local radio stations urging drivers to stay away.

1982-83. WALTER ROY BEAUMONT, Company Secretary

June. The Harrogate Council Housing Services Committee agreed to carry out renovation of council houses in Ambrose Road, Curfew Road, Southgate and Quarry Moor Lane at a cost of £300,000.

The Civic Society inaugurated the annual Helen Whitehead Conservation Awards for outstanding environmental improvements in Ripon during the previous 12 months. Three categories of improvements were considered for commendation: the best new building to be erected which harmonised with its surroundings, the best restoration of an old building and the best general environmental improve-

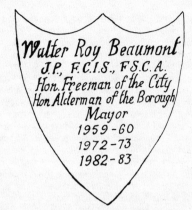

Mayor 1959-60, 1972-73, 1982-83

ment. No award was made in the new building section: Quarry Moor Development Association received first place in the general section for its voluntary work in clearing the site for recreational use and building a trim-track; King's Bakery, restored after being damaged by a gas explosion, was judged the best example of restoration work carried out in 1981. The work was supervised at the Bakery by the York architects, Greenwood and Nicholas, who received the overall award of the Helen Whitehead Silver Salver to hold for one year. The salver was given by Dr John Whitehead, Chairman of the Society, in memory of his wife, a former Honorary Secretary. The awards were presented by Lady Graham, who had graciously accepted the Presidency of the Society in succession to her husband, the late Sir Richard Graham.

September. The 150 men of the 11 Field Squadron Royal Engineers, who had returned to Claro Barracks after three months' duty on the Falkland Islands, were welcomed by the Mayor at a parade on the Market Square. The Dean led prayers for those who had suffered during the conflict. School children were given a half-holiday and Jet Provosts from R.A.F. Leeming flew over the square, wings dipped in salute. A crowd of over 2,000 watched the men as they moved off the square and exercised their right as Freemen of the City to march through Ripon with bayonets fixed, led by the regimental band.

November. Ripon Y.M.C.A. reopened at the end of a two-year rebuilding programme. The refurbishment had been under the leadership of Mr Colin Standbury, the development officer. The youth club had closed down in 1980, and the buildings were in a poor state of repair. The Manpower Services Commission provided the labour; the Yorkshire Humberside Trust gave £17,000 toward the cost of repair, leaving £15,000 to be found. The total was reached after Councillor R. W. Bracken gave the Y.M.C.A. £2,500 from the Mayor's Appeal Fund. The facilities, which are now used by many groups in Ripon, included a community hall, coffee lounge, youth club, sports and activities area, and an arts and crafts room.

Councillor Mike Falkingham, Mayor of Ripon 1976-77, died suddenly of a heart attack aged 47 at his home in North Road.

December. The Committee composed of representatives from organisations opposed to N.Y.C.C. proposals for an inner relief road and including the two County Councillors for Ripon, renamed itself the Rescue Ripon Group. The Group decided to retain the services of Mrs Ann Moon, a town planner, who had battled against the Ipswich bypass, campaigned for a lorry-ban on the A58 between Wetherby and Leeds, and fought against the Aire Valley trunk road.

January. Disputes again broke out between the Ripon Ramblers' Association and local farmers over the harassment of walkers using alleged public footpaths in the Studley Royal area. The Association asked for an inquiry under the Wildlife and Countryside Act (1981) into rights of way in the area, in order to get the closed paths reinstated.

The Harrogate Council agreed to take over the installation and maintenance costs for the lamp which was moved to the home of new Mayors of Ripon each year. This tradition had continued since 1892, but the costs had increased in recent years. In 1982, maintenance had cost £300, and the Electricity Board had charged £126 for connecting the supply to the lamp.

The Archdeacon of Richmond, the Venerable Paul Burbridge, was appointed Dean of Norwich Cathedral. The move brought to an end his 20-year long association with the Church in Yorkshire, first at York Minster and later at Ripon Cathedral.

February. Two masked raiders armed with sawn-off shotguns entered the Bondgate Post Office shortly before 6 pm, just after the postmaster Mr Jack Whippey, 47, had opened the safe to cash up for the day. His wife was serving their last customer, Mrs Burton, when the men ran in. One of them grabbed £7,600 from the safe and the other ordered Mr and Mrs Whippey and Mrs Burton into a back storeroom. Mrs Burton ran out of the back door to the garage next door to call for help. One of the raiders followed her and fired his gun; fortunately he missed and ran back into the shop. Both men escaped in a get-away car driven by a third man.

Lady Graham of *Norton Conyers* received the O.B.E. from Prince Charles at Buckingham Palace. The award, announced in the New Year Honours List, was in recognition of her services to the mentally ill in North Yorkshire.

March. The Ripon Conservative Association selected Mr John Watson, the sitting M.P. for Skipton, to fight the new Skipton and Ripon seat in place of Dr Keith Hampson. The recent reorganisation of Parliamentary Constituencies meant that the old Ripon constituency lost the Otley section and was now joined to a modified Skipton constituency. Dr Hampson who until then had represented Ripon was later adopted by North West Leeds.

Councillor Jack Briscombe at last agreed to become Mayor of Ripon for 1984 after having previously turned down 15 offers. He said 'I'm delighted. I've done everything else in local government, but to be Mayor would be the accomplishment of my life'.

April. Canon Duncan Thomson, headmaster of the Ripon Cathedral Choir School, died after a long illness at the age of 58. He was ordained in Gloucester in 1951 and came to Ripon in 1953 as a minor canon. In 1957 he became chaplain at Aysgarth Preparatory School, returning to Ripon in 1960 as the headmaster of the newly-established choir school.

1983-84.   JOHN BRISCOE BRISCOMBE, Outfitter

Coun. J.B. BRISCOMBE
Elected
Alderman 1961

Mayor
1983 to 1984

Born 1916. Son of John Briscoe Briscombe, Councillor and Alderman, to whose business in Kirkgate he succeeded. Educated Cathedral Boys' School and Grammar School. 1939-45 served with Royal Army Service Corps. Elected to Council 1950 and to Harrogate District Council 1974. After declining on 15 occasions, he acceded to the wishes of councillors and citizens and accepted the mayoralty in 1983, a difficult year dominated by controversy over the inner relief road. He was a governor of the Grammar School, the County Secondary and other schools. Feoffee of Jepson's Hospital and a trustee of the Hospitals of St Mary Magdalen and St John to which he was devoted. A supporter of the City Band, the Football Club, the Cage Bird Society and the Children's Sports Day. "Jackie" Briscombe was one of the best known personalities in the city and, like his father, was always to be seen with a pink carnation in his buttonhole. He died in 1984.

May. A three-year programme of extensive renovations to *Markenfield Hall* near Ripon for the seventh Lord Grantley were completed with the advice of Mr John Weaver and the late Mr Gilyard-Beer, F.S.A., of the Ancient Monuments Inspectorate: the entire work was directed by Mr John S. Miller, the Harrogate architect. The east wing of the early 14th-century fortified manor house was rehabilitated as a home for Lord and Lady Grantley, the Great Hall and its undercroft repaired and the medieval kitchen converted into a self-contained cottage. Among many interesting discoveries was the survival of part of the medieval panelled ceiling in the Chapel. The building was to continue to be open to the public.

June. Councillor Jack Briscombe, Mayor of Ripon, England, welcomed Mr Thomas E. Jones and his wife,

the Mayor and Mayoress of Ripon, Wisconsin, U.S.A., at a reception at the Town Hall. Mayor Jones, a professor of German in his home town, was on a goodwill visit.

The Ripon Canal Society organised a series of action weekends during the summer clearing the canal and locks of rubbish and debris. In July, a Manpower Services Commission scheme was put into operation to rebuild the two locks. The work was planned in two stages: the first stage, lasting six months, would involve clearing stones from the lock chambers; the second stage (planned for 1984-85) would concentrate on rebuilding the locks and installing lock-gates.

Three old cine-films were discovered in the vaults of Ripon Town Hall. The earliest film showed the Highland Games held on Ripon racecourse organised by the Highland regiments from South Camp in 1916. Another film, commissioned in 1923 by the Council for publicity purposes, featured beauty spots in and around Ripon. The third film, made in the 1930s, showed the Mayor and Mayoress attending a gala on the Market Square with dancers and a German band. The films had been developed on a celluloid base which becomes unstable on prolonged storage. Mr Peter McNamara of Ripon College who found the films had copies made on a modern base, and it was hoped that they would form the nucleus of a Yorkshire Historic Film Library.

The Ripon City Centre Study, designed to show possible ways in which land alongside the proposed IRR between Westgate and Coltsgate Hill could be developed, was published by the Harrogate Planning Department. The Borough Council would finance the proposed car parks and service roads; housing and commercial development would depend on private investment. Comments were sought from the public and the Harrogate Council adopted a modified scheme in June.

June. The Harrogate Public Works Committee decided to go ahead with the replacement of the derelict Alma Weir on the River Skell (which had become one of the city's worst eyesores) with a gauging weir which would measure the flow of water. The £45,000 costs would be shared by the British Water Authority who would pay £25,000 and the Borough Council who would pay the rest.

July. Outline planning consent was given for a scheme to develop the cleared Bedern Bank site with a housing and shopping complex. The area had been unused for over 25 years since the demolition of property to make way for one of the several discarded W.R.C.C. relief road schemes of the 50s and 60s.

September. The eight almshouses of St Anne in High St Agnesgate, built in 1869, were reconditioned to provide modern accommodation for four elderly Ripon citizens and were reoccupied in 1983.

With the local unemployment rate running at 7.6 per cent, Harrogate Council's Community Projects Schemes were welcomed in response to the problem of the long-term unemployed. Schemes co-ordinated by the Borough Chief Engineer, Mr Alan Benton, involved projects in Ripon, Harrogate and Knaresborough, and would employ a maximum of 90 people. Ripon projects included the River Skell Improvement Scheme and the Ripon Canal Scheme, the latter being carried out with the British Waterways Board and in liaison with the Ripon Canal Restoration Society.

The Mayor came under a vote of censure at a meeting of the City Council for his support of the IRR. In July, he had displayed a pro-road poster in the window of the Mayor's parlour in the Town Hall and he had angered many people in August when he refused to attend the Quarry Moor open day because the Rescue Ripon Group were manning a stall to raise funds to fight the road scheme. The motion of no confidence was withdrawn after the matter had been fully debated. The Council later voted seven to four to donate £2,000 towards the legal costs of the Rescue Ripon Group for presentation of their case at the public inquiry.

October. The long-awaited public inquiry into the N.Y.C.C.'s proposals for an inner relief road began on 4 October. Two hundred objectors paraded with anti-IRR placards outside the Hugh Ripley Hall when the Inspector, Mr Maurice Astrinski, arrived. On the previous evening there had been a tumultuous public meeting at the Town Hall when the Mayor had closed the main door to prevent too many people entering the building, and the police had to be called in to control the disappointed campaigners locked outside.

Mr David Woolley, Q.C., represented the N.Y.C.C. and in his opening speech outlined the case for the proposals. The 1978 survey of traffic showed that in that year 13,000 vehicles per day had an origin or destination in Ripon and 5,500 per day were through vehicles. It was claimed that 2,000 of the through vehicles would use a Harrogate southern bypass if built, leaving only 19 per cent of the total traffic to use a Ripon bypass: 13,000 would still seek access to the central area. The Council's case was that a bypass could not be justified on economic grounds and that an IRR would cater for all traffic; it would take pressure away from the Cathedral and the Market Square; allow derelict areas to be developed, only three listed buildings would be lost and relatively few small businessmen would be displaced; the effect on the hospital would be acceptable; redevelopment would lead to improved parking facilities and traffic management would solve traffic problems in the Market Square. Various expert witnesses were called to substantiate the case in detail. The County Council was supported by the Dean and Chapter, the Ripon Chamber of Trade, the Ripon Development Association and a number of individuals including Mr John Richmond, an ex-Mayor and former County Councillor for Ripon.

The main case for the opposition was presented by Mr David Pedley, a solicitor, and Mrs Ann Moon, consultant town planner, for the Rescue Ripon Group. The Group's alternative proposals had been published in a document 'Ripon Rescued'. It was claimed that an outer bypass combined with inner traffic management and city centre redevelopment could give all the advantage claimed by the County and District Councils to be possible only through the IRR proposal. Mr Gavin McPherson, the Rescue Ripon Group's consultant engineer, maintained that there were two crucial questions which needed to be answered; these concerned the degree to which a Harrogate southern bypass would affect the traffic passing through Ripon, and the desirability of traffic management measures and associated environmental improvements in the city centre. If the County Council had miscalculated and overestimated the Harrogate bypass's effect, then the County's case for the IRR collapsed and Mr McPherson claimed that his analysis showed they had done both. Opposition came from the following: County Councillors John McGarr and F. W. Spence; owners of property involved in both the road proposals and the Ripon Centre Study; the Ripon Civic Society, the York Georgian Society and several conservationists. At the end of the inquiry all parties agreed that the Inspector, Mr Astrinski, had conducted the proceedings fairly and had given all participants an opportunity to express their views.

The Public Inquiry into the Harrogate District Council's plans to develop the Ripon city centre opened on 29 November. Mr David Woolley, Q.C., told the Inspector, Mr Maurice Astrinski, that the Council had no intention of going ahead with the plan if the IRR was not approved. Five experts presented evidence for the scheme. Mr Keith Roberts said that the existing road networks to the west of Ripon were not adequate to serve the area once it was developed. Westgate already carried 50 per cent more traffic than was suitable, and if the scheme went ahead the number of vehicles would increase by a further 700 per day. Mr Colin Brown, Assistant Planning Officer, explained that the Council's Compulsory Purchase Order covered 38 separate plots of land and outlined three main areas: area servicing of Market Place stores, housing and shopping developments. Mr Dennis Mason, traffic consultant, pointed out that the existing parking system in Ripon was very unbalanced with the majority of parking spaces on the east side of the Market Place. The proposals would include 300 car-parking spaces, of which 213 would be for public use, making an overall gain of 64 places. Mr Ian Cartwright said that the pattern of ownership was so fragmented that improvement could only be achieved by compulsory purchase, but he was sure that the plans were economically viable and would prove attractive to both private investors and developers.

Mrs Ann Moon gave evidence on behalf of the Rescue Ripon Group and, while agreeing with the concept of the area being tidied up and put back in full-time use, opposed the plan in principal because it was built around the proposed IRR. The Inspector's Report and the Minister's decision were published in July 1984, when the Secretary for the Environment, Mr Patrick Jenkin, ruled against the IRR because it would radically damage the character of the city. He also refused permission for the Compulsory Purchase Orders needed to implement the Ripon City Centre Study.

In December 1985 the County Council decided to build a major bypass at a cost of two-and-a-half million pounds, following along the line of the disused railway, and a greatly reduced inner relief traffic system, to be completed by 1989.

November. Mr Alan Oliver, a Ripon postman, was appointed to the post of Ripon Hornblower. He started playing the cornet at the age of eight and played the bass euphonium in the Ripon City Band, of which he had been a member for 21 years.

December. Mr John Metcalfe and his wife presented to the city a watercolour of Ripon Cathedral, painted by the local artist George Jackson and given to them as a wedding present. Mr Metcalfe lived in Ripon in the early years of his life and his grandfather was one of twin brothers who founded furnishing and drapery firms. The other twin was Mayor of Ripon in 1909.

January. D. S. Textiles of Bradford applied to the Harrogate Council for permission to develop a site at the rear of Queen Street with a frontage on the entrance to the bus station. The plans were for three retail shop units with office and storage space above. The area behind the new shops and those already situated in Queen Street would be used as a service area. The scheme was generally welcomed as it would tidy up another of the derelict sites in the centre of the city.

Mr Tom Gowland, who died in September aged 93, bequeathed £1,000 to help to restore the medieval Leper Chapel of St Mary Magdalen, and £1,000 to the Cathedral. He had lived and worked in Ripon for about 70 years as a solicitor before his retirement, and when he was a young man he worshipped in the Leper Chapel. He and his father built up the firm of Edmundson and Gowland, which amalgamated with Hutchinson and Buchanan in the 1960s. Mr Gowland was a fine local historian who wrote on the medieval administration of Ripon and district.

Mr Patrick Webb became Clerk to the City Council in succession to Mrs Joan Connor who had retired after ten years' service. Mr Webb was also invited to be Sergeant-at-Mace, thus becoming the first person to hold the two appointments at the same time.

Mr Joe Kennedy, County Librarian, reported to the County Library and Archive Committee that the public area of the Ripon Library, built in 1937, was only 1,250 square feet, and ought to be four times larger to serve a city of over 13,000 people. The Committee decided that a new library for the city would not be considered before 1989.

Mr Joe Cooper, Headmaster of Ripon City School, announced that he would retire at the end of the year after ten years' service. He had broadened the curriculum, started a thriving computer course and reorganised the maths and library departments, and campaigned for the introduction of comprehensive education in Ripon.

April. Forty volunteers completed a training course for the National Trust to prepare them to conduct guided tours of Fountains Abbey and the Studley Royal Estate under the leadership of Miss Mary Mauchline, historian, Mr W. T. C. Walker, architect and a leading authority on the estate, and Miss Beatrix Molesworth, naturalist.

1984-85. JOHN McGARR, Civil Servant

Mayor 1977-78, 1984-85

May. The Ripon Police and Prison Museum was officially opened by Mr Kenneth Henshaw, Q.P.M., Chief Constable North Yorkshire Police, in the presence of the Mayor and Mayoress and other invited guests. After the opening ceremony the Hornblower, the successor of the early law officer, 'set the watch'. The museum, which was housed on the first floor of the old cell block of the Ripon Liberty Prison in St Marygate, displayed memorabilia, artifacts, documents and prints with particular reference to Victorian prisons and the development of the police force. In July the Ripon Pottery, who occupied the ground floor, offered to sell the building to the Museum Trust. An anonymous friend of the Trust purchased the property to allow negotiations to be carried out with the Harrogate Borough Council, who took over ownership and granted a 25-year lease on the whole building to the Trust in January 1985. The first six months of that year were occupied in restoring the ground floor and one new gallery was opened in July.

More than 250 people attended a farewell evening held in the Dalton Hall of the Choir School in honour of the Very Revd Edwin le Grice, Dean of Ripon, on his retirement after 16 years. The Cathedral choir, under the direction of Mr Ronald Perrin, sang two anthems and the Bishop of Ripon, the Rt Revd David Young, presided at the formal presentation ceremony. The Chairman of the Select Vestry, Mr Jim Davison, presented the Dean with a cheque from the Cathedral congregation. A glass bowl with Peter Kearney's engraving of Ripon Cathedral on it was presented to Mrs le Grice by Mrs Dorothy Thornewill, a Friend of the Cathedral for many years.

July. A black case was found by a verger in the entrance to the Cathedral during the Ripon Grammar School Commemoration Service at which the guest preacher was the Rt Revd David Jenkins, who had recently been appointed Bishop of Durham. The Mayor and many other civic and church dignitaries were present. The verger alerted the police, who in turn called the bomb squad. P.C. Tony Lockwood removed the case and found that it was the official container for the Mayor's ceremonial chain which the Sergeant-at-Mace had left behind the door after the Mayor had donned the chain for the service.

August. The Harrogate Planning Committee gave permission for the development of the old Ripon railway station and surrounding land on Ure and Hutton banks to provide offices, industrial units and 22 bungalows. The original application for 30 homes in the form of flats, detached and semi-detached dwellings was modified after objections raised by residents of Ure Bank Top.

September. The Royal Shakespeare Company made history with their first-ever performance in Ripon, and their first performance in a cathedral. The Cathedral was transformed with soft and colourful carpets replacing the rows of pews and spotlights dangling from scaffolding beside the nave pillars. The audience followed the actors around the various sets resting on tables or carpets and the Company invited audience participation for several scenes in the productions of *A Winter's Tale* and *The Crucible*. Both plays were on the examination syllabus for Ripon schools that year.

The Very Revd Christopher Campling was installed as Dean of Ripon in the Cathedral. Extra seating was provided to accommodate the large congregation for the one-and-a-half-hour service of collation, induction and installation. The Dean was collated by the Bishop to the benefice of the Cathedral which includes Littlethorpe, Sharow, Copt Hewick, and Marton-le-Moor; he is responsible for the spiritual care of the three parishes. When the Lord Lieutenant had read the Royal mandate, the Vice-Dean led the Dean, the Precentor and representatives of the Select Vestry to the Dean's Stall in the choir where he was installed.

1985-86.   JOHN (JACK) THOMPSON, Stationer

Born 1914 at Houghton le Spring and educated at the Grammar School there. Joined the Royal Air Force in 1933 and served for more than 20 years; 1939-45 in the Far East, West Africa and the Middle East as a Flight Lieutenant. Retired to take up business and become a stationer in Ripon. Elected to the City and Harrogate District Councils in 1976. Mayor of Harrogate 1980-81. As Mayor of Harrogate, supported an appeal for the mentally handicapped and as Mayor of Ripon the 'Ripon in Bloom' Committee. Governor of the Grammar School and the City School. A member of the City Club and of the Cricket and Rugby Clubs.

In the earliest discussions concerning the commemoration of 1100 years of Ripon's history in 1986 the hope was expressed that a royal visit might be included in the celebrations. The announcement that Her Majesty Queen Elizabeth would distribute the Royal Maundy in the Cathedral on 4 April 1985 was therefore received with great joy. Intense and careful preparations followed and on a pleasant day in a dismal spring the crowded streets were bedecked with flags and bunting, a perfect background for the Yeomen of the Guard as they paraded from the Square to the Cathedral.

The Queen and HRH The Duke of Edinburgh travelled by train to Harrogate where they were received by the Lord Lieutenant of North Yorkshire, the Marquess of Normanby, the Mayors of Harrogate and of Ripon, and other dignitaries. They proceeded to Ripon by car to be welcomed by crowds before entering the Cathedral for the Office of the Royal Maundy. The splendid service was sung by the Cathedral choir and the Gentlemen and Children of Her Majesty's Chapel Royal, St James's Palace. The Duke of Edinburgh read the first Lesson. All the seating in the Cathedral was arranged east to west, with the 59 men and 59 women recipients of the Maundy spread at intervals along the aisles, so that all present had a clear view of Her Majesty as she distributed the purses of Maundy Money from trays carried by Yeomen of the Guard, assisted by the Lord High Almoner, the Bishop of Rochester. Particularly charming were the pupils of Ripon schools, chosen to be Children of the Royal Almonry, who accompanied Her Majesty carrying the traditional posies.

After the service there was an informal and unexpected 'walkabout', to the delight of the people waiting in front of the Cathedral. The Queen and the Duke then attended a reception at Minster House, where they were introduced by the Dean to members of the Cathedral staff and congregation who had been involved in the organisation of the ceremony. The Royal party proceeded to the Town Hall by car where they were the guests of the Mayor and Council at a civic lunch in the Council Chamber attended by civic heads from the district and county. On behalf of the City the Mayor, Councillor John McGarr, presented the Queen with a Chillingham horn mounted with a Ripon spur.

When the Queen and the Duke had acknowledged the cheers of the crowd in the Market Place they left by car for Fountains Abbey, where they were able to see some of the work being undertaken by the National Trust.

The planning and organisation of festival events to commemorate the 1100th anniversary
of civic life in Ripon has been the responsibility of:

The City of Ripon Festival Trust 1986
Chairman: Mr B. Price

with the following sub-committees:

Civic, Religious and Royal Events and Visitors
Chairman: Mr W. J. Baily

Environment and Buildings
Chairman: Dr J. K. Whitehead

Exhibitions and Displays
Mr J. Cooper

Fund Raising
Chairman: Mr B. Elsworth

Historical and Archives
Chairman: Mr P. MacNamara

Performing Arts
Chairman: Mr D. McAndrew

Publicity and Advertising
Chairman: Mr R. Wardroper

Sporting Events
Chairman: Mr J. H. Richmond

Appendix One
THE FALLEN OF WORLD WAR I, 1914-18

Harold Akers
Herbert Akers
J. W. Ambler
George Anderson
Albert Arnett
William Arnett
John Ashton
Robert Aslin
Frederick Atkinson
George Atkinson
Albert Baines
Bernard Baines
P. O. Baines
G. W. R. Beacher
J. H. Bellerby
Charles Bendelow
W. Benson
W. R. Benson
Robert Bickersteth
Alfred Blackburn
Fred Blackburn
George Blackburn
R. S. Bland
Bernard Booth
T. Buck
J. R. Burgess
G. E. Burnett
H. Burnley
C. F. Burton
W. E. G. Burton
B. T. Butler
James Campbell
William H. Cargan
J. Carney
V. C. D. Boyd Carpenter
Arthur C. Carter
Tom Cartman
Stanley Casling
J. Clarke
W. T. Cole
C. Compton
H. Compton
Richard Connor
William Connor
James Corker
Fred Cousins
G. E. Cousins
Percy Cousins
Robert Cousins

W. Cullen
Edward Cust
James Dalton
Percy Dawes
J. A. Dennison
G. R. Dixon
Bernard Ellerker
Arthur W. Ellerker
George Ellerker
N. B. Elliott-Cooper
C. F. Elsy
George English
R. W. English
James I. Farmer
J. S. Firth
John B. Fisher
Francis Walter Ford
T. G. Fox
William French
Robert Fuller
Charles Geldart
F. C. Geldart
William Geldart
Albert Victor Gill
Henry Gilling
F. W. Goodger
William Gott
Arthur Grange
A. Granger
E. C. Griffiths
James Grundy
Albert Hainstock
John Handley
James Hardcastle
J. W. Hardcastle
Percy Hardcastle
T. E. Hargrave
Robert Harper
Joseph Harrison
Lewis Hayton
Eric Heatherington
J. D. W. Heavisides
Herbert Hebden
Arthur W. Herdman
John Hewson
William Hewson
Clarence Hillery
Frederick H. Hobson
W. W. Hodgson

Hubert Hollox
H. B. Hornby
Alfred Horner
William Horner
C. N. Houseman
Alfred Hudson
F. W. Hudson
Arthur Hunt
F. Hunt
Hanley Hutchinson
Albert Hyatt
Christopher l'Anson
John F. l'Anson
J. W. Ingleby
Harry Jackson
J. W. Jackson
George Jarvis
Harry Jarvis
J. H. Jarvis
Richard Jefferies
Ingleby S. Jefferson
F. W. Judson
W. B. Kay
W. Kay
T. Kerton
Alan Kilding
Harry Kilding
J. W. Kilding
G. H. King
Katherine Kinnear
John L. Kinnear
Thomas C. Kirk
Norris Kitchingham
George Kitchingman
William Kitchingman
C. W. Knaggs
Harry Knowles
Albert Lacey
F. Lancaster
H. Leckenby
James Leeming
F. S. Lickley
J. B. Lumb
John Lynch
Reuben A. Mangin
P. I. Marston
A. W. Mason
Arthur Mason
Cyril Mason

THE FALLEN OF WORLD WAR I, 1914-18 (continued)

W. Masterman
John A. W. Mawson
E. S. Meggison
F. C. Metcalfe
G. H. Metcalfe
James Metcalfe
Alfred Monger
M. C. Morton
Fred Moorey
Fred Mudd
C. E. Naylor
T. C. Naylor
W. T. Neave
H. Nellis
Charles E. Nicol
Reginald M. Owen
Robert D. Oxley
R. Palmer
Alan F. Parker
E. T. Parker
J. Parker
P. Parkinson
G. F. Parvin
J. P. Patrick
J. A. Peacock
Walter Peacock
G. W. Pratt
J. W. Pratt
George Precious
J. T. Prest
F. Prest
W. H. Pybus
Alan Pyman
M. L. Raphael
W. Reddish

Cyril Render
Donal B. Renton
F. Reynard
George Reynolds
John Reynolds
F. W. Richardson
Gordon Richardson
W. C. Richardson
E. R. Robinson
George A. Robson
Thomas L. Rogers
George Rumfitt
Harry Rumfitt
J. W. Sawyer
Ernest Searle
Harry Sefton
W. Sefton
Tom Sheldon
Wilfrid Sherwin
James Sibald
A. Simpson
Frank Simpson
William Simpson
T. Smithson
R. A. Snow
E. Spence
F. C. Squires
J. H. Storey
Peter Sutcliffe
Thomas Swainson
William Swires
J. T. Sykes
Arthur Taylor
E. E. Thistlethwaite
Frank Thompson

Gilbert Thompson
Howard Thompson
A. Thorogood
William Thorpe
Edwin Tiffney
Wynn C. Tilly
W. Topham
Herbert F. Trevor
H. Trow
Christopher Turner
F. W. Turner
Herbert Unwin
S. Vickerman
Tom Wait
Joseph Walker
R. Walker
G. H. Ward
A. E. Watson
G. E. Webster
Herbert Webster
John Webster
A. S. Wells
Herbert Wells
Charles Wharton
George Wharton
J. A. White
Frederick Willows
Arthur Windsor
C. Winsor
R. H. Wise
Thomas Wise
Fred Wright
Herbert Wright
Thomas Young

Appendix Two
THE FALLEN OF WORLD WAR II, 1939-45

Harry Anderson
James Arkle
Frederick Beckwith
Gilbert Benson
Jack Benson
John Benson
Leonard Boniface
George Bowser
James Bradley
Geoffrey Braithwaite
Leslie Briscombe
W. E. Browning
John Bull
Thomas Burdes
K. Alan Burini
William Campbell
George Cartman
Harry Clegg
Charles Cowell
Bernard Cundill
Frank Darbyshire
Frank Eccles
Harry Ellerker
Samuel Elsy
Harold Fawbert
William Flockton
William Gorman
Albert Grange
Ernest Grange

Robert Green
Christopher Haithwaite
Robert Haithwaite
John Hall
Clifford Harniess
Charles Henstock
Gilbert Hislop
Marjorie Hodgson
Kenneth Holroyd
Richard Hornby
Archibald Hudson
J. Hunter
John Hunter
W. Jackson
John Jervelund
Cecil Jolly
William Julian
William Lonsdale
Ian MacGill
Alfred Marlow
Austen Metcalfe
Charles Metcalfe
Ernest Metcalfe
George Metcalfe
John Metcalfe
Robert Metcalfe
Gordon Myers
George Myers
G. Myers

Harold Nelson
Norman Orton
Frederick Prest
Robert Prince
Herbert Ramm
Isaac Rawson
James Robb
John Rowatt
Thomas Rowland
John Simpson
William Simpson
George Simpson
Norman Skirrow
Robert Spetch
Geoffrey Stainthorpe
James Starkey
William Sullivan
Ronald Tate
John Thornton
Ronald Thornton
John St L. Thornton
Ernest Thwaites
Edward Vickers
Richard Vickers
Lawrence Waddington
John Ward
F. Watson
James Wilkinson

Appendix Three
MAYORS OF RIPON 1887 — 1986

1886-87	John Baynes	1937-38	John Ireland McHenry
1887-88	John Baynes	1938-39	Frederick Isaac Trees
1888-89	H. Mann Thirlway	1939-40	Frederick Isaac Trees
1889-90	Thomas Hargrave	1940-41	Frederick Isaac Trees
1890-91	Thomas Smithson	1941-42	Margaret Sara Steven (Nov.-May)
1891-92	Thomas Smithson	1941-42	William Russell Dixon (June-Oct.)
1892-93	Joseph Brooks Parkin	1942-43	Arthur Nettleton
1893-94	Francis Smith	1943-44	Arthur Nettleton
1894-95	John Baynes	1944-45	Leavens Marson King
1895-96	1st Marquess of Ripon	1945-46	William Russell Dixon
1896-97	Thomas Williamson	1946-47	William Russell Dixon
1897-98	John Banks Lee	1947-48	William H. Clayden
1898-99	Arthur Wells	1948-49	William H. Clayden (Nov.-May)
1899-1900	Richard Wilkinson	1949-50	Frank Charles Lowley
1900-01	John Spence	1950-51	Frank Charles Lowley
1901-02	John Spence	1951-52	Frank Charles Lowley
1902-03	William Topham Moss	1952-53	William Maylott Eccles
1903-04	William Topham Moss	1953-54	William Maylott Eccles
1904-05	John Banks Lee	1954-55	Cecil Augustus Fearn
1905-06	George Simpson	1955-56	Cecil Augustus Fearn
1906-07	John Banks Lee	1956-57	William Norman Wells
1907-08	Herbert Morris Bower	1957-58	William Davies Toulman
1908-09	Herbert Morris Bower	1958-59	William Davies Toulman
1909-10	Francis George Metcalfe	1959-60	Walter Roy Beaumont
1910-11	Walter Fennel	1960-61	James Miles Coverdale
1911-12	Walter Fennel	1961-62	James Miles Coverdale
1912-13	Walter Fennel	1962-63	Cecil Augustus Fearn
1913-14	Thomas Harrison (Nov., Dec.)	1963-64	Wilfrid Henry Parnaby
1914-15	Edward Taylor	1964-65	Wilfrid Henry Parnaby
1915-16	Frederick William Hargrave	1965-66	Neville Stephenson
1916-17	Frederick William Hargrave	1966-67	Neville Stephenson
1917-18	Frederick William Hargrave	1967-68	Frederick Walter Spence
1918-19	Frederick William Hargrave	1968-69	Frederick Walter Spence
1919-20	George Hotham Newton	1969-70	Luigi George Handel Feather
1920-21	George Hotham Newton	1970-71	Luigi George Handel Feather
1921-22	Walter Fennel	1971-72	Norman Wilfrid Pollard
1922-23	William Hemsworth	1972-73	Walter Roy Beaumont
1923-24	William Hemsworth	1973-74	Walter Jack Baily
1924-25	William Hemsworth	1974-75	Edward Iver Jones
1925-26	Charles Harker	1975-76	John Henry Richmond
1926-27	Charles Harker	1976-77	Michael Frederick Falkingham
1927-28	Thomas Fowler Spence	1977-78	John McGarr
1928-29	Thomas Fowler Spence	1978-79	Frederick Walter Spence
1929-30	Sidney George Moss	1979-80	Walter Jack Baily
1930-31	John Proudfoot	1980-81	Barrie Price
1931-32	John Proudfoot	1981-82	Robert Winster Bracken
1932-33	Richard Thorpe	1982-83	Walter Roy Beaumont
1933-34	Richard Thorpe	1983-84	John Briscoe Briscombe
1934-35	William Russell Dixon	1984-85	John McGarr
1935-36	William Russell Dixon	1985-86	John Thompson
1936-37	John Ireland McHenry		

Appendix Four
HONORARY FREEMEN OF THE CITY OF RIPON

1896   The Most Honorable George Frederick Samuel, Marquess of Ripon, K.G., in the County of York

1897   The Right Honorable H. E. B. Viscount Mountgarret of Nidd Hall

1903   The Honorable and Very Reverend W. H. Freemantle, D.D., Dean of Ripon

1905   The Right Reverend W. B. Boyd Carpenter, Bishop of Ripon

1945   Miss Amy Heslop, Matron of the Ripon and District Hospital 1924-45

1949   The Chief Royal Engineer, the Officers and other Ranks of the Corps of Royal Engineers

1951   Charles Harry Moody Esq., C.B.E., D.Mus., F.S.A., F.R.C.O., Hon.R.C.M., F.S.A.

1953   Her Royal Highness The Princess Royal, C.I., G.C.V.O., G.B.E.

1958   Charles Harker Esq.

1958   William Russell Dixon Esq., O.B.E.

1965   The Royal Air Force Station, Topcliffe

1971   Colonel Sir Malcolm Stoddart-Scott, O.B.E., T.D., D.L., M.D., M.P.

1982   Councillor W. R. Beaumont, J.P.

1982   W. H. Parnaby Esq., B.E.M.

Appendix Five
RIPON TOWN CLERKS 1887-1974

1881   Matthew Kirkley

1920   J. H. Gough

1942   K. D. Hanna

1946   J. R. Nicholson

1948   J. A. Berry

1955   J. Rennison

1958   W. M. Claye

1960   J. A. Berry

CLERKS TO THE RIPON CITY COUNCIL

1974   Mrs Joan Connor

1984   P. Webb

Appendix Six
RIPON SERGEANTS-AT-MACE 1887-1986

1887   T. Precious

1904   T. Hammond

1935   E. Staples

1956   E. Bourke

1970   C. Hawley

1978   T. Harding

1980   D. Marshall

1984   P. Webb

Appendix Seven
RIPON HORNBLOWERS 1887-1986

1887	Jesse Davidson
1894	John Masterman
1903	Edward Heward
1916	Thomas J. Hawley
1922	Harold Blackburn
1941	Thomas J. Hawley
1954	R. Bruce
1955	Cyril Hawley
	John H. Ellis
1961	Cyril Hawley
1968	Brian Waines
1972	George Simpkin
1974	Philip Harrison
1976	Paul Richmond
1978	Derek Tyerman
1984	Alan Oliver

Appendix Eight
MEMBERS OF PARLIAMENT FOR RIPON 1887 — 1986

1886   John Lloyd Wharton (Unionist)

1906   H. F. G. Lynch (Liberal)

1910   Hon. E. L. Wood (Unionist)

1925   Major J. W. Hills (Conservative)

1938   Christopher Yorke (Conservative)

1950   Colonel Sir Malcolm Stoddart-Scott (Conservative)

1973   David Austick (Liberal)

1974   Dr Keith Hampson (Conservative)

1983   John Watson (Conservative)

Appendix Nine
WEST RIDING COUNTY COUNCILLORS FOR RIPON 1887-1974

1887	Marquess of Ripon
1901	Lord Mountgarret
1912	W. T. Moss
1930	T. F. Spence
1937	S. Brayshay
1946	C. T. Wade
1949	Major E. B. Eccles

Appendix Ten
NORTH YORKSHIRE COUNTY COUNCILLORS FOR RIPON 1974-1986

1974	W. R. Beaumont
	W. H. Parnaby
1977	W. R. Beaumont
	J. H. Richmond
1981	J. McGarr
	F. W. Spence
1984	J. McGarr
	F. W. Spence

Appendix Eleven
BISHOPS OF RIPON 1887-1986

1884   William Boyd Carpenter

1912   Thomas Wortley Drury

1920   Thomas Banks Strong

1926   Edward Arthur Burroughs

1935   Geoffrey Charles Lester Lunt

1946   George Armitage Chase

1959   John Richard Humpidge Moorman

1976   Stuart Hetley Price

1977   David Nigel de Lorentz Young

Appendix Twelve
DEANS OF RIPON 1887-1986

1876   William Robert Freemantle

1895   William Henry Freemantle

1915   Charles Mansfield Owen

1941   Godwin Birchenough

1951   Frederick Llewelyn Hughes

1968   Frederick Edwin le Grice

1984   Christopher Russell Campling

Sources consulted for the period 1887-1986

Council Minutes, Ripon City Council.

Archive material deposited in the Ripon Community History Project Centre in the College of Ripon and York St John.

Papers relating to the Public Inquiry on the Inner Relief Road 1984-85.

The *Ripon Gazette*, the *Ripon Observer* and the *Yorkshire Post*.

Inscriptions: Ripon Cathedral, Ripon War Memorial and Ripon City Cemetery.

Ripon Millenary 1886 (1892).

Robinson's *Ripon & Wensleydale Directory* (1906).

Ripon & Claro Household Almanac (1918).

Freemantle, Revd W. H., *Presentation of the Town Hall to the city of Ripon by the Marquess of Ripon K.G.*, (1897).

Williamson, Alice J., *Williamsons with particular reference to Tom Williamson and His Times* (1931).

Rogers, P. W., *A History of Ripon Grammar School* (1954).

Wilkinson, A. M., *Ripon College 1862-1962, The First Hundred Years* (1963).

Smith, Percival, *The Jepson Story* (1966).

Ripon Civic Society, *Ripon, Some Aspects of its History* (1972).

INDEX

Harrogate Road, 50, 52, 94, 96, 128, 129, 148
Hartland, Mrs Elizabeth Harnet, 120
Hartley: Edward, 95; R., 109
Harwood, J.H., 86
Haslam, Revd A.B., 2
Hawke, Lord, 21
Hawley: Cyril, (Hornblower), 149, 160, 171, 172,
    178; Thomas J., (Hornblower), 103, 110, 134
Hawthornthwaite, C., 111, 158
Haxby, Albert and Mrs, 72
Heath's Court, 5, 48
Hebden, Mrs Sarah, 3
Hellwath Bridge, 136
Hemsworth: A.W., 81; William, (Mayor), 21, 61,
    70-6, 77, 78, 79, 90, 111; Mrs, 74, 90; family,
    83
Hen and Chicken Inn, 17
Henderson, A.D., 89
Henry of Battenberg, Princess, 28
Hepworth & Co. (brewers), 9, 17, 18, 63, 75, 96,
    142, 164
Heslop, A., 26
Hey, Dr Samuel, 107
High Berrys, 101
High Cleugh, 19, 36, 64, 95
High Common Farm, 176
High Mill, Skellbank, 21, 23
High St Agnesgate, 7, 22
High Skellgate, 14, 17, 19, 28, 45, 56, 73, 77, 88, 95,
    103, 131, 157
Highfield: 5; estate, 96, 111
Highland Laddie Inn, 152
Highways Yard, 100
Hill: H.W., 121, 132; Mrs K.E., 7, 94; J.P., 106;
    Thomas, 1; W.S., 122
Hill Crest, 64
Hillborn, Miss, 94
Hills, Major J.W., 77, 81, 85, 90, 93, 96
Hinton, Patrick, 179
hiring fair (Martinmas), 25, 46, 75
H.M.S. *Burdock*, 104
hockey clubs, 74, 118, 123
Hodgson: J. Vincent, 111; Sister Marjorie, 111
Hodkin, Revd Hedley, 92
Holland, Miss Barbara, 132
Hollin Hall, 35, 109, 110, 149
Holmes, Arthur, 165
Holmfield: 105, 116; estate, 112, 114, 117, 120, 121
Holy Trinity church, 23, 25, 32, 62, 65, 68, 71, 76,
    79, 88, 90, 96, 102, 107, 117, 129, 140, 143, 178,
    180
Home for Girls, 45, 63, 73, 78, 94, 111
Homing Society (pigeons), 89, 90
Hooper, Revd G., 73
Horn, The Ripon, 22, 76, 99, 104, 110, 172
Hornblower, The, 1, 6, 44, 54, 56, 64, 70, 73, 76,
    89, 103, 136, 149, 154, 155, 160, 164, 170, 174,
    189
Horse Show, 5, 15, 28
Horticultural Society, 70, 87, 117
Hosband, Revd A.E., 184
Hospital, Cottage (later General), 5, 19, 36, 39, 41,

(Hospital,Cottage;cont'd)
    45, 48, 66, 68, 71, 75, 77, 78, 80, 83, 85, 86, 89,
    90, 96, 117, 118, 124, 142, 152, 153, 165, 183
Hospital, Isolation, (St Wilfrid's), 83, 106, 121,
    133, 137, 152, 165
Hospital, Lark Hill, 45
House of Correction, 145, 177
housing, 17, 23, 26, 40, 46, 58, 62, 65-6, 68, 71, 74,
    76, 77, 79, 80, 82, 83, 84-5, 86, 89, 92, 94, 95, 96,
    97, 105, 106, 110, 111, 112, 113, 115, 116, 117,
    118, 120, 121, 123, 124, 125, 127, 129, 131, 133,
    134, 136, 139, 142, 146, 147, 148, 149, 152, 154,
    164, 168, 170, 173, 179, 181, 182, 185, 187, 190
Housing Improvement Trust, 76, 83, 84, 92, 97,
    114, 124
Howard, Edward, (Hornblower), 25
Hudson: Percy, 111; Ted, 181; T.H., 148
Hugh Ripley's House, 53, 57, 59, 61, 71, 158
Hughes, Very Revd Frederick Ll., (Dean), 125,
    132, 133, 147, 148, 152, 157, 159, 163
Humphreys, Mrs Feodora, 168
Hunt, Derrick, 128
Hunter, Mary Ethel, 86, 94, 184
Hurst: J.S., 17, 45; Joseph, 161
Husband: Dr Charles, 5, 12, 101; Dr J.C.R., 78,
    93, 101, 107, 124; Nina, 124; General, 65
Hutchinson: Charles Barstow, 179; William
    Hanley, 35, 73
Hutchinson and Buchanan, 179, 189
Hutton Bank, 123, 190
Hutton Conyers, 69

Ibbetson, Christopher, 144
Industrial Society, 8, 44
Ingham: Major F.R., 138; W.L., 148; Mrs, 133
Ingilby, Lady, 162
Ingram, Miss, 79-80, 83
Ingram's Place, Stonebridgegate, 83, 103
Ireland's Court, 5
Irving, Eric, 122
Irwin, Lord *see* Wood, Hon. Edward
Isherwood, Mrs., 58

Jackson: George, 89, 105, 143, 189; Sir Percy, 93,
    99
Jackson & Co., 26-7, 39
Jacob, Naomi, 7, 92, 98, 155
Jameson, Lt J.L., 55
Jefferson, Ingilby S., 34
Jeffry, Christopher, 34
Jennings, Mr, 36
Jepson, Zachariah, 14
Jepson's Hospital Bluecoat School, 9, 14, 22, 34,
    53, 61, 62, 63, 69, 76, 78
Jobling, Frederick, 164
Johnson: Miss M.W., 111, 118, 151; Richard,
    (Mayor), 34
Johnson's Court, 95
Jones: Alfred, 34; Edward Ivor, (Mayor), 171-3;
    Philip, 162; Thomas E., 187
Josephs, Stanley, 183
Judson: C.W., 38, 40, 44; Thomas (two), 38

LIST OF SUBSCRIBERS

Miss K. M. Abbott
Mr & Mrs R. W. Abbott
Miss Theresa Adams
Mrs C. E. A. Alder
J. W. Alves
R. A. Alves
K. A. Anderson, Scrap Metal
   Merchants
V. &. J. Anderson
J. M. N. Anderson
R. J. Ankcorn
Richard D. Andrews
R. C. Appleby
Edward Archer
J. S. Armstrong
Askham Bryan College
P. L. Astin
Douglas T. Atkinson
Jack & Evelyn Baily
Patricia M. Baker
Dr Katherine M. Barran
Miss L. J. Barran
Bernard A. Barton
Major J. P. Baslington
Joel & Judith Bastow
Mrs E. M. Bean
W. R. Beaumont
W. Roy Beaumont
David H. Bell
Carol Bellis
Dr & Mrs C. J. Bennett
Andrew Benson
D. G. W. & M. E. Benson
Mr & Mrs K. Benson
John R. Benson
J. A. Berry
Patrick Bickersteth
Miss C. E. Birkinshaw
David Birkinshaw
Mr & Mrs N. S. Birkinshaw
Mrs Anne H. Blackburn
M. W. Blackburn
Joanne Catherine Blenkey
Claire Elizabeth Blenkey
Kenneth J. Blundell
P. J. Borchard & Co. Ltd
Anthony H. Boynton-Wood
Cllr Wg Cdr R. W. Bracken
Patricia M. Brady, Yorkshire
   Tours
Amy Louisa Bridges
A. M. Briggs
Miss E. Briggs
Elizabeth S. Briscombe
Marion L. Briscombe
Mrs Suzanne P. Briscombe
G. L. & J. Briscombe
R. E. Britton

Jack Broughton
Robert Edward Broughton
Miss Barbara B. Brown
C. F. Brown
John A. Brown
R. Chilton Buchanan
R. R. Buchanan
A. Marion Burnett
Dr & Mrs T. P. Burton
Roland Calter
Robert C. Calvert
D. W. M. Cameron
R. & E. D. Cansfield
S. & M. Carr
Mary & Frank Carter
Richard Carter
Stephen Carter
A. Cartman
Nell Cartman
Mrs Bessie Chapman
Mrs J. Chapman
Chapter, Ripon Cathedral
John Richard Child
Mr & Mrs J. R. Chester
Miss R. Chester
A. G. S. Chisenhale-Marsh
Jill Elizabeth Clark, R.G.N.
R. & F. Clarke
Dr P. E. G. Clements
Judith A. Close
Miss M. E. Coggan
College of Ripon & York
   St John
Mrs M. T. Colley
Mark Taylor Collinson
Paul Taylor Collinson
R. E. J. Compton
Mr & Mrs Edmund Cooke
Mrs E. M. Cooke
H. & D. Cousins
L. S. Couldwell
W. D. F. Coverdale
I. Cowan
Miss M. Craig
Mr & Mrs W. M. Craven
Mrs Caryl Crompton
Gordon Crompton
Simon Crosfield
J. & M. Cullingworth
John George Cuss
J. G. Cuss
Dorothy Cox
I. J. Day (née Bellerby)
Maj.-Gen. Sir Charles Dalton
Michael Danischewsky
Cllr & Mrs Bernard Darbyshire
David Darbyshire
J. Darnbrough

John Barry Darwin
Mr & Mrs W. Davill
Mr & Mrs K. Davill
Mr & Mrs J. Davison
Miss Joanna M. G. Dawson
The Dean of Ripon
John A. Dean
Joy Norton Dean
M. C. Deeming
Joan Dix
Rose Mary Dixon
Mrs N. J. Dixon
Evelyn Dodd
J. T. Donoghue
C. D. Drummond
Thomas Liddle Dunning
Mr & Mrs J. Crossley Eccles
W. Maylott Eccles
B. Elsworth
A. W. Emmerson
Sqdn Ldr W. R. Evans,
   A.E., R.A.F. (Retd)
J. M. Fardell
Donald Fergusson
Allan Fieldhouse
Mrs I. Fieldhouse
G. Finch
Ms Caroline Fleming
Dr C. H. Fletcher
John E. Fletcher
Dr & Mrs W. A. Forster
Mr & Mrs W. J. Foster
Mrs A. Foxton
Mr & Mrs P. G. Freeman
Jennifer Fryer
Susan Furness
Marjorie Gage
Ernest Gamble
Mr & Mrs P. Garside
R. M. Gaunt
Douglas H. Geldart
Harry & Margaret Gott
V. E. Gott
Beatrice Graham
E. I. Graham
The Lord Grantley, M.C.
Mrs Constance Grayson
Mrs R. M. Green
Dr Robert H. Griffiths
J. F. Groundwater
Z. M. Groves
Mr & Mrs N. H. Grundon
Mr & Mrs David Grundy
A. C. Gyte
Halifax Building Society, Ripon
   Branch
Miss Margaret Hammonds
J. N. T. Handley

Mr & Mrs P. Hanson
Mr & Mrs D. Hardisty
Mr & Mrs C. L. Hardisty
The Earl and Countess of
 Harewood
Douglas Harris
C. W. Harrison
David D. J. Harrison
George R. Harrison
Harrogate Borough Council
Harrogate District Resort
 Services Department
Barrie Hartley
Christopher Stuart Hartley
J. D. Hartley
Mrs K. B. Hartley
Guy L. Hartley
Brian C. Hawthornthwaite
Constance E. Hawthornthwaite
Mr & Mrs A. Hayden
Andrew R. Henderson
G. W. Herbert
Miss Herron
John Holdsworth
Eric & Sandra Hopper
The Cathedral Choir School,
 Ripon
Christopher Hodgson
H. Holdridge
J. F. Horner
Mrs Barbara Hornsby
Mrs Mary Hudleston
Mr & Mrs W. Hudson
Bryan H. & Ruth A. Hunter
Barbara Hutton
W. B. Imison
Nicholas Inchboard
Mr & Mrs J. E. & V. Ingram
Ian James Irving
Miss Winifred Jackson
Mrs Wyn James
Beechy F. Jarrett
Geoffrey W. Johnson
Peter Arthur Johnson
Margaret and Stanley Josephs
M. Julian
Mrs Marika Kelsey
R. J. Kelsey
Mrs Dorothy A. Kent
 (née Handley)
Mr & Mrs Eric Kenyon
Mr & Mrs R. I. Kerr
Mr & Mrs John A. Kirkman
Mary Pamela Kitching
B. C. & E. M. Knowles
Mrs E. S. Krenz & Children
Mr & Mrs K. Lang-Burns
Emma Lambden
Mr & Mrs D. Lawrence
Edwin Harrison
Jane Lee
Dr & Mrs R. A. Lee

Department of Adult and
 Continuing Education,
 University of Leeds
Miss D. A. Leeming
Mr & Mrs J. M. Lennard
Mrs Charles Leveson-Gower
T. G. Levitt
Peter C. Lilley
Angus & Rosemary
 Livingstone
Guy Livingstone
Zoe Livingstone
Thomasina Livingstone
Michael Lofthouse
John-Paul Looney
Elliott-Michael Looney
Mr & Mrs G. W. Lowe
J. David Lowe
Capt. & Mrs P. L. Lyons
T. & D. O. McCarthy
The Revd Canon Ronald B.
 McFadden
D. M. McFarlane
Colin & Sylvia Mackay
Anne Macnamara
Jean R. MacQuarrie
L. P. & R. M. Maister
Mrs A. Martin
Roy F. Martin
R. H. & A. V. Martin
Eileen Mason
Wing-Cdr Peter Masterman,
 R.A.F.
Cllr Ron May, Mayor,
 Richmond (Yorks.)
Mrs D. M. Mellor
A. E. & J. E. Merrin
F. M. Metcalfe
Robert Metcalfe
Mrs P. R. Milburn
Isabel Milestone
Arthur H. Mills
Air Cmmdre Wm C. Milne,
 R.A.F. (Retd)
J. Milner
I. M. Miskin
William Mitchell
Margaret Moreham
Mr & Mrs B. Moriarty
Mrs M. H. Morland
John Mortimer
Mrs M. I. Moss
W. L. Mothersdale
J. F. Muirhead
The National Trust (Fountains
 Abbey & Studley Royal)
Mr & Mrs H. V. Nelson
Roy & Winifred Nelson
Mrs J. M. Newsome
Mr & Mrs J. Nicholson
Gladys Nicholson
Mr & Mrs G. H. Nicholson

Graham & Thelma North
North Yorkshire County
 Record Office
Mrs Nora Leslie O'Flanagan
E. D. P. Ottevanger
Mr & Mrs J. Ounsley
Brian M. Parker
J. E. Parker
Freeman W. H. Parnaby, B.E.M.
Thomas Partrick
Cllr & Mrs C. H. Pawson
E. Pearson
J. H. Pearson
Jean & John Penketh
Mr & Mrs Norman Pickersgill
Frazer Lloyd Porter
Mrs D. Portwood
Vera Postill
Barrie Price
Elizabeth Price
Mr & Mrs W. H. Proctor
The Pullan Family
Miss Janet Pybus
Martin Rae
Philip Ramsden
R. G. Raw
Mr & Mrs C. S. A. Rawlinson
Mr & Mrs F. Rawlinson
N. J. A. & K. M. Rawlinson
Brenda Reeves
Mr & Mrs A. Renton
John & Barbara Richmond
Dale & Kay Braeuninger
W. H. Rickard
C. Rickard
Ripon City School
Ripon College Library
Ripon Gazette
Ripon Historical Society
Ripon Piscatorial Association
The *Ripon Spa Hotel*
K. B. Rimmer
A. & B. Roberts
Mrs Patricia Ann Robinson
Ann & Bill Robinson
W. R. & S. Y. Robinson
Christopher Roe
Mrs Margery Rolfe
Edward J. Rose
Mr & Mrs C. G. W. Rosher
Mr & Mrs J. R. Ross
Raymond Rumbold
M. V. W. Sach
The Sadler Family
Peter & Jane Sanderson
Mr & Mrs M. W. Sanderson
F. N. Schofield
Mollie Schofield
F. & M. V. Schornagel
R. S. Scorer
Joyce R. Scott
Phyllis Sheen

Cllr James Simpson
A. J. Sleat
Mrs Geoffrey Scrope
Ann Shepherd
B. C. Simpson
Sister Alice Simm, S.S.P.
Miss Beverley Kaye Skaife
George & Eve Skaife
Miss Nicola S. Skaife
Jennifer Lynne Slater
David & Maureen Small
Mrs M. G. Small
Leon Smallwood
Christopher N. Smith
Ms Deborah Smith
Miss Joan Smith
Mr & Mrs J. B. E. Smith
L. V. & M. E. Smith
Moira Smith
Priscilla J. Smith
S. Anthony Smith
Stephen A. Smith
Jacqueline Ann Smithson
F. G. & M. Sowray
F. W. Spence
Mrs Leslie J. Spence
Cllr John S. Spooner, J.P., A.C.P.
Neville Stephenson
Edwina & Derek Stevens
I. L. Stockdale
H. J. Stokell
Mrs C. A. Stokell
Simon P. Stockill
Mrs Doris M. Stocks
E. M. Storr
Mr & Mrs A. Stride
Eric Malcolm Sturdy
Mr & Mrs D. G. Suddards
Stella Swales

Rachel Swann
Mr & Mrs John Sylvester
Mr & Mrs D. P. Taylor
Fred Castle Taylor
G. Alec Taylor & Iris Taylor
Joseph Taylor
Mr & Mrs M. H. Taylor
Mr & Mrs L. M. Tebay
Mr & Mrs G. Tempest
Malcolm Cooper Tempest
Mrs A. D. Tetley
Paul F. Theakston
Richard J. Thomas
A. & J. Thompson
Mrs Beryl Thompson
John Thompson, Mayor of Ripon 1985-86
Julian & Diane Thompson
Peter & Morven Thompson
Celia Thomson
Dorothy Thornewill
M. A. Thorp
George E. Thorpe
Brenda P. Thwaites
Barry & Dorothy Titterington
J. C. Toulman
W. B. Trenholme
Janet Tweed
David K. Uffindall, J.P.
Alison Vague
M. P. & C. Viner
Brian Waines
Bruce Waines
C. D. Waite
Don Waite
Hazel & Roy Waite
Mr & Mrs Edward Walker
Geoffrey M. Walker
W. T. C. Walker
N. G. Walmsley

Bryan & Margaret Warburton
Mr & Mrs Geoffrey Wardman
The Warehouse
Allan H. Warren
Mr & Mrs S. P. Warwick
Joseph A. Waterworth
Dr & Mrs Clyde B. Webb
Patrick Webb (Sergeant-at-Mace)
Mrs P. M. M. Webb
Keith C. Webster
Mr & Mrs R. A. Wells
Leslie P. Wenham
E. Pauline West
Mr & Mrs A. White
Mr & Mrs P. D. Whitehouse
E. H. Whittaker
J. A. Whittaker (Bushy)
J. E. Whittaker
Susan & Bryan Wilkinson
Dr & Mrs Richard Wilkinson
Philip & Joanne Wilkinson
Fay & Gordon Wilks
Martin Willey
Ann Williams
F. Williams
T. T. Williams
D. I. Watson
V. L. & L. Winterburn
Christina D. J. Wood
Mrs Ronald Wood
Mr & Mrs R. D. Wright
Yorkshire Archaeological Society
Mr & Mrs C. W. P. Young
The Rt Revd David Young, Bishop of Ripon
J. M. Younge

Plan of the centre of Ripon reproduced from the 1983 Ordnance Survey map.